Restore Your Life

Restore Your Life

A Living Plan for Sober People

Anne Geller, M.D., with M. J. Territo

A Philip Lief Group Book

BANTAM BOOKS
NEW YORK · TORONTO · LONDON · SYDNEY · AUCKLAND

For Alexis and Emma

RESTORE YOUR LIFE: A LIVING PLAN FOR SOBER PEOPLE
A Bantam Book/April 1991

Grateful acknowledgment is made for permission to reprint from the following: The AA Preamble, copyright © by The AA Grapevine, Inc.; reprinted with permission. "Recommended Dietary Allowances," 9th edition, 1980, with permission from the National Academy Press, Washington, DC. Daily Eating Guide (Table 3), copyright © 1989, CSPI, 1501 16th Street N.W., Washington, D.C., 20036, reprinted from the New American Eating Guide. Used with permission.

The Twelve Steps are reprinted with permission of Alcoholics Anonymous World Services, Inc. Permission to reprint the Twelve Steps does not mean that AA has reviewed or approved the content of this publication, nor that AA agrees with the views expressed herein. AA is a program of recovery from alcoholism. Use of the Twelve Steps in connection with programs and activities which are patterned after AA but which address other problems does not imply otherwise.

Book design by Jeannette Jacobs.

Library of Congress Cataloging-in-Publication Data

Geller, Anne.
  Restore your life : a living plan for sober people / Anne Geller with M. J. Territo.
    p. cm.   Includes bibliographical references and index.
  ISBN 0-553-07153-X
  1. Alcoholics—Rehabilitation. 2. Narcotic addicts—Rehabilitation. 3. Alcoholics—Life skills guides. 4. Narcotic addicts—Life skills guides. I. Title.
  HV5275.G45 1991
  362.29'18—dc20   90-49869
                                                                                    CIP

Published simultaneously in the United States and Canada

PRINTED IN THE UNITED STATES OF AMERICA

BVG   0 9 8 7 6 5 4 3 2 1

Contents

Foreword

by Anne Geller, M.D.

You're sober. You've stopped drinking or using drugs, perhaps for the first frightening time, perhaps for the second or the fifth time.

As you well know, giving up alcohol or drugs took a great deal of courage. But did that single act make you a sober person?

Speaking as a recovering alcoholic, a physician, and the director of the Smithers Center, a treatment center for substance abusers, I must say *no*. To become a truly sober person—someone leading a normal, healthy, productive life without using mood-altering chemicals—you need a *living plan*, that is, a simple, organized way to conduct your life. Sobriety may begin, often dramatically, with throwing away your bottle, pills, powder, or needles. But it by no means ends there. It is an ongoing proposition, one that encompasses millions of moments of everyday living. And it is here, in the ordinary tests of daily life, that I have seen so many recovering people falter. It is where I faltered myself in the first three years of my recovery.

Sobriety requires more than courage. It requires skills and knowledge that you, an addict, do not have, indeed cannot have, when you make your brave leap into abstinence. But once you have stopped drinking or using drugs, you *can* acquire the skills and the knowledge that will enable you to plan your sober life. It would be presumptuous of me to put a timetable on building a stable sobriety. But my own experience and the experience of my patients have shown me that it takes most people about three years to be comfortably and solidly sober. This building period is difficult and demanding, but rewarding, too, as you count the milestones in your transformation from user to sober person.

My own journey was not entirely smooth. During the first three years of my recovery, as I struggled to stay sober and rebuild my life, I searched hard for information about how to conduct my life as a sober person. Even with the resources available to me as a physician, I found very little. This was more than a decade ago, but the same is true today. That is why I have written this book. *Restore Your Life* is a guide to building a secure and calm environment in which you can make the change from addict to sober person. No other book about recovery gives you the wide range of information—about health, emotions, stress, family, friends, and work—that you will find here.

I don't mean to imply that there are no other good or useful books about addiction and recovery. Anyone who's been in a bookstore lately knows there are shelves full of books to choose from. There are books about the disease of addiction, and guides that tell you how to give up addictive substances, or how to find a treatment program. For families of addicts, there are books on staging interventions and getting help for their loved ones and themselves. Celebrities tell how alcohol or drugs ruined their lives and how they got sober. Many of these book are excellent. There are also scores of books that focus on the spiritual aspects of sober living, and I have found comfort and wisdom in many of them. But while I agree that fostering spiritual growth is a vital part of your new life in sobriety, it is not the whole of that new life, just as the decision to become sober does not automatically make you a sober person.

Most of your days in sobriety, as they are in any normal life, are taken up with mundane tasks—driving to work, preparing dinner, picking up the kids from soccer practice. You have to cope with traffic jams, difficult bosses, burnt potatoes, and overexcited children. Such everyday annoyances are among the countless events that can precipitate a relapse. As every recovering person knows, almost any stimulus, physical or emotional, can trigger a desire to drink or use drugs again—a callous remark, too much time on your hands, or a precipitous dip in your mood brought on by a drop in blood sugar. But knowing what will happen to you as you go about your daily life, why it happens, and what to do about it will decrease your chances of relapse and enable you to create a comfortable and stable sobriety.

No matter how you became sober—whether you signed yourself into a treatment center or began by attending a self-help meeting—you will find in this book the information that will allow you manage the moment-to-moment business of sobriety. This information will be most helpful to those of you who have just become sober and to those who have not yet achieved three years of solid sobriety. I do, however, recommend the book to anyone in recovery. Even if you have celebrated your fourth or fifth anniversary of sobriety, reading it may give you insight into why your first years in recovery were so difficult, and it may give you some new ideas for an even better sober life.

There is only one requirement for using this book well: a firm commitment to sobriety. You do not have to have been in a treatment program, although you can use it in conjunction with one or when you leave a program. You can use it to supplement your participation in an anonymous self-help group. Use it in any way that helps you.

At the Smithers Center, in both the inpatient treatment center and the outpatient programs, we teach the principles you will find in the book. While most of our patients come from New York City and the metropolitan area, people come to Smithers from all over the United States and from abroad. We work with all kinds of people—from wealthy celebrities to welfare recipients, from truck drivers to nuclear physicists. Our patients have one thing in common, however: They have stopped denying their disease and admitted their powerlessness over their addiction. Using the same principles you will find in this book, thousands of Smithers patients have restored their lives, as you will see from the many inspiring stories I will tell.

To use the book successfully, you too must already have given up drinking or using drugs, and you must understand that you can never drink or use drugs again. You have a chronic disease, and you must learn to live with it. That's why I call this book a *living* plan.

A sober life has many components, and to design a living plan that works for you, you must become acquainted with all of them. A healthy body is essential. Your addiction has caused some degree of physical damage, and your body must heal, a process that can be disconcerting and uncomfortable if you don't have some understanding of what is happening to you and why. A stable mood is also a primary goal in sobriety, but your mood, especially in the first three to six months, will often be unstable because of the chemical changes taking place in your brain. For many people, this emotional volatility can be one of the most frightening aspects of early sobriety. Stress can also contribute to your emotional ups and downs, so I have included information on avoiding stress and on coping with those stresses you cannot avoid.

Repairing your relationships—with family, friends, and coworkers—will be another important component of your sober living plan, and I offer a chapter on each aspect of your interpersonal dealings, as well as one on sex in sobriety. In another chapter I focus on the process of self-examination that will help you learn what can trigger a relapse for you. You will also learn how to maintain a healthy body and a stable mood through sensible medical care, good nutrition, regular exercise, adequate sleep, and by overcoming your addiction to nicotine.

A book of this length covering so many topics may seem daunting to those of you in the first six months of sobriety, when completing even a simple task can sometimes seem overwhelming. I urge you to read the book in small doses, concentrating on whatever is troubling you most at the moment. And remember that you may not be able to change all these aspects of your life immediately. But try to keep this book always at hand. If you feel yourself in danger of drinking or using again, dip into Chapter 12, Relapse: Avoiding the Pitfalls. If there is a lot of tension at home, try Chapter 8, Banking the Home Fires: Rebuilding Your Family Life. By attending to your most pressing problems as they occur, you will gradually become acquainted with the principles of the book. As you settle into sobriety, you will be able to absorb and retain more of the information. You will read sections, not because of urgent need, but in order to move ahead with creating your living plan. No one, no matter how long they've been in recovery, need read the book from front cover to back, although I do recommend reading it all, in whatever order makes the most sense for you.

I have also written this book for the families and concerned friends of recovering people. It will help them to understand the process of recovery, so that they can support the recovering people in their lives. It will also enable them to understand how the addiction has affected their lives, so that they can recover along with their loved ones.

No matter how much damage your addiction has done—to your health, your emotions, your family, your career, your finances—you can pick up the pieces of your life and build a strong, healthy sobriety. I have done it, and I have been inspired and strengthened by my patients who have done it. But sobriety doesn't happen magically, and it doesn't happen overnight. It takes effort and time—and it takes a plan, so that that effort and time is spent profitably. Armed with knowledge, understanding, and preparedness, you *can* restore your life.

Restore Your Life

Chapter One
The Stages of Recovery

**What Happens to You Physically and Emotionally from the
First Three Months Through the Next Three Years**

While every recovering person is unique, recovery itself has clear stages, and every recovering person goes through them. Among my many patients, there has never been an exception, although it may take one person a bit more or less time than another to move from one stage to the next.

What follows is a brief outline of the stages, so that you can see how they unfold. It is important for you to understand—whether you are reading this in the first week of your sobriety, or in the eighth month, or the second year—that recovery is a process, one that continues throughout your sober life.

The initial stage of recovery, which takes about three months, is one of convalescence as your body and brain begin to recover from the ravages of alcohol or drugs. Wide and unpredictable mood swings are inevitable during this stage, and nearly everyone experiences some degree of physical discomfort. You know you are leaving this stage when you start to lose the feeling that you are recuperating from a long and devastating illness.

The next stage of recovery, which also lasts about three months, is one that I liken to walking through a long tunnel. The light at the end is visible, but the path to it is not entirely certain. Being inside the tunnel is strange and uncomfortable. Your senses sometimes feel deadened, sometimes heightened. But you keep moving, although it may not always feel as thought it's in a forward direction. Eventually you reach the light, and the world beyond looks clear and bright. For many people, leaving this second stage of recovery is a time of great joy and hope.

For the remainder of the first year (about six months), recovery is less fraught with drama and danger. The changes you experience are

1

fewer and more subtle. You feel well physically and your emotions are for the most part stable, but you still unexpectedly find certain tasks or situations difficult. However, you now accept the fact that your disease makes certain demands of you, and you begin to think of these requirements as a normal part of your life.

These first three stages, that is, the first year, are what I mean when I refer, throughout the book, to early recovery.

By the time you celebrate you first anniversary in sobriety, you are well on your way to seeing yourself as an abstinent person. Hopefully with the help of this book, you have created a living plan, and you have a normal daily routine. You have the skills you need to maintain your sobriety one day at a time and can start to look ahead and plan for the future. The great challenge of the next two years of sobriety—and beyond—is to continue to improve your living plan, keeping it strong enough and flexible enough to sustain you for the rest of your sober life.

If you are in the first months of your recovery you will naturally want to read the whole of this chapter (at your own speed, of course) so as to understand what to expect, physically and emotionally, during the coming year. If you have already passed through some of the stages, you will still find it useful to read the entire chapter, both to reinforce your vision of recovery as a process and to understand more fully what happened to you at the earlier stages.

This chapter is a description of the stages of recovery; detailed advice on coping with the difficulties of the various stages would dilute its purpose. If you have a particularly worrisome problem and need advice immediately, please consult the appropriate chapter, as listed in the table of contents.

The First Three Months

Although each recovering person experiences the process of recovery differently, there is one thing everybody feels at the beginning—an enormous sense of relief. For the first time in months or years, you are free of the endless need to keep feeding your addiction to alcohol or drugs.

Now that the noise and inner turmoil of your addiction have subsided, you have a new sense of inner quiet and peace. You also have the ability to think and contemplate in a way that was impossible when you were dependent on alcohol or drugs. On the other hand, you may be troubled by one or more of the generally unpleasant symptoms that often occur during the first months of recovery.

Some of you may suffer from troubling physical reactions—shakiness, blurred vision, queasiness, itching, muscle cramps. As your appetite returns, you may become concerned about gaining weight. If you experience memory loss, you may be worried that you have caused permanent damage to your brain. You may find yourself prone to sudden, disconcerting mood swings. Your initial feelings of triumph and elation may turn to depression as you face up to the damage you've inflicted on your family and friends, your career, your body.

As upsetting or frightening as these symptoms may be, they cannot begin to compare with the pain of being chemically dependent, nor do they seem quite so distressing when measured against the freedom that comes from being clean and sober.

The Body

To adjust itself to the absence of drugs or alcohol, your system must undergo a series of acute physical changes. It takes time before your brain; liver; stomach and intestines; heart, blood vessels, and lungs; muscles; and sexual organs can resume their normal functions. And, without the dulling effects of alcohol or drugs, you begin to feel the full extent of the damage your body has sustained.

But the *good* news is that some of the ill effects—the bloating, blotchiness, bloodshot eyes and bruises—subside quickly, often within four days to two weeks after you stop drinking or using. Over the first three to four weeks, the change in your appearance, visible proof that you are recovering, can be quite startling. At the Smithers inpatient treatment program, we demonstrate that change by photographing residents on the day they begin their treatment. When they are about to leave the facility, we ask them to compare their "day one" photographs to the way they look after twenty-eight sober days. The difference in their "before and after" appearances is always inspiring proof of the power of sobriety. Photographs can be a helpful tool in your recovery, too.

Your improved appearance is the outward sign that your body is beginning to repair itself. You may also experience unexpected relief from complaints you thought were chronic, such as nausea qr diarrhea. But you may develop pain or other troublesome symptoms that can surprise and upset you if you're not prepared for them.

Lydia, two weeks sober after twenty years of heavy drinking, complained that her sleep was interrupted every night by a painful muscle spasm that traveled from the arch of her right foot up through her calf. The spasms occurred just as she was drifting off to sleep, and could last for as long as half an hour, during which time Lydia alternately massaged her leg and swore. To make matters worse, the spasms often occurred again just after she'd fallen back to sleep.

Lydia became apprehensive about bedtime, and she was tired and irritable during the day because she wasn't getting enough sleep. Her counselor suggested that she begin a bedtime routine that included doing some gentle stretches, taking a warm bath, eating a calcium-rich snack, and wearing a pair of warm socks to bed. When Lydia tried this regimen, her spasms became much less frequent, although they didn't disappear completely until she had been sober for more than a year.

While not medically serious, Lydia's spasms were very disconcerting, the more so because she hadn't expected any physical difficulties once she became sober. Other symptoms of which my patients have complained are muscle weakness and unpleasant sensations such as numbness, twitching, "pins and needles," and itchiness. Pain under the right ribcage, the result of a fatty liver, is also common.

In Chapter 2, I will describe in greater detail the effects that alcohol and drugs have had on your body and your brain. For now, keep in mind that you are recovering from a serious illness. You wouldn't expect to bounce back immediately from a heart attack or major surgery, and the effects of alcohol and/or drug dependency can take an equally grave toll on your body. Even though you are not bedridden, even though you may be able to hold down a job and care for your family, you must remember that you have a chronic, potentially life-threatening disease. The physical symptoms of withdrawal can be frustrating, annoying, at times even unbearable, but be patient. Allow your body the time it needs to heal.

Sleep

Nearly everyone in recovery has some problem sleeping during these first months, especially in the first few weeks. You may have difficulty falling asleep or staying asleep. Your sleep may be frequently interrupted by vivid dreams and/or frightening nightmares. In the morning you're likely to be tired, out-of-sorts, and sluggish. As a result, it may be hard for you to concentrate, and you may find yourself feeling drowsy in the middle of the afternoon.

The first few nights of sobriety, when you are still in withdrawal, can be especially traumatic. Gail, a paralegal in her late twenties who had been drinking heavily for several years, was in danger of losing her job when she entered our inpatient treatment program. The first night in the detox ward, Gail got no sleep at all. Every time she closed her eyes, horrid pictures of leering men seemed somehow to be imprinted on her eyelids.

Gail was, in fact, experiencing a perceptual distortion of a print by the seventeenth-century Dutch painter Jan Steen, which hung on the wall of her living room. The leering men she saw were images from that painting, a scene of peasants in drunken revelry, magnified and distorted by the process of withdrawal and by her own fears. The images so terrified Gail that she forced herself to stay awake the whole night.

On the second night, the leering men were gone. But despite her fatigue, Gail couldn't fall asleep until dawn. Even then she was soon awakened by a vivid and frightening nightmare. For the next couple of nights, she slept fitfully and was frequently roused by fearful, anxious dreams. By the fifth night, however, she was able to sleep though the night and experienced no further sleep disturbances.

Of course, your sleep difficulties may not be so rapidly and completely resolved. Disruptions generally diminish, after the first several extremely distressing nights, although you may have trouble sleeping well into the first six to twelve months of your recovery.

The Emotions

In the first months of recovery, you are like a piano with a faulty damper pedal. You have no mechanism for modulating the force of your emotions. Modulation of emotions depends on a balance in your nervous system. Your addiction—whether to alcohol, tranquilizers, cocaine, opiates, or barbiturates—has disturbed that balance, and it takes some time before a healthy equilibrium can be restored. As a result, you may find yourself feeling suddenly depressed or anxious. Or you may be irritable, tense, and easily upset by an offhand comment or a trivial incident. Some of you may find the utter unpredictability of your emotions even more unsettling than the emotions themselves.

Sam's experience is a good example of how abruptly a recovering person's mood can shift from one extreme to the other. A businessman in his mid-thirties, Sam joined an outpatient treatment program when he stopped taking cocaine. For the first couple of days, he was extremely anxious and touchy. He continued going to work but found he couldn't sit through meetings, couldn't answer the phone in his office, and couldn't face returning telephone calls.

Because his sense of time was distorted, he had difficulty pacing himself. Sometimes an hour rushed by in a blur; at other times each minute dragged on and on. However, by the end of his first drug-free week, the worst of Sam's anxiety and excitability had passed, and he entered a period of calm and contentment. He felt a renewed energy for his work and found that his relationships with his wife, Jane, and his eight-year-old son, Josh, were starting to heal.

On his first sober Saturday morning, Sam drove Josh to baseball practice. They laughed and joked together on the way over to the field, and Sam was feeling great as he joined the other parents seated on the bleachers. Then the coach assigned Josh to the bench for the first inning, and Sam was suddenly overwhelmed with sadness and despair. He could barely keep himself from crying. He wanted to rush over to his son and comfort him, even though Josh seemed unconcerned about being kept on the sidelines.

Throughout the day, Sam continued to find himself on the verge of tears—when a door slammed unexpectedly, when Jane touched his hand, when he misplaced his car keys. That evening, he and Jane went to see a film, a thriller, not at all the kind of movie that provokes tears. But Sam began to weep so unrestrainedly that he and Jane had to leave the theater.

Jane was confused by Sam's crying jag. Was he hiding something from her? Had he lost his job? Was he having an affair? Sam assured his wife he was not keeping anything from her, but he felt an almost overwhelming need to explain his emotions, not only to Jane but to himself as well.

Sam had no idea that his sudden, painful mood swings were normal in early recovery. His emotional balance, which had been disrupted by his drug dependency, was further disturbed when he stopped using cocaine. Fortunately, a doctor at the clinic where he was being treated was able to reassure him.

Feelings of sadness and despair similar to Sam's are common during these early months of sobriety, as are anger, shame, remorse, and self-pity. In fact, these last four emotions are almost universal among newly recovering alcoholics and users, and they cannot help but cause pain to you and those around you. But facing up to these unpleasant feelings is a first, necessary step toward regaining your emotional balance. Your willingness to do so is also an important sign that you have truly begun to accept your powerlessness over your addiction, one of the most important steps toward true sobriety and Step One of the twelve-step program of Alcoholics Anonymous.

In these first, difficult months of recovery you need not, indeed *should* not, dwell on your bleak or terrible feelings. But you also must be careful not to ignore them. These emotions are a part of how you feel about yourself, and they won't disappear simply because you refuse to examine them. To the contrary, if you try to deny their existence, they will surface in unexpected ways that can threaten your sobriety. It is far better to work through your rage or regrets. Only then will you be free to put the past behind you and move on.

Catherine's story shows how the best of misguided intentions can undermine even a steely determination to stay clean. Catherine was a suburban mother of three school-age children and a super-organized homemaker. She was one of those women who could always be counted on to organize a charity fund-raising event, to provide an extra tray of brownies for the soccer team bake sale, to serve up a last-minute, elegant dinner for unexpected guests. Catherine's problem was that she relied on Valium and vodka the way other people relied on her.

The morning she woke up too hung over to drive herself to her daughter's school play, Catherine decided to join Alcoholics Anonymous. With the support of her AA friends, she was able to stop drinking and taking tranquilizers. She quit over a long weekend, when her husband James was home to take care of their children and other adults were available to help her.

Catherine had a rocky three days, but by Monday, she was once again feeling strong and in control. Her cheerful facade was firmly back in place. She drove James to the train station, dropped her kids at school, and rushed off to a library book-fair meeting.

Three weeks later she fell apart. Suddenly one afternoon she became overwhelmingly depressed. She felt utterly incapable of performing even the simple, familiar task of picking up her daughter from ballet class. She couldn't think, couldn't act. All she knew was that the urge to take a drink and swallow a pill was almost irresistible.

Fortunately, Catherine was able to stave off her craving long enough to phone Nicholas, an AA friend. After arranging to have someone else meet Catherine's daughter, Nicholas hurried over to be with Catherine. He stayed with her, alternately talking and listening, until her husband arrived home. Shortly thereafter Catherine decided to enter an inpatient treatment facility, where she could focus exclusively on her own needs and attend to her recovery without having to be competent and in control.

Catherine had made a strong commitment to sobriety, and she was able to ask for help, which safeguarded her from drinking or taking drugs again. But the need to maintain an unflappable public image had caused her to jeopardize her sobriety by ignoring the powerful emotional and physical demands of recovery.

For Catherine, who could not permit herself the luxury of being less than a flawless mother, wife, or neighbor, a resident treatment program provided a place where she did not have to be perfect. I don't mean to imply that the only sure path to recovery is through such a program.

But however you choose to begin being sober, allow yourself the time and emotional latitude to grapple with the painful feelings that are bound to plague you during your first weeks and months of freedom from addiction. Ignoring or suppressing your difficult emotions can threaten your sobriety.

Thinking, Memory, and Perception

Alcohol and drugs alter not only the brain's mood-regulating function, but its thinking, concentration, and memory functions as well. Physiological withdrawal temporarily throws the mind and body into a state of imbalance—a reaction to the absence of a daily dose of drugs or alcohol. In the early months of your recovery, you are likely to have difficulty learning and remembering new concepts, names, or facts. You may have trouble with simple, everyday details, such as directions, appointments, or where you parked the car last night. You may find yourself confused about issues that in the past seemed perfectly clear, or have difficulty thinking about or doing more than one activity at a time. You may even have uncanny, unsettling experiences that make you doubt your sanity.

Steve, a forty-year-old sales manager for a nationwide shoe company, had been a heavy drug user, taking marijuana, cocaine, Quaaludes, alcohol, and anything else that came to hand. For years, he had been plagued by blackouts, but he'd shrugged them off, telling himself blithely that they happened to everybody—until his final blackout, when he stood behind a podium to address a large audience. He didn't know who the audience was, and worst of all, he had no idea what he was in the middle of telling them. With that cunning so many addicts have, born of years of practice in tight situations, he immediately faked a heart attack. Fortunately the doctor in the emergency room where he was taken had some training in addiction medicine and ordered a test of Steve's blood alcohol level. When the results showed him at nearly double the legal limit, she referred him for treatment.

After five totally drug-free weeks, Steve's memory was still not restored. He was back at work, but not entirely sure of himself. Dictating a letter one afternoon, he glanced up and noticed a look of bewilderment on his secretary's face. "What's up?" he asked cautiously.

She hesitated, flushed, and then said, "Well, you dictated the exact same letter yesterday."

"Well, at least I'm consistent," he joked.

As soon as his secretary left, he called his doctor for an emergency appointment. "What seems to be the matter?" the doctor asked.

"Only that I seem to have lost my mind, that's all."

Of course, Steve was not crazy. His memory system was still short-circuited. While such events can be alarming, they are not signs of permanent brain damage.

You should also be aware that you may experience perceptual distortions, including the sensation that you are witnessing a scene from above or outside it, rather than participating in it. Or you may be disconcerted by a profound sense of *déjà vu*—the feeling that you have previously been involved in a particular circumstance or conversation, when in fact the event is altogether new to you. You may also experience some degree of paranoia, in which you become unreasonably suspicious of other people.

Because your brain is likely to interpret incorrectly much of what is happening around you, you may develop phobias. That is, you become irrationally fearful of situations that did not bother you at all before you became sober—crossing a busy street or riding an elevator, for example. You may also feel that the world does not seem quite real. These faulty perceptions can, of course, make you anxious. But be assured that as your brain adjusts to sobriety, such distortions diminish and eventually disappear.

Because your nervous system is so unbalanced during these first months, your judgment is poor. Making decisions and sensible choices is virtually impossible while your brain and body are changing so rapidly and unpredictably. Your judgment and ability to analyze will be restored, usually by the time you've been sober for one year. But it is a good idea to postpone major life decisions, if at all possible, until you have achieved a full year's sobriety.

The first three months of recovery are a time of acute abnormality, and you should not expect—nor be expected—to function well. Your physical and emotional states are in a constant state of flux. Frequently, especially if you have gone through an early period of euphoria, your expectations for your recovery may be too high. In these early days, when you're at your most fragile, trying to live up to unrealistic goals may trigger powerful cravings for alcohol or drugs.

You may find yourself wondering, *Is this what I get from sobriety? Is this what it feels like to be "normal"?* You may well decide that if such is the case, you're not altogether sure you want to be sober.

In fact, what you are feeling—the sense of disorientation, the negative emotions—is *not* normal, except within the limited context of the early months of recovery. But your body and brain do adjust to the lack of alcohol and drugs, and eventually you regain your balance.

The Next Three Months

The most descriptive word I know for this next period of recovery is a term frequently used at Alcoholics Anonymous meetings—"mocus." I'm not sure where the word comes from or who first made it up, but in AA it's used to mean feeling muddled and out-of-focus, woolly-headed, as if your brain is surrounded by clumps of cotton.

These are months of overall, gradual improvement as you solidify your recovery and develop the living plan that works for you. You make progress in your life, although sometimes the progress may seem slow or halting. You still frequently feel out-of-sorts and unsure of yourself, your perceptions, and your behavior. Your mocus feelings may lift at times, only to descend again for no particular reason, leaving you stuck in a thick, impenetrable fog. But on the whole, you feel stronger and more in charge of your life.

The Body

In this second stage of recovery, your physical condition improves steadily. Muscle cramps are less frequent and less acute, though your muscle strength and endurance is still below par. Symptoms of nerve damage—numbness, tingling, itching—decrease. Your liver, if you were a drinker, gradually resumes its natural function.

Your immune system grows stronger, and you are far less prone to minor infections. You are also less susceptible to colds, viruses, and low-grade fevers. Your skin tone and appearance continue to improve. Your appetite begins to regulate itself as you adjust to a normal eating pattern. Most people find that sexual function—desire, as well as the ability to maintain an erection and/or reach orgasm—is restored during this period. For those who continue to be troubled by sexual problems, Chapter 9 is devoted to restoring your sex life.

Sleep

Sleep problems generally diminish during this second stage of recovery. You have fewer disturbing dreams and nightmares, and less difficulty falling and staying asleep. But don't be discouraged if you're among those who continue to experience sleep difficulties. About fifty percent of my patients still complain about the unsatisfactory *quality* of their sleep during this period.

Normal sleepers pass through several stages of sleep each night.

However, only in the deepest stage is the body able to restore and refresh itself. Even though you may have several hours of uninterrupted rest each night, you may be reaching only the shallower sleep stages. Consequently, you feel tired and irritable and find it hard to concentrate the next day. As time goes on, you will probably see an ongoing improvement; if you are still troubled by wakefulness, you may get relief from the suggestions in Chapter 14.

Emotions

Your emotions continue to be volatile, although the swings from high to low won't be as violent as they were in the first stage of recovery. But you may still have bouts of anger, shame, remorse, guilt, and self-pity. You may also experience unexpected periods of anxiety. These mini-explosions of emotions may be unrelated to any specific anxiety-producing event or activity. Nevertheless, they can make for uncomfortable minutes, even hours, of pure panic, accompanied by physical symptoms such as rapid heartbeat, sweating, and flushes.

During this second stage of recovery, you may become emotionally trigger-happy. You're likely to be easily excitable, irritable, impatient, and impulsive. You may suddenly have an almost undeniable urge to stalk out of a room in the middle of a meeting, while only seconds before you were absorbed in what was being discussed. You may inexplicably explode with anger while engaged in pleasant conversation with a friend. Your tolerance for frustration will be low. Normally annoying situations such as waiting in line at the bank or searching for a parking space can become major hurdles that seem impossible to cope with.

Although your mood gradually improves, episodes of depression may still come upon you out of the blue. These unexpected, extremely uncomfortable feelings of melancholy and despair are hazardous to your sobriety. In search of fast relief, you may be tempted to turn to what you know best—a stiff drink, a snort of cocaine, a couple of pills. That's why the living plan you will be developing during these months is so important. Knowing what you will do at such difficult times will help you get through them with your sobriety intact. I'll talk more about depression and other dangerous emotions in Chapter 5, where you will also find out what to do if your depression continues to be severe, constant, and unrelieved after eight to twelve weeks of sobriety.

You are also likely to be spending a good deal of time reviewing your life. Your self-esteem may have been buoyed by the act of getting sober and surviving the first tough weeks. But the process of examining your past often brings up deep feelings of regret, remorse, shame, humiliation, and embarrassment. You may also be feeling guilty, not only about your past actions, but also for having a chronic, life-threatening disease in the first place. Under the weight of these feelings, your fragile self-esteem may begin to crumble and perhaps nearly disappear. Relapses can occur at any time in recovery, but during this period they are frequently related to low self-esteem.

Jim, a middle-aged departmental manager at a large corporation in New York City, is an example. He was in his fifth month of sobriety when he was asked to write an important report. He worked hard and stayed late at the office every night for a week, writing and revising until he was sure he'd put together an accurate and comprehensive presentation.

Several days after Jim handed in the report, his boss summoned him to the executive suite and pronounced Jim's report "terrible, a total disaster." Jim had left out critical information, the boss added, and misinterpreted some of the data. In short, the report was unusable. To add to Jim's misery, his boss went on to say that over the last three years, his work had been substandard. If he didn't shape up quickly, he warned, Jim would be out of a job.

Even though he knew his work had improved greatly since he'd become sober, Jim said nothing to defend himself against his boss's harsh words. Nor did he mention that his instructions for preparing the report had been unclear and ambiguous. Instead, he stumbled out the door, feeling utterly crushed and humiliated. All afternoon he brooded in his office, berating himself both for his poor performance and for not speaking up on his own behalf. By the end of the day, he'd concluded that he was an utterly worthless human being.

Why bother staying sober? he asked himself. He didn't even *deserve* to be in recovery. Instead of going home, he headed straight for his favorite watering hole and proceeded to get thoroughly drunk—and continued to do so for many weeks.

As Jim discovered, failure to act positively in situations that threaten your self-esteem can be very dangerous. In Chapters 5 and 12, I'll talk more about how to build and bolster your self-esteem, and how to deal with those circumstances that undermine your wavering sense of self.

Thinking, Memory, and Perception

Although your ability to concentrate improves by the time you have been sober for six months, you may be hard pressed to remember facts or skills that you learned while you were still drinking or using drugs. Work-related tasks that you repeatedly performed in the past may suddenly feel strange and confusing. Having to relearn these routines can be frustrating and time-consuming.

You may also have problems orienting yourself in space, which can contribute to your feeling mocus. The familiar suddenly seems unfamiliar. One morning a patient of mine who had been commuting to work for years from the same train station went to the wrong platform and ended up many miles in the opposite direction from where he was supposed to be. Another patient missed the highway exit he had been taking for the fifteen years he had lived in the same town.

You may note an improvement in your ability to analyze and solve problems, but in all likelihood your judgment is not yet entirely reliable. You may continue to have difficulty sorting out and weighing facts, and this can lead to ill-considered snap decisions.

The strange perceptual distortions, paranoia, and phobias of the first few weeks will now decrease or disappear, but you may still have trouble accurately assessing and controlling the way you react to the world around you.

Gail, the paralegal who hallucinated about men leering at her when she was in alcohol withdrawal, described her perceptual state after four months of sobriety. "When I was in withdrawal, I was terribly frightened by my hallucinations. But I knew I was sick and that there was an explanation for what was happening to me. What happens to me now is different. I can be feeling perfectly okay, and then, out of the blue, for a few hours everything seems to be happening at a distance. It's as if I'm enclosed in a glass bubble and the rest of the world is outside. Then suddenly everything snaps back to normal again. I worry that I may have permanently damaged some part of my brain."

Moments of unreality, when your relationship to the world doesn't seem quite right, are not unusual. I reassured Gail that her minor perceptual distortions were not a sign of brain damage. They do go away, usually by the time you've been sober for a year.

The Remainder of the First Year

You continue to see improvements in your physical and emotional well-being throughout the first year of recovery, but the changes are less dramatic than those you experienced in the first six months. Your muscle strength and endurance may not be all that you'd like them to be, and your mood remains somewhat unstable. Your memory may continue to play tricks on you, learning new skills or facts may still be a challenge, and your ability to tolerate and respond appropriately to stress is still impaired. For the most part, however, you are feeling quite well.

What follows are some pitfalls to watch out for during these months.

At a therapy group for spouses of people in recovery, Clara talked about what was happening to her husband Herb. "I don't understand it," she said. "He's acting the way he did when he was drinking, but he doesn't act drunk, if you know what I mean."

"Maybe he *is* drinking," Vivian suggested.

Clara shook her head. "No, I really don't think so."

"You've been fooled before," Vivian reminded her. "We all have."

"I know, I know," Clara said with a sigh. "That's why I'm so confused. I used to know when Herb was drinking, even when he denied it. His mood would change. He'd be more expansive and silly, sometimes even vulgar. He'd hog the conversation and get into an argument if anybody contradicted him. A real social asset," she added wryly. "But this time it *is* different. This time it's more like he has a perpetual hangover," she explained. "He's grouchy and touchy and terribly down on himself. If one of the kids is cheeky, he yells a blue streak. The kids are keeping out of his way. I'm keeping out of his way. I can't understand this mood change. Everything was going so well."

Clara has just given a flawless description of a dry drunk, an episode during which one is plagued by all the disagreeable symptoms of an active addiction with one major exception—the person is not drinking or using. A dry drunk can sneak up on you for any number of reasons—a cold, an infection, a case of the holiday blues, or the stress of caring for a sick child. Suddenly you're in a foul mood. And because your disease has left you emotionally vulnerable, your bad mood quickly spirals downward. If you don't defuse a dry drunk, it can turn into a real drunk. For advice on how to defuse a dry drunk, consult Chapter 12.

Another potential threat to your sobriety is the "pink cloud," a phenomenon that frequently occurs in the second six months of sobriety. You wake up one morning to discover that your mocus feelings have finally faded and the world is suddenly a wonderful, exciting place to be. Colors are bright, sounds melodious, and coupled with this renewed appreciation of the universe is the feeling that you're flying high. Life is fantastic, and it will remain fantastic forever.

By now you're sufficiently removed from your drinking or drug-taking to realize how truly destructive your addiction was. You remember not only the excitement of getting high but the dreadful hangovers; not just the thrill of buying and hiding your supply, but the strangling need for booze or drugs. Consequently, you feel an exhilarating sense of relief, headier even than that which you experienced in the very early days of sobriety. You've had a narrow escape, but you've survived. You're flying high again—but this time you're sober and it feels terrific!

If you've landed on a pink cloud, enjoy the ride. You've earned it. But tuck away in the back of your mind the knowledge that the feelings won't last forever. Life *is* wonderful, but it is not quite as wonderful as it may seem to be on a pink cloud. Sooner or later, reality will inevitably reassert itself, and you'll suffer a disappointment or find yourself in a stressful situation.

Unless you're aware that your pink cloud is only temporary, you may be unpleasantly surprised when it evaporates. One of the joys of sobriety is that you're able to feel the highs of life as well as the lows. So float luxuriously on your pink cloud, but keep close at hand the parachute that will allow you to land safely when the time comes. Without that parachute—the awareness that the cloud will eventually vanish—you may crash to earth with a painful bump that could lead to a relapse.

Overconfidence is perhaps the most dangerous trap you can stumble into during these second six months of sobriety. You've licked your addiction, and you've never felt better. Much of your sense of well-being comes from feeling normal, rather than crazy or weak or bad, as you may have considered yourself when you were in the throes of your addiction. In fact, you may be feeling so good that you begin to think you *are* normal, even to the extent that you think you can drink like a normal person. Although no one is helped by dwelling constantly on his or her disease, it is crucial never to forget that you are an alcoholic or addict. If you do forget, you can easily be seduced by a false sense of security, as Joanna was.

Joanna had spent four weeks in an inpatient treatment program and was in her eighth month of sobriety when her husband, Dave, asked her to give a dinner party to entertain several of his business associates. Dave had attended the family program at Joanna's treatment center, so he knew that alcoholism was a disease. He'd also been warned about the hazards of keeping liquor in the house before Joanna had completed at least a year of sobriety.

Nevertheless, he insisted that they serve wine with dinner. And because he refused to believe she could be harmed by taking "just a few sips," he convinced Joanna that she could share a glass of wine with their guests. To protect her sobriety, he would buy only enough wine for the evening so that none would be left over to tempt her. Joanna was feeling so good about her recovery that despite all she'd learned, she let herself believe that Dave was right. She had a glass of wine at dinner and was very pleased to see she had no trouble stopping after that one glass.

A month later Joanna and Dave gave another dinner party where they again served wine, and Joanna again permitted herself "just one glass." Later, as she was clearing up, she noticed that a few sips were left in the bottle, so she finished it off while she was loading the dishwasher. Two days later she stopped at the liquor store, bought another bottle for herself, and polished it off before the kids got home from school. It took no more than a couple of weeks before she was back to sneaking gulps from a bottle of vodka throughout the day. Joanna reentered treatment shortly after this relapse, and with much hard work she regained the ground she'd lost. The episode was not a total loss. Both she and Dave now have a much more realistic picture of her disease and how to live with it, and she's been sober for three years.

Should you also suffer a relapse, you too can start over again—and the sooner you recommit yourself to sobriety, the better off you are. Best of all, of course, is to stay sober. One way to preserve your sobriety is never to get so secure about your recovery that you prematurely expose yourself to risky situations before you are strong enough to make the right choices.

After the First Year

"So," [said the doctor]. "Now vee may perhaps to begin. Yes?"

Thus ends Portnoy's Complaint, a novel by Philip Roth. The main character, Alexander Portnoy, has spent nearly three hundred pages baring his soul on the analytic couch, and all the psychoanalyst can say is, "So." But what was the significance of Portnoy's lengthy recital of his painful—if sometimes comical—revelations, if this is only the beginning?

Your recovery, after the first year, is like Portnoy's complaint. You may think you've completed the process, but in fact, you're just getting started.

Anyone who has achieved a full year of sobriety deserves congratulations for an excellent beginning, but it is nonetheless only a beginning. The fact remains that you still have a disease. Because you've been sober for a year does not mean your recovery is finished. A stable, comfortable lifelong sobriety is a day-to-day proposition, a continuous chain of new beginnings.

Your main task in your second and third years of sobriety, and beyond, is to build a good sober life on the foundation you have laid in your first year of abstinence. This book is designed to help recovering people lay that solid foundation, but it is still relevant to those of you who have already celebrated your first or even your second, third, or fourth anniversary in sobriety. Some of the information in it will be new to you. You may not have incorporated some of the components of the living plan—for example, a nutritious diet or regular exercise—into your normal routine. Or you may find help for a persistent problem—your sex life, for instance. But most important, your experiences of the early stages of recovery will be kept fresh in your mind. Reading this book as you work to consolidate the gains you have already made can shed new light on the difficulties you encountered on the way to your first or second anniversary in sobriety. This new understanding can make the work of later sobriety—making amends, helping others with their recovery— richer and more rewarding.

Whether you stopped drinking or using yesterday or more than two years ago, sobriety means putting the past behind you. Yesterday is over. You did not drink or use drugs then, but today is a new day in sobriety. And tomorrow is another. With each new day you have the opportunity to remain sober and add another link to the never-ending chain of new beginnings that makes a sober life.

And so, then, let us begin.

Chapter Two
How Alcohol and Drugs
Have Affected Your Brain
and Body

To begin, you must know where you are. You must know what has happened to you as a consequence of your alcohol or drug abuse, both to your physical self and your emotional self. In this chapter and the next I will discuss what went wrong and why, in all areas of your life. Until you identify and analyze the problems you brought into sobriety, you cannot formulate a plan for solving them. Because these two chapters deal with the early weeks and months of sobriety, they will be of greatest interest to people in the two earliest stages of recovery. But even if you have achieved a sobriety of more than three to six months, any information that adds to your understanding of recovery is valuable. And it is unlikely that you have read or heard much of what is contained in these two chapters elsewhere.

You don't need to read a book to know that alcohol and drug abuse has negative effects on your brain and body. You find that out in your first days of sobriety, when you feel so rotten, mentally and physically. But what you probably don't know, even if you have been sober for six months or longer, is why you feel so awful at first. Why are your emotions erratic and your thought processes sluggish? Where does the dull ache on the right side of your body come from? How long will it take before your fingers stop feeling numb?

These are the types of issues I will address this chapter. I think it is important for you to have this information in order to better understand the mental and physical consequences of your addiction to alcohol or drugs, and to be reassured that the vast majority of these consequences are neither serious nor irreversible. Most are minor ailments that disappear in time, as long as you remain sober. Even when there is more serious damage, to the heart, for example, the condition often improves considerably with proper medical care and continuing sobriety.

I have divided this chapter into two main sections. The first describes the results of using alcohol and drugs on the brain and nervous system. Every abused drug affects the brain, and so I recommend this section to every reader. The second section discusses the other physical effects of the most commonly abused drugs, beginning with alcohol, followed by subsections on cocaine, prescription drugs, hallucinogens, drugs that are smoked, and drugs that are injected.

Much of the information in the second section may not apply to you. You may never have had a respiratory problem, or you may never have abused prescription drugs. So you might decide to treat this second section as a reference guide and refer only to those areas that are of particular concern to you. Also, because alcohol damages every system in the body, I've gone into some detail about its effects. Even if you've never used alcohol, you may still be interested in reading about its physical consequences for the information I have included on how the body works.

How Alcohol and Drugs Have Affected Your Brain

Getting messages to and from the various parts of your brain is a complicated process. Each of the many billions of neurons, or nerve cells, in your brain is surrounded by a network of dendrites, short branch-like fibers that accept incoming electrical impulses from other cells. Once received by the dendrites, outgoing impulses leave the neuron via the axon, a single long fiber that extends from the cell body. Each axon ends in a web of terminal fibers, which have several axon terminals. The junction at which a dendrite from one cell meets an axon terminal from another is called a synapse. At each synapse there is a minuscule gap, known as the synaptic cleft. Because electrical signals cannot cross this cleft, chemical compounds called neurotransmitters are released from the axon terminal to ferry messages across the tiny divide. Anything which interferes with these neurotransmitters can short-circuit the transmission of messages in your brain. (See the diagram on the next page.)

Mood

Although your brain needs only small amounts of each neurotransmitter, these amounts are precisely regulated and carefully bal-

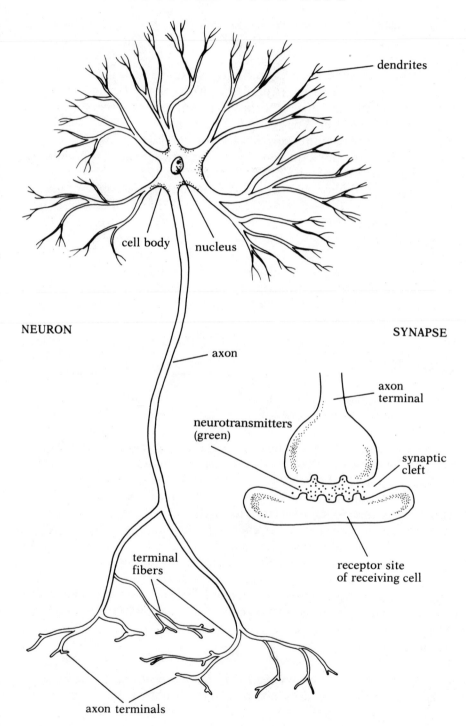

dendrites

cell body   nucleus

NEURON

axon

neurotransmitters
(green)

terminal
fibers

axon terminals

SYNAPSE

axon
terminal

synaptic
cleft

receptor site
of receiving cell

anced. Even small changes can have very large effects on your mood. All drugs that make you euphoric interfere with your neurotransmitters. Different drugs play different tricks, but they all produce substantial changes in your brain chemistry.

Exposing your brain to large quantities of alcohol or drugs is a lot like dumping garbage into the ocean. At first, the nutrients provided by the decaying wastes may cause the plant and animal life to flourish. But the garbage has also disturbed the balance of nature. In time an overgrowth of algae consumes all the oxygen, so that the fish begin to die. As they float belly-up and decay, more waste and more pollution is created. If the dumping is discontinued, the ecosystem may be restored to normal. But the process takes time, and there's no guarantee that the ocean will ever be the same again.

Similarly, your brain becomes "polluted" by alcohol and drugs; the natural balance of its chemical messengers is disturbed. When you stop drinking or using, the alcohol or drugs are soon eliminated from the brain and body tissues. But the disruption of the neurotransmitters' fragile equilibrium continues for quite some time, which is why you're likely to have mood swings, depression, anxiety, fear, and panic attacks.

Let's look at the neurotransmitter called dopamine which is involved in a number of activities in the brain. You may have heard of it in relation to Parkinson's disease, a condition that causes persistent shaking and loss of muscle control. People with Parkinson's disease seem to be lacking dopamine in certain regions of their brains. This deficiency can be corrected to some extent by a drug called L-dopa, which replaces the missing dopamine.

People with schizophrenia, on the other hand, are thought to suffer in part from an excess of dopamine in other areas of the brain. Tranquilizers such as Thorazine, which decrease the amount of dopamine in the brain, can also decrease the hallucinations and delusions that are symptoms of schizophrenia.

However, doctors must be careful to prescribe the precise drug dosage that alleviates a patient's symptoms without causing any further dopamine-related disturbances. Some Parkinson's patients suffer from hallucinations when they take too much L-dopa. And for some schizophrenics, too high a dose of Thorazine can cause symptoms similar to those of Parkinson's disease. If carefully regulated drug use for serious medical conditions can cause such problems, imagine the havoc unregulated drug use can create in your brain.

Cocaine is one of the drugs that's known to increase dopamine levels, and it's not unusual for people who use a lot of cocaine to develop paranoid delusions. Although the worst of the delusions generally disappear soon after they stop using, cocaine addicts often continue to feel suspicious of and anxious about other people for quite some time thereafter. This residual effect may be related to long-lasting changes in the dopamine system.

Such was the case with Lloyd, a crack addict who spent much of the last weeks he was using cowering in his bedroom closet, convinced that his landlord and the FBI were coming to get him. Shadows at the windows and noises in the steam pipes confirmed his suspicions. To outsmart his persecutors, Lloyd turned his apartment into a fortress. He tacked up sheets over the windows, barricaded the doors with furniture, and turned his bed on its side to prevent anyone from hiding under it. The kitchen was littered with broken dishes that Lloyd had thrown at "them" as "they" tried to climb in through the window.

Lloyd's parents finally managed to get inside the apartment and had their son admitted to an inpatient treatment program. The worst of his paranoia subsided quickly, and after two weeks he'd stopped believing that people were out to get him. He had come to understand that his delusions had been caused by his use of crack. But he nevertheless continued to feel uneasy after he left the hospital. The shapes and shadows that danced on the windows after dark made him jittery. He wasn't so nervous that he needed to throw plates or cover the windows with sheets, but he was still so jumpy that he didn't want to be alone in his apartment.

To get himself through this difficult time, Lloyd arranged to stay with a friend. It was about six weeks before he felt confident enough to return home, and another three or four weeks before he regained his delusion-free, pre-crack state of mind.

Cocaine isn't the only culprit as far as dopamine levels are concerned. Alcohol, tranquilizers, and sedatives have also been shown to alter the dopamine system, which may explain why some people develop hallucinations or delusions while they're coming off these drugs. You may not have such extreme psychological symptoms, but in early sobriety you may experience a tendency towards misperceptions, odd visual sensations, and distrust of others, all of which may be related to minor changes in your dopamine levels.

Alcohol and drugs also affect other neurotransmitters. For example, alcohol and drugs reduce the amount of available norepinephrine in the brain. Researchers have found that people who are depressed have low levels of available norepinephrine. Therefore, it is not surprising that episodes of depression are common in early recovery. Abused drugs also interfere with the neurotransmitter system GABA, which is involved in the regulation of anxiety. This interference may be related to the unexpected bouts of anxiety that occur in early recovery.

Although your emotional reactions may depend to some extent on whether you drank or the particular drug you took, after withdrawal from alcohol or almost any drug, you're likely to experience some mixture of anxiety and depression. If you've been using alcohol and/or sedatives, for example, you'll probably be more prone to periods of severe anxiety during early recovery. On the other hand, coming off stimulants such as cocaine and amphetamines may make you more susceptible to depression. Former marijuana users usually describe themselves as suffering from a low-grade mixture of anxiety and depression, often accompanied by perceptual distortions. And people who've stopped taking painkillers most often seem to experience anxiety and depression, along with an increased sensitivity to pain. All these reactions can persist for more than a year, although they do decrease during the first year of recovery.

Perception and the Senses

In addition to regulating mood, the brain also controls how we perceive the world around us, and how we respond to the stimuli we receive. As a result, brain disturbances caused by alcohol and/or drugs often show themselves through the symptoms of abnormal perceptions and sensations.

The perceptual changes and problems that are so common during early recovery can be very alarming, especially if you're not prepared for them. I've had many patients tell me that the world seems out of focus, or that they feel as if they're seeing life through a fog. There may be moments when the fog momentarily lifts and their vision clears, but it soon returns. My patients have also reported that they have difficulty maintaining their sense of self. They feel detached and distant, as if they aren't occupying their own bodies; they are observers who aren't really present in their own lives. This sense of dislocation is sometimes accompanied by a sense of *déjà vu* or by the feeling that the world with which they are familiar has suddenly become unfamiliar.

At the same time, recovering people often feel overwhelmed by the sheer number of sensory messages they're receiving. It's as if the brain's circuits have been temporarily overloaded; its ability to modulate sensations has been impaired by chemical imbalances.

Sometimes this flood of sensations can take on a mystical or spiritual significance. While transitory, such events can have a long-lasting positive impact. My patients have often told me of experiences that made them feel at one with the universe or more spiritually aware and open than ever before. Their experiences led to a genuine spiritual awakening which changed the way they viewed the world and themselves in it.

Kirk, a forty-three-year-old biology professor, had the worst six weeks of his life after coming off alcohol and Valium. He was constantly anxious. At night, while he tried in vain to fall asleep, he could feel an army of ants marching up and down beneath his skin. At odd and unpredictable times his muscles twitched and fluttered. "I'd feel a strange sensation in my biceps, and when I'd roll up my sleeve I could actually see the muscle beating like a pulse, as if it had a life of its own."

New York City, where he'd lived all of his adult life, became a nightmare for him. He couldn't bear the din of police sirens, car alarms, screeching brakes, and blaring radios. "I felt I was being electrocuted by noise." Desperate to get away from it all, he drove with a friend to an isolated cabin in Vermont for a week of cross-country skiing. "It was another world up there," Kirk recalls. "The only sound was our footsteps crunching in the snow. We didn't talk much. It seemed a pity to break the silence."

The full days of skiing so exhausted him that he actually began to sleep at night. The ants were still on the march, and the strange pulse in his biceps still throbbed, but he was much less bothered by either symptom. His anxiety began to abate as he focused on the basics of life—keeping the cabin warm, preparing food, and exercising.

One afternoon he took a long walk by himself and came upon a tiny frozen pond in a clearing in the woods. The sun was shining brilliantly on the ice and on the snowy branches. When he stood still, the silence was absolute. "I was overcome with a feeling of utter peace. The light on the ice was so intense that I felt it flooding through me. I felt transparent and in perfect harmony with the universe. I don't know whether the episode lasted several minutes or only a few seconds, but I'll never forget it. Afterwards, I felt so grateful to be alive and to have been permitted such an unclouded experience of an all-embracing force outside myself. I'm not religious, but I do believe there's a higher power in the universe. Call it nature, call it God, whatever—I *felt* that power. Now when I'm bogged down in self-pity or involved in petty squabbles or fed up with the rat race, I think back to that moment beside the pond. It helps me keep my perspective on life."

Like Kirk, you may be hypersensitive to all kinds of stimuli. Your responses can vary and affect you differently from one day to the next. To one person, the fact that colors seem extra bright can be thrilling; to another, a light pat on the arm can feel like a punch; to a third, a keen awareness of aromas can be tantalizing one day and nauseating the next. These perceptual fluctuations can be very distressing because you have no way of knowing from one moment to the next what sensory messages you'll be getting. You feel as if you don't quite have control of either your inner self or your external environment.

While this hypersensitivity affects almost everyone who enters treatment, it's most common among people who are recovering from dependency on alcohol, tranquilizers, or marijuana. It seems like a mild form of the disorders seen in people who've sustained damage to the temporal lobe of the brain. But unlike victims of brain damage, recovering alcoholics and addicts can expect this problem gradually to diminish and finally disappear, usually within four to six weeks.

You may feel other abnormal sensations such as numbness, tingling, and itchiness, which may be caused by the distortion of messages in the brain itself, or by damage to the peripheral nerves in the part of the body experiencing the abnormality. Alcohol, more than any other drug, affects the nervous system. When you drink to excess, the alcohol destroys the protective sheath that surrounds the nerve endings. The nerves which carry sensation from the skin and organs to the brain conduct electrical currents abnormally, resulting in the peculiar sensations I've just mentioned. I've had patients, for example, with such severe cases of itchiness that they scratched themselves until they were bleeding. But they had nothing at all wrong with their skin. They were scratching at an illusion caused by the scrambled signals emitted by the brain and/or nerves.

The time it takes for your nerves to be restored to health depends upon how much damage they've sustained. For some people, the unpleasant symptoms will subside within four to six months. Other recovering alcoholics, who have incurred greater injury, may have to endure these strange sensations for up to a year or two.

Your eyesight may also be affected in early recovery. Most frequently, I hear complaints about blurred vision. But some patients are troubled by black spots or wavy lines in front of their eyes. Others find even ordinary light to be uncomfortably bright. While these visual distortions can be annoying, they are not the result of permanent damage to the eye itself. They are usually due to temporary harm to the visual nerve, or to distortions of sensory information within the brain itself.

The brain can also garble audio stimuli, so that even moderate noise levels seem too loud, or you may hear sounds that others do not. What you're experiencing are *not* hallucinations, but rather sensory distortions that will disappear once your brain regains its equilibrium. How long this may take depends upon the drug you've been using and your own particular sensitivity, but usually you can expect relief within four months after stopping use of the drug.

Of all the senses, taste seems to be the one that improves immediately. I hear many patients exclaim how much they're enjoying food again—how really terrific it all tastes. At least in this one area, you can expect to be pleasantly surprised at the outset.

Memory, Thinking, and Concentration

Nobody thinks clearly when drunk or high. Most people don't expect to, but they do assume that their logic and reasoning powers will improve when they get sober. While it's certainly true that most former drinkers and users *are* able to think better when they're not under the influence, chemical dependency can have serious long-term effects on memory, thinking, and concentration.

It is the very delicate memory system that presents the most problems during recovery. Memory is one of the first functions to be affected by changes in or trauma to the brain, including the normal physical changes that occur as you age. And it's especially sensitive to the effects of alcohol and drugs. In early recovery, or the first year, memory lapses can take many forms. You may find yourself wondering whether you remembered to lock your front door, or turned off the iron. You may have worrisome moments in social situations when you suddenly can't remember the name of someone you met just a few minutes earlier. You also may not be able to recall what you discussed in a phone conversation you had that morning. In general, your long-term memory—your ability to remember what happened or what you learned in the past—will not be affected. But your capacity for remembering recent events and for learning new skills and information will almost always be diminished by alcohol or drug dependency.

A blackout—a period of time of which you have no recollection whatsoever—is the most dramatic manifestation of how alcohol and sedatives affect the memory while one is actively drinking or using. A blackout may occur because the amount of alcohol or sedatives in your blood shuts down your memory system before you pass out. Or you may suffer a blackout because your tolerance has become so great that while you can walk, talk, and even work under the influence, your very delicate memory system can't tolerate the alcohol or sedatives and therefore stops functioning. A blackout is always a sign of excessive drinking or sedative use. Repeated blackouts are a sure sign of alcoholism or addiction to sedatives.

Blackouts can last for only a moment or for entire days and weeks during which you attended meetings, played tennis, cooked meals, or bought a new car that you couldn't afford. You can come out of a blackout and find yourself in a strange place, without a clue as to why or how you came to be there. And you can perform very complicated tasks during a blackout, even though your memory function is disturbed.

If you've ever suffered a blackout, you probably know yourself how frightening it can be to "lose" a chunk of time in your life. But *once you stop drinking or using, you'll never suffer another blackout*. Blackouts occur only when alcohol or drugs are present in the brain. The fact that you have had one or more blackouts does not mean that you will be more or less prone to memory problems than any other user. However, for a while in recovery, you are likely to have trouble recording new information.

All drugs produce some short-term memory problems, but alcohol causes the most severe of these. In fact, I don't believe I've ever treated a heavy drinker who didn't have significant memory problems after he or she first became sober. Most drug users find that their memory improves greatly within four to eight weeks, but among alcoholics, it can take a year, or even two, before their short-term memory returns to normal. Even then, some alcoholics will be left with a slightly impaired short-term memory function. However, as you grow older, it will no longer be possible to tell which of your memory lapses are due to your drinking and which are the result of the normal process of aging.

A very small percentage of recovered alcoholics actually sustain severe permanent damage to the memory system, a condition known as "Korsakoff's psychosis" and commonly referred to as a "wet brain." People who suffer from Korsakoff's psychosis have lost the ability to remember what is happening in the present or to master new information. They can recall only those past events that occurred before their memory systems were permanently injured.

In his book *The Man Who Mistook His Wife for a Hat*, the neurologist Oliver Sacks tells the story of Jimmie, an ex-navy man who has an extreme case of wet brain. Some time around 1970, Jimmie's memory was completely destroyed by alcohol, thereby wiping out all his recollections of anything that had happened to him between 1945 and 1970, along with his ability to record any new information. For Jimmie, the year is and will always be 1945, and he's about to celebrate his twentieth birthday. Confronted with concrete evidence to the contrary—newspapers or magazines displaying the current date, or his own aging face reflected in a mirror—Jimmie is momentarily puzzled. Seconds later, he forgets the incident, and is happy once again.

Most of us know when we're having memory lapses, but we're often far less aware of having trouble thinking clearly or solving problems. My patients don't often complain that their brain isn't working properly. But because of interrupted connections in the brain, most people have weakened problem-solving abilities in early recovery. Some recovering people find it hard to concentrate on a given subject or activity because their brains are hyperactive and easily irritated. So don't be alarmed if your mind wanders, or you find reading, writing, listening, or even watching television too taxing during your first months of sobriety. Your ability to pay attention and to concentrate will take about three months to restore itself. But problem-solving—whether it is a physical problem such as figuring out how to install a seat for your toddler on your bicycle or a life problem such as whether or not to leave your job—will remain difficult for the first year of recovery.

Ed told this story at an AA meeting when he had been sober for five months. "There I was, sitting on the floor of the den surrounded by wood, clutching some 'easy assembly instructions' in my sweaty fist. I was so frustrated I didn't know whether to kill or cry. Then Rita, my friend who lives down the block, walks in. 'Didn't I leave you in this position two hours ago?' she asks. Now that was a really dumb thing to say. That woman will never know how close she came to annihilation. So I started to mouth off about the Japanese who can't write instructions in plain English. 'This is the hundredth time I've followed the instructions for this goddam sliding file cabinet,' I squawked. 'It won't slide and it won't hold files. Maybe the Japanese keep files upside down, but I don't.' So Rita walks over to the box the whole mess came in and turns it over. She reads very slowly, 'Made in the U.S.A.' All the while, she's keeping one eye on me, the way you do when you think someone's maybe a little psycho and you don't know which way they're going to jump. Then she gets down on the floor, turns some of the pieces around, bangs them together and presto, a sliding file cabinet. Still keeping her eye on me, she backs out of the door. But she pops back in again and says, 'Ed, I think you need a meeting.' So here I am."

Rita gave Ed the same advice I would have given him. A self-help meeting is an excellent place to vent your frustrations with problem-solving in early sobriety.

One last word about memory problems: Recovering alcoholics in particular may temporarily have trouble keeping themselves oriented. As a result, they can lose their bearings and find themselves, for example, wandering lost through a building that should be familiar. The reason for this damage to geographical memory is not known, but the problem usually corrects itself or at least improves within the first three to six months.

How Alcohol and Drugs Have Affected Your Body

Alcohol

Of all the drugs people abuse, alcohol causes the most *physical* damage:

1. Alcohol inhibits good nutrition. An average drink—a glass of wine or beer or a shot of hard liquor—contains 80 to 100 calories. Most people require approximately 1,500 to 2,000 calories a day, so five drinks can supply about one-third of their daily calories. Because heavy drinkers get so many calories from liquor, they tend to skip meals and to snack instead on non-nutritious foods. Alcohol also irritates the stomach, another reason why alcoholics frequently lose their appetite for balanced meals that include meat or other forms of protein, grains, vegetables, and fruits. Consequently, they may not take in enough protein, vitamins, and minerals.

2. Alcohol consumes oxygen. Ethyl alcohol, the active ingredient in all alcoholic drinks, is a simple substance that is soluble in water. It can therefore travel throughout the body and lodge in any body part. Once lodged, it must be broken down. To do this, it steals vital oxygen from that organ's tissue. Over time, this oxygen deprivation damages the tissue and thus the organ itself.

3. Alcohol interferes with the delicate membrane that surrounds each cell. It can so badly damage cell membranes that cells begin to leak, which can result in the loss of minerals vital to proper functioning, especially in the brain, nerves, and muscles. Alcohol also interferes with the absorption of vitamins and minerals through cell membranes in the stomach and intestines. Consequently, whatever nutrients *are* taken in may not reach the parts of the body that depend on them.

4. Alcohol indirectly causes other kinds of bodily injuries. (For that matter, so do all abused drugs.) When people drink too much, they lose control of their muscle coordination and movements. Their reaction times are also impaired, so that they're much more prone to have accidents, cut or bruise themselves, strain muscles or break bones.

Now let's take a closer look at how alcohol affects each of the body's systems.

The Digestive System

These are the parts of the body—the mouth, esophagus, stomach, intestines, and bowel—responsible for ingesting and digesting the food that fuels your body. What you eat, or don't eat, also affects the digestive system, so I've included in this section a description of the effects of alcohol on the appetite and nutrition.

The Mouth and Esophagus

Any kind of chemical dependency seems to be incompatible with good preventive dental care. No matter what drug they've been abusing, most of my patients have teeth and gums that are in terrible condition. (But that need not continue, as you will learn in Chapter 13.)

Alcohol is particularly harmful to the gums, for two reasons. First, the mucous tissue of the mouth is fragile due to poor nutrition. Second, alcohol prevents the body's clotting mechanism from functioning properly. The result is that most heavy drinkers bleed from the gums when they brush their teeth. Canker sores and other gum and mouth infections are also common, frequently a result of poor hygiene. Some alcoholics also complain of a coated tongue, which may be a sign of B vitamin deficiencies.

Alcoholics who smoke heavily also have an increased risk of cancer of the mouth and the upper part of the esophagus, due to the combined effects of alcohol and nicotine on those parts of the body. An irritated esophagus is also quite common, especially among those who drink hard liquor. When the esophagus is inflamed, it can produce a burning sensation in the throat, which is made worse in turn by the vomiting that frequently occurs among heavy drinkers.

A patient of mine named Eric once graphically described how in the months before he finally stopped drinking, he would spend most mornings "in a prayerful attitude" in front of the toilet bowl. "I'd kneel on the floor with a huge glass of whiskey and water by my side, waiting for the vomiting to stop so I could get some booze inside me. Sometimes it took four or five tries before I could get any of it to stay down. Then I needed at least four shots for my hands to stop shaking, and another two before I was ready to face the world. The liquor hurt going down, and it hurt coming up. My throat felt like it was on fire, but I still kept drinking."

When Eric first got sober, his inflamed esophagus made it hard for him to swallow. For three or four days he was so sick that all he could get past his aching throat were a few sips of water. But within two weeks, he was able to eat whatever he wanted.

The Stomach, Intestines, and Bowel

Heavy drinking can irritate and inflame the stomach, frequently causing gastritis, an inflammation of the stomach lining. This is often the condition that brings alcoholics to see their doctors, and may be the first step that leads to a diagnosis of alcoholism.

Gastritis is a direct consequence of alcohol sitting in the stomach. It can be exacerbated by a predisposition to excess stomach acidity, as well as by vomiting. Among people who have a tendency toward ulcers, the gastritis may be severe enough to cause a gastric or peptic ulcer, or possibly even internal bleeding. Blood-streaked vomit or dark black stools are the warning signs of internal bleeding.

Alcoholics often experience irritability in the intestines and the bowel. Diarrhea, nausea, and vomiting are very common and often continue for the first four to fourteen days of sobriety. But the first three to four days are usually the worst. After that, the digestive system calms down and begins to function normally.

The Appetite and Nutrition

Newly sober alcoholics often suffer from some nutritional deficiency, usually because their diets have consisted mainly of carbohydrates and fats. A few alcoholics have so limited their protein, vitamin, and mineral intake that they actually develop primary malnutrition, the kind of severe malnutrition seen in developing countries. Others may be suffering from secondary malnutrition—they've taken in sufficient food, but their bodies can't properly process the nutrients. Thus, they may be seriously deficient in the B vitamins, in vitamins A and K, in magnesium and/or calcium.

Lack of B vitamins contributes to malfunctions of the brain and nervous system and inhibits the formation of red and white blood cells. Vitamin A deficiency causes vision problems, particularly poor night vision. Insufficient vitamin K, which is vital to blood clotting, causes easy bleeding and bruising as well as poor clotting and healing. Loss of calcium can cause bones to thin and weaken and consequently be more easily fractured. Low magnesium can contribute to irritability of the nervous system and may cause twitching or seizures.

Alcoholics may also be seriously deficient in protein. Alcohol interferes with the process whereby protein is broken down into amino acids so it can be used by the body. Lacking protein, the body can't build or repair muscle tissue, and protein deficiency often contributes to muscle tissue loss.

Most alcoholics compound their nutritional defiencies by continuing to eat poorly even though they have stopped drinking. And improved nutrition is often viewed as unimportant even by those who have achieved a sobriety of a year or longer. For information on good eating practices to start as soon as possible, consult Chapter 15.

The Liver

The liver is like an enormous chemical factory that controls most of the chemical processes of the body. The liver breaks down the food you eat into chemicals that can be used by the body, turning complex carbohydrates into simple sugars, proteins into amino acids, and fats into fatty acids. It also controls the level of many hormones, which regulate such responses as your reaction to stress and your sexual behavior. Moreover, it is responsible for breaking down the vast majority of drugs into inactive substances that are then eliminated by the body.

When confronted with a load of ethyl alcohol, your liver moves to process it immediately, first breaking it down into a toxic substance called acetaldehyde. Your body does not allow this poison to accumulate, so your liver must further occupy itself in breaking down the acetaldehyde into carbon dioxide and water. This conversion uses up a great deal of oxygen and interferes with your liver's ability to perform its normal functions. As a result, a liver that is liberally supplied with alcohol may be able to process only a small part of the nutrients in your food.

People who drink more than two drinks a day on a regular basis may begin to accumulate some fat in their liver. But at greater levels of alcohol intake, the liver becomes very much like that of a Strasbourg goose, overfed to make pâté de foie gras. Almost all alcoholics who come into treatment have some degree of fatty liver, although they may not know it unless they feel some fullness or tenderness under the right rib cage. Some people have such an enlarged liver that it occupies a big part of the abdominal cavity, stretching the capsule (the covering of the liver) and causing pain.

If all that's wrong with your liver is an accumulation of fat, you can expect it to return to normal on its own once you stop drinking. Depending on how enlarged it's become, this process usually takes three to four months.

Many heavy drinkers also suffer from an inflammation of the liver called alcoholic hepatitis. (This disease differs from infectious hepatitis, which is caused by a virus.) It is possible to have alcoholic hepatitis and not know it. You may feel generally unwell, out of sorts, tired, and without an appetite. You may even have tenderness under the right rib cage, and your skin may be slightly yellow. Often alcoholic hepatitis isn't diagnosed until a heavy drinker checks into a hospital for some other reason, and tests show that his or her liver enzymes are abnormal. Like the fat accumulations, the inflammation will gradually subside and disappear, generally within four to six months after becoming sober.

People who continue to drink and suffer bouts of liver inflammation may develop a condition called cirrhosis (cirrhosis is the Greek word for scar tissue). Any severe, untreated inflammation causes cells to die and to be replaced by scar tissue, in the same way that a scar forms on your skin when you've had a bad cut. The liver can lose a lot of tissue and still continue to function. But there can come a point when the liver is so scarred that liver failure occurs. When this happens, fluid begins to accumulate in the body, which is why people with liver failure usually have hugely distended abdomens, swollen ankles, and thin arms and legs. If they continue to drink, they will certainly die.

There is no way to know whether you have cirrhosis or just a fatty liver unless you have a liver biopsy. But in either case the remedy is the same—stop drinking and your liver will get better.

As I explained earlier, one of the functions of the liver is to break down complex carbohydrates into simple sugars, which the body uses for energy. If the liver is too busy processing alcohol to take care of carbohydrates, the simple sugars the blood needs will not be produced. The result is that some alcoholics may have low blood sugar (hypoglycemia), which is one reason why people go into an alcoholic stupor. Not only are they knocked out by the alcohol, they're also knocked out by their low blood sugar.

It may take four to fourteen days after you stop drinking for your blood sugar to test at normal levels, and four to eight weeks before your body can properly regulate your blood sugar level again and keep it stabilized. But time, sobriety, and a healthy diet will cure alcohol-related hypoglycemia.

Another function of the liver is to break down excess hormones into inactive substances. This function is often curtailed in heavy drinkers, both male and female. As a result they may have abnormally high levels of certain hormones, especially the female sex hormone, estrogen, which is present in both men and women. In some alcoholics, this excess estrogen produces a red network of dilated capillaries—tiny broken blood vessels—on the nose or upper chest. In others, it takes the form of the classic W.C. Fields red nose. Once these capillaries become dilated, they remain so, and the network is often visible on people who haven't had a drink in years. The redness may fade, but it won't disappear.

Women who have high estrogen levels may develop irregular menstrual cycles. Some men whose estrogen is elevated may grow extra flesh around their breasts, or may lose body hair. Eric, the man I mentioned earlier who had a severely inflamed esophagus, also showed some of the physical effects of poor liver function, as well as other signs of deterioration due to his thirty-five years of hard drinking. One morning, about two weeks into his sobriety, he had what he called "an unveiling." He stripped down and took a long, close look at himself in the mirror.

"I knew I was no thing of beauty, and sex had been out of the question for years, but I had no idea how bad I looked. I had boobs! Nothing to turn you on, just these saggy bags. Plus I looked like something out of a Tom and Jerry cartoon, where Tom's been squeezed through a vacuum and everything's been sucked out of his top half and settled in his bottom half. No shoulders, arms like twigs, and these folds of fat around my belly."

Eric also noticed that his skin was gray and dirty-looking, covered with blotches and small red veins. "Especially on my chest, if you can call it that. And no hair. Gone, not even a few gray strands left. And I'm only fifty-one! I looked like my grandpa when he died. He was eighty. Died from the drink, like everyone in the family."

Eric's palms were flushed, too, a further sign of a distressed liver. The redness in his palms faded over the next two to three months, but they always retained a somewhat red color. Still, once he stopped drinking, his liver began to resume its regular functions. His hormone levels returned to normal, and the food he ate was processed properly. Eventually, with good food and exercise his physical condition improved. As he developed his chest, the increased padding on his breasts became barely noticeable, although it never went away entirely. Although Eric was never invited to appear on the cover of *Gentlemen's Quarterly*, he did turn into a healthy man who cared about his appearance.

The Heart and Blood Vessels

The heart and blood vessels—the arteries, veins, and capillaries —are responsible for pumping blood and other fluids through the body. The amount of work it takes for these organs, known collectively as the cardiovascular system, to accomplish this task is measured in two ways—heart rate and blood pressure.

Your heart rate is the number of times your heart beats over a set period of time, usually one minute. The lower your heart rate, the less work your heart does to pump the blood through your body. Blood pressure measures the force with which your heart pumps blood against the walls of the blood vessels. If the walls of the blood vessels are blocked (by a buildup of cholesterol, for example), your heart has to exert more force to pump the blood through them. High blood pressure means that your heart must work harder to do its job.

While alcohol can seriously damage both the heart and the blood vessels, its effects are reversible when you stop drinking—unless you have had a heart attack or a stroke. The permanent damage caused by a heart attack or a stroke cannot be undone, but your heart and blood vessels can recover to the fullest extent possible as long as you stay sober.

Alcohol damages the blood vessels, and potentially the heart, principally by causing high blood pressure. When you drink, your blood pressure goes down. The following morning, however, there is a rebound effect: your blood pressure (along with your heart rate and your temperature) rises to a higher-than-normal level. If you keep drinking large amounts of alcohol, your blood pressure remains abnormally high.

The heart is a muscle, and one way alcohol affects it is by weakening the muscle tissue itself. Heavy drinking also increases low density lipoproteins, the so-called bad cholesterol. If the blood vessels leading to the heart are clogged with LDL cholesterol, the risk of heart attack increases. And by interfering with the normal functioning of heart muscle, heavy drinking can produce an irregular heartbeat.

Often people who aren't alcoholics but who have overindulged, perhaps over a holiday weekend, may complain of palpitations or an irregular heartbeat. In hospital emergency rooms, this phenomenon is known as "holiday heart." But in long-time alcoholics, the heart muscle can become seriously weakened. This can result in heart failure—in some cases, even among people as young as thirty.

William was twenty-eight and seemed in good physical condition. A former high school basketball and baseball player, he had started drinking beer as a teenager with his buddies after their games. As he got older, he devoted fewer hours to sports and more time to drinking beer. His evenings were often spent hanging out with his buddies, consuming many cans of beer. On Saturdays, he and the guys played softball or basketball, depending on the season. After the game, they'd spend the rest of the afternoon and evening drinking. But William never thought of himself as a drunk. He didn't get rowdy; he didn't fight; he didn't miss work. He was just a regular guy who drank eight to twelve or more pints of beer a day.

William first noticed some physical difficulty when he started to get winded while playing basketball and had to drop out after the first half—sometimes the first quarter. Then, increasingly, he began to experience breathlessness while climbing stairs. He was alarmed enough to consult his doctor, who sent him to the hospital for further tests.

William was told that he had a dilated heart, caused by the amount of beer he was drinking. The heart muscle had weakened and expanded, and was therefore unable to pump blood through his body, especially when he exerted himself. His condition, which used to be known as "beer-drinkers' heart," can develop from drinking other alcoholic beverages, but most commonly strikes people who drink large quantities of beer.

William was very upset when his doctor informed him that he had to give up all forms of alcohol. "But I'm not an alcoholic," he protested. "I only drink beer."

Nevertheless, he heeded his doctor's warning that if he continued to drink, his physical condition would continue to deteriorate. Athletics were so important to him that he was highly motivated to stay sober. He went into treatment and stopped drinking. I'm not sure he ever accepted that he was an alcoholic, but he did come to accept the fact that he could never drink again.

People are often confused about the effect alcohol has on the heart because they've heard drinking can help prevent heart attacks. It is true that *light* drinking—one drink or less per day—seems to guard against heart attacks in some cases. However, as soon as you begin drinking more than two drinks a day, your risk of heart attack rises. Among those who drink more than six drinks a day, the risk of heart attack is dramatically increased.

One drink a day or less also seems to have a slightly beneficial effect on the blood pressure. However, more than two drinks per day increases the risk of high blood pressure. The more you drink, the higher your blood pressure can rise. Stopping drinking generally causes the blood pressure to decrease. Former drinkers who have been on medication for high blood pressure often find that they can maintain a normal pressure without medication.

Alcoholic drinking also greatly increases the risk of a stroke, especially for people over fifty. However, once you stop drinking, your risk decreases to that of the rest of the population.

The Respiratory System

The lungs are the primary component of the body's respiratory, or breathing, system. Because of lowered body resistance, alcoholics tend to get a lot of respiratory infections such as colds, flu, and bronchitis. But once they become sober, their body's ability to repair itself returns, and the incidence of respiratory infections—indeed of all infections— decreases. However, since the vast majority of alcoholics are also smokers, they may continue to have respiratory problems. Smoking is the major reason for chronic lung problems in abstinent alcoholics. In Chapter 17, I'll talk more about the consequences of smoking for recovering people.

The Muscles, Bones, and Joints

Muscles work by responding to electrical impulses that originate in the brain. These impulses are passed along a complex chain of nerves until they reach the targeted muscles, which then perform the desired actions. However, if your muscles don't get the message your brain is sending, they aren't able to obey the commands. Most abused drugs, and alcohol in particular, interfere with the transmission of electrical impulses from the brain by cutting the vital nerve connections along the pathways to the muscles. Alcohol also attacks the muscles directly by destroying muscle cells.

It can take from one to six months to reestablish proper communication between the brain and the muscles. Symptoms of poor brain-to-muscle transmission include unexpected fatigue and the inability to accomplish familiar physical tasks.

One of my patients went on a weekend hiking trip four weeks after she stopped using alcohol and cocaine. "By the middle of the first afternoon I just couldn't go on. My legs were shaking from exhaustion. The leader and another man had to carry me to the nearest campsite, which was much more crowded than the one we'd been heading for. The others were very kind, but I'd ruined their weekend. I couldn't understand it. I'd been feeling so well, and I could easily have gone the distance and more before I started drinking and drugging."

Another patient had been the star pitcher of his company's softball team. He'd been sober six weeks when the season began, and he fully expected to pitch better than ever now that he was off the sauce. But he found that he was walking every other man, because he just couldn't get the ball over the plate. It was well into the summer before he found his throwing form again.

In addition to poor brain-to-muscle communication, you may also experience one or more of the following muscle problems. Painful spasms of single muscles or whole muscle groups are common. These are caused by the accumulation of blood containing lactic acid in the muscles. Lactic acid, the residue left in the blood when the muscles have used up the sugar stored there for energy, causes cramps in nondrinkers who exercise too vigorously. But alcoholics can get cramps even without exercising because their flabby muscles can't pump out the used-up blood.

Uncontrolled muscle movements are another common disorder. Unbidden by you, your leg or arm may suddenly kick up or fling out to the side. These spasms can be merely annoying, or can cause more serious problems by disturbing your sleep or keeping you from falling asleep. When they occur just before or during sleep, they indicate that your brain is overactive and still sending signals to your muscles after you've closed up shop for the night. You may experience still another particularly uncomfortable and upsetting sensation—a powerful, uncontrollable twitching under the skin, like Kirk's, due to increased muscle excitability.

Even if you experience none of these muscle disturbances, you'll probably have sustained an actual loss of muscle tissue, especially if you've been drinking and/or using drugs for more than a year. Your physical condition will be weaker than it should be. Your endurance and your ability to perform short, fast spurts of activity will also be curtailed. Weakened muscles are also less able to protect joints and ligaments (the bands of tissue that connect one bone to another), so it's easier to slip a disk or tear a ligament.

Fortunately, loss of muscle tissue doesn't have to be a permanent condition. A regular exercise program can rebuild muscles. But be sensible and take care when you begin to exercise. Start slowly and work up gradually. If you exercise too vigorously while your body is still in a weakened state, you may sustain muscle and/or ligament problems such as shin splints, tennis elbow, or a strained back. I will discuss exercise in detail in Chapter 16.

Besides muscle problems, you may also suffer from joint pain. When you were high, you may have put yourself in contorted positions and you're only now becoming aware of the pain these distortions have caused to your joints. Because you're no longer putting such stresses on your body, this type of joint pain should clear up within four to eight weeks. However, if you have discomfort as a result of arthritis or general joint inflammation, it won't disappear after you become sober. Many chronic conditions, although made worse by drinking, are not caused by alcoholism. Your arthritis may improve with sobriety, but you cannot expect complete relief.

Alcohol also leeches calcium from the body, so that the bones can become thinner and more porous (a condition known as osteoporosis). In menopausal women, who lose calcium anyway because of a drop in their estrogen levels, the additional loss of calcium from alcohol use may cause bones to become especially brittle and liable to fracture from even minor injuries. Alcohol-related nutritional deficiencies may also rob bone ends of the necessary nutrients, which in turn affects the joint surfaces so that movement becomes painful. In rare cases, the pain is so severe that a joint replacement is necessary. However, if you build up your bones through exercise and sufficient calcium intake before the age of thirty-five, you will have a better structure to resist the loss of calcium during menopause.

When Aileen, a forty-two-year-old nurse, entered my office I noticed that her right hand and arm were in the type of case used for a Colles's fracture of the wrist, a condition rarely seen in a woman as young as Aileen. Before I could comment, she said, "That's right, it's the old ladies' fracture I've got."

Elderly women with osteoporosis are particularly susceptible to hip and wrist fractures. The wrist fractures come about when they put out a hand to save themselves from a fall and their brittle bones snap at the wrist. Although we all automatically shoot out a hand to break a fall, normal bones rarely fracture in this way. A sprained wrist is the usual consequence.

"The orthopedist says I have osteoporosis," Aileen continued. "My periods stopped a year ago. He says it may be because I'm drinking too much. That's why he sent me to you. Isn't that ridiculous? He says my bones belong to a seventy-year-old. First he insults me by calling me an alcoholic, then he tells me I have the body of an old woman. He shouldn't be practicing medicine with those attitudes." I interrupted Aileen's rampage to ask for the orthopedist's telephone number. I wanted to call and congratulate him on his astute diagnosis. Aileen barely paused to spit out the number, but eventually she ran out of steam. "So what do I have?" she demanded belligerently.

Sober now and working in a detox unit, Aileen remembers the day we met. "I came to see you in a rage so that I could sue Dr. Forbes for malpractice. I fully expected you to tell me that his suggestion was outrageous, yet somewhere inside I knew my body was falling apart. I knew it was the alcohol. I kept trying to suppress that terrifying thought and yet I wanted the nightmare to end. That's really why I came."

Aileen stopped drinking, but her periods did not return. She consulted her gynecologist, who confirmed that she was in early menopause and prescribed hormone replacement therapy. She also added sufficient calcium to her diet, and began exercising regularly. With this regimen, Aileen was able to mitigate the effect of excessive drinking on her bones. She should not have to worry about incurring another Colles's fracture for several decades, if ever.

The Bladder and Kidneys

By and large, alcohol does not have a significant impact on the bladder or the kidneys unless you have a pre-existing condition that's exacerbated by your alcoholism or by the physical neglect and deterioration that go along with it. However, alcoholics do tend to contract infections of the bladder and the urethra, due to their generally lower resistance to infections.

When you drink heavily, you urinate often. Alcohol is a diuretic —that is, it increases urination. However, once a load of alcohol has left your body, there's a rebound effect and you start retaining water. This accounts for the bloated, puffy look that's so common among alcoholics. You lose this excess water when you stop drinking. Indeed, in the first three to five days of sobriety, you may find yourself making more than a few extra trips to the bathroom, but you'll soon see a marked difference in your appearance.

The Sex and Reproductive Organs

Achieving satisfactory sexual and reproductory function is a complex process that depends on both mental and physical well-being. It involves not only the mind, but also the testes or ovaries, the nerves that lead to the sexual organs, and the pituitary gland that controls sex hormone levels in blood. For things to go well in the bedroom, *all* these systems must be functioning properly.

All drugs, including alcohol, affect the emotional aspects of sex, which I will discuss in Chapter 3.

Males Alcohol attacks the testes directly, killing cells which produce testosterone, the male sex hormone. It also destroys sperm cells and lowers sperm count, which may result in diminished fertility.

Low testosterone levels, which can also be seen in heavy social drinkers, may contribute to decreased interest in sex as well as to performance difficulties. In several experiments, healthy young men who were given enough alcohol to make them drunk every night for two weeks showed marked decreases in their testosterone levels. For these subjects, testosterone levels returned to normal within days after the experiment ended. However, they had been drinking to excess for only two weeks. For men who have been drinking alcoholically for years, it may take four to six months before testosterone levels return to normal. In some men, damage to the testosterone-producing cells in the testes may be so extensive that testosterone remains permanently low.

As I mentioned before, by damaging the liver, alcohol can also impair the body's ability to break down estrogen. In some men, like Eric, the combination of increased estrogen and decreased testosterone can produce feminization. Feminization does not change the direction of your sexual interest. That is, heterosexual males do not develop homosexual interests. But your libido may diminish, and you may lose body hair and develop a more feminine distribution of fat, especially increased breast tissue.

Alcohol can also harm the pituitary gland, which normally monitors and regulates sex hormone levels, so that it fails to perform these tasks, allowing sex hormone levels to move either above or below their normal ranges.

And finally, alcohol attacks the nerves going to and from the penis which carry skin sensations to the brain and provide the stimulus for erection. Because of this impaired nerve function, men may be unable to get or maintain an erection.

Alcohol's damage to the sex and reproductive systems is so extensive that about 50 percent of alcoholic males coming into treatment centers have experienced some significant potency problems. Most recover, but about 5 percent remain permanently impotent because of severe organic damage. This small group comprises mostly older alcoholic men who have been drinking to excess for decades.

Clearly, alcohol and sex don't mix well. With abstinence, however, your interest in sex and your ability to achieve and maintain an erection and to reach orgasm will improve. Without alcohol, your testicular cells revive, your pituitary resumes normal functioning, and your nerve endings regenerate. This process can take from two weeks to a year, depending on the extent of the damage you have sustained.

Females Women coming into treatment for alcoholism typically suffer from loss of libido as well as from difficulty in becoming aroused and in reaching orgasm. These problems may be masked by increased sexual activity during the course of their addiction, which is the result of intoxication and is generally not satisfying. Moreover, fertility may also be affected. Less research has been done on performance difficulties in female alcoholics, but some of alcohol's effects on women's sexual and reproductive organs are known, even though the causes and implications of these effects are not yet fully understood.

Alcohol harms nerve endings around the clitoris. This damage can deaden sensation, diminishing arousal and vaginal lubrication and also impairing the sensory feedback which fuels orgasm. Combined with an increased susceptibility to vaginal infections, lack of vaginal lubrication can make intercourse painful.

During the first four to six months of sobriety, women characteristically experience a low level of desire and arousal. They want, and have, less sex. It can take from six months to more than a year to begin having normal, comfortable sexual relations, but as long as you remain sober, your sexual performance will improve.

Reproduction Alcohol directly damages the ovaries. In pre-menopausal women this results in fewer eggs and more cycles in which eggs are not produced. Both these circumstances result in diminished fertility. Menstruation may also be irregular and may sometimes disappear entirely. I have seen many women, some as young as thirty, who have not had a period for several years due to their drinking. Most women with irregular or stopped menstrual cycles can expect to return to a normal cycle in three to four months.

With abstinence, fertility will improve and return to normal, generally once your menstrual cycle has become regular again. You can then expect to have no further reproductive difficulties unless you have a problem that is unrelated to your drinking. If you become pregnant, you can also expect to deliver a normal baby if you maintain abstinence throughout your pregnancy. There is no evidence that an abstinent alcoholic woman has any greater chance of having an abnormal baby than a woman who has never had a drinking problem.

While alcohol can diminish fertility in both males and females, it has even more severe effects after conception occurs. The majority of babies born to women who were using alcohol or drugs to excess during a pregnancy are normal. But there are some serious risks associated with using alcohol or drugs during pregnancy.

Women who are alcoholics have more miscarriages and premature deliveries than non-alcoholics. However, the most serious risk of drinking during pregnancy is fetal alcohol syndrome. Babies born with this syndrome have characteristic facial features—wide-spaced eyes, small noses, thin lips—and associated mental retardation. The chances of having a baby with fetal alcohol syndrome, while small (about two or three in one thousand), increase with the amount of alcohol drunk during pregnancy.

While fetal alcohol syndrome itself is comparatively rare, babies born to mothers who were drinking heavily during pregnancy are more likely to have fetal alcohol effects, such as lowered birth weight, poor functioning at birth, irritability, and a possible reduction of intellectual abilities.

Some babies born to alcoholic or drug-using mothers are themselves physically dependent on the substance they have been getting through their mother's blood. They may go through physical withdrawal after birth.

If you were using alcohol or drugs during a pregnancy, you will probably be worried about whether your child was affected. If your child is growing well, eating well, sleeping well, and getting along well in school and with his or her friends, stop worrying. You don't have to wonder when your child gets a seventy-five on a test if she might have scored an eighty if you hadn't been drinking during your pregnancy. If your child is not much of an athlete, your job is not to agonize over whether his clumsiness was caused by your addiction. This will not help either of you.

Because there are so many factors involved—genetics, maternal nutrition, use of nicotine, exposure to chemicals and pollutants, to name a few—there is no way of knowing whether or not a child's particular abnormality (unless there is a sure diagnosis of fetal alcohol syndrome) is a result of having been exposed to alcohol or other addictive drugs in the uterus. All you can do now is resolve that you will never take that risk again: stay sober and be there, all there, for your children.

The Immune System and the Blood

Alcohol and other drugs are immunosuppressants—that is, they weaken the body's immune system, whose job it is to identify viruses and bacteria as foreign invaders. This recognition triggers a defensive response that includes an outpouring of white blood cells that neutralize and eliminate the invaders. When the immune system is weakened, the body can't properly defend itself against disease. Infections are more frequent, wounds heal more slowly, and recovery from any disease, even a common cold, takes longer.

Drinking and taking drugs per se don't expose you to AIDS, and you can't become infected with the AIDS virus unless there are other risk factors involved, such as sharing infected needles or having sex with someone who has AIDS. But lowered body resistance can weaken your ability to fend off the AIDS virus if you *are* exposed to it.

Alcohol also affects the blood cells, mainly because excessive drinking promotes poor eating habits, as I discussed earlier. Inadequate nourishment causes a decrease in the number of disease-fighting white blood cells and a subsequent deterioration in the body's defenses. As a result, a heavy drinker's skin and mucous membranes become fragile and are more likely to be penetrated by bacteria, viruses, and fungi, leaving alcoholics subject to skin ailments such as boils, pimples, athlete's foot, and other bacterial or fungal infections.

The blood's red cells carry oxygen to the body tissues. An abnormally low number of red blood cells indicates a condition called anemia. There are different types, but the two most common are iron deficiency anemia and vitamin deficiency anemia. Iron deficiency anemia is frequently seen in women who are menstruating heavily or in people who have lost a great deal of blood.

Some alcoholics may develop iron deficiency anemia because they have heavy blood loss due to poor clotting. But they're more likely to suffer from vitamin deficiency anemia because their diets are low in folic acid, a B vitamin that's essential for cell growth and for building the antibodies that fight disease. Folic acid deficiency is frequently the reason that many newly sober people feel tired and run-down. But this is rarely serious and can be easily corrected during the first three to four weeks of sobriety with an improved diet and a daily multivitamin supplement, as I will discuss in Chapter 15.

Drugs Other Than Alcohol

While alcohol does the most harm to the most parts of the body, other abused drugs also damage the various body systems. In the discussions that follow, if I don't mention a particular body system in relation to a drug, it means that drug has no known effect on that system.

There are two areas in which most abused drugs cause harm: the liver and the immune system. While alcohol does the most extensive damage to the liver, other abused drugs also affect this organ by training it to rid your body quickly and efficiently of all drugs, including any nonaddictive prescription medication you may be taking. This can affect your future medical care. Abused drugs can also weaken your immune system, making you more susceptible to disease and prolonging the time it takes for you to recover from illness or injury. Alcohol and drugs have a similar effect on the immune system. For a more complete discussion of these effects, please refer to the previous section on alcohol and the immune system on pages 42–43.

Cocaine

Unlike alcohol, which has a cumulative effect on the body, it is thought that most of the harm caused by cocaine occurs during the time you're high on it. Because cocaine abuse is a relatively new phenomenon, its long-term effects are not yet known. It is thought that the amount of cocaine and the method by which you ingest it determine the extent of the problems you may incur. When you freebase cocaine rather than snort it, or when you smoke crack, more of the drug gets into your body.

The Heart and Blood Vessels Cocaine stimulates the sympathetic nervous system (which sends nerve signals to the heart, muscles and glands), causing a reaction which mimics the fight-or-flight response. Snorting a line of coke can be the physiological equivalent of coming face to face with an armed burglar in your apartment. Your heart beats wildly and your blood pressure rises rapidly. Your breathing rate increases and your temperature goes up.

From the description above you can see that cocaine puts a sudden, overwhelming demand on your heart and blood vessels. Your blood vessels may become so constricted that your heart may not get enough oxygen and you may suffer a heart attack. Or the conduction of electrical impulses within the heart can go awry, causing your heart to beat erratically. If sufficiently severe, both these conditions can be fatal. In any case they are serious.

Fatal heart attacks due to cocaine use sometimes occur in older users with pre-existing heart disease. But they have also struck down people barely out of their teens, like Len Bias, the young basketball player, who was the victim of such a heart attack.

If you haven't had a heart attack, you are likely to have experienced chest pains while using. These may persist for three to five days and for up to two weeks after you stop taking cocaine. Persistent chest pains after this period may be a sign of serious heart damage, and you should consult your doctor immediately.

The sudden rise in blood pressure that accompanies cocaine abuse can also cause strokes. A severe enough stroke can sometimes result in permanent paralysis. Also, if there is a weakness in the blood vessel walls (an aneurysm), a fatal hemorrhage can occur when the weak portion bursts due to the sudden rise in pressure. Unfortunately, there is no way of knowing whether you have such a weakness until you suffer the consequences.

Regular cocaine use can cause your blood pressure to remain at a higher-than-normal level even during those periods when you are not actually using the drug. When you give up cocaine entirely, your blood pressure will return to normal.

The Brain Cocaine brings on excessive stimulation of the brain and can cause epileptic-like seizures, during which your limbs shake convulsively and you lose consciousness. If you have had repeated seizures, you may have incurred some brain damage. More likely, you may have sustained some physical injury—broken limbs, sprained muscles, or cuts and bruises—during a seizure. Although your brain chemistry will still be abnormal in the ways described in the first section of this chapter, when you stop using cocaine you are no longer at risk for seizures.

General Nutrition Nutrition is usually poor among cocaine users, not only because cocaine suppresses appetite but also because users are so focused on getting their drug that they neglect essential functions like eating. If they do eat, they choose foods that are convenient rather than nourishing. They frequently lose weight and muscle tissue and can become vitamin deficient. If this has happened to you, proper nutrition and regular exercise will correct these conditions in the first one to six months of sobriety, unless the damage has been unusually severe. Please read Chapters 15 and 16.

The Nose and Mouth Cocaine is a local anesthetic and also constricts the small blood vessels in areas it contacts. (For these reasons it has been used in eye surgery for over a century.) When used repeatedly, cocaine causes the cells in the affected areas to die from lack of oxygen. The dead cells become irritated and swell, giving you the characteristic "cocaine sniffles" and the congested nose that come from snorting cocaine regularly. Eventually, so many cells may die that your septum—the thick membrane between the nostrils—may become perforated, often leaving a large hole which requires surgical repair.

The mucous membranes also suffer when they come into contact with cocaine. Irritated, bleeding gums, dental abscesses and even lost teeth are common features of chronic cocaine use. Once you stop using, your gum problems will clear up, and you can substitute artificial replacements for your lost teeth.

The Lungs Smoking crack produces the same debilitating effects on the delicate membranes of the lungs as snorting it does in the nose. In addition, the inhaled air is hot, causing further inflammation and damage. As a result, you may experience decreased lung capacity, shortness of breath and sometimes asthma-like attacks. These symptoms usually disappear within three to six months of staying sober, but I have seen some severe cases where it took patients up to a year before they were able to exercise without becoming breathless. In rare cases, lung capacity is permanently decreased.

Sexual Function Cocaine does not have the long-lasting effects on the ovaries and testes that alcohol does, and as far as is known, it does not affect your sex hormones. However, heavy cocaine users frequently experience a loss of sexual desire, which often persists into the first one to two months of sobriety and may be related to the general lack of energy many cocaine users experience when they first become abstinent.

Because cocaine is a local anesthetic, it causes numbness when it is rubbed directly on the penis or into the vagina. Some people use cocaine this way because the loss of sensation prolongs intercourse by retarding orgasm. While the anesthetic effect wears off in one or two hours, serious skin tears may occur during intercourse, and since no pain is felt at the time, the activity continues and the tear worsens. Such tears provide an entry point for AIDS and other infections.

In some people, cocaine use seems to increase compulsive sexual behavior of all kinds. Users experience a need for more and more sexual stimulation and engage in such practices as repeated intercourse with many different partners, constant masturbation, sexual behaviors outside their usual range, sadomasochistic activities, and other bizarre and dangerous practices. While hazardous sex is a likely consequence of all drug use, the combined drug effects of cocaine—increased energy, disinhibition, poor judgment, sexual sensation-seeking and compulsiveness—increase the likelihood of contracting a sexually transmitted disease, including, of course, AIDS.

For most people, intense preoccupation with sex ends when they stop using cocaine. In a few cases, it may persist and professional treatment may be necessary, as I describe in Chapter 9.

Headaches Recovering cocaine users frequently complain about headaches in the first one to twelve weeks of abstinence. The exact physiological cause of these headaches is not yet known, but they do decrease in frequency and intensity over time and rarely persist after the first six months of abstinence.

Other Effects Cocaine can also cause an overactive bowel and a powerful, uncontrollable twitching under the skin. Both these problems, which can be quite intense during the first three to four days after withdrawal, improve and generally disappear within two weeks of becoming sober.

Most cocaine users, in the first four to fourteen days of sobriety, feel sleepy and extremely lethargic. This is a rebound effect, resulting from intense cocaine-induced activity in the brain and body. In heavy users who lost weight during their drugging days, this loss of energy and also of muscle power can persist for up to four to six months.

Prescription Drugs

As many of you are all too aware, some valid and important medicines can become abused drugs. Sleeping pills, tranquilizers, and pain medication fall into this group.

Sleeping pills, also known as hypnotics, include such drugs as Dalmane, Doriden, Halcion, Nembutal, Noludar, and Restoril. Fiorinal, a drug prescribed for headaches, contains a substance that places it in the hypnotic category and is also potentially addictive. Tranquilizers, also known as anti-anxiety drugs, are mostly variations of a single chemical group, the benzodiazepines. Common benzodiazepine tranquilizers include Ativan, Librium, Serax, Tranxene, Valium, and Xanax. Of course, many other drugs fall under both these headings, but I've listed the ones you're most likely to have encountered.

Most of the problems caused by sleeping pills and tranquilizers are the result of how they act on the brain, the nervous system, and the muscles. The effects of overusing these drugs can be quite severe and may last a surprisingly long time. They include mental cloudiness, poor concentration, distractibility, memory difficulties, and sleep problems, as well as mood swings, anxiety, depression, and irritability. Muscle twitches, spasms, and jerks are also common and may continue for several months. You may also be bothered by odd skin sensations, numbness, and tingling, as well as blurred vision and distorted hearing. These drugs also interfere with functions that are regulated by the brain, such as the body's response to stress and sexual function, both of which can be impaired.

Roland was a retired historian who came to see me because he was alarmed by his reactions to a prescription drug. He had begun taking Dalmane after his wife died because he was having trouble sleeping. Every night for ten years he'd taken two 30 mg Dalmane capsules, never more. But a few months before I met him, he'd begun to feel foggy during the day, and a couple of times he'd lost his balance and begun to stagger, "as if I were drunk," as he described it.

He felt his worst in the morning, which was when he did most of his work on his book about the Crusades. He frequently lost track of ideas and worried that his thinking was muddled. Toward late afternoon he regained his normal clarity, but by then his stamina was flagging. After all, he was eighty-five.

Fearful that he was becoming senile, Roland went to his internist, who sent him to a neurologist. After a careful workup, the neurologist advised Roland to stop taking Dalmane, which he did. But without the medication, he couldn't sleep. He was agitated during the day and couldn't concentrate. His mind raced, and his heart beat wildly. Five days later, he started taking the Dalmane again, and the symptoms immediately disappeared. This instant relief convinced Roland that he was an "addict."

Very few people walk into my office freely admitting they are addicted to any drug, but Roland did. Because of his age, he had certainly become physiologically dependent on his daily 60 mg of Dalmane, and he was certainly experiencing withdrawal symptoms. But he'd never used more than prescribed, he'd never increased his dose, and he didn't take the medication to get high. I explained to him that he was *not* an addict, that physiological dependence alone did not make him one.

We agreed on a schedule for reducing and ultimately discontinuing his use of Dalmane. During this period he kept a diary in which he recorded his exact symptoms, the precise time they occurred, and many other details of his daily activities. Because of his lifelong habit of keeping careful records, he was temperamentally suited to this task and found it very reassuring. Over a twelve-week period his symptoms gradually diminished and disappeared, as verified by his remarkably precise diary. Today he is symptom-free, working well, and his book is about to be published.

At twenty-four, Natalie lives the kind of life little girls dream about when they put on their first pair of ballet slippers. A lead dancer in musicals, she is pretty, charming, and successful. She's frequently seen at fashionable parties and night spots, and she's traveled and performed all over the world. Because she's so young and exuberant, Natalie may seem to have nothing in common with Roland, but, in fact, they do share several important traits. Both are extremely disciplined and very demanding of themselves. If anything, Natalie is the harder taskmaster. Despite many dreadful hangovers and sleepless nights, she had never missed a performance, a rehearsal or even a class.

Unlike Roland, Natalie had used just about every available mood-altering substance—except alcohol, which would have made her put on weight. But it wasn't her "recreational" drug use—at that point cocaine and heroin, which she snorted—that brought her into treatment. It was Fiorinal, which she'd been taking for headaches.

The more Fiorinal she took, the more frequently her headaches seemed to occur, and yet the drug seemed to be the only remedy for the problem. On good days she was taking seven or eight tablets, and on bad days up to ten. She could barely keep going. "I look and feel like I'm ninety years old," she complained when I first saw her. She did look extraordinarily haggard and worn. Not ninety perhaps, but certainly a lot older than twenty-four.

While she was detoxified in the hospital, Natalie attended Cocaine Anonymous meetings. She realized that she had to stop using drugs, and after she was discharged she brought her considerable determination and discipline to bear on the problem. She found time in her crowded schedule to attend a self-help meeting each day and to come twice a week for outpatient treatment. But though her headaches weren't as severe as before, they still bothered her often enough that she consulted a headache specialist. She was reluctant to use even the non-addictive medication he prescribed, but she finally did agree and found that the medication gave her great relief without affecting her sobriety.

During her first sober six months, Natalie experienced periods of anxiety and moments when she lost track of herself. "I'd be in class or at a rehearsal and suddenly realize I had no idea what I was doing, as if I'd been on automatic pilot." She was also aware that her coordination wasn't at its best. "It was a very subtle thing. My turns were a fraction off. I wasn't as precise as I can be."

But after two years of sobriety Natalie looks and feels wonderful. "I'm dancing at my peak now," she told me happily. I asked her if she still made the rounds of the parties and clubs. "Of course," she said. "I go just about everywhere I used to, and I'm having more fun than ever, but I go with people who don't drink or do drugs. I've met some fascinating people who wouldn't have had anything to do with me when I was using."

Painkillers are the third type of potentially addictive prescription drugs. All addictive pain medication is related in some way to opium, which is one of the oldest treatments for pain. Opium derivatives and synthetic opium-type drugs include codeine, aspirin and Tylenol with codeine, Darvon, Demerol, Dilaudid, morphine, Percocet, Percodan, and Vicodin. Heroin and methadone also fall into this category. Although these drugs differ from sleeping pills and tranquilizers, they also have long-lasting effects, mainly on the brain, nervous system, and muscles.

Withdrawal from pain medication can cause flu-like symptoms, with muscle aches and joint pain and sometimes painful muscle spasms.

Feelings of depression, irritability, and low energy may continue for four to six months. Your body's temperature can also be erratic, causing sweats and/or chills. The production of endorphins, the body's natural pain reducers, may be lowered so that pain now seems more intense.

Hallucinogens

Hallucinogens include marijuana, hashish, LSD (acid), PCP (angel dust), and plant derivatives such as psilocybin (magic mushrooms). The long-term medical effects of these drugs are largely confined to the nervous system, in part because they can be stored in the fatty tissues of the brain for long periods of time. This accounts for the phenomenon of flashbacks, brief episodes when former users feel as if they're high again even though they haven't used.

Drugs That Are Smoked

Formerly heavy users of marijuana may suffer from irritability, poor concentration, depression, and sleep problems for several weeks after they stop using. The lack of energy and motivation they experience may continue for the first three to six months of recovery but will eventually improve. People who use marijuana often have an increased appetite, especially for sweets and snacks, but their desire for nutritious, balanced meals will return when they stop using the drug. The question is still being debated whether these hallucinogens can cause any permanent brain damage, but most former users can expect total recovery.

Finally, although it is still an area of medical controversy and study, some experiments have suggested that marijuana may cause changes in the chromosomes which carry the genes that convey hereditary characteristics.

Heavy marijuana smokers are subject to all of the same lung and respiratory problems as tobacco smokers: frequent respiratory infections and an increased risk of cancer and of emphysema, a debilitating disease that results from a loss of lung tissue. Furthermore, because marijuana cigarettes are rarely filtered, they can cause serious lung damage with fewer doses than tobacco cigarettes.

Injected Drugs

Anyone who injects any drug directly into his or her veins, whether it's heroin, cocaine, or a prescription painkiller, will suffer complications and difficulties resulting from the injections themselves. The drugs are often mixed with potentially dangerous substances such as talcum powder or quinine, which can block capillaries, thus causing tissue damage and preventing blood and oxygen from reaching vital organs, including the heart, lungs, and brain. The needles used to inject the drugs are often contaminated with bacteria that cause infections and viruses, including the AIDS virus, which can be transmitted by sharing a needle with an infected user.

If you have ever been to a wedding or any party with a large buffet you know the stuffed, uncomfortable feeling that comes from filling your plate over and over, tasting a bit of this, nibbling a bit of that. After reading this chapter, you may well be experiencing a similar discomfort. But once you digest the material you will undoubtedly feel better.

At most buffets, there is one memorable dish. From this vast array, the one I'd like you to remember is that the majority of alcohol- and drug-related complaints disappear, or at least diminish significantly over time, as long as you stay sober.

Time will do much of the work of healing your brain and body, but your life plan can facilitate that work. For example, eating well and exercising regularly, discussed in Chapters 15 and 16, can help you to regain your energy, strength, and endurance. Preventive medical and dental care, as outlined in Chapter 13, can safeguard your improved health. And strategies for stabilizing your mood, found in Chapter 5, can help you cope while your brain function returns to normal. With a well-designed life plan, you can work *with* time to mitigate the effects of alcohol and drugs on your brain and body.

I have noticed that while the mental and physical consequences of their addiction may be the first ones that my newly recovering patients confront, it doesn't take them long to realize that their alcohol or drug use has had other serious results. They soon begin to see that the emotional aspects of their lives are as damaged and in need of healing as their brains and bodies. As with the mental and physical consequences, to begin that healing they must understand what has happened to them. In the chapter that follows, I will discuss the effects of addiction on family life, sexual relations, and friendship.

Chapter Three
How Alcohol and Drugs Have Affected Your Emotional Life

Family, Sex, and Friendships

The effects of your addiction on your emotional life are fewer than the physical consequences I talked about in the previous chapter. But they're more complicated because they concern other people, who are never as predictable as one's liver tissue, for instance. Yet a healthy emotional life is crucial to sustaining your sobriety. If your home life is tense, if you are anxious every time you climb into bed with your spouse, or if you continually dread an angry phone call from your one-time best friend, your sobriety will be in danger. Time can help heal emotional wounds, but not to the extent that it repairs your brain and body. Therefore, your living plan must *actively* promote your emotional well-being. But before planning those actions, you must know the extent of the damage to be repaired, which is what much of this chapter is about.

Emotional relationships are delicate and require a great deal of fine-tuning. Even if you have been sober for more than a year, it is very likely that this area of your life still needs some work. During early recovery, when you are often concerned simply with getting from one day to the next without drinking or using, you can start this work, but beware of making your family the focus at this point in your sobriety.

Your family, sexual partner, and friends also need to understand how your addiction has affected them and their relationship with you. For this reason, I have devoted several sections of this chapter to readers who are close to a person in recovery.

Your Family Life

Your family is affected first and worst by your addiction. Long before anyone outside your family even notices that you have a problem, family members may already have stopped communicating with you and with one another, and begun to develop potentially destructive coping behaviors. And even when your problem has become apparent to virtually everyone in your life, it is frequently a family member who takes the first steps toward getting you help.

My patients often assure me that sure, they *use* drugs or alcohol, but they certainly don't have a drug or alcohol *problem*. As proof, they tell me how well they're doing at work—they've earned raises, promotions, citations. Any trouble they may be having on the job is attributed to stress or some other unusual circumstance. In such situations, it's only when I speak to a family member that I get the real story.

Ken, a young doctor who was doing his residency in surgery, was referred to me for an evaluation by his hospital chief of service. The chief wasn't sure that Ken had a drug problem, but he frequently seemed tired and there were rumors that he partied a lot. Twice recently, he had arrived late in the operating room, quite a serious matter for a doctor in training. The first time, Ken had apologized profusely and explained that his three-month-old son had been up sick all the night before with a virus. He and his wife had taken the baby to the emergency room at dawn. The chief had excused Ken, but the second time he was late, the older doctor had become concerned.

When Ken called to make an appointment, I told him I wanted to see his wife Emily, too. That was impossible, because she had to take care of the baby, Ken replied. I explained that I wouldn't see him without his wife. The next day they both showed up at my office. I saw Ken first, alone, and he told me that his son had been sick. He said that he did party some, but very rarely now that he was a father. And yes, he'd tried cocaine a couple of times, but it wasn't a big deal.

Ken was articulate, contrite, and plausible. Perhaps he was telling the truth, and his tardiness and fatigue were caused by the combined demands of his medical training and the stress of his son being ill. But I reserved judgment until I could hear what Emily had to say.

She sat silently in my office for a long moment. Then she took a deep breath and launched into her story. "I can't cover up for him anymore," she said. "Sooner or later, cocaine is going to destroy Ken's career. I hope it's not already too late."

She told me she had promised Ken not to say anything to me today if he stopped using. "But he got high again last night, so now I'm off the hook. Maybe he really wanted me to tell you. This has been going on for years. He started using coke in his first year of medical school, only occasionally then, but now coke is all he thinks about. As soon as he gets his paycheck, he's off to buy more. He stays out all night and then goes straight to the hospital in the morning. My parents have been paying the rent and giving me money for the baby. Ken hardly notices our son. When I went into labor, Ken begged off duty for two days, but he wasn't with me. He left the house when my water broke, and I didn't see him for three days. I feel so alone. I just don't know what to do anymore."

To the outside world, Ken was healthy and successful, with only a minor problem at work. But what wasn't apparent to his supervisor, or possibly even to Ken himself, was all too obvious to his wife, who had already been deeply hurt by his cocaine use. Emily's response—covering up for Ken—is one of the most frequent reactions among family members when someone they love is abusing alcohol or drugs. Although Emily didn't hide Ken's problem from her parents, other spouses very often do try to conceal their partner's addiction from everyone outside the home. The other common response among family members is to deny what's happening, not only to others, but to themselves as well.

Both of these protective mechanisms have the same result: The family begins to isolate itself. The big family secret must be kept. It becomes more and more impossible for you to speak frankly with people outside the family. Family members hesitate to invite anyone home because they're never sure whether the dependent person is high or drunk, or how he or she will behave. Planning or attending social occasions becomes a nightmare, because there's always the fear that the user will turn up intoxicated, or not show up at all.

Gradually the family gets used to and develops a way to cope with the dependent member. First the family members notice that the user's moods are unpredictable and they begin to avoid him or her. The dependent person spends more time away from home, either in an attempt to hide from the family how much he or she is drinking or drugging, or to avoid the angry or rejecting reactions of the family members.

As the disease progresses, the unpleasant incidents increase. Some family members may begin to argue with the dependent person about the substance abuse. Others, hoping the problem will solve itself, may try to ignore the upsetting behavior. Still others come up with rationalizations. Mom's had a couple of bad breaks on the job; the teenage son got dumped by his girlfriend; as soon as they recover from their disappointments, the drinking and/or drugging will stop.

Almost all family members eventually feel that they're in some way responsible for this terrible situation. They think: *If only I loved her more, cared more about him, did more for her, understood him better, we wouldn't be in this mess*. Eventually virtually every family member comes to feel a mixture of anger toward and embarrassment about the dependent person's behavior.

They recognize that the chemically dependent person is unreliable. Dad can't be counted on to come to his son's school play or to supervise his scout troop camping trip—even though he promised he would. But Dad made those promises when he was in a blackout, and now he doesn't remember. His son finally stops asking and starts making excuses to others.

A husband cancels or refuses invitations to family celebrations because his wife is too drunk or hung over to leave the house. His parents and siblings feel hurt by what they take to be his rejecting behavior, and he gradually loses touch with them.

And so the family builds its life around the dependent person, excluding him or her from any responsible position. At the same time, family members are acutely aware that they are living with a time bomb that can explode at any moment, and this causes everyone a great deal of anxiety.

The Spouse

The husband or wife usually starts off thinking that the chemically dependent person's behavior is a temporary aberration that will go away. They remind themselves that earlier in the marriage he or she was decent, reliable, fun, warm, outgoing. This newly volatile mate, who's nervous one minute and depressed the next, who's angry and accusing, seems like someone entirely different from the person in the wedding picture.

When Irene and Chris got married during their last year of law school, everyone talked about how lucky Chris was. Irene was the star of the class—beautiful, brilliant, clearly destined for greatness. She was even-tempered, funny, and not a bit impressed with herself. Easygoing Chris, who marveled at his good fortune, had always done well enough, but he never shone like Irene. Some of her friends wondered what in the world she saw in him, but their relationship seemed to be close and happy.

After law school, they both settled into jobs they had wanted— Irene in the corporate division of a prestigious law firm, and Chris in the public defender's office. They'd been married three years when they decided to have a baby. But as much as they tried, Irene didn't become pregnant. She began to drink—first a glass or two of wine at dinner twice a week, then every day. It was only one or two drinks at first, but soon it became four or five or more.

Chris drank with her, but not nearly as much. He had no idea how much she was actually putting away, nor did he know what to do about her angry, drunken tirades or her fits of inconsolable weeping. Whether he argued or tried to comfort her, she'd become enraged. She attacked him, usually verbally, sometimes physically. So Chris learned to play possum, and like a Mafia figure he'd read about in a novel, always to position himself near an exit. But like many spouses of alcoholics, he felt responsible. "I really believed it was my fault," he told me. "Through some dreadful defect in my character, I'd transformed this lovely, laughing woman into a raving lunatic."

Chris was not alone in his reaction. Let me describe a typical morning-after scene played out in the homes of so many chemically dependent people. The husband or wife is outraged, hurt, and humiliated by the behavior of the night before. The dependent person is guilty and full of shame, even though he or she may not remember exactly what took place. They trade recriminations; the dependent person promises it will never happen again. But it does happen just the same—or worse. And the episodes continue, only more often.

As the alcoholic or addict continues in a downward spiral, the tone of these arguments changes. The spouse's nagging becomes at once more insistent and more hopeless. The dependent person's responses grow more irate and indignant. Then, frustrated by being so out of control, his or her anger turns to accusation: If it weren't for your constant criticism, I wouldn't have to drink/smoke dope/take downers. Now the vicious circle is complete.

While some spouses continue to badger and find fault as the behavior of the chemically dependent person deteriorates even further, others grow increasingly hurt and withdrawn until they become emotionally detached from their mate. I've seen this reaction in both men and women, but husbands, more than wives, often respond by leaving their marriages. Women, who realistically may have fewer economic options and are also more conditioned to be caretakers, tend to stay on.

Unfortunately, it's the rare spouse of a chemically dependent person who manages to find his or her way into a self-help group such as Al-Anon or Nar-Anon, or who manages to get the family into treatment, with or without the chemically dependent person. When families do get help, they begin to understand that they have to live for themselves and not for the dependent person. Their attitudes and behavior change accordingly.

Chris had never told any of his friends about Irene's drunken episodes, and none of them had seemed to notice. Socially, Irene's facade was fairly intact. On a couple of occasions she had publicly embarrassed Chris, but her wicked witch of the west act was purely for domestic consumption. Professionally, her facade was unblemished. At work she was still the competent, successful attorney.

One evening, Chris and Irene attended a party to celebrate the birth of their friends' first child. Angry and bitter because she couldn't get pregnant, Irene started drinking at home and continued to drink at the party. Several hours later Chris found her, weeping and incoherent, surrounded by a group of their friends. While a couple of the women led Irene to the spare bedroom, the hostess took Chris aside and told him, "She's an alcoholic."

Chris surprised himself when he replied, "I know." Though he had never before thought that of Irene, suddenly everything was clear.

"I know all about it," said Liz matter-of-factly. "Don's an alcoholic, too. He's on his best behavior tonight, because he's just become a father. But once you all clear out, he'll start in on the whiskey and pass out in no time flat."

"Can't you do anything to help him?" Chris asked.

"I've tried every blessed wrong thing and then some, but you can learn from my mistakes." She paused and looked at him shrewdly. "Of course you think it's your fault."

Chris nodded. It was as if Liz had read his mind.

Then she told him about Al-Anon. When Chris made a face, she said, "Forget your prejudices. Don't tell me you've never taken a case where you knew the client was guilty. You defended him anyway because the guy has a constitutional right to an attorney. Come with me to a meeting tomorrow. You can do this, too, you'll see."

Chris went along with Liz to Al-Anon, and though it took time, he did come to see that he wasn't responsible for his wife's alcoholism. Irene didn't get sober until much, much later. But that night was the beginning of Chris's recovery.

The Children

Children have many different ways of coping with a chemically dependent person. There are some, perhaps naturally more resilient or self-sufficient, who seem to go about their business regardless of the chaos at home. They do their schoolwork, make friends, and have a life apart from their family. Eventually they emerge as apparently healthy adults.

Donna was one of these unusual children. I first met her at age fifteen, when she brought her mother Racquelle into treatment. Racquelle was only thirty-two, and she and Donna looked more like sisters than mother and daughter. I saw immediately that Donna was in charge. Calmly and competently, she helped her mother tell the story of her alcoholism. When Racquelle faltered, Donna put a protective, maternal arm around her. When Racquelle wept, Donna comforted her. I wondered who comforted Donna.

Donna told me about the many nights she'd dragged her mother home from the bars. She described the time she found Racquelle in the back room of a gin joint, surrounded by a group of rowdy, excited men. "I walked in just as one of them was unzipping his fly. I was sure they were going to rape her."

But somehow the presence of a young girl shamed them, and they slunk away. After this incident, Donna enlisted the help of Racquelle's best friend, and together they got her to go to an AA meeting.

"She stayed sober for a little while, but then she kept slipping. She really tried, though," Donna said loyally.

Despite the disorder of her home life, Donna was an excellent student. She had a ninety-five average, played on the basketball team, and was hoping to get a sports scholarship to college. Racquelle was very proud of her daughter. "Where I come from blacks don't go to college. I didn't even graduate from high school. But Donna's going to make it—in spite of me."

What made Donna a survivor? It's hard to say for sure, but I believe it helped that both she and Racquelle had a wide network of supportive and concerned friends and family. Donna had plenty of people to talk to about her problems with her mother. Also, Racquelle's alcoholism was very much out in the open, and Donna didn't seem to feel stigmatized by it.

Racquelle finally did get sober the fall Donna left for college. Donna is doing well in school, and she doesn't seem to bear the psychological scars that mark many children of alcoholics. Perhaps she's one of those fortunate individuals who are born with a sense of balance. Certainly she was the most impressive teenager I've ever met.

Unfortunately, most children don't have Donna's support network or her ability to cope so healthily with her mother's addiction. They are seriously scarred by having lived in a family in which one or both parents are chemically dependent. As we know from studies of children of alcoholics, many respond to living in an alcoholic home by adopting inappropriate behavior patterns that can continue into their adult lives. Because virtually all of these studies have focused on the children of alcoholics, in this I refer to the chemically dependent parent as an alcoholic. But the problems are much the same no matter what substance the parent is abusing.

One response that I typically see in many children is to take over whatever role the alcoholic would normally play in the family. Most often it's the older children who assume this responsibility, but the middle children, too, can fill this role if the alcoholism occurs or continues after the older sibling(s) leave home. For example, if Dad is the alcoholic, one of the older boys may begin to do the chores around the house and to watch over Mom. He may even escort his mother to social events, acting as substitute husband. Similarly, if Mom is an alcoholic, an older daughter may take the place of her mother. If her father is the alcoholic, she may take on a lot of her mother's functions because mother is focusing all of her attention on Dad.

Because they're so busy coping at home, these children necessarily miss out on a lot of other activities, especially with their friends. They appear to be very mature, but that maturity is in part an illusion. Children from "normal" homes have a chance to be carefree; they also have people they know they can depend on. The children of alcoholics are denied both of these fundamental aspects of a healthy childhood, and they miss an essential part of growing up.

Some children, bewildered and confused by the disorder in the home, start to feel very anxious, which can show up in any number of ways. Their grades drop. They stop participating in peer activities, or they begin to have a hard time relating to other children. In fact, one indicator of alcoholism in a household is a formerly well-adjusted, competent child who has begun to have problems in school or in relationships. Children of alcoholic families also express their distress by becoming withdrawn, moody, and depressed. They often act out through rebellious or destructive behavior, or even run away from home.

Abby, a single parent who attended the Smithers outpatient treatment program, insisted that her drinking hadn't affected her daughters, ages twelve and fifteen. She had never drunk in front of them, she assured me, nor had they ever seen her drunk, and they were both doing well in school. She saw no reason for them to attend the meetings of alcoholics and their families at our clinic, but my staff and I insisted they do so.

At their first meeting, the two girls sat silent and withdrawn. They showed no reaction to what the others were saying until another teenager began to talk about how hurt and frightened he'd been by his father's drinking. The twelve-year-old began to sob, quietly at first. Then the older girl began to cry, too. She turned to her younger sister and said, "I never knew you felt how awful it was. I never talked to you about it because I wanted to protect you."

Abby had sincerely believed that her daughters were unaware of and unaffected by her drinking. And on the surface, they seemed to be doing well. Now sober two years, Abby dates her recovery from the moment her last illusion—that her children hadn't been touched by her disease—was shattered.

Neglect and emotional trauma aren't the only ways in which children suffer when an addicted mother or father is unable to function as a parent. Children may also become victims of direct psychological and/or physical abuse. Some children and their families may need professional counseling to overcome the effects of such traumas, as I discuss in Chapter 8.

When Sobriety Hits

One of the hardest lessons you, the recovering person, and your family will have to learn is that life at home does not automatically and immediately return to normal (if indeed there ever was a "normal") the moment you become sober. Most families mistakenly believe that the troubles at home are caused solely by the behavior of the chemically dependent person. Everyone assumes that once the problem goes away, so too will the friction and tension within the home. Unfortunately, it doesn't work this way. The addiction did not happen overnight, and it took a long time for the family to develop ways to cope with the addiction. Now it takes time to unlearn those behaviors and learn new ones.

At a group therapy meeting, Angela, the wife of a recovering alcoholic, confessed, "As soon as Vito's out the door for work, I make the rounds checking all his old hiding places for bottles. I look inside the toilet tank, behind *War and Peace*, his favorite book, under the bottom shelf of his tool cabinet. I feel terribly guilty all the while I'm doing this. One of the kids caught me the other day and said, 'Ma, you look like you've been shoplifting or something.'

"I know that if he found out he'd be terribly hurt . . . maybe he'd even start drinking again. But I can't stop myself, even though he hasn't touched a drop in four months."

Sandra, another group member, admitted that she had followed a similar ritual when her husband first got sober. "Now . . ." she stopped, suddenly embarrassed.

The group gently urged her on.

"Now I sometimes *wish* he would drink again, and I wonder if I'm setting him up to do it. When he was drinking I knew what to expect. Step over the body on the way to make breakfast. Check to see he hadn't peed on the carpet—leaves a nasty stain if you don't get to it quickly. I didn't even have to make up a story for the children, they knew exactly what was going on. Now he's actually sitting and having breakfast with us instead of lying there on the living room floor. I used to enjoy having the newspaper all to myself in the morning. Now I have to beg one of the sections from him."

The resentment in Sandra's tone was evident. Giving up the newspaper really bothered her, just as Angela found it hard to break her habit of checking for hidden liquor. When lives are changing day by day, if not hour by hour, any point of familiarity, even one that's connected with the addiction, can seem comforting. Family members must adjust not only to the sobriety, but also to changes in the small, seemingly unimportant routines that they've come to take for granted.

If you're the newly sober person, you have to keep in mind that you're still not quite well. As I said in Chapter 2, throughout the first year of recovery your behavior can be unpredictable, further aggravating family tensions and possibly arousing suspicion that you may have once again begun drinking or using. Moreover, as thrilled as your family may be about your new sobriety, their happiness can't immediately erase all the years of anger, humiliation, shame, and disgust. If every day for the past five or ten years, they have lived in dread of your drunks or highs, that dread will linger on, no matter how much they love you and want to believe in you. For many months to come, they'll worry: *Will he be okay today? Will she come home drunk? Will I find him passed out on the sofa? Will Mom be acting weird when I bring my friends home after school?* Their long-standing fears, concerns, and suspicions won't disappear overnight.

You're bound to be disappointed if you think your family should now trust you implicitly. This is especially true if you've had sober periods in the past when you made your family many promises that you ultimately broke. As confident as you may be that *this* time is different, your family members have to see for themselves that you're now truly committed to recovery.

Virtually no newly recovering family wants to talk about the fact that life at home is still less than perfect. No one wants to say or do anything that could be even remotely construed as a reason for the newly sober person to start using or drinking again. This artificial, fragile harmony can lead to resentments that get bottled up, only to emerge later on in an explosion of anger or in some other more subtle, equally dangerous and upsetting way.

Another problem faced by families of newly recovered people is that family members are accustomed to having someone in the role of the sick person. The chemically dependent person in one way or another has engrossed the attention of the entire family. Now the family lacks a focus. Along with a collective sigh of relief that the person has become sober, they may also experience a kind of letdown. Parents and siblings may not know what to do with their free time, or how to relate to one another.

It's been my experience that family members are often less than pleased when the recovering person begins to reclaim his or her appropriate role in the family. The son who has been a substitute father may be angry when his father comes back sober and prepared to take his rightful position. The wife who singlehandedly bore the entire financial burden of the family and has come to like the responsibility may now resent having to share the load. If the newly sober husband used to handle the family finances by himself, husband and wife may battle for control of the money. Many issues, large and small, will have to be discussed and renegotiated. All the family members will have to work at arriving at a new, more comfortable arrangement.

The newly sober person is often very eager—too eager—for things to be as they "should." You fall all over yourself trying to make amends for the difficulties you created during your addiction. You work overtime, trying to be "good." But your family needs time to readjust—and you need time to recuperate before you try to repair all your damaged relationships.

When Martha came home from the treatment center, she promised her three teenagers that now that she was sober, they would be spending lots of time together. And that very first weekend she made good on her promise. She bought tickets for the Friday night high school basketball game, planned a shopping expedition for Saturday, and invited her sister and her family to come for Sunday lunch.

But her kids had other ideas. Her oldest son had already arranged to go to the game with his pals, and her younger son had been invited to sleep over at his best friend's house that night. Her daughter was planning to go to a Sweet Sixteen party on Saturday afternoon. And none of them had any desire to see their young cousins, whom they'd nicknamed "the brats."

In her eagerness to compensate for all the times she'd neglected her children when she was drinking and taking tranquilizers, Martha ended up feeling rejected and unneeded by her kids. She was tempted to comfort herself by pouring a drink, but she called her sponsor Jane instead. They talked about the value of taking things slowly, and Jane suggested that Martha get to know her kids better, to find out what they really needed from her. Perhaps they wanted help with their college applications, or maybe her daughter needed advice about what to wear to the Sweet Sixteen. Or maybe what they needed most was just for Martha to be sober.

In Chapter 8 I discuss strategies for improving your family life.

Your Sex Life

If there's one word to describe the sex life of the chemically dependent person, it's catastrophic. The following stories, told at a couples therapy group, are typical of what goes on in the bedroom when one member of a couple is chemically dependent.

• It's been three months since Andy and Judith had intercourse. The last time they had sex, Judith was so angry at Andy because of his drinking that she seethed all the way through and started a fight the moment they were finished.

• Lou admitted that although he usually saw his wife Vera for the bright, accomplished woman he'd married, her drug use often enraged him. The worst night had been the one when he'd dragged her from a friend's apartment as she was pathetically offering herself to another man in exchange for "just one more hit." Lou had been so angry that when they got home he was uncharacteristically brutal to Vera in bed.

• Stephanie had come to the meeting without her husband Walt. At previous sessions they had claimed to be having an absolutely harmonious and satisfying sex life. But on this particular evening, Stephanie spoke bitterly about Walt's infidelities, his compulsive womanizing, and his apparent inability to stop cheating on her, even though he was no longer using cocaine. Stephanie had pretended to be having a wonderful sex life in the vain hope that wishing would make it so.

After hearing what these partners of former users had to say, another group member remarked, "I didn't think anyone had a worse sex life than my husband and I do. I'm sorry for everyone's troubles, but I have to admit it's a relief to hear that other people are in the same boat."

It's important to remember that, to one degree or another, most substance abusers have followed a pattern of sexual behavior that began when they sneaked a beer or a swig of vodka to ease the awkwardness and anxiety of their first sexual encounters. The alcohol eased their inhibitions, and made them feel more relaxed and outgoing. It was easier to make contact, to initiate and respond to sexual advances. Eventually, getting high, whether on alcohol or other substances, became a routine part of any sexual encounter.

The fact that alcohol inhibits sexual performance has long been noted. "Drink, sir," says the porter at Macbeth's castle, "is a great provoker of three things . . . nose-painting, sleep, and urine. Lechery, sir, it provokes and unprovokes: it provokes the desire, but it takes away the performance." In the twentieth century, more than one scientific experiment has demonstrated the truth of Shakespeare's words. In one study, a group of college students watched erotic films while consuming increasing doses of alcohol. Their sexual responses were measured, both psychologically by their responses to a questionnaire, and physically by the extent of tumescence in the penis and clitoris.

As the level of alcohol in their blood rose, the students reported that they were feeling more and more erotically stimulated. But their actual physical arousal diminished measurably. Put simply, though they felt sexier, their ability to perform was in fact greatly reduced.

These students weren't substance abusers, but their responses illustrate how people are sexually affected when they get high. The more they drink, the less they can do. Despite the claims of a popular bumper sticker, beer drinkers don't make better lovers.

Although the debilitating sexual pattern that affects most substance abusers usually begins with alcohol, any drug that's abused ultimately results in diminished sexual performance, desire, and relations. No matter what drug you use, the decline progresses in much the same way, although heroin and heroin-type drugs make you lose interest in sex much earlier than any other drug. But since alcohol is the first and most popular drug that's used in sexual situations, let's look at how its abuse can destroy your sex life.

Alcohol depresses sexual performance in three ways. First, it reduces your physical capacity to have and/or keep an erection, or to reach orgasm. Second, it lessens your overall sensitivity. Alcohol is an anesthetic that dulls the senses and decreases your responsiveness to touch. As a result, your brain receives fewer of the pleasurable sensations that are evoked by sexual contact. Finally, when you're drunk or high, you're less able to pick up on your partner's responses. It's hardly surprising that intoxicated people make clumsy and inconsiderate lovers.

As you become more mired in alcoholism, you need to drink more and more in order to perform and enhance all your activities, including sexual encounters. It becomes increasingly likely that sex will occur not while you're just a little high, but when you're grossly drunk—so drunk that you fall asleep or pass out in the middle of the act. Your response says nothing about your actual interest in sex. It's a physical reaction to the high level of alcohol in your body. Needless to say, such a development can be extremely disconcerting for your partner.

The poor judgment and disinhibitions that are associated with being drunk often lead people into sexual situations that are humiliating and embarrassing. This is especially true when the encounter takes place while you're blacked out. Waking up and finding yourself in bed with a stranger can be more than embarrassing—it can be terribly frightening. You can't remember what happened the night before. You don't even know if you actually had sex. If you did, you don't know what the act involved. The person beside you may be physically repulsive, or you may feel threatened by him or her. These experiences are painful and possibly dangerous, but you're doomed to repeat them as long as you continue to drink.

Nancy, a journalist in her mid-thirties, was no stranger to being greeted by unpleasant surprises the morning after. "I have a whole lot of what I call my 'Goldilocks and the Three Bears' stories, as in: I wonder who's been sleeping in my bed. I try to remember those stories every time I think it might be nice to have just one drink. The best incident —or the worst, depending on how you look at it—happened when I was visiting some friends in southern California. The night I arrived we smoked pot and went off to a party at a sculptor's house. He was into primitive art, and the patio and pool were surrounded by huge, forbidding stone figures he'd done. I was jet-lagged, and I'd already had the pot, but I started knocking back Scotch as soon as we got there. I must have gone into a blackout pretty soon, because I can only remember bits and pieces of the rest of the night.

"First, I was in a clinch with someone, male I think, but it could have been a rubber sea lion for all I knew. Next, I was holding on for dear life to one of those grotesque stone faces. Its eye, the one I could see, was staring at me malevolently. Someone—definitely male this time—was screwing me from behind. Then I was in the swimming pool with all my clothes on, and some naked guy was trying to peel off my jeans.

"The next thing I remember is waking up in this strange room. It was dirty and full of tacky old furniture. I knew it wasn't the sculptor's place, but otherwise I didn't have a clue where I was. There was no one else in bed with me, which was a great relief. Suddenly I heard someone banging on the door and shouting, 'Police! Open up!' I managed to drag myself out of bed, even though my head was pounding and my vagina was so sore I could hardly walk. There were some women's clothes— not mine—piled on a chair. Whoever they belonged to was several sizes bigger than me and from the Mother Earth school of dressing. I did the best I could with them and opened the door. Two uniformed cops burst in.

" 'Where is he?' one demanded.

" 'Where's who?' I asked.

" 'Donald Duck,' wisecracked the other cop. 'Your boyfriend. Just tell us where he is and we won't bother you anymore.'

" 'But I don't know where he is,' I insisted. 'I don't even know who he is.'

"I shouldn't have said that because one of them turned nasty. 'Cut the crap, lady!' he yelled and grabbed my arm. 'Maybe you'll remember more down at the station.'

"Twenty-four hours and what seemed a lifetime of humiliation later, my friends took me home. As I was leaving, the nicer cop said to me, 'You should check yourself into that Betty Ford place. The next time you might not be so lucky.' "

Despite deep disappointments and even danger, until she became sober, Nancy continued to seek solace in sex, as do many people in the throes of an addiction. When your life feels in a mess and getting progressively worse on all fronts, a new sexual relationship can seem to offer promise of salvation. You blame your drinking on your partner— or your lack of partner—and find hope of getting sober in the arms of your new love. In fact, these intensely troubled relationships only bring more problems to your already troubled family and social life. Getting involved with somebody new does nothing to stop you from using drugs or drinking, but your addiction blinds you from seeing the truth.

The worse the addiction becomes, the more the mechanics of performance suffer. Sex becomes increasingly unsatisfying. Alcoholics commonly respond to this situation in two ways. Some cling to sex as their only source of gratification, even in the face of so much evidence to the contrary. Other alcoholics isolate themselves and have even fewer social encounters, sexual or otherwise. Sex for them becomes a distant memory, replaced entirely by the bottle.

Either way, a disrupted sex life is widespread among people who seek treatment for their alcoholism. On a questionnaire filled out by incoming patients at our clinic, over eighty percent reported sexual dissatisfaction in the previous year, and over fifty percent reported one or more physical sexual problems related to alcohol. Men usually cited the failure to maintain an erection, while women complained that they couldn't achieve orgasm.

As I explained in Chapter 2, the physical problems usually correct themselves during the first year of recovery. But many of the psychological issues, which are related to long-term use of alcohol during sex and to the trauma caused by failed or unwanted sexual encounters, can persist long after the physical difficulties have been cleared up.

Continued psychological difficulty with sex is often tied to a phenomenon called "state dependent learning," which works as follows: When you learn a skill while under the influence of alcohol or drugs, you may not remember how to perform that skill when you're sober—even though you'll be able to do it again the next time you're intoxicated. Similarly, if you've always performed a particular action while under the influence, it may seem unfamiliar or hard to duplicate when you are sober.

Researchers have demonstrated this phenomenon in many experiments, but in real life it's most often observed in the area of sex. People who have used alcohol since the very beginning of their sexual activity may never have experienced sex while sober. For recovering people who don't have a regular partner, the mere thought of attempting to make sexual contact without alcohol can create tremendous anxiety. And for those with regular partners, sex can feel strange and awkward.

The recovering alcoholic isn't alone in feeling awkward about sex. For years, his or her partner has been having sexual experiences that have produced mostly negative expectations. Many alcoholics are dimly aware that they're less than perfect partners. But few truly realize how unpleasant it can be to have had repeated sex with someone who's drunk, gross, greedy, uncoordinated, and likely to pass out in the middle of the act.

Leo, who entered treatment after years of heavy drinking, vividly described this scene with his wife Joan. When he opened his eyes, the morning sun was blazing in through the bedroom window. His wife lay next to him in bed, wide awake and tense with fury. Joan's mood was all too familiar. Lately, she was like this so often he could almost smell her anger. He didn't know exactly what had happened the night before, but he had the general idea—he had behaved badly in bed.

As consciousness crept up on him, Leo became aware that his knee was throbbing, but he hadn't the foggiest notion why. All he could remember was arguing with Joan about ordering a second bottle of wine at dinner the night before. Maybe he'd had a few brandies, too. Now, his bladder full to bursting, he gingerly rolled out of bed and hoped Joan wouldn't attack him. She didn't—until he limped back from the bathroom. Then she sat bolt upright in bed and let him have it. "You don't even remember, do you, you sadistic, selfish son of a bitch?" she yelled. "When we got home last night I thought you were out, so I went to take a bath. I thought it might relax me, though how I'm supposed to relax living with a pig like you, I don't know. Well, you weren't out. You came charging into the bathroom and jumped into the tub with me and cracked your knee on the soap dish. But that didn't stop you. You went at me like a madman, grabbing me by the shoulders and trying to ram yourself into me. You almost drowned me. I screamed, but you wouldn't stop. I finally managed to break away, but you chased me into the bedroom and wrestled me down on the bed. As soon as you were finished with me, you passed out. Next time I'm going to cut off your dick, Leo. I swear I will."

Such scenes are common in marriages in which one partner is chemically dependent. And even though the sober spouse may understand that it's the booze or drugs that cause the unpleasantness and violence, he or she nevertheless feels abused, violated, and traumatized. Most partners also end up feeling very resentful and many suffer from low self-esteem, even if they know rationally that the addiction and its consequences have nothing at all to do with them.

The result is that many partners of users approach sex warily. Over the years, they've learned how to protect themselves from disappointment and revulsion. Their protective mechanisms are still operating, even after the chemically dependent person has gotten sober.

Jennifer started drinking and smoking marijuana in high school when she went out on dates. In college she occasionally added cocaine to her repertoire. She found that the added confidence she got from being high made it easier to handle her anxieties about sex, even with her fiancé David, with whom she was very much in love. She promised herself that when she got married she would stop drinking and getting stoned before she and David made love. But the couple of times she tried having sex while sober, she felt so uncomfortable that she could hardly respond to David's caresses.

Not wanting to ruin their otherwise wonderful relationship, Jennifer went back to her old habits. Over the next seven years, she became increasingly dependent on alcohol and drugs, until David threatened to leave her if she didn't seek treatment. In the year before she checked into our clinic, their sex life had been almost nonexistent. Ever more preoccupied with her addictions, physically ill and mortified by all the weight she'd gained, Jennifer had gradually lost interest in sex.

After many distressing and humiliating experiences, including one session when she had urinated on the bed while they were making love, David had moved into the guest bedroom. Finally, convinced that David's threat wasn't an idle one, Jennifer agreed to get help. In her first weeks of treatment, she made so much progress that both she and David began to feel very optimistic about saving their marriage. At the end of her month-long stay at Smithers, Jennifer was looking and feeling better than she had in years.

On her first Saturday home, she and David spent most of the afternoon together in the kitchen. David, whose previous culinary experience had been limited to putting a frozen dinner in the microwave, cooked her an elaborate meal. He made bad puns in a ghastly French accent as he chopped and diced and dirtied almost every pot and pan in the house. Jennifer enjoyed not only David's antics but the meal as well, even though the Hollandaise sauce was curdled. They were feeling close and sexy when they went to bed.

Unfortunately, their lovemaking fared little better than the Hollandaise. No matter how hard she tried to relax, Jennifer was tense and unresponsive until David's ardor disappeared. They lay silently side by side for a long time. Finally Jennifer turned to David and said, "I guess I'm really still hung up about sex."

When Jennifer next saw her AA sponsor, she shyly broached the topic of her sex life. As it turned out, her sponsor had been through the same sort of experience herself and was able to direct David and Jennifer to a therapist who specialized in sexual problems. Through therapy, and with David's support, Jennifer learned how to put her old inhibitions to rest so that she could enjoy lovemaking in sobriety.

As I mentioned in Chapter 2, cocaine use often leads to compulsive, and often risky, sexual behavior. In early sobriety, coke addicts may remember their superhuman sexual exploits euphorically and yearn for that level of intensity of experience again. This is an extraordinarily dangerous fantasy to indulge.

Mario, a thirty-year-old schoolteacher with a quiet charm, was a sexual giant only in his daydreams. His fantasies were fairly routine—an unending powerful erection, mind-blowing orgasms, whimpers of exhausted gratitude from a roomful of voracious women, doomed to playing with themselves and each other until he should come and satisfy one and all with his electrifying organ. Then he discovered cocaine, and his fantasies became real—or appeared to. "I'm not," he said, "sure if I got many grateful whimpers because I don't think I was listening, but there were a lot of available partners, no inhibitions, and plenty of energy. Until the coke ran out."

For three weeks Mario struggled to stay off drugs and put sex out of his mind. Then he had a glass of wine with a friend in a restaurant. Up to that point, he'd been enjoying himself and amusing his friend with tales of the idiocies of the school system when suddenly he became obsessed and oppressed by an intrusive sexual fantasy, which would not go away. "I had to have it. The high, the uninhibited sex. I needed that experience again." He made some lame excuse to his friend and bolted off to call his old connection. No answer. Frantic, Mario went to "the jungle," a section of town where it was easy to score. He wound up in a crack house with some clapped-out users—scraggy, exhausted, riddled with pimples and bad breath. "Like figures in a painting by Edvard Munch," he described them. But he was undeterred by the seamy surroundings. He had his orgy then. The compulsion was on him. He could not stop himself. "Fantasies don't have flaws," he explained, "and they never smell bad. When you're high on cocaine you don't notice the flaws either. Usually. This time, though, reality was so strong it penetrated the euphoria and stayed in my mind afterwards. I'd like to bottle that rancid smell and uncork it whenever I get a sex and cocaine fantasy again."

Though some people like Mario are driven by sexual compulsion, fueled by selective euphoric memories, others find that cocaine itself becomes the obsession, the orgasm, and the orgy. Sexual activity, certainly with other people, becomes a distant memory. "For months after I came off the cocaine, I had sexual dreams about masturbation," one young man confessed. "How infantile can you get? There was a lot of competition in my CA group about who could come up with the most bizarre, dangerous, or revolting sex stories. It took me a long time to realize that half of us didn't have any stories at all."

In Chapter 9 I will talk about how to develop a satisfying sex life in sobriety.

Your Social Life and Friendships

Many people begin to use alcohol or drugs in social situations where others are also drinking or using drugs. If one is shy or awkward, going to parties or meeting large groups of new people can be very painful, especially in adolescence. Many of my patients have told me that when they took their first drink or toke of marijuana at a stressful social occasion, they suddenly felt more at ease. They could chat and laugh and feel as witty and attractive as anyone else in the room. In short, they were transformed into more socially comfortable beings.

Gillian, a good friend of mine who's been sober and in AA for twenty years now, described to me how a few drinks could change her from wallflower to social butterfly. Gillian's father was a diplomat, and as a gawky, self-conscious teenager she was frequently required to attend official functions. She dreaded these stiff, staid occasions, where she didn't know what to say and blushed bright red if anyone spoke to her. She longed to hide behind her mother's skirts like a three-year-old, even though she was already several inches taller than her mother.

One day a kindly friend of her father's noticed her discomfort and offered her a small glass of sherry. Not knowing what else to do, she gulped it down, and a moment later a miracle occurred. Gillian's tongue was loosened and she stopped worrying about what everyone else was thinking. She couldn't wait to drink another glass of that marvelous stuff.

Far from dreading these parties, she began to look forward to them. After a few sherries she could be warm and charming to anyone. She would jabber away in her schoolgirl French to imposing Africans in colorful robes; she managed to coax a smile from the dour Austrian whose thickly-accented English made him sound like a character in a comic operetta. Both she and her parents were complimented on how much she'd grown up, and soon she was much in demand among her parents' circle of diplomatic acquaintances. After that Gillian never looked back. She knew alcohol would always help her through a difficult situation and never again—until she became sober—did she attend a social occasion without it.

All adolescents go through periods of feeling shy and clumsy in social situations, and many teenagers experiment with alcohol and drugs to ease their discomfort. The difference between those who grow up to be social drinkers and those who develop an addiction, as Gillian did, is the intensity of the alcohol's transforming effect. For those who experience a real metamorphosis, it becomes difficult even to consider going to a party without being high. They begin to think of alcohol and drugs as a regular and essential part of their social interaction, as part of what allows them to have fun.

At first, there are some wonderful, memorable times. As the drug or alcohol use increases, the good times become fewer, but the drug or alcohol use nevertheless continues and increases. You may start out cheerful and extroverted, perhaps the life and soul of the party, but as you get deeper and deeper into trouble with alcohol or drugs, you become a problem to yourself and to others. You become aggressive or morose. You do foolish things, create embarrassing scenes.

As you progress into chemical dependency, you become increasingly reluctant to accept invitations from people who don't drink or do drugs. Little by little, your circle of friends narrows to include only people who drink or do drugs as much as you do. My patients often tell me they don't drink or do any more drugs than their friends—and they don't.

This selection process is compounded by your increasingly unreliable behavior. Friends will put up with the occasional broken appointment, the odd drunken evening, the occasional outburst of unprovoked aggression. But sooner or later, all but the most dedicated friends will drop you. Social isolation is a common aspect of the advanced stages of chemical dependency.

Given the demands you place on those closest to you, it's not hard to understand their withdrawal. You insist that your behavior be tolerated, even when it's cruel and rejecting. Then you require that they listen gratefully and sympathetically to your tearful confessions. You expect an unrealistic level of support. The odd telephone call at 2:00 A.M. may be condoned, but when you start to call twice a week, even the most caring of friends will back off.

When your demands aren't met, you become angry and reproachful. Sometimes, because you were in a blackout, you don't remember the malicious insults you hurled at your best friend the night before, and you're mortally wounded when he doesn't call to see how you are the next day. Your friends' apparent rejection plays into your diminishing self-esteem. You become defensive and bristly. You assume an attitude of "I can take care of myself." You assure yourself that you don't need anyone else.

Some of my patients do have a concerned network of friends. On the other hand, I've treated some very personable and lovable people whose only friends were the drinking buddies they had met in bars. I've also had patients who had been drinking or using for so long that no one in the world, not even their families, cared about them.

Whatever your individual situation, your social circle is certainly smaller and more limited than it was before you became addicted. Those friends who haven't yet given up on you are probably very cautious. Having been hurt in the past, they may not want to get too involved with you anymore. They may be skeptical about your promises to stop drinking, to change. And their reactions are entirely normal.

Because I treat so many single people, I've seen many patients who had developed a close, dependent relationship with a best friend or lover. Many studies have shown that spouses of the chemically dependent are likely to be children of alcoholics. I've noticed that this is also true of many friends, either of the same or opposite sex, who have become the primary caretaker of the chemically dependent person.

When Juan threw Ramona out of their apartment because she'd gotten high on crack and had sex with another man, her friend Mercedes took her in. When Ramona was fired from her job for being late once too often, Mercedes listened to her rail about how unfair her bosses had been. And when Ramona was drugging too much to hold down any job at all, Mercedes lent her money until she could "get back on her feet."

Evening after evening, Ramona sat in Mercedes's apartment, high on crack and complaining about how she was exploited by men and discriminated against at work. Ramona was convinced that Hispanic women got a raw deal all around, and much in Mercedes's life made her agree with her friend. This was the bond that drew the two women together: They were both trying to maintain their independence in a culture that had little tolerance for independent women.

There was something else that drew them together. Mercedes's father had been an alcoholic. Her mother, exhausted by the demands of twelve children and a drunken husband, had been ill for much of Mercedes's childhood. The oldest girl, she took on the responsibility of caring for her older brothers, looking after the little ones, and nursing her mother. She shopped, cooked, cleaned, and mopped up after her father when he was drunk and sick.

Mercedes was only nineteen when he died of complications from alcoholic liver disease. She knew that the alcohol had killed him, and for this reason she drank very little herself and never used drugs. She knew that most of Ramona's troubles were caused by her crack use and not because she was a Hispanic woman. But Mercedes was so used to taking care of people that it felt natural to take care of Ramona. She never told Ramona how much the drugging worried her. Ramona was her first real friend, and she didn't want to lose her.

In time, Ramona's addiction got worse, and she began shooting heroin as well. Once vivacious, exuberant, and enthusiastic, she became morose and apathetic. Put off by her bitterness and anger, her friends stopped coming around to visit. Mercedes, in the meanwhile, was making new friends. She had worked her way up to a managerial position in the department in which she had started out as a secretary. She became active in an organization that promoted the interests of Hispanic women. But as Ramona continued to use crack and heroin, Mercedes continued to take care of her.

Then Mercedes began dating Miguel, a lawyer she'd met through her work with the feminist group. Miguel couldn't figure out Mercedes's relationship with Ramona, especially since Ramona had taken to stealing money from Mercedes to pay for her drugs. But Mercedes continued to support Ramona until one day Ramona stole a necklace that had been a gift from Miguel. That was the last straw. Mercedes was finally able to see how low Ramona had sunk. She also saw that Ramona was past helping herself. She had to be the one to do something—and not only for Ramona's sake. She loved her friend, but she was beginning to see how much the relationship was costing her.

She investigated treatment centers and found a way to get medical coverage for Ramona. Then she confronted her friend and gave her a choice: Go into treatment, or leave the apartment and never come back. Ramona, who had hit rock bottom and was terrified of losing her last ally, agreed. Mercedes stood by her during treatment, and Ramona got sober. The two have now reestablished their friendship on a healthier, more equal footing.

When You Get Sober

When you first get sober and look around to see who's left of your old friends, you may find very few people willing or able to support your sobriety. Certainly, your old drinking or drugging pals can't be of any help to you, and you can put your recovery at risk by continuing to associate with people who are still drinking or using. If they are your only friends, you'll have to build a new support system. The self-help groups—AA, CA, NA, and the others listed in Appendix C—are very useful in this regard. The people you meet at the groups may be your only friends during the early stages of your recovery. I have more than a few patients who date all their friendships from the day after they got sober.

At the beginning of your sobriety, self-help meetings may be the only social situations where you feel comfortable. Because you never learned how to be at ease in groups without being high, you're likely to find other social gatherings very stressful. You may also worry about what to do or say if you're offered a drink or drugs. Don't hesitate to say no to parties and other social events if you feel apprehensive. In fact, turning down invitations may be part of what you need to do to stay sober.

It's interesting to me that newly sober people often talk about how socially awkward they feel, and yet those feelings seem at odds with their actual behavior, which seems relatively smooth and open. Many, many times I have heard people at self-help meetings describe—with great eloquence and ease—how uncomfortable they feel in groups. This discrepancy often stems from the fact that they aren't used to feeling the normal, limited amount of discomfort that many people who don't drink or use feel in social situations. The difference is that over the years, people who are not chemically dependent have acquired coping skills that you don't possess. But you can acquire them, and you will, as you become more comfortable in sobriety.

Building new friendships and rebuilding old relationships is a slow and gradual process. It may be a year or more before you've formed a nurturing social network. Former friends who were driven away by your addictive behavior and have since formed other, more satisfying friendships may not be interested in resuming the relationship. Their rejection can be very distressing, and you may be tempted to take a drink to erase the pain. Consider instead *why* they wrote you off in the first place, and what you can do to reestablish connections with the people who are willing to do so.

If you're fortunate enough to have old friends who want to continue the relationship, it may still take some time before they feel that they can trust your sobriety. You'll have to be patient until they come to terms with the fact that your relationship is on a different footing than it was in the past.

When my son was young I used to read him a book he loved called *Who Will Be My Friends?* It's the story of a little boy who's moved into a new neighborhood. Though he wants to make friends, he's not sure how to go about it. He tries to get the mailman to play with him, but the mailman's too busy. The cat's too preoccupied with her ball of string. Finally he spots some children playing ball, one of his favorite games. When he tells the children he can run and throw, they invite him to play with them, and soon they become his friends.

This children's story contains much wisdom for adults, and particularly for newly sober adults. You'll sometimes be disappointed when you try to make friends, but when you get involved in activities you enjoy, you'll find other people who share your enjoyment. These people will be your friends.

For more help with rebuilding your social life and your friendships, see Chapter 10.

The success of your family life, social life, and sex life are closely tied to your ability to establish and maintain intimacy. It is within intimate relationships that one's emotional life can take root and blossom. But when you're addicted, you can't be intimate with anyone. Your drug becomes your only true love object, and your emotional life becomes warped and sterile.

You view other people only as they relate to the primary purpose in your life—getting and using your drug. They become objects, to be manipulated, placated, avoided, defended against, or used in the service of your addiction. You make no real contact with others; you can't participate in the give and take that intimate relationships require. You register others' pain only as something that interferes with your freedom to get or use your drug.

Becoming sober offers the possibility of intimacy, of a new and more nurturing emotional life. In the beginning, however, you'll still be preoccupied with your drug—not with getting it, but with avoiding it. Your primary purpose in the early weeks and months of your sobriety is to stay sober. Sometimes intimacy and emotional connectedness, no matter how eager you are for them, must be sacrificed to that end. But as your sobriety develops and stabilizes, so do your prospects for intimacy and emotional growth. Indeed, the ability to become connected again—to family, friends, a loving partner, to all of life—is what sobriety is all about.

The core of this book, Chapters 8 through 10, is dedicated to helping you restore your emotional relationships. And Chapter 11, which deals with sustaining sobriety on the job, covers a related issue. While perhaps not strictly emotional, your relationships with coworkers, as well as your feelings about your work itself, are pivotal to your self-image as an abstinent person. Putting in order all these aspects of your life—family, sex, friendships, and work—can easily occupy you not only in the first year of your sobriety but well into your second and third years of abstinence, perhaps beyond. And the work you do in these areas is central to the living plan I introduce in the next chapter.

Chapter Four
A Living Plan to Keep You Healthy, Happy, and Sober

Unpredictable. Chaotic. Excessive. These three words best describe your life when you were drinking or using drugs. In sobriety, your life will be the opposite—stable, ordered, and temperate.

This does *not* mean that your sober life will be dull, monotonous, or boring. There will be moments of intense joy in sobriety. There will be spontaneity and surprises—some pleasant, some not so pleasant. But no matter what happens, now that you are no longer at the mercy of the disordered chemicals in your brain, you will be the one to decide how you want to spend your hours, days, and weeks. As you well know, you cannot control your addiction, but you can take charge of your life.

Much of your day-to-day existence has already begun to fall into place simply by virtue of your being sober. But you may still be left with habits and routines which are neither useful nor productive. There are also gaps in your life, formerly occupied by drinking or drugging, which you will have to fill. Changing your habits and occupying those now-empty hours requires careful thought and planning—a living plan. Your plan will be comprehensive, encompassing all aspects of your life. It is not meant merely to fill empty hours, but to help you create an entirely new life which promotes your physical, mental, and spiritual health as well as your sobriety.

After six weeks without a drink, Nancy, whose disastrous one-night stand you read about in Chapter 3, found herself ambivalent and even disappointed with sobriety. "So I'm sober. What else is new?" she said flippantly to her therapy group.

"I get up in the morning. I know who I'm in bed with—me. Well, actually that's nice," she admitted. "I get dressed, which only takes half the time it used to because I can find things in my apartment, and I don't have to use six pounds of makeup to look alive. Then I eat breakfast. Me, who used to gag just watching people come out of a coffee shop in the morning. I stay at work all day—no slipping out for a few quick belts."

Nancy had arranged to take only local assignments for the first three months of her sobriety. "Work is a lot easier now that I know what I'm doing most of the time. I don't mix up my notes and quotes anymore. But I'm not exactly covering the most exciting stories. That's okay for a while, I guess, but I miss being in the thick of things. After work I go to an AA meeting. I like them—the stories are great, but it seems as if there's a kind of group censor operating. People go only so far in what they say. When I tell my story," she said, grinning in anticipation, "I'm not leaving anything out." Nancy paused. "Oh, hell. I mean it's all okay, but I feel so flat most of the time. I'm doing what everybody else is doing. I'm just one of the crowd."

"So you need to be drunk to be unique?" one group member challenged.

"Well, no, not drunk," Nancy answered uncertainly. "But I miss the excitement, the turmoil, the sense that something unexpected could happen at any moment."

"Like spending the night in jail?" another member who knew her story asked.

Lloyd, the young man from Chapter 2 who became so paranoid on crack that he barricaded himself inside his apartment, was also in Nancy's group. "It seems to me," he said, "that you're romancing booze the way I romance coke. I forget about being so paranoid and think about how much energy I used to have. But you can't have one without the other. You can't have your kind of artificial excitement without getting yourself in deep trouble, and I can't have my kind of supercharged energy without being paranoid. I'm working on accepting my human limitations and looking for a different kind of energy. Maybe you could do something like that."

Eric, whom you also met in Chapter 2, let out a long, low whistle. "Nancy, it sounds like you're headed straight for a slip." Eric spoke bluntly, but his face wore a look of deep concern for Nancy.

Nancy did have her slip, not then, but six weeks later when she went on her first out-of-town assignment since becoming sober. She got drunk again and found excitement. But it was more than she bargained for. Shaken, but defensive and defiant, she returned to the group. "How was I to know he was a sadist? He wasn't dressed in black leather and studs. He was wearing a boring gray suit. He never said a word about whips and chains. He was amusing and pleasant."

"How would you know?" Eric asked wearily. "You were drunk."

After this encounter, Nancy made a new commitment to sobriety. This time, she decided to celebrate the ordinary—a sober day, a sober week, a sober month. She began to work on her living plan in earnest, making sure to include plenty of special events, either for herself alone or with friends—a theater party, curry at her favorite Indian restaurant, a facial. Soon she found herself looking forward to these celebrations. After a particularly satisfying—and sober—weekend, she reported to the group, "I think I'm beginning to enjoy myself sober."

As it was for Nancy, it may be difficult when you first become sober to accept the importance of making a living plan. You may think that being sober is enough, that your life will inevitably fall into place just because you've stopped drinking or using. Abstinence alone does a great deal, but it cannot turn you into a truly sober person. You must do that yourself through a self-designed program for healthy living.

If you have achieved a year or more of sobriety without having made a plan, you may question the value of doing so now. But a systematic, organized way of sober living can only make sobriety better—and easier—for you. It may enable you finally to stop smoking or to lose those extra twenty pounds. Or you may find that having a living plan provides a secure base from which you can tackle some of the tough problems you have set aside—changing jobs, perhaps, or making amends to your sister. Whatever outstanding business you have in sobriety, a living plan can help you bring closure to those situations. And it can help you build a fuller, richer sobriety.

Moderation

No single living plan works for everyone, but I can suggest a general principle that applies universally: *moderation*. Think of it this way. If you eat an enormous dinner, you're likely to spend an uncomfortable, restless night. If you exercise for eight hours at a stretch one day, you'll be sore and achy the next. Most people can cope with occasional overindulgence or excess, but, in early sobriety, a lack of restraint may put you at risk of drinking or using again.

Because your body and mind are in a state of flux, too much food or exercise and lack of sleep can be particularly risky. At this early stage, your brain is likely to misinterpret certain familiar signals. Hunger or fatigue can send you looking for a pick-me-up drink or drug. Overstrained muscles may push you to medicate yourself with a shot of alcohol or a tranquilizer. Surrounding yourself with chaos can make you feel anxious by reviving, consciously or unconsciously, memories of the years before recovery when everything was left to the last minute and your days were disordered and frenzied because you were too busy drinking or doing drugs to make plans. In order to truly recover, you first need to create for yourself a secure, reliable environment.

Creating Your Plan

Your new living plan, which may be the first regular routine you've ever followed, will help you greatly to regain your sense of emotional balance. But in your eagerness to move ahead, you may pack your schedule too tightly, as most newly sober people do.

Planning your workday is easier than filling free time. At the office or on the job, you're governed by a more-or-less predetermined schedule and set of responsibilities. You must arrive by a certain hour, and you have particular tasks to perform. However, your leisure time is full of possibilities, and you are apt to think you can—or perhaps should— explore them all. A good rule of thumb is to make a list of what you'd like to do—then cut it in half.

Newly sober people are often unsure about how to organize their free time. As one of my patients explained, "I didn't realize how much of my time I spent waiting to get high—first thinking about it, yearning for it, then scoring, then finally using. As soon as I came down, I'd start thinking and waiting all over again. Life went on around me, but I was oblivious. Now I have all this extra time, but I can't let myself drift through the day anymore, because when I do, I feel a lurking sense of danger. So I plan every minute. But that seems artificial, too. I guess the problem is that I never really had a life without drugs."

Without the familiar crutch of alcohol or drugs, you may have difficulty choosing among the bewildering array of recreations or hobbies. So you take a smorgasbord approach—a little bit of this, a smattering of that, until your schedule is too crowded to be enjoyable.

You may also be locked into habits or patterns of behavior that seem too much a part of you to change, even though they long ago ceased to be rewarding. For example, you may continue to go bowling every Wednesday, when you have stopped caring about the game. Or you may meet the same group of people at the same restaurant each week, as you have done for years, even though the conversation bores you to tears. On the other hand, you may have given up former pleasures or ruled out new possibilities because you were preoccupied with alcohol or drugs. When you're using, almost any activity that takes you away from your high can be irritating or bothersome.

In sobriety, however, you should try to start out with no preconceived notions about what you do or do not enjoy. You may be surprised to find yourself delighting in all kinds of pastimes that would have bored you to tears when you were using.

Flexibility is another important element. Your life plan is not carved in stone. Rather, it's a set of options that will change as you change and grow in sobriety. Try to avoid thinking of those options as obligations that must be carried out precisely. If you allow the guidelines to rule your life, you're likely to feel guilty when you don't follow them.

Guilt, one of the most easily and commonly evoked emotions among recovering persons, erodes self-esteem, which is precisely what your life plan is meant to enhance. But if you beat yourself over the head every time you deviate from your agenda, you may wind up taking a drink or using drugs again in order to blot out your guilt. Becoming a slave to your plan undermines your efforts to be healthy, happy, and sober.

Dashing madly from one place to the next is another trap to avoid. When you schedule your activities and appointments, give yourself a generous helping of in-between time. This is especially helpful to remember as you block out time for self-help meetings. If you arrive flushed and panting just as the meeting is about to begin, you won't be able to focus on the discussion (or on yourself) for a good fifteen or twenty minutes. Similarly, if you make a date to meet someone or be somewhere immediately after the meeting, you may have to rush right out and thus miss the opportunity to quietly reflect on what you've just heard. In either case, you've cheated yourself of the chance to relax and truly be a part of the group.

Besides these general guidelines—being open-minded, flexible, and time-conscious—there are a number of other specific elements you should incorporate into your sober living plan. We'll discuss each point in greater detail in later chapters, but let's briefly look at them now. The simplest way to start your plan is to create a physical structure for your day, by eating regular meals, establishing a usual bedtime, and exercising regularly.

Eat Regular Meals

Now is neither the time to be dieting stringently nor to be indulging your every whim for fattening foods. Developing regular, healthy eating habits in early sobriety is crucial not only for nutritional reasons, but also for stabilizing your mood, for supplying you with adequate energy throughout the day, and for providing you with set periods when you can socialize or relax by yourself.

Your day should begin with breakfast, a meal you may have forgotten existed. Breakfast means more than a few quick sips of coffee as you dash out the door. You should plan to get up early enough to spend twenty or thirty minutes leisurely eating your food, reading the newspaper, listening to the news, or talking to your family.

Although grabbing lunch on the run is sometimes unavoidable, don't let it be part of your daily routine. Your new life has to allow you time out in the middle of the day to unwind, get some fresh air if possible, and eat a nutritious, but not heavy, meal.

Try to plan your dinner so that you don't wind up eating five minutes before bedtime. Try also to use this meal as a time to relax or to socialize with family or friends. Your schedule will occasionally have to vary, sometimes of necessity and sometimes because of a special occasion. But do try to establish a practical schedule from which you can deviate now and then.

In Chapter 15, I will discuss what constitutes a healthy diet.

Establish a Regular Bedtime

Alcohol and drugs have not only interfered with your sleep patterns, but have also upset the normal biological rhythms that determine when you feel sleepy and when you feel awake. A good way to normalize both is to set a regular hour at which you go to bed. Your routine should include a half-hour or so to relax before you go to sleep. Falling into bed as soon as you've finished dinner, on the heels of a phone conversation, or after an evening devoted to helping your daughter with her science project doesn't do a thing to promote a healthy night's rest.

Be realistic about your bedtime. This may sound obvious, but it's not smart to get into bed at ten o'clock in order to be up at seven if you need only eight hours sleep. You're likely either to spend half the night anxiously tossing and turning or to wake up earlier than necessary. Think about how much sleep you need, and whether you prefer the extra "down time" at night or in the morning.

Exercise Regularly

Regular exercise is essential in order to condition your body, increase your energy, and help you get a good night's rest. If you've previously enjoyed some physical activity, whether bicycling, tennis, swimming, or aerobics, it shouldn't be too hard for you to reestablish an exercise routine. But those of you who feel faint at the mere thought of vigorous exertion may have to make more of an effort to apply yourselves, as Alan did.

Alan loathed physical exercise in any guise. As a kid, he'd suffered from such poor hand-eye coordination that playing games or sports was always an ordeal. So he exercised his intellect instead and grew up to be a pudgy, paunchy banker. When he was in his late thirties, he became addicted to the painkillers that had been prescribed for his chronic lower back pain.

When he became sober, he began exercising out of desperation. His back hurt badly, and he could take nothing for the pain. His doctor suggested that he enroll in an exercise program specifically designed for people with back problems. In the class Alan learned strengthening and relaxing exercises that helped significantly. By the end of the course he was able to walk comfortably, which he hadn't done in years, so he added a regular walking program to the exercises he had learned in the class. To his surprise, Alan found himself looking forward to his workouts. "Of course it's a mindless bore, but I feel so good afterwards," he admitted.

Not only did his back condition improve, but he also lost weight, which further helped alleviate the pain. In less than a year he was feeling so much better that he decided to take a vacation in the Bahamas. "I love the beach," he told me, "but I never dared show myself in a bathing suit except when I visited my mother in Miami. At least there I didn't feel out of place because all the seventy-year-olds were as flabby as I was. Now," he finished with a mischievous grin, "I can take off my clothes anywhere."

For exercise haters like Alan, or for people who are in poor condition, walking is an excellent way to ease yourself into fitness. The speed and length of your walk will depend on the shape you are in; what's important is that you walk regularly for a set length of time.

The key point about exercise, whether you're happy walking or aspire to run a marathon, is that you make it a regular part of your weekly routine. You will feel so much better if you do. Chapter 16 will go into more detail about how to set up an exercise plan.

If you eat right, get a good night's sleep, and exercise regularly, you'll do much to restore your physical and emotional well-being. But there are additional ways to foster your emotional stability:

Avoid Unnecessary Stress

"Avoid stress!" one patient spoke out angrily in a group I was addressing. "That's like saying 'Take two aspirins and call me in the morning.' How can you avoid stress? Being alive is stressful. Driving to work is stressful, working is stressful, families are stressful, staying sober is stressful. Show me a person without stress and I'll show you a corpse," she challenged.

She's right, of course. You can't eliminate stress entirely, but you do need to look at what causes the stress in your life and take steps to relieve those pressures. Stress reduction can mean the critical difference between staying sober and having a relapse. Although your ability to tolerate stress will increase as the weeks and months pass, in early recovery (the first year) you must try to avoid stressful situations. Later on in your recovery, after you have been sober for about a year, you can learn better how to deal with the stress you do encounter.

Of course, the circumstances that produce stress are different for each person. But there are some obvious stimuli that affect everyone in recovery. Overextending yourself physically is one of them. In early sobriety, you tire easily and undoubtedly find it hard to bounce back from a too strenuous day. Fatigue can affect your ability to concentrate, so you make mistakes and become angry with yourself, which can cause even more stress.

Psychological pressure is yet another cause of stress. It can come from a variety of sources, but one that many recovering people encounter is a hazard I spoke of earlier: overestimating what you can reasonably do in the course of a day or a week. If your goals are unrealistic, you're likely to be left with a list of errands, chores, phone calls, and appointments yet to be completed. The list can get very long after a while, and ultimately you feel anxious and overwhelmed by all that remains to be done. Learning to set a manageable agenda is far preferable to succumbing to the stress of trying to do it all.

Many recovering people are also prey to the psychological stress of responsibilities long neglected, such as unfiled tax returns or unpaid bills. While it is not necessary and probably not possible to take care of all your overdue obligations at once, neither is it a good idea to push thoughts of these troubling matters to the back of your mind where they'll fester and nag at you when you least expect it.

You can reduce your anxiety by making whatever arrangements are necessary to postpone fulfilling your obligations. For example, you only add to your fear and distress by continuing to ignore unpaid taxes. If you can bring yourself instead to call the Internal Revenue Service, you may be able to arrange to defer payments, and thus lessen your stress.

Hard as you may try, it is sometimes impossible to avoid stress. Some situations—divorce, a serious illness in the family, a layoff at work—are so fraught with anxiety and uncertainty that stress is inevitable. If you're faced with such problems you'll find it extremely helpful to make a special plan to help get you through this particularly trying time. The most important component of any arrangement you make is to find someone to talk to about what's going on. Trying to go it alone when you are unavoidably under stress can badly threaten your sobriety. I will discuss this and other aspects of handling stress in Chapter 6.

Postpone Major Life Changes

Major life changes include quitting your job, leaving your spouse, moving house, returning to school, starting a new career, embarking on a new relationship, or having a child. Even though such changes can often have a positive effect on your life, making these moves produces stress. In early recovery, your reaction to stress is unpredictable, and what may start out as a legitimate effort to improve your life can end up being a disaster. You should make every effort possible to postpone such undertakings until you have achieved at least a year of sobriety.

Effecting a major life change requires you to make a great many decisions, large and small, along the way. Because your ability to judge and analyze is not at its best, you may not make sensible choices, and you may become overwhelmed by the sheer number of alternatives facing you. Postponing these big moves will cause you far less anxiety than trying to cope with the consequences of decisions you made when your judgment was impaired.

Another excellent reason to avoid making major changes in early recovery, when possible, is because your perspective is likely to evolve as you remain sober. A boring job or volatile relationship that seemed intolerable in your first weeks of sobriety may feel quite manageable by the time you're three months sober. Biding your time and being patient doesn't mean you're ignoring the situation. When you consciously choose to postpone action, you are taking a *positive* step along the path of your recovery.

Diane, a talented graphic artist, had often thought about turning her hobby of designing jewelry into a business, but her cocaine use prevented her from taking such an ambitious step. Her job at an advertising agency was the only stable point in an otherwise chaotic life, and she also relied on what she earned there to buy her drugs.

But when she became sober, her job seemed dreary and confining, and she began to think more and more about setting up on her own. Ben, a sculptor she met at CA, persuaded her to wait. "I'd lost my agent because of my addiction and decided to strike out on my own when I'd been sober four months," he told her. "I didn't know how to handle my time—either I couldn't fit everything in or I didn't have anything to do.

I also had to pay the rent, so I started taking my portfolio around to the galleries myself. I knew there would be lots of rejections and also some hard bargaining to do if someone did want to show my work. Somehow I got the idea in my head that I would be sharper if I blew a line or two before I went. You can write the ending of that story yourself."

Diane was convinced. She waited until she had eighteen months solid sobriety behind her before she started her business. Three years later, it's an unqualified success. "It was hard at first," she admits. "I wasn't exactly overwhelmed with orders. Weeks could go by without a single phone call, and after three months I wasn't sure I could stick it out. My savings were dwindling fast. But I had my friends in CA, my sober routines, and a little perspective. I knew things could never get so bad that using wouldn't make it worse. After six months business began to pick up, and within a year I knew I was going to be able to make the business work. I might not have—no, I definitely wouldn't have—made it if I'd started the business earlier in my sobriety."

Join and Attend a Self-Help Group

Becoming a member of Alcoholics Anonymous (AA), Cocaine Anonymous (CA), Narcotics Anonymous (NA), or any of the twelve-step self-help groups founded on the AA model can be one of the most important tools of your recovery. (Here and throughout the text I will refer to the various organizations—AA, CA, etc.—as self-help groups or anonymous or twelve-step self-help groups to avoid repeating the list with each reference.)

Nowhere else can you find the company of sympathetic peers who understand exactly where you have been. And there is no better place to find a wide range of role models for successful sobriety. Joining a self-help group also gives you the opportunity to find new and sober friends who can help you in your recovery. And one of the most supportive sober relationships I know of is between a self-help sponsor and a newly sober person. A sponsor is someone who is available to you whenever your sobriety is in danger and who can offer much insight into what a sober life is.

Many people are reluctant to join a self-help group, citing religious reasons or personal misgivings, for example. I will discuss this resistance as well as sponsorship and other aspects of self-help groups in Chapter 7. But for now I urge you to set aside your reservations and avail yourself of the unique opportunity self-help groups provide for everyone in recovery.

Now let's go on to another equally important component to your plan: caring for your health.

Avoid Nonessential Medications

Because so many changes are taking place in your brain and the rest of your body during the early days of sobriety, medicines can affect you in unexpected ways. You'd therefore do best to avoid over-the-counter medications, and to be very cautious about taking prescription drugs unless they are absolutely necessary for your health. Essential medicines include antibiotics to fight infection, insulin for diabetics, and high blood pressure medicine. You need to be especially wary of any medication that affects the brain.

However, common sense and moderation dictate that you don't immediately race into the bathroom and throw out all the pills and liquids in your medicine chest. Instead, discuss your situation frankly and thoroughly with your doctor. If the two of you decide that a particular medication is necessary for your good health, then by all means take it. On the other hand, you and your doctor may determine that a medicine you once needed—anti-depressants or a drug to lower blood pressure—is no longer called for now that you are sober.

Chapter 13 provides a further discussion of medications.

Set Up a Systematic Health Care Program

Many newly recovering alcoholics and substance abusers find themselves paying frequent visits to the doctor because they're suddenly paying attention to all the aches and pains they were previously too numb or high to notice. Taking proper care of these ailments is part of the process of regaining your health.

You should also now begin to make a habit of regular preventive health care. Have someone you trust recommend a doctor who can give you a complete physical workup if you haven't had one in the past year. If you're a woman, you should have a gynecological checkup, including a Pap smear to test for cervical cancer, and a breast examination to check for lumps that may be the first sign of breast cancer. You should also visit a dentist to have your teeth cleaned and checked for cavities and other dental disease, and to receive instruction on the proper care of your teeth and gums.

*   *   *

In this chapter I have given you only a summary of the main components of your sober living plan. In the chapters that follow I'll go into greater detail about what you need to know in order to formulate your plan and put it into action. After you've lived with your plan for a while, you'll begin to see how it can help you establish healthy attitudes and behavior. These patterns will guide you not only in the first year of sobriety, but for the rest of your life. By altering *how* you approach a problem and act on it, you also alter how you feel, not only about yourself but about life in general.

The desire to stay sober has given you the motivation to develop a saner, more peaceful way to live. With your sober living plan, you can move away from the anguish and pain of your addiction and develop a new lifestyle. And as you do, you gain a sense of perspective that enables you to grow to your full potential.

Chapter Five
Sobriety's Ups and Downs

Establishing a Stable Mood

If there is one aspect of early sobriety that disturbs virtually all of my patients, it is the often astonishing rapidity with which their moods and emotions change. Because they don't know how they're going to feel from one moment to the next, they find it hard to make progress in their lives. That's why I've put stabilizing your mood at the top of the list of life-plan components. Until you begin to feel more comfortable with your moods and emotions, it can be difficult to move ahead with creating your life plan.

While you were drinking or using, you masked all your emotions. Feeling happy was cause for celebration—and a few drinks. When you were anxious, you reached for your Valium. A snort of coke could banish the blues in a second. Then, any emotion provided an excuse to drink or use. Now that you're sober, you're suddenly bombarded by feelings. At times they come at you with a strength and intensity that can be positively frightening. Some of them you may not even be able to name.

Back in Chapter 1, you met Sam, who experienced several confusing mood swings on his first Saturday without cocaine. He started the day full of hope, but by mid-morning he was almost in tears because his son was benched during baseball practice. He nearly cried again that afternoon when he misplaced his keys. Later he actually did break down in the middle of an adventure movie.

Such volatile and unpredictable mood swings are upsetting in and of themselves, but they also pose a threat to your sobriety. In the grip of an intense, unfamiliar feeling it is very easy to convince yourself that a drink or a pill would put you on an even keel again. That's another reason it is so important to do what you can to stabilize your mood while your brain chemistry is returning to normal.

And what can you do? First you must learn to recognize and acknowledge your feelings as they occur. You also need to know how to defuse the negative moods that can put you in danger of a relapse.

These skills will serve you long after your moods are no longer as fickle as the wind. No matter how long you have been sober, whether it is nine months or three years, you will still have feelings that upset you. You will be anxious at times, depressed at times, angry at times. The further you progress into sobriety and the more you put your life in order, the more your moods and emotions will have definable antecedents. But traceable or not, upsetting feelings are among the ordinary vicissitudes of life, and you must know how to contend with them in a way that safeguards your sobriety.

Getting to Know You

Just as people are born with different color hair and eyes, their nervous systems also have varying degrees of sensitivity. You can see proof of this in any hospital nursery. Some newborn infants lie peacefully in their cribs, while others are restless and active. As people grow to adulthood, their personalities and patterns of behavior are shaped by an interaction between their genetic predisposition and whatever happens to them as they mature. In other words, individuality and self-image are formed by a combination of nature and nurture.

No evidence exists that one type of personality is more likely than another to become chemically dependent. Years ago there was talk of the "addictive personality," but most of the studies that defined this so-called personality were conducted while the subjects were in the throes of their addiction. The fact is that people who are drinking or using behave with remarkable similarity. What these researchers were seeing were the symptoms of the disease—the personality of addiction, as it were, rather than the addictive personality. When the researchers looked at people *after* they'd become clean and sober, they noted that their personalities were actually extremely dissimilar. Findings now indicate that except for a slight tendency to be more impulsive and easily frustrated, substance abusers are indistinguishable from a comparable group of nonaddicted people.

What this means is that once you've achieved a stable recovery, you have every reason to believe that your moods and behavior won't be any different from anyone else's. However, initially you may have difficulty getting reacquainted with how you feel and behave under normal, sober circumstances. Some of my patients have had to think back twenty and thirty years to their early adolescence in order to remember what they were like before they started drinking or using drugs. While you may not have to go back that far, you'll probably have to do some digging to discover who you are now that you're sober.

Irene, the lawyer who also had a problem with infertility, told me when she had been sober for three months, "I've recently gone through several versions of my past. The one I stuck with the longest was the lonely, vulnerable child inside the charming, competent adult. But now I know that I'm basically a stable person. I don't get too anxious, even when I have to argue a tough case in court, and I'm not usually down. I've had good luck all my life—with friends and grades, and a husband who loves me and understands my disease. But I'm always waiting for my luck to run out. I watch myself like a hawk. Did I deliver a weak summation to the jury? Is my new suit the wrong color? Will I ever become a partner? Why wasn't Chris crazy about the new pasta dish I cooked? Did I put in too much basil? Does Chris really love me?

"Any critical remark or mistake, no matter how minor, gets me thinking along those lines. What I need to work on is learning that I can't be perfect. That's why not being able to get pregnant has been such a blow to me. It's something I couldn't do, no matter how hard I tried. I have to learn to be merely human and allow myself to fail occasionally without thinking it'll be the end of the world."

Lloyd, the recovering crack addict whom you also met earlier in the book, and whose paranoid delusions were so strong that he barricaded himself in his apartment, had a very hard time figuring out who he was in sobriety. After three months he said, "I really don't know if I have a personality. I started doing drugs when I was thirteen, and most of what I did and felt back then had more to do with the drugs than with me . . . whoever me is. My parents split up when I was twelve. When they got divorced I was sad and angry, and the way I coped was by lashing out at everyone and everything, especially them. Helping me get straight is just about the first thing they've done together in the last ten years.

"Now I'm so confused . . . sometimes I feel sort of empty inside, like I don't have any feelings. Other times I feel okay, like a real person. It's that emptiness that's the real bitch. When I'm in that mood, nothing matters. Staying straight is pointless. But I've learned that when I hear myself say that, I have to get myself to a safe place right away."

Whatever your situation, whether you have a fairly good grip on yourself like Irene, or whether you're still searching, as Lloyd is, recovery is an opportunity to get to know yourself again, a chance to embark on a journey of self-exploration.

A good way to begin is to keep a diary of your emotions. For three of four days, keep a pad and pencil handy and jot down your feelings as they occur. If you can identify a particular person, place, or activity that seems related to that emotion, note it as well. Be as specific and detailed as possible, both when naming your feelings and their antecedents. Try to avoid using the words good and bad to describe how you are feeling. When you felt good, were you joyful, elated, carefree, or content? When you felt bad, were you depressed, sad, tense, or worried? Note your physical surroundings, too—where you are, the weather, the time of day, the season. Do these factors or any others contribute to the way you are feeling? Think about the situations you are in, too. Which ones bring out the worst in you? Which bring out the best? Don't attempt to analyze your feelings as you jot them down, or try to do anything about them. Simply observe how you are feeling and the circumstances in which the feeling occurred.

For those of you in the early stages of recovery, this may be a difficult task because your emotions fluctuate so much. At times you'll feel frustrated, but you'll also discover unexpected pleasures. After keeping your journal for a few days, you will notice how much easier it is for you to identify your emotions as they occur. There's no need to continue with such a detailed record, but do take a few minutes once or twice a week to update your journal. If you began your record in early sobriety, periodic reviews will show you how your mood has stabilized, and how much more familiar you are with your emotions and their possible antecedents. Anyone who keeps such a journal for a year, no matter in what stage of sobriety it was begun, will have gained a great deal of self-knowledge, an indispensable tool for any sober person.

Why You Have Negative Moods and Emotions—and What to Do About Them

Everybody is in a bad mood some of the time. People who have not been chemically dependent accept this and have strategies—some more helpful than others—for coping with their negative moods. Some wait it out. Some put their fist through a wall. Others go for a swim or to a movie. Alcoholics and addicts take a drink or a drug. That is no longer an option for you, but very likely you don't know what else to do when a negative mood hits. In early sobriety the problem is compounded by your emotional volatility and by the fact that you may seem to be in a bad mood a lot of the time.

You experience so many negative emotions in early recovery because the neurotransmitter systems that produce euphoria have been overstimulated by your alcohol or drug use. Now that you are sober, those systems must regain the ability to operate without chemicals. Be cause the systems are not working properly, your good feelings are few and your defenses against bad feelings are weak. Your brain is so excitable that the abnormal activity in the brain itself can trigger powerful and unpleasant emotions. And a minor event that would cause no disturbance in a brain that was functioning well can produce a prolonged or intense emotional reaction in early recovery.

You also frequently feel that your mood will be with you forever, that getting out from under it is impossible. But it's not. Eventually your mood, no matter how unpleasant, will pass. If you can endure it for a day or an hour or even a minute, it will change.

I am often struck by how easily people can see the end of disagreeable circumstances: a day at work when things are going badly, a weekend visit of relatives they don't like, the tedious school play in which their child is making a five-second appearance. They can tolerate such situations because they have a fixed beginning and end.

But black moods have no such clearly defined timetable. They can't be counted on to arrive precisely at 1:42 P.M. on Thursday and depart by 11:02 A.M. on Friday. But that does not mean they will go on forever. These moods eventually do dissipate—unfortunately, they are on a schedule that we can neither control nor predict.

When he was drinking, Patrick always felt as if he were living under a black cloud of gloom, irritability, bitterness, and hopelessness. When he got sober, the black cloud was replaced by one that was pink and glowing, and Patrick was ecstatic. Then without warning, about six weeks into his recovery, the dark cloud once again descended for a few days, then lifted, only to return a month or two later. This pattern continued over the next two years.

"Each time I got depressed, it was as if I'd felt that way forever, and that I'd always feel that way. Then one weekend when I was at the beach, after I'd been fine for three or four months, the despondency suddenly hit me again. I woke up feeling terribly low, but I still managed to drag myself out for a swim. Afterwards, sitting in the sun, I saw a flock of sandpipers feeding at the shoreline. As the water receded, they all ran forward on their fragile legs and pecked like mad for whatever goodies the wave had brought them. As the next wave moved towards the shore, they raced back to the dry sand, then forward again when it was safe. They were in constant motion, like leaves swept back and forth by a changeable wind.

"I watched them for a long time, and I began to feel lighthearted. I realized that my depressions came and went like the waves. If I kept running ahead of them, I could reach dry land and wait for them to recede again. Only an hour or so had passed since I'd awakened feeling so rotten, but the change in my mood was remarkable. I was able to look back over the two years of my sobriety and see clearly for the first time that it hadn't been all doom and gloom. I'd had many long periods that were good, interspersed with shorter, darker times. But eventually those dark moods always subsided. At that moment I resolved to hang in there a day at a time, to ride the waves without allowing them to knock me over. I've stuck to that resolve, and I'm a lot better off for it."

When you're in the grips of any negative mood, you can do one of two things: You can *fuel* it, or you can *defuse* it. The former allows you to behave in ways that are guaranteed to make you feel and behave even worse, until your negative emotions threaten to boil over. The latter means you don't allow yourself to behave in ways that feed your mood. You may not be able to alter the mood itself, but you can prevent it from escalating into a full-scale disaster—and may even cut it short. Although is is often helpful to determine later on whether or not an external circumstance caused or contributed to your mood swing, such analyses are not helpful when the feelings are actually upon you.

Let's watch Tony, a recovering cocaine addict who has been sober for eight months, fuel a negative mood. It was late on a Friday afternoon, and for no reason he could determine, Tony was feeling anxious and edgy, ready to pounce on anyone or anything that crossed his path. He snapped at the company accountant when she came into his office to discuss a billing error, and when she responded angrily, his mood darkened. Later, on his way home, he got stuck at a broken traffic light. The driver in front of him seemed oblivious, so Tony leaned on his horn, but to no avail. As Tony impatiently watched the clock on the dashboard, a full minute passed before the driver finally ran the broken light. Tony zoomed after him through the intersection.

When he got to the expressway, the bumper-to-bumper traffic was moving sluggishly. About a mile later, it came to a complete stop. Tony was beside himself. *Why me?* he raged. *Why does this always happen to me?* He shook his fist at the car ahead of him; he punched his horn in short, angry bursts. Then he glanced to his right and noticed that the driver was grinning at him. Even more infuriated, he glared again at the dashboard clock. This time five minutes went by before the traffic started moving freely again.

By the time he arrived home, Tony was consumed with rage. As soon as he walked in the house, his eight-year-old son Ricky asked him for help with his math homework. Tony loudly launched into a ten-minute tirade about the need to be self-sufficient, to get homework done on time, about the lousy grades Ricky had received on his last math test. He wound up his lecture by telling his son what a disappointment he was. Ricky slunk away in tears while Tony's wife Elaine, who'd caught the end of Tony's outburst, wondered aloud whether the family had been better off back when Tony was still using and paid very little attention to them. "At least then you kept your big mouth shut," she shouted before she went upstairs to console Ricky.

Tony slunk outside, feeling furious and ashamed of himself. He knew his reaction to Ricky's request was inappropriate, and now he'd succeeded in both hurting his son and alienating his wife. But there seemed to be nothing he could do to sidetrack his mounting fury.

Probably, Tony couldn't control the fact that he found himself in a tense, anxious mood. Nor did he have a clue as to what had caused it. But he could have taken some positive action early on to defuse his anger and handled the situation much differently, as follows:

It was late on a Friday afternoon, and Tony was feeling anxious, irritable, and tense. Unpleasant though the mood was, he reminded himself that he'd felt this way before and it always lifted, usually within a few hours, and inevitably after a good night's sleep. Then the accountant, whose brittle, sarcastic manner always put him on edge, walked into his office to discuss a billing error. Tony told her politely but firmly to please leave the papers on his desk, because he couldn't deal with the matter until Monday.

Knowing that the traffic was bound to be heavy, Tony decided to wait awhile before heading home. He snacked on an apple and worked the newspaper crossword puzzle, which not only gave him a chance to relax in quiet, but also quelled his end-of-the-day hunger. When he finally got into his car, the first thing he did was tune in to his favorite radio station, which was playing a soothing Bach cantata.

At the intersection before the entrance to the expressway, he was stalled by a broken traffic light, and the car ahead of him wasn't moving. Tony began to drum his fingertips on the wheel, but stopped and told himself, *"This will pass. It's no use getting excited about a minute more or less."* The expressway, once he finally reached it, was jammed, and his temper started to rise again. But instead of dwelling on how much longer it would take to get home, Tony turned his thoughts to the much more pleasant question of where to take his wife to dinner on her birthday.

When he arrived home, he told Elaine and Ricky that he was feeling crummy and wanted to go for a run before dinner. "Could you help me with my homework first?" Ricky asked hopefully. Tony felt his temper rising. Hadn't he just told the kid he wasn't feeling well? But he bit back his angry response, took a deep breath, and promised to help Ricky over the weekend. As expected, the run helped calm his nerves, so that Tony was able to get through dinner without fighting with Elaine. He spent the rest of the evening reading and watching TV with his family, and by Saturday morning he was feeling much better and able to help Ricky with his homework.

Because he had experienced these moods in the past, Tony knew that even simple requests could dangerously escalate his emotions. He had learned that by putting people off, as calmly as he could manage, he was able to save himself and others a lot of anger and aggravation. He had also learned that the best way for him to deal with such moods was to "pull a Greta Garbo"—to tell everyone involved that he wanted to be left alone. Physical exercise, whether running, swimming, or even a five-minute walk around the block, was also very helpful. When he could take some quiet time alone, his dark moods usually disappeared in a few hours or by the next day.

By making the choice to defuse his anger and anxiety, Tony did not end up feeling ashamed or bad about himself. Like Tony, as you struggle to stay sober a day at a time and protect your still-fragile self-esteem, you too can avoid behavior that threatens your recovery by taking positive steps to defuse your negative moods.

The Four Negative Moods Most Dangerous to Your Sobriety

Anxiety/Irritability

When you're feeling anxious, tense, irritable, or jumpy, it can help to remember that it's not the mood itself that's so dangerous, but rather what you may do to escalate the mood—for example, what you say to anyone unlucky enough to cross your path, or the drug or drink you then take to assuage your guilt and shame.

What usually works best to defuse anxiety and irritability is removing external stimuli and immersing yourself in whatever calms and comforts you. For Tony, this meant temporarily shutting himself off and getting involved in a physical activity. For you, it may mean a hot bath, a bowl of soup, or an hour spent reading, playing the piano, sewing, or chopping wood. The point is to change the way you respond when you're having such feelings, and to change your internal monologue so that the voice inside you comforts rather than chides.

Depression

When you're feeling down, so low that you have no energy and can't get moving, you can easily make the situation worse by settling in and getting cozy with your depression, as Harriet did. She especially hated rainy mornings, when she would want nothing more than to huddle under the covers. On one typical rainy day, she dragged herself out of bed and into the shower, all the while wondering whether the slight dryness in her throat meant she was coming down with a cold. As she was getting dressed, she impulsively decided to call in sick. Then she put on her pajamas and climbed back into bed.

But instead of falling back to sleep, she guiltily began to think about everything she could be doing now that she wasn't going in to her office. By mid-morning she was feeling so wretched that she crawled out of bed, moseyed into the kitchen, and tried to drown her sorrows in a plate of bacon and eggs, followed by a buttered sweet roll and two cups of coffee. But the high-fat, high-calorie brunch only made her feel worse. "Half the day gone, and I've eaten my total calorie allotment for the next two days," she berated herself. "And I haven't accomplished a thing today. I'm the world's worst loser. Why do I always feel depressed? Why didn't I plan this day better? Why don't I ever do anything worthwhile?"

Harriet had crawled right into the pity bag, as it's known in the self-help groups. The pity bag is an infinitely expandable object, and there are many ways to make it bigger. In fact, you can get it to grow so big that it threatens to swallow you up. Here are some of the ways my patients have inflated their pity bags: playing sad records, cataloging past failures, and making a list of all the ways they were less privileged, less successful, and/or less attractive than their friends and associates.

Once inside the pity bag, you can easily turn a mild case of the blahs into a deep pall of gloom and despair. You become totally convinced that no creature on earth is less fortunate than you. You're absolutely worthless—so worthless there's no point in staying sober. So you take a drink or a pill or a hit of cocaine.

Obviously, crawling into the pity bag can be very dangerous. So how do you get out? Better yet, how do you prevent yourself from creeping in there in the first place? To begin with, you can remind yourself that this isn't the first time you've felt depressed, nor will it be the last. Then take a minute or two to reflect on how long your depressions usually last. They may go on for a few hours, maybe a couple of days or even a week.

When you wake up feeling grim and cheerless, you're better off getting out of the house than staying in bed. Even if you have to force yourself to do so, getting up, dressing, and eating a nutritious breakfast will probably begin to dispel your mood. And once you get going, the activities, interactions, and amusements of the day will often serve to distract you. Yes, the mood will still be upon you, but you won't be feeding it and thereby making yourself feel even worse.

Perhaps you remember Jane Craig, the conscientious, ambitious news producer played by Holly Hunter in the film *Broadcast News*, who starts every day feeling miserable and blue, crying at her desk in the quiet, empty newsroom. But the minute her phone begins to ring and her colleagues arrive at the office, as soon as the pressures and pleasures of the workday take over, Jane's tears dry up—like magic.

Jane claims that she's "depressed all the time," but she forgets about it when she throws herself into the job she loves. When you see this happen again and again throughout the movie, you start rooting for Jane to realize that she's not "depressed all the time." And neither are you, despite the fact that when you're blue, you can't seem to remember all the times when you were happy or excited or even just feeling neutral.

Several studies have shown that depression is alleviated by activity. When you do nothing, as you're inclined to do when you're depressed, you end up feeling worse. Unlike anxiety and irritability, which are usually worsened by exposure to external stimuli, depression frequently dissipates when the environment is stimulating. Instead of sitting alone and isolated, thinking about how lonely and miserable you are— get involved! Exercise can also help lift your spirits and may even shorten your periods of depression. Whatever takes you outside yourself and gets you involved, whether it's a physical or mental activity, or a group situation, will improve your spirits.

Very occasionally, despite your best efforts, depression does not abate. Please consult pages 103–106 for advice on getting help if you need it.

Anger

People in early sobriety are particularly sensitive to criticism, to any failure or perceived failure, or any kind of slight. Faced with such circumstances, they may either explode in a furious outburst or bottle up their rage and say nothing. Both of these responses are frequently cited by my patients as relapse triggers.

Even under normal circumstances, anger is an emotion that requires a lot of modulation. Many people react angrily when criticized or slighted, but they've learned to temper their responses with such thoughts as *He's right, I really did make that mistake*, or *Boy! Larry sure got out of the wrong side of bed this morning! Too bad he had to take it out on me*. First, they use this sort of inner monologue to keep themselves from flying off the handle; then they promise to correct the error, or they avoid Larry for the rest of the day. But in early recovery you're not likely to think so clearly when you're in an angry mood. And even if such responses do occur to you, they probably won't dampen the intensity of your reaction.

An angry mood can also be fueled or defused. If you're given to heated outbursts as a way to express your anger, fueling it may lead you to say or do things of which you'll later feel ashamed. If you tend to repress your rage, then fueling your pent-up feelings may cause you to feel bitter and full of self-pity. But if you defuse your angry mood, you can avoid falling into either of these traps.

Quite probably you've gone through periods when you've been tense and simmering for hours or even days, when you're ready to explode at the slightest provocation. Consider these typical scenes: You feel your fist clenching when someone pushes ahead of you on the coffee line, and you're ready to haul off and slug him. A colleague preoccupied with her work fails to say good morning as you pass her desk. You take offense and snidely remark, "Too busy to say hello?" You may find yourself imagining any number of situations in which you become justifiably angry. It's almost as if you're just waiting for the opportunity to let someone have it.

One of my patients imagined himself making loud, self-righteous speeches to his frequently broke brother-in-law, who had just asked him for yet another loan. In his fantasies, he was delivering these speeches before an audience of applauding family members. Another patient dreamed of telling off an officious, nit-picking supervisor after she had caught a mistake that he had made. Such imagined scenes are good tip-offs that you're in an angry mood.

Recognizing your angry mood is the first step in defusing it. Many people don't realize when rage is driving their behavior. They believe their anger is justified and appropriate, that external events are motivating their mood. But you cannot recognize an angry mood for what it is if you're involved in rationalizing your behavior. All of us have indulged in telling ourselves, *It's no wonder I got mad—he snubbed me. She criticized me. They made me do it wrong.* But as a recovering person, you can't afford the luxury of ignoring or making excuses for your anger. You have to watch for and acknowledge that undercurrent of anger, so that it doesn't lead you into potentially harmful situations.

Let's consider the difference between unassigned rage and the anger you feel in response to a specific, annoying event when you're otherwise in a neutral mood. For example, feeling neither particularly good nor bad, you arrive at the mall to do some shopping. A man rushes past and pushes you out of his way so that you drop your packages. "Idiot!" you mutter. For a moment you're angry, and justifiably so. It's normal to feel riled when someone is rude and inconsiderate. You're not expected to smile and ignore such an incident. But it wouldn't be normal for you to run after the person who shoved you, to punch him in the arm, or scream and yell and get yourself into an agitated state.

When you're feeling calm and at peace, your reaction is likely to be appropriate. But if you're in an angry mood, a minor incident can be enough to make you fly off the handle in a major way. The key is to recognize your angry mood and take steps to defuse it. But how can you do that?

First of all, don't allow yourself to stay angry. A patient of mine, Joe, described how he got into an ugly encounter one Saturday morning when he was full of unaccountable rage. When Joe went outside to tidy up the lawn, his elderly neighbor Russell leaned across the hedge that separated their properties and began complaining because Joe's maple tree was shedding leaves all over his yard. "I want you to cut down that darn tree," grumbled Russell. "I've told you that every fall since you moved into your house."

Joe's temper was already near the boiling point, and Russell's annoying comment was the last straw. "Listen, you stupid old man!" he exploded. "Don't you ever talk to me about that tree again! I'm never cutting it down, and that's final!"

With that, knowing full well that Russell hated the noise of the hedge clippers, Joe stormed into the garage to find the extension cord so he could run them. All the while he couldn't stop thinking about what he could have said . . . should have said. *That silly old fool should mind his own business. A little leaf-raking sure wouldn't do him or his spare tire any harm*, Joe told himself. *What's he got to do all day anyway?*

Remembering the incident, Joe commented that by the time he got around to trimming the bushes, he was shaking with such built-up rage that it was a miracle he hadn't cut off one of his fingers.

I explained to Joe that the next time he found himself in a similar situation he should short-circuit such thoughts and think about something else instead. This is good advice for you as well. Instead of dwelling on what you perceive as the injury that's been done to you, walk away from it. If you don't leave the incident and your anger behind, you'll only succeed in fueling your anger—and harming yourself.

You can also defuse your anger by *not* talking about it with other people. Don't force your spouse or lover to listen to a fifteen-minute tirade about what a jerk your boss is, or how your sister has ruined another weekend by making family plans without first consulting you. Not only does reciting your grievances fuel your fury but it also provides you with an audience whose remarks will only add to your ire.

You should also remove yourself from situations that are likely to provoke you. Become aware and make a list of the kinds of circumstances that set you off—then stay away from them. The time may come when many of these situations no longer upset you, but for now, while your emotions are volatile, avoid as much aggravation as you can.

Distract yourself. Diversion is one of the best ways I know to defuse an angry mood. You'd be amazed at how quickly an angry state of mind, like depression, subsides when you get absorbed in an attention-consuming activity. Physical exercise is especially good because it induces a more tranquil mood. So instead of running the hedge clippers in order to further inflame Russell and yourself, get your bike out of the garage and take a long ride. By the time you get home, you're sure to be feeling better.

Lately we've heard a lot about how "it's okay to be angry," about giving oneself permission to be angry because repressing anger can be bad for one's physical and mental health. Indeed, there's nothing wrong with anger itself, or with acknowledging that a specific situation or certain people make you angry. (In fact, as I said earlier, I recommend that you know what your triggers are.) But you must also realize that taking action while you're angry can lead to risky, foolhardy behavior. When your brain is flooded with intense emotion, you can't make coherent, logical, well-judged responses. Wait until you can contemplate the situation calmly. It's okay to *be* angry; it's not okay to *act* when you're angry.

It's equally harmful not to act at all when you've been wronged. If someone makes an unkind remark to you, claims credit for work you've done, steals your girlfriend, tells a lie about you, acts dishonestly or behaves badly to you—your anger is appropriate. And if you don't express that anger, you'll begin to feel bad about your inability to react.

Unexpressed legitimate anger can lead to low self-esteem and depression. Allowing yourself to be trampled on without responding properly is just as bad as losing your temper in an incoherent blaze of emotion. As difficult as it may be, you owe it to yourself to tell the other person how you feel about what he or she has done, and what you intend to do in response to those actions.

Let's say, for instance, that you've just received a memo written by you that's being circulated under your supervisor's signature. You're livid—and rightly so. *Of all the nasty, underhanded tricks*, you think. You're so angry that you want to stomp down the hall to Virginia's office and tell her what a creep she is. Instead, you stop for a moment to consider whether an angry scene will do any good. You take a few deep breaths, count to ten (or twenty or thirty, if need be), and go back to work. When you go home, you have a good dinner and spend a relaxing hour listening to music. Then you sit down and make a plan of action, thinking through and writing down exactly what you want to say to Virginia in the morning.

The next day you're nervous, but you've carefully rehearsed your speech. You walk into Virginia's office and say, "Virginia, it makes me very angry that you circulated my memo under your name. If you ever do that again, I'll have to talk to the department manager. I keep copies of all my work, so I can easily prove what's mine. I want an apology, and I want you to inform everyone in the department that I actually wrote that memo."

If Virginia doesn't agree to your demands, you may decide to take your case to your manager. You still may not get full credit for your work, but you'll have taken steps to right the wrong done to you. You will have acted calmly, rather than in the heat of the moment. You will not have allowed your anger to draw you into a name-calling match that could have cost you your job. Nor did you spend the evening stewing over the incident and wind up taking a drug or drink. Dealing with your anger can be very difficult, especially when you're in the grips of a negative mood. But if you work to recognize and defuse it, your rage won't get the better of you.

Boredom

When people are out of touch with what they're feeling, when they're depressed, when they want some excitement, or when they want to drink or use, they often say they're bored. They may use the word when what they really mean is they're lonely or afraid. When my patients tell me they're bored, I begin to listen very carefully because boredom is a code word—a signal to me that something else is going on. Usually, that something else is dangerous.

One hot, sunny Saturday afternoon in July, Cal, two months sober, was feeling bored. He hadn't gone to the ball game because his buddies all drank a lot of beer at the stadium. He couldn't visit his sister because he had smashed his car while driving drunk. He wasn't with his girlfriend because she'd walked out on him after he had slugged her during another time he had been tanked.

He flung himself around the apartment, finally settled down and watched half an inning of the game on TV, then ran the radio dial from one end to the other. He kept looking at the phone, willing it to ring. When it stayed silent, he picked it up and idly dialed a few numbers. No one was home. "Who would be inside on a day like this?" he muttered to himself. "Only a dork like me. Twenty-four years old. No ball games, no wheels, no booze, no girlfriend, no nothing."

He couldn't take another moment alone in the empty apartment, so he went out, with no particular purpose in mind. When he left his building, he turned right, thinking, *What the hell? Right's as good as left.* Two blocks later he found himself in front of the Dew Drop Inn, one of his favorite old hangouts. He peered through the window; the bar looked cool and dark and inviting. The ball game was playing on the TV set over the bar. *Might as well go in and say hello*, he figured. *Watch a little of the game with some company.*

Needless to say, Cal's story didn't end happily that day.

That's not to say that we don't all have moments of sheer, utter tedium. I still remember how, as a child growing up in England, I had to listen to the king's speech every year after Christmas lunch. There were a million things I would rather have been doing—playing with my toys, eating my Christmas sweets. But instead I had to sit quietly and listen to the boring old king. All of us have such moments in our daily lives, when we have no choice but to submit to boring situations: We have to sit through the union president's crashingly dull annual speech. We have to listen to our daughter practicing her scales on the piano. We have to grin and bear it as our spouse or lover launches into a story we've already heard countless times.

But except for such unavoidable instances, as a recovering person you can't afford to let yourself be bored. When you begin to think, *I'm bored*, when you find yourself craving thrills and drama, you need to stop and consider what your boredom is really all about. Do you want to use again? Are you missing the excitement and turmoil? Are you longing for the highs, the lows, the intrigue, the accusations, the preoccupations that made your days feel so full? Perhaps you're lonely because your telephone hasn't been ringing lately. Have you suddenly realized that all your friends are users or drinkers, and you're pretty much on your own? Or is the problem that you don't know what to do to fill your time because for years your only leisure activity was getting high?

A few minutes of soul-searching will help you identify the real feeling masked by your boredom. Other times you might not be able to get to the heart of what's actually troubling you. In either case, the remedy is the same. *Do something.* Do anything . . . except take a drink or a drug. But don't just sit there and be bored. If you're lonely, plan to get out, meet people, and make new friends. Your self-help group is always a good place to start. Or join a group that sponsors activities you enjoy—a choral group or a cycling club, for example. If you're restless and edgy, get some exercise. A bicycle ride, a game of tennis, a brisk walk, or a run can do wonders.

If you're feeling bored because your life seems to lack excitement, do something a little bit crazy—take your kids to the amusement park and ride the roller coaster, rent a hot air balloon and have a picnic in the sky, play hooky from work and go to the movies in the middle of the afternoon. If you're at a loss as to how to fill your free time, sign up to go hiking, or learn Chinese cooking, car repair, ice skating, or a foreign language. In many cities you can find enjoyable, inexpensive classes especially geared for adults who want to meet people. If you can't think of a subject that interests you, open the school catalog, close your eyes, and point to a spot on the page. Or go to a library that uses the Dewey Decimal System to classify its books, pick a three-digit number between 000 and 999, and see what books are on the shelf at that number. Let's say you chose 812, which happens to be the Dewey designation for drama. Read a play, go to the theater, or audition for a local amateur dramatics group.

When Arnie was smoking pot, he spent most of his free time zonked out in front of the tube. After he got straight, watching TV bored him, but he couldn't think what else he wanted to do on the evenings he wasn't at a self-help meeting. Nothing excited him. Then one day, waiting in line to get some cash from the bank machine, he noticed a flyer advertising carpentry lessons. He had always liked doing things with his hands; maybe this would be fun. He called the number as soon as he got home, and a friendly-sounding woman answered the phone, which intrigued him all the more. The woman told Arnie he could come around to the workshop anytime. Arnie took her at her word and went right back out.

The shop was filled with the fresh scent of sawdust and glue. Arnie watched the owners, Sara and Christy, demonstrate how to make tongue-and-groove joints, and immediately fell in love with the place. He signed up for lessons with Sara, starting the next day, and the workshop quickly became like a second home to him. He also turned out to be a very good carpenter, so good that his friends began asking him to do work for them. Arnie eventually worked out a deal with Sara and Christy to use some of their space for his own projects, in return for helping them around the shop.

Going to meetings, joining a group, or taking a course may sound like a lot of bother. But consider this: When you're bored and do nothing to alleviate that feeling, if you sit home alone with nothing to occupy your time, you may as well be issuing an engraved invitation for trouble. And sooner or later, trouble will show up, and you'll find yourself using again.

Getting Help If You Need It

In the first year of recovery, a very small percentage of people (less than three percent in the Smithers outpatient department) suffer prolonged and immobilizing depressions or anxieties. These individuals may require one-on-one psychotherapy, and perhaps even medication to relieve these severe symptoms. If you've had persistent depression for eight to twelve weeks that's preventing you from sleeping or eating and interfering with your work, family, and social relationships, then you should arrange for a consultation with a psychiatrist who's knowledgeable about alcohol and drug abuse. The American Society of Addiction Medicine, listed in Appendix C, can help you locate such a psychiatrist.

To help stabilize your mood you must first learn to recognize your emotions as they occur and then turn away from behaviors that fuel your negative moods and embrace those that defuse them. At first, the actions you take to accomplish these goals may make you feel uncomfortable, awkward, and embarrassed, as if you're trying to learn how to walk on your hands when you already have a perfectly good pair of feet. But if your feet are moving you in the direction of the liquor store or the cocaine dealer, then you must learn another way of walking.

After the day she'd had at work, Libby knew she should have gone to an AA meeting. She was feeling angry and extremely irritable thanks to all the screaming that had gone on at the office over unmet deadlines and unhappy clients. Her secretary had broken down under the strain, so on top of everything else, Libby had had to spend twenty minutes with her in the ladies' room, trying to get her to calm down and stop crying. Now she was home, lounging in her favorite armchair, watching a M*A*S*H rerun. All she needed was to phone down to the liquor store and have them send up a bottle of gin, and she would be right back to her old routine.

That thought alone was enough to get Libby out of her chair, away from the phone, and headed for the front door. "One step at a time," she said as she threw on her coat. "One foot in front of the other." As she closed the apartment door behind her, she felt her spirits lifting. Her step was almost sprightly as she made her way to the church basement where her AA group met.

The steps you take to protect your sobriety gradually come to feel more natural. You become less conscious of forcing yourself to make mood-defusing choices. By the end of your first year of recovery, you do this automatically—a sign that you've begun the process of integration. You start to see yourself as a nondrinker or a nonuser. You no longer behave as if you're an abstainer. Another aspect of the integration process is that you're able to link the "old you" with the "new you." You begin to look back on your drinking or drugging, not with horror as a part of yourself to be violently rejected and denied, but with detachment, as a manifestation of yourself that you've now outgrown.

In your second year of sobriety you may enter a period of deeper reflection and introspection. You may look at your moods and feelings, your behavior, reactions, and attitudes with an eye toward greater understanding and continuing growth and change. When your mood has stabilized, you can also begin to assess and set new goals for yourself. This process is known as "taking an inventory," and is one that will continue throughout your life.

As you approach your third anniversary in sobriety and your sense of yourself becomes more secure, as you learn effective ways of handling the mood swings and minor crises that are a part of your life, you begin to achieve a balance in your life, a "serenity," as it's called in the twelve-step self-help groups. This doesn't mean that you'll never again be unhappy or anxious or blue. But you have developed a solid framework for living, a stable, well-constructed base from which you can continue to develop.

From within that framework you have the means—and the desire—to "give it back," that is, to give to others, perhaps those who are just starting their journey into sobriety. You may decide to become a sponsor or do other Twelfth Step work. Now you can do this without fear of endangering your own sobriety: You may enrich it in the bargain.

All of this takes time, and you can't rush the process of change, which is both gradual and sequential. Introspection can be very fruitful when your moods have become more stable, when your cravings have abated, and your old habits have changed. But when your emotions are still volatile, your thinking disordered, and your judgment impaired, self-reflection is useless and possibly even dangerous.

"Utilize, don't analyze," is another of those on-target self-help sayings. Understanding and insight are wonderful, and self-exploration can be most enriching when you're able to take advantage of it. But insight itself doesn't change behavior.

I've treated many people in early recovery who came up with a variety of explanations for their negative moods, ranging from parental neglect when they were children to being rejected by a lover. One patient even attributed his deep unhappiness to the fact that ten years earlier he'd failed to make the college varsity football team! All of them were convinced of the truth of their conclusions at the time they arrived at them, only to revise their opinions at some later point in recovery because they'd turned out to be "soluble in sobriety."

In your first year of sobriety, you should focus on taking action to relieve your negative moods and leave the analysis for later on in recovery when your insight is greater and truer.

And remember—you'll make mistakes. Sometimes you'll snap at people, talk out of turn, act in the heat of anger, or nurse a blue mood. Your behavior can't—and won't—change overnight. But if you keep at it, if you learn from your mistakes rather than being discouraged by them, you'll soon see the fruits of your efforts. And you'll be well on your way to calm and comfortable emotions that can support a lifelong, life-enhancing sobriety.

Beyond your first year in sobriety, you can keep using the principles you learned in this chapter. You will continue to have negative moods that need to be defused to protect your sobriety. And you will want to extend and refine your strategies for enhancing your positive moods. Also, as you grow and change in sobriety, your emotional capacity does likewise. Continuing to observe your emotions and their antecedents expands your self-knowledge, helps you enjoy this new emotional depth, and reduces your potential for relapse.

One major cause of negative moods throughout sobriety is stress. The following chapter will discuss ways of avoiding, minimizing, and coping well with stress, and I hope will further stabilize your emotions and help you sustain the healthy, stable life you deserve.

Chapter Six
Keeping the Pressure Off

How to Cope with Stress

According to Hans Selye, the physician and researcher who first popularized the concept, stress is "the nonspecific response of the body to any demands made upon it." What Selye means is that when you find yourself in demanding circumstances, your body undergoes a number of physiological changes. Any difficult situation that you encounter is called a *stressor*, and your body's response is the *stress*.

In everyday conversation, we use the word "stress" to describe not only the physiological symptoms but also the sources of our stress, and the feelings of tension and pressure related to it. However, in this chapter we will be discussing stress as it is defined above.

Whenever you respond to a stressor, which can be anything from hitting a pothole you didn't see to being yelled at by your boss, you undergo an increase in heart rate, respiration rate, blood pressure, and alertness, as well as a rise in adrenaline and corticosteroids, both hormones produced by the adrenal glands. In addition to these changes, we each have our own characteristic personal responses. For example, a friend might jiggle her leg or have sweaty palms, whereas you may grind your teeth or tense certain muscles. You might also develop negative thought patterns, which are often repetitive and/or obsessional.

In extreme cases, you realize that your heart is beating faster or that you have become more alert. You *know* you're experiencing stress. In other, more commonplace circumstances, or when your body has adapted to an ongoing stressor, you may not be aware of your physical responses. But you can train yourself to notice the signs. By becoming conscious of your distinctive stress responses, you can become more sensitive to those conditions that cause you stress. This awareness can enable you to avoid some situations and to cope better with those stresses you cannot avoid.

I've often heard people sum up someone else's addiction with the comment, "No wonder she became an alcoholic. She was always under so much pressure." The speakers were well-meaning and concerned, but not well-informed. I know of no evidence which indicates that an addiction can be caused by stress, in and of itself. However, we do know that *stress can bring on a relapse*. Thus, for the sake of your recovery, as well as for your physical and mental health, it's doubly important that you learn to recognize and minimize stress.

And not only in early sobriety. Seth, a surgeon, had been sober for eighteen years when, at the age of fifty-nine, he learned that all surgeons practicing in the affiliate group to which his hospital belonged must be recertified by the age of sixty. The fact that he was director of surgery and former president of the medical board at his hospital did not exempt him from either the written or the oral recertification exams. Preparing for the exams meant spending his nights and weekends studying. It also meant the possibility of failure, a humiliation which overshadowed even the fear of losing his job and income.

On the one hand Seth acknowledged that some surgeons, to the detriment of their patients, did not keep up with the rapid development of medical information. On the other hand he knew that the exams did not test surgical skill or the experience and understanding that developed over a lifetime of practice. Secretly, he was filled with overwhelming fury and felt personally insulted by the hospital licensing board edict. His vast skills and knowledge, so painstakingly acquired, were being demeaned by a multiple choice questionnaire suitable for young surgeons just out of training. He raged, and he sulked, but he studied. He spoke to no one about how he felt, not even his wife, who unwittingly added to his stress by complaining that she never saw him anymore. The night the exams were over he went out and got stupefyingly drunk. Three months later, in a rehabilitation center, he learned that he had passed.

It is painfully evident from Seth's story that stress can threaten even a long-established sobriety. Learning and using this chapter's techniques for minimizing and managing stress will serve you throughout your sober life.

Chronic Stress

This type of stress is usually the result of a series of unpleasant events that continue over time, and to which the person must adapt him-

or herself. Chronic stress may be a factor in many physical and psychological ailments, such as ulcers, headaches, muscle tension, diarrhea, anxiety, and depression, to name just a few.

It can be produced by a variety of sources, some of them unavoidable. Perhaps the most extreme example of unavoidable chronic stress was that endured by the inmates of German concentration camps during World War II. Other more commonplace circumstances are the long-term illness or slow death of a loved one.

But much chronic stress is attributable to external causes, which can be avoided, and to internal causes, which can be altered. Internal causes include frustration, insecurity, boredom, overcommitment, an excessive need for control, and perfectionism. People who have such feelings or character traits find themselves in an almost constant state of stress.

When exposed to a severe, ongoing stressor, the body's first reaction is to try to adapt by gradually dampening its physiological responses. Although this initially enables you to cope better, you ultimately pay a price. If the adaptation fails, you begin to feel exhausted and burntout, and may even suffer a nervous breakdown in an extreme case. Or you may somehow continue to manage, but at the expense of your psychological or physical well-being.

Acute Stress

This second type of stress is precipitated by an unexpected, and, sometimes, a dangerous event. Being reunited with someone whom you thought was dead, for example, can be as great a shock and produce as intense a physiological reaction as witnessing a fatal accident. Simply *hearing* about an especially traumatic event can also cause acute stress.

A car accident, however minor, usually provokes an acute stress reaction. Even a near miss can cause a shock wave of adrenaline coursing through your body. Your scalp tingles. An electric jolt runs down your arms and legs. You are intensely, unpleasantly alert.

Abe, a recovering cocaine addict, described his reaction as something like using cocaine, but without the euphoria. On the expressway one morning he was rear-ended by a truck when he slowed down for a pothole. Although he was bruised and shaken up, he was not seriously hurt. But his car was totaled. Abe thought he was handling the incident pretty well until the truck driver, after swearing a blue streak at Abe, took off without exchanging registration or insurance information. "That's when I lost it," Abe told me. "I started screaming like a maniac and running down the expressway after him."

The physical response to acute stress prepares the body for fight or flight. A gazelle that suddenly comes face-to-face with a lion on the African veld will respond with a rapid increase of adrenaline in its blood. This in turn will raise its heart rate, constrict the arteries going to its skin and intestines, and divert blood to its muscles. The gazelle is thus prepared to run like the blazes from its natural enemy. The lion, unexpectedly encountering the gazelle, experiences the same set of physiological reactions. But instead of being primed to flee, the lion is being prepared to pounce on its prey. Although the eventual outcome of their confrontation is likely to be quite different for each of them, the response of their bodies is remarkably similar.

Human beings faced with an unexpected stressor experience the same rise in adrenaline and change in blood distribution. In addition, more blood is sent to the brain, which prepares people to deal with the situation with their intellect as well as their bodies.

In some instances, the acute stress response can prove very useful. Before you give any kind of performance, whether it's playing the organ in church, taking an oral exam, or delivering a report to a committee, you undoubtedly experience some degree of acute stress reaction. Your pulse rate quickens, your mouth gets dry, your muscles tense, and you become extremely alert. Your increased mental awareness enables you to put forth your best effort.

But all of us sometimes produce acute stress responses that are unnecessary. I call this the *paper tiger* response. Say you arrive home after dark and park your car in the driveway. As you walk towards the house, you hear a rustling noise in the rhododendrons. You see a shadow moving. Your heart begins to pound, your mouth feels like cotton, and you're poised to leap for safety. And then . . . the neighbor's cat bolts out from behind the shrubbery. Your stress response immediately begins to subside, and you walk calmly, if sheepishly, to your front door.

A second glance would have told you that whatever was hiding in the bushes was too small to be a real threat. But you didn't look twice. You reacted instinctively. All too often when we're faced with paper tigers in ordinary life, we neglect to check more carefully. Instead, with no benefit to ourselves, we suffer through the whole stress reaction. Later in this chapter, I'll talk about how to identify those situations in which you don't have to fight or flee, but can instead turn around and coolly walk away.

One lesson that can be learned from the lion and the gazelle is that the same event can have different meanings, depending on your point of view. It's the same with many stressors. A source of stress for one person may be exciting or challenging to the next. For example, one of the most "stressed-out" people I know is a writer named Steven, who lives on a sailboat in the Mediterranean, taking care of it for its owners. This arrangement gives him the freedom to pursue his writing, which is very important to him. Unfortunately, Steven has an overpowering need to be sure everything is always perfectly under control. Every morning he makes long lists of everything he plans to accomplish that day. A typical list would include a reminder to check fifty feet of anchor chain, grease the stern gland in the exhaust system, repair the storm sail, make plastic casings for the mooring lines, and clear out the starboard locker.

What Steven consistently ignores is the fact that no human being alive could accomplish all these chores in a single day. And so, Steven is never to be found lounging on the deck in the evening, enjoying a glorious sunset. He's too busy worrying and castigating himself for not having completed his allotted tasks. Interestingly, Steven experiences no stress at all when he sits down to write, an activity that's highly stressful for many people. But because of his psychological makeup, he ends up being tormented by a potentially idyllic lifestyle that many would envy.

Some people can manage to make the most pleasurable situations stressful. Spend a couple of hours at your local tennis courts, and you'll probably notice that most of the players are enjoying themselves. But there are likely to be two or three at all levels of play, from the most incompetent on up, who work themselves into a fury. They throw their rackets down and swear every time they miss a shot, fault a service, or generally fail to achieve the perfection to which they aspire. For such people, an hour of tennis becomes a source of great tension, rather than a way to relax and get some exercise.

Why You Must Reduce Stress in Your Life— And How to Do It

In your first year of recovery, you'll respond unpredictably, and usually poorly, to the stressors in your life. This is partly a physical phenomenon, the cause of which has not yet been discovered. But researchers have found that during this period your general stress response (which we discussed earlier) is unstable. There's no telling how you may react when you encounter unforeseen circumstances.

By the time you reach your second year of recovery, your physical ability to withstand stress improves. However, you still may not have learned to respond appropriately to stressful situations. When you were drinking or using, you coped with stress by turning to the bottle or a pill. Even after a year or more of sobriety the chances are good that you have not yet developed reliable alternative strategies for coping with stress. Yet stress reduction remains a key factor in preventing relapses.

The following is an example of how acute stress can affect those in early recovery. Eric, for instance, prides himself on his no-nonsense approach to life. "No excuses, no whining," he always says. "I always look at it straight, and tell it straight—at least as straight as a devious-minded alcoholic can." After a rocky first two weeks of sobriety, Eric, a sixty-year-old building contractor, was adjusting well to recovery. He told me that he felt "not wonderful, but a helluva lot calmer than I ever did when I was boozing."

He was feeling good enough to spend a long weekend in the country with his daughter's family. Bonnie and her husband rarely got to go out by themselves, so Eric volunteered to take Bobby, his five-year-old grandson, into town for pizza and ice cream while the couple went to dinner. On the drive home Bobby was chattering away excitedly when he suddenly screamed, "Stop, Granddad, stop!"

Eric caught the eerie reflection of a pair of eyes in the glare of his headlights and slammed on the brakes. But he was too late. He heard a soft thud before he could bring the car to a complete stop. "You hit it!" Bobby wailed.

Eric parked on the side of the road, and he and Bobby went to investigate. Their flashlight shone on a raccoon, lying quietly in the rough gravel. Bobby reached out to touch the animal, but Eric grabbed his hand. "If it's alive, it could bite you. Animals do that when they're hurt," he explained. He peered closer, realized the raccoon was dead, and gently told his grandson so.

"He's not dead," Bobby insisted. "I'm going to take him home and feed him. He'll like that."

It took Eric quite a lot of persuading before his grandson would believe him. Trying to be as kind and patient as possible, he helped Bobby fashion a makeshift grave and together they said a short prayer over the animal. But when they got back in the car, Bobby was inconsolable.

"You killed him, you killed him," he cried over and over again.

Eric was so shaken he could hardly drive the short distance to his daughter's house, and he didn't get a wink of sleep that night. Bobby's accusations kept ringing in his ears. The next day, the boy seemed to have forgotten the incident, but Eric couldn't. Pleading an emergency at one of his construction sites, he cut his visit short and left.

"I couldn't tell my daughter I was upset about a damned raccoon. Animals get run over all the time out there. She would have thought I was some kind of nut case," he told his group a few days later. But he was still upset by the episode, and continued to be haunted by it for several weeks.

Because Eric was in early recovery, this exposure to acute stress became a period of chronic stress for him. If Eric had known more about stress and his response to it, he might have gotten over it much more quickly. Of course, I don't mean to imply that you can anticipate or prevent such random events. But you can modify your response to *all* stressors so that if you do encounter one that's unexpected, you won't develop the kind of long-lasting problem that Eric did. You can also identify the stressors in your day-to-day existence. In the long run, these will cause you far more trouble than a few isolated, chance incidents.

The first step is to learn to recognize your characteristic stress responses. Try to pinpoint your earliest reaction to any stressor. (It may help to jot down your observations.) Does your eyelid twitch? Do you tense your neck muscles? Do you bite the inside of your lip? Do you drum your fingers on the nearest surface?

Once you recognize your telltale signs, you can match them with specific occurrences. Does your eyelid twitch when your boss asks you to step into her office? Do you tense your neck muscles when the kids are driving you crazy with their noise? Do you bite your lip when you're stuck in rush-hour traffic? Do you drum your fingers when your spouse criticizes you? Now that you've established the link between cause and effect, you can begin to plan a stress reduction program.

Here are three ways to reduce stress effectively:

• You can actively avoid the source. (Of course, this isn't always possible.)

• You can identify stressors of your own making—what I referred to earlier as paper tigers—and reframe them, that is, see them for what they really are.

• You can alter the way your body reacts to stressors.

How to Avoid Stress

"Easy does it."

This famous self-help slogan succinctly sums up how you can shield yourself from tension and pressure: Make things as easy as possible for yourself. Turn your back and walk away from stressors whenever possible. You can't do this for the rest of your life, but during your first year in recovery the following are things you must do.

Postpone Major Life Changes

In Chapter 4 I talked about this in reference to your overall recovery plan. But I'd like to remind you—by telling you about several of my patients—that major life changes can be a major source of stress.

Doris, a fifty-three-year-old recovering alcoholic, had scheduled a face-lift, then changed her mind a week before the operation was set to take place. "I don't know the old me yet," she admitted. "And I'm sure not ready to adjust to a new me. Besides, suppose something went wrong—what a great excuse to get drunk! And now that I know about the dangers of pain medication, I don't want to put myself at risk for an optional procedure."

Jonathan, a chemical engineer, turned down a transfer to London after much soul-searching. "I've wanted to live there all my life—and visit the pubs, of course," he added. "I know that eventually I can make the right connections to be comfortable and sober there. But right now I need my sponsor, and my wife and I are getting a lot out of family therapy."

Lloyd's parents wanted him to go to college in the fall, now that he's made a commitment to stay off crack, but Lloyd has decided to wait a year. "They were really ticked off about that," he told his group. "They'd tried so hard to get help for me. Hell, they practically broke down the door of my apartment to get me into treatment. So now I sort of feel I should go, just to please them. But I also know that the pressure of getting good grades and making new friends without getting into drugs again would be too much."

Irene, the recovering alcoholic who couldn't get pregnant, didn't rush out and register with adoption agencies as soon as she stopped drinking. Not until she had been sober for eighteen months did she and her husband feel ready to begin adoption proceedings.

Of course, sometimes you can't put off making an important decision that will radically alter your life circumstances. Mitch, for example, *had* to leave his marriage because his alcoholic wife was regularly beating him up. "It was okay when I was on drugs. I thought I deserved it then," he said. But now that he was clean, the situation was intolerable. After thoroughly discussing the move with his counselor and his brother, he left.

Brenda, whose stage name was Fanny LeFevre, quit her job as a nightclub dancer. "There was no way I could stay sober in that joint," she realized. Because she'd never done any other kind of work, quitting wasn't an easy decision. But with the help of her sponsor, she applied for and was accepted into a training program to become an electrician.

Both Mitch and Brenda recognized that their sobriety would be threatened if they didn't improve their circumstances. But by seeking the support and heeding the input of counselors, sponsors, and family members they were able to make their difficult transitions. Through careful planning, they were eventually able to decrease their stress.

Organize Your Time Carefully and Sensibly

If you try to do too much, you may wind up feeling like Steven —frustrated, worried, self-critical, and pressured. A well-organized daily plan should enable you to accomplish what you have to and still allow for "downtime," when you can recharge yourself by reading, knitting, watching television, or whatever it is you enjoy. As I mentioned in Chapter 4, your schedule should also allow you plenty of time to get from one place to the next. That way, if you do get stuck in traffic, you can sit back and listen to the car radio, instead of feeling your adrenaline soar as you worry about being late.

Give yourself a few minutes to catch your breath between commitments. Window-shop or read for a while after lunch. If distance permits, take a leisurely walk from the office to your self-help meeting instead of driving or riding the bus. Rather than rushing home to prepare dinner, visit the park with your daughter after you pick her up from the day-care center.

Keeping your schedule manageable will go a long way toward reducing stress. If you're always running around, trying to keep up, you'll only succeed in increasing the pressure you put on yourself while your recovery is still fragile.

Start to Rebuild Your Self-Esteem

One of the best ways to do this is to work the Fourth Step of the anonymous self-help programs, and make a "searching and fearless moral inventory" of yourself. Surprisingly enough, taking such an inventory doesn't increase stress, as you might think. On the contrary, it can actually help you feel calmer and more in charge.

Now that you're sober, you'll still continue to be troubled by the shame and mortification of much of what you did as an active addict. The sense of worthlessness that accompanies these feelings is a stressor for a great many recovering people. So is your attempt to bury your emotions. But if you're to revive your self-respect and sense of worth, you must face up to them no matter how painful that may be.

I suggest that you draw up two lists. One should include all the things you've done that make you feel bad about yourself. The other should note all your positive qualities, as well as everything you feel good about having achieved. These lists are an important first step in alleviating the humiliation and remorse with which you've been burdening yourself. Seeing it all before you, written down in black and white, will help you begin to establish a sense of proportion in your life—a sense that is crucial to your self-esteem.

Easy Does It—But Do It

Identify whatever it is that's been keeping you up nights. Even if you've been avoiding these distressing issues (and wish you could continue to avoid them), you're much better off exposing them to the light of day and figuring out how to deal with them.

I know many newly abstinent people who haven't filed tax returns for several years, who owe thousands of dollars on their credit cards, who haven't paid their bills, who have borrowed heavily from family or friends. One patient in a precarious financial situation told me he had put off coming home at night because the mere thought of seeing his mail on the doormat made him so intensely anxious. Not that he opened it—that was unthinkable. He'd simply scoop everything up and stuff it into his desk drawer. Another patient in similar straits used to deposit her mail directly into the garbage chute of her apartment building.

These ostrich-like maneuvers do *not* help. The anxiety, which can't be disposed of as easily, gnaws its way into every pleasure, forcing the thought of that dreadful thing—whatever it is—into your consciousness, usually when you're alone and defenseless. You need a friend or perhaps a professional advisor to help you examine this nameless monster—whether it's a financial matter, a legal question, or an interpersonal issue—that you can't face alone. In any case, find someone to take a clear-eyed look at it with you; then make a plan to correct the problem. Your plan may involve a decision to postpone taking the necessary action until some specific future date when you've achieved a longer and stronger sobriety.

Chances are that part of your anxiety is tied to the fury, blame, and scorn you expect to be heaped upon you when you finally do something to resolve the matter. Quite possibly you've even written an imaginary script, as so many of my patients have, that ends with your complete degradation.

Check out your script with a friend. See whether he or she agrees that your imagined ending is the only possible outcome. This is called reality testing, and the mere act of doing it often brings considerable comfort. Once you formulate and start to enact your plan, you'll feel even more relief. I suspect you'll also be pleasantly surprised, because it's been my experience that people rarely encounter the response they've most dreaded.

Wait to Make Amends Until You're More Secure in Your Sobriety, but Make Your List Now

The Eighth Step of the anonymous self-help programs is to make a list of all the people you've hurt and become "willing to make amends to them all." While putting matters right can help enormously in alleviating your guilt and shame, the stress engendered by confrontations with people you've hurt may be more than you can tolerate in early sobriety. Postpone these encounters unless they're absolutely necessary.

You can, however, begin to compile a list of the specific actions you might take when you feel ready. The very act of digging out the details of what you've actually done from beneath the debris of guilt and self-reproach can help shrink those feelings to a more manageable size. It's also very useful to discuss your "sins" with your self-help sponsor or a sober friend. Often you'll find that your misdeeds are neither as unique nor as horrifying as you had imagined.

Sometimes the opportunity to square things up will arise naturally and spontaneously. If this happens, take advantage of the situation. But don't rely on chance. Take as much time as you need to prepare your strategies, even though you may not use them exactly when or how you had expected.

If you have already achieved a year or more of sobriety, it may be time to consider putting into action some of the plans you already have for making amends. But before you do, make sure you reassess your proposed strategies. If you have not yet made any provisions for making amends, now is the time to think seriously about how you might do so.

Oliver's story illustrates the value of being prepared, the wisdom of waiting, and the pleasure to be derived from making amends later in sobriety.

At twenty-eight, Oliver had been a scientific researcher at a major university. The project he worked on was funded by a government grant that had been awarded to Professor Donaldson, the head of the project, and a man whom Oliver greatly admired. As Oliver's drinking got worse, the quality of his work deteriorated. Lacking the necessary patience and ability to concentrate, he took to working on only the most superficial aspects of his share of the research. But before his diminished capacities became obvious to his coworkers, Professor Donaldson accepted a chair at another university. He generously turned over his own grant money to Oliver, so that he could continue his work until he was awarded a research grant for himself.

Oliver deeply appreciated the opportunity, but he couldn't follow through properly. His brain was so dulled by alcohol that it was actually painful for him to think. After a year of fruitlessly forcing himself to come in to work with ever-worsening hangovers, he resigned from the lab, on impulse and without offering any explanation. He told himself he was taking a sabbatical to "find himself." But in truth he traveled around aimlessly, taking odd jobs to support himself, and drinking more and more.

Finally, after suffering severe convulsions, he was admitted to a hospital for detoxification. After he was released, he suffered several relapses, but eventually he achieved a full year of sobriety. During that time he compiled his list of people to whom he had to make amends. High on that list was Professor Donaldson.

The case against Oliver was impressive. He had taken Donaldson's grant money, but had done little work and written no papers. He had hidden his lack of progress and abandoned the entire project without personally informing the professor. (Donaldson finally heard about Oliver's departure from the department secretary when he phoned to find out why a letter to Oliver hadn't been answered.) To make up for all this, Oliver felt he had to speak to Donaldson in person; a letter or phone call simply wouldn't suffice. But he didn't feel capable of facing Donaldson quite yet, so he put his plan on hold.

Two years passed, and Oliver had begun to establish himself in an entirely different field. He happened to be in a hotel one afternoon for a business meeting when he saw a notice about a scientific conference also being held there. Professor Donaldson was to be the keynote speaker. Oliver rearranged his schedule in order to attend Donaldson's lecture.

Afterward, his heart pounding, he made his way toward the podium, all the while worrying about how Donaldson would react to his greeting. Would he turn on his heel in utter contempt as soon as he recognized Oliver? Would he spit in his face? Would he expose him before the entire roomful of people for the incompetent ingrate he was? Finally, Oliver reached the stage. He nervously tapped Donaldson on the shoulder and managed to choke out a hello.

Donaldson turned around, and a moment later his face lit up with pleasure. "Oliver!" he declared. "How wonderful to see you. I feared you were dead."

It was quite by chance that Oliver was able to meet personally with Professor Donaldson, and their reunion was very different from the humiliating scenes he had imagined. But without having made up his mind and formulated a plan to see Donaldson in person someday, Oliver might not have made the effort to go to the lecture; nor might he have found the courage to come forward and speak to the professor. As it turned out, Professor Donaldson was primarily relieved to see Oliver.

But even if he had reacted otherwise—even if he had berated Oliver for his shabby behavior—Oliver's self-esteem would have been strong enough at this point in his recovery to withstand the assault of Donaldson's justifiable anger. He could now acknowledge and apologize for his mishandling of their project without jeopardizing his sobriety. However, had he happened upon Professor Donaldson in his first year of recovery, Oliver would have been wise to wait for another opportunity to make his amends.

Establish Your Priorities

Your first priority in recovery is to stay sober. No matter how you order your list of other priorities, you must eliminate those items that may threaten your sobriety in any way. Making a list of what's most important enables you to focus on the matters that are truly significant and to eliminate those that are trivial.

Identifying Paper Tigers

Earlier I mentioned that often you come upon situations that appear to be stressors until you examine them more closely. But a second look at these paper tigers enables you to perceive them in a different light and modify your responses accordingly.

For example, Bruce, a recovering cocaine addict, had spent the better part of the morning trying to figure out why his boss had given him the cold shoulder when he'd walked into the office. Had his weekly activity report been handed in on time? He checked with his secretary. It had. Had the contracts gone out to the new supplier? They had. Bruce couldn't think of a single job he'd left undone. But he did remember a remark he'd made the week before to his colleague Max, about the fact that his boss had all the charm of a hungry alligator and about the same amount of brains. Had Max repeated the comment to another of their associates? Could it have gotten back to the boss?

"The boss didn't say good morning to me today," he confided to Max over lunch. "He just scowled and walked right past me."

"Well," Max drawled in his Southern accent, "I guess he hasn't been sayin' much of anythin' to anybody this week. Haven't you heard? Seems his lady love upped and left him. Took his Porsche with her. Burned rubber all the way down the driveway." Max paused for effect and grinned conspiratorially. "He's one unhappy alligator."

Bruce didn't say a word, but his sigh of relief could be heard halfway across the employees' cafeteria.

Instead of creating a paper tiger by assuming the boss was angry with him, Bruce could have had some alternative thoughts about the boss's bad temper. For example, someone else in the office could have screwed up. Or the boss's ulcer might have been acting up. Or perhaps he'd overdrawn his bank account. By considering many alternatives, not just his own possible lapses, Bruce might have spent a far more productive morning.

Paper tigers come in many guises. Here are some ways to identify them:

Recognize That You Are Powerless, Not Only Over Alcohol and Drugs, but Also Over Many Other Aspects of Your Daily Life

As it happens, Steven, my writer friend who boat-sits in the Mediterranean, isn't a recovering addict. But he has a problem that's common to many people who have been chemically dependent: the need to control everything.

Step One of the self-help programs deals with the important issue of control and power. To work this step, you must admit that you are powerless over alcohol and/or drugs and that your life has become unmanageable. You are indeed powerless over alcohol and drugs, but you're also powerless over many other far less momentous but nevertheless annoying circumstances—late buses, rude shop clerks, careless drivers, and so on. Accepting this fact enables you to relax and put to much more constructive use the time you would otherwise have spent fuming and tense.

For example, instead of pacing up and down in front of the bus stop, you could take a few minutes to think about a point made by a speaker at your last self-help meeting. Rather than arguing with the salesman who's been rude to you, you can leave the store and take your business elsewhere. Instead of leaning on your horn when someone passes you on the inside lane, you can draw a deep breath, turn on the car radio, and remind yourself to drive defensively.

In your first year of sobriety, you simply cannot say the serenity prayer too often. You have probably already used it many times, but it bears repeating here:

"God grant me the strength to change the things I can, the courage to accept the things I cannot change, and the wisdom to know the difference."

Saying these words to yourself whenever you're having a difficult moment can help transform an upsetting situation into one that you can handle.

Trying to control everything and everyone, on the other hand, leads only to frustration. You cannot control circumstances or inanimate objects, nor can you control people. There is a self-help slogan that says, "Let go and let God." Letting go requires practice, but doing so will repeatedly save your sobriety.

Stop Trying to Please All the People All the Time

Low self-esteem understandably causes many recovering people to fear the disapproval of others and robs them of the ability to say no. Because you don't want to disappoint anyone, you overload your calendar and then find yourself burdened with commitments you can't possibly fulfill.

When you try to gratify every demand that's made of you, you create lots of paper tigers. For instance, there's the caller at the other end of the telephone line whom you imagine will be angry when you turn down his or her request. Now think for a moment about what *your* expectations are when you ask a favor of someone. Aren't you aware in advance that that person may have a previous engagement that prevents him or her from saying yes to you? And when the answer is no, though you may be disappointed, don't you usually accept the response calmly and without anger?

Your family, friends, and colleagues won't resent your honesty when you decide not to take on a responsibility you know you can't handle. But they will be annoyed and possibly angry when you don't honor obligations you've undertaken. You do risk their disapproval if you stand them up without notice, if you're habitually late for appointments, or if you regularly miss deadlines.

Remember—the ability to say no is crucial to your sobriety, and the time to start saying no is now.

Analyze Every Demanding Situation

When you feel yourself getting worried, tense, or anxious, ask yourself what could be the worst consequences of a given situation.

Say, for instance, your good friends have just given birth to their first child. They've invited you to attend the baptism and a buffet lunch afterwards. But your family has planned a birthday party for your father on that very same day. You consider juggling the two engagements, but your friends live 100 miles away from your parents' house. You can't go to the baptism, but you're worried about calling your friends to tell them. You become increasingly tense and upset because you don't know what to say.

Now, let's examine what could be making you so anxious. Are you scared your friends will be irritated, disappointed, or even relieved that you can't come? Are you concerned about what they'll think of you? Will they suspect you of making up an excuse because you don't really want to come? Will you lose their friendship if you're not present at this important celebration?

Ask yourself, what's the very worst that could happen? They would never speak to you again. Is that really very likely? And if it is, are they the kind of people you want for your close friends? Or are you really worried that they'll fly off the handle or berate you for being irresponsible? In that case, what would be your response?

First, consider what the odds are that they would be upset with you. You would be one guest at a large gathering; it's doubtful they would be seriously put out. Are they likely to be disappointed then? Yes, because they value your friendship. What could you do to assure them of your good will? Perhaps you could phone them on the day of the baptism from your parents' home and congratulate them. You could arrange to see them and the new baby some other time. Or you could offer to run an errand or buy a special gift for the baby to let them know you care.

Without this step-by-step analysis, you'll become increasingly distressed whenever you so much as *think* about picking up the phone. But once you've thought it through and answered all these questions, you'll be able to make your phone call without expecting the roof to cave in on you.

It can be very difficult to think calmly when you're feeling extremely anxious about some pending matter. So if you find yourself caught up this way, talk to a friend. You may discover that you're terrified of yet another paper tiger.

Learn to Be Assertive

There are two parts to assertive behavior. First is the ability to communicate honestly and directly, instead of passively or aggressively. Neither silent defiance nor active belligerence is a productive defense in the face of a paper tiger, but good communication skills are.

The other half of being assertive is recognizing what your rights are, which is often difficult when you're in early recovery because of low self-esteem. So here's a partial list of what you're entitled to; all of these are essential for your sobriety. You have the right to:

> Say no.
> Change your mind.
> Ask for help.
> Reject advice.
> Respond to criticism.
> Protest if you're treated unfairly.
> Take time for yourself.
> Be wrong.

This is by no means an exhaustive list. In fact, I suggest you supplement it with whatever feels appropriate to you. Once you understand what your rights are, you then have to claim them, calmly and directly.

When You Leave Work, Close Up Shop for the Day

When your workday is finished, you should be finished with work. You've done as much as you can for that day. It's fruitless to dwell on what you *could* have accomplished, or to be like Steven and miss the glorious sunset because you're worried about everything you left undone. There will always be some task you didn't have time for. But you can't live each day with a sense of incompletion.

The same principle applies when you go to sleep. Don't turn off the light and lie in bed stewing about all your unfinished chores. Know that you've done as much as you possibly could for one day.

Changing Your Body's Response to Stressors

You can safely avoid some sources of stress. You can identify a paper tiger when it's there, but one may not always be present. For those stressors that remain, you can change the way you respond.

While you should strive to avoid stress whenever possible, especially in the first year of recovery, you must also learn to distinguish between those stressors you must avoid because you have no control over them and those where you have some ability to affect the outcome. It is not healthy to continue to avoid stressors that you can do something about, and it can even create more stress. For example, if you avoid standing up for yourself in a situation where someone continually puts you down, you are liable to feel worse about yourself rather than better.

* * *

Kerry, who was being treated for alcohol and cocaine addiction when I met him, had noticed that he developed a squint whenever he was feeling particularly stressed; he called this reaction his tip-off. He told me that to help himself relax, he liked to record those events or thoughts that were making him unhappy, then come up with an amusing explanation for each item. Here's a typical example:

Stressor	*Explanation*
Kit rushed by me in hall, didn't stop to say hello.	She needed to get to the bathroom—on the double.
Boss didn't smile.	Boss never smiles.
Wife prefers the cat to me.	Cat is softer, prettier, and doesn't talk back.
Children would rather talk to their friends than me.	Friends understand Nintendo. I don't.
Nobody commented on my report.	It was so good they were stunned into silence.
Nobody ate the breakfast I cooked.	They're junk cereal junkies.
Everyone expects me to do something. I can't do it all.	The cemeteries are full of indispensable people.
Nobody identifies with me when I speak at AA meetings.	Keep talking. Somebody there is on your wavelength.

Kerry was under a lot of pressure, and he couldn't joke it all away. He was the only child of elderly, ill parents who depended on him both emotionally and financially. He had his own family to support and nurture, plus his recovery to work on. He'd done what he could to avoid sources of stress and to identify his paper tigers, and he, quite admirably, used his sense of humor to maintain his perspective when he felt himself getting tense and uptight. But there are several more helpful ways to modify your body's response to stressors.

Take Time for Yourself

As an addict, you had plenty of time for your drug or your bottle, but that's not at all what I mean by taking time for yourself.

First, you have to find out what you enjoy. If you're like many newly recovering people, you're probably out of touch with what gives you pleasure. You've been so preoccupied with your dependency that you could hardly spare a minute for anything else. But now that you've reclaimed those endless hours that used to be wasted on drinking or drugging, you should dedicate some part of each and every day to doing nothing but having fun. This is one of the most effective stress reducers I know.

Make an Effort to Stick to Your Plans for Diet, Exercise, and Sleep

As I discussed earlier, you need to eat well, get regular exercise, and get a good night's sleep in order to help yourself relax. An alert mind and a healthy body can do wonders for minimizing stress.

Learn Some Relaxation Techniques

Relaxation training, meditation, self-hypnosis, biofeedback, and yoga are all effective stress reduction techniques. In fact, I have been so impressed by how helpful such techniques have been to people in early sobriety that we now include meditation and relaxation training as part of our inpatient treatment program at the Smithers Center. Besides reducing stress, these disciplines can also promote better sleep and help you cope with chronic pain without medication that can harm your recovery. To get started in these disciplines, you may need a few sessions of professional instruction, or you may want to consult some of the many excellent books, audio, and videotapes that are also available. In Appendix A you will find a small sampling of instructional materials.

Even if you don't study or practice some systematized form of relaxation, you must learn to STOP, sit down, if you can, and take three or four slow, deep breaths whenever you recognize a stress response. Deep breathing slows down your heart rate and helps you feel calmer, so that you can take a moment to think about what's happening.

Deep breathing is a skill you can learn easily and then practice anytime. First, slowly breathe in through your nose. As you breathe in, imagine that you're filling not just your chest, but your entire abdominal cavity with air. Your belly should expand as you inhale. Pause for a second when you've taken in as much air as you can, then begin slowly to exhale the breath through your mouth. Think about trying to empty your entire abdominal cavity of air. Your belly should contract as you breathe out. Repeat two or three times.

At first this technique may feel a bit complicated or forced. But if you stick with it, you'll find that the pattern will soon become second nature, and that you've armed yourself with a simple and effective tool for reducing tension.

Change Your Internal Monologue

Most of us have a stream of thoughts, or an internal monologue, that runs through our heads whenever we're not actually involved in an activity that engages all of our attention. This inner voice can either exacerbate or reduce stress. We can also consciously rewrite and redirect the monologue.

To see how this works, let's look at a typical stress-inducing scene. Lynn is all set to leave for work one morning when she discovers that she can't start her car. She calls the AAA, and a serviceman arrives an hour later. He manages to get the car going but tells Lynn she needs to check with her regular mechanic to find out why the battery ran down. Lynn cancels her morning appointments and takes the car over to the garage, where she has to wait for an hour and a half in a messy lot while the mechanic repairs the battery.

He also points outs to her that the inspection sticker is due to expire in three days. Lynn drives to the inspection station, where she's informed that she'll have to leave the car for a couple of hours. She walks over to a nearby coffee shop, calls her office to cancel her afternoon appointments, and eats a tuna fish sandwich. When she returns to the inspection station, she learns that her car needs a steering adjustment and two parking lights. Back she goes to the garage, where she waits for two more hours while the work is done. Then it's back again to the inspection station—which is now closed for the day. Lynn puts her head down on the steering wheel and begins to cry.

Throughout all of this, thoughts have been running through Lynn's head: *I've got to get the inspection sticker before I go on vacation next week. I have no time. When will I make up today's appointments? Why does this always happen to me? Why doesn't the mechanic run his business more efficiently? Why can't I be more assertive? Why did I let my husband talk me into buying a second-hand car? He's so cheap, and now my whole day has been ruined. I'll never get everything done.*

This self-punishing monologue has only increased Lynn's stress. She might not have been able to do anything differently to change the situation, but she could have changed the things she said to herself: *Okay, the day is shot. Stay calm. Tomorrow is another day. There's going to be a long wait at the garage, that's the way the guy operates, but I wouldn't trust anyone else with my car. Good thing I put those files in my briefcase last night. While I'm waiting, I can find a quiet coffee shop where I can read them and get started on my report. Thank heavens I'm going on vacation soon—plenty of swimming, sailing, and sun. Maybe I can start working on my suntan while I'm stuck sitting around at the lot.*

By calmly accepting that her day is shot and deciding to make the best of it, Lynn can reduce her stress even if she can't entirely eliminate it. Yes, she has to make arrangements to reschedule her appointments, but she can also catch up on some paperwork and spend a few hours outdoors, away from the hustle and bustle of the office. It may not be the best of days, but she won't be in tears by the end of it.

When you catch your inner voice making a bad situation worse, rewrite the script. Remind yourself to stay calm, take a few deep breaths, then do whatever you must to minimize the stress.

Talk Things Over

One of the best ways to reduce stress is to share your concerns about the cause with someone. Now, more than ever, you need to be able to unburden yourself. When you hoard your troubles, you usually increase the feelings of strain and pressure.

If you're in a self-help program, find a sponsor. Sponsorship is one of the best benefits of being in such a program. By agreeing to be your sponsor, the person you have chosen promises to be available whenever you have to talk. You won't get a professional opinion, but you don't need one. You'll get a listening ear and the kind of wisdom that comes from achieving sobriety. If you're not in a self-help program, ask a close friend or a family member to make him- or herself available to you in this same way.

Fatigue, hunger, loneliness, anger, criticism, overwork, illness, accidents. These are some of the stressors that come readily to mind, but I'm sure that even if I were to write down every one I'd ever heard, each of you could make your own contributions to the list. But all stressors have one trait in common. They can trigger a well-worn circuit present in the brains of all chemically dependent people: "I feel terrible. I need to make it go away *now*."

Even though you know that the instant relief promised by your favorite drink or drug is only temporary, your desire for it becomes overwhelming. By now, this urge is almost instinctive, a reflex conditioned by the thousands of times in the past that you've sought release this way. As we've seen throughout the chapter, stress causes your instincts to move front and center. A comfortable sobriety therefore depends on your diligent efforts to reduce stress—by avoiding your personal sources of it, by identifying paper tigers, and by changing your body's response to those stressors you cannot avoid.

Chapter Seven
One Day at a Time

Joining and Getting the Most
Out of Your Self-Help Group

Taking the First Step. Twelve Stepping. Working the program. One day at a time. Throughout these chapters, I have been using phrases associated with the twelve-step anonymous self-help programs. Many of you are already attending self-help meetings regularly and with enthusiasm. Others of you may have reservations that are hindering your full participation in a program, and still others may be shying away from self-help meetings altogether for one reason or another. But there is much to be gained from self-help meetings, even if your preconceptions or first experiences seem to be telling you otherwise, as mine did.

When I was training as a medical resident in neurology at Bellevue Hospital in the 1960s, a great many of our patients were suffering from the consequences of alcoholism. They had a variety of problems, including blood clots on the brain from having been in accidents or fights, nerve injuries from having passed out in odd positions, and motor impairment due to the effects of alcohol on the brain. We corrected whatever medical problems we could, treated our patients with thiamine and multivitamins to help mend the nerve damage, and referred them to a neurosurgeon when necessary. But we never concerned ourselves with the underlying cause of their ailments. We just patched them up and sent them back out . . . to drink again.

From time to time an earnest-looking man would come to our ward. He carried a book which he called the "Big Book" of Alcoholics Anonymous. He'd make his rounds, talking to as many patients as could or would respond to him. My colleagues and I were tolerant of this visitor, but we weren't really interested in his message. We were giving our patients wonderful (or so we thought) medical treatment, and that's all that concerned us. We never stopped to wonder about what would happen to them once they left the hospital. We never thought about the real reason they had been admitted to our ward in the first place—their alcoholism.

But after a couple of months of watching this man, I became curious about the organization he represented. Several of the patients he'd spoken to hadn't returned to the hospital with their usual regularity. I began to think that maybe, just maybe there was something to this Alcoholics Anonymous. I had a couple of chats with our visitor, and finally I asked if I might observe a meeting. He told me that an AA group met every evening at 7:30 P.M. at a nearby church and that everybody was welcome.

I was so ignorant about AA that when I went to that first meeting, I thought I was going to a branch of the Salvation Army. I expected there to be people in uniforms playing drums and trumpets and singing hymns, all the while trying to persuade me to believe in God the way they did. When I arrived at the church I found the side door with a sign that read, "AA meeting, 7:30 tonight." I hesitated, sure that passersby were watching me and thinking that I was one of "them." I even strolled up and down the street a couple of times to make sure the coast was clear before I scurried inside.

When I walked into the meeting room several people came up to me, introduced themselves, and made me feel welcome. I was so eager to assure everyone that I was a medical doctor who was here to see how AA worked, and to deny that I'd ever had or ever would have a drinking problem, that I hardly heard a word anyone said.

I was surprised to see that the others present looked like a pretty respectable, even congenial bunch of people. They were standing around drinking coffee, chatting and laughing a lot. I was immediately drawn into a conversation, a rare occurrence among strangers at a gathering in New York City. But I still felt an underlying tension. When would the sales pitch start? When were they going to begin the God-talk? And when would they sing the opening hymn?

There were no hymns. At exactly 7:30 P.M., everybody found a seat, and the chairperson read the preamble. I listened to the words, surprised by what I was hearing.

"Alcoholics Anonymous is a fellowship of men and women who share their experience, strength, and hope with each other that they may solve their common problem and help others recover from alcoholism.

"The only requirement for membership is a desire to stop drinking. There are no dues or fees for AA membership. We are self-supporting through our own contributions. AA is not allied with any sect, denomination, politics, organization, or institution; it does not wish to engage in any controversy, neither endorses nor opposes any causes. Our primary purpose is to stay sober and help other alcoholics achieve sobriety."

No mention of God there, I thought. No arm-twisting either. I decided they must leave all that for the end of the meeting. After the preamble, the chairperson introduced Esther, the speaker for the meeting. Esther, who had been sober for ten years, then proceeded to tell the story of her drinking days. It was one of the funniest tales I'd ever heard, presented with marvelous zest and an apparent capacity for total recall.

As Esther spoke, I looked around at the others. They were obviously enjoying her story very much, and at various points many of them nodded their heads in recognition. I'm sure that we would happily have listened to her all evening, but she ended her talk after speaking for precisely thirty minutes.

At the fifteen-minute coffee break that followed, I was surrounded by people who asked if I was new, if I'd been to any meetings before. No one asked whether I was an alcoholic or implied that I might be. Instead, they either told me a little bit about themselves or offered an anecdote about their own drinking and how they'd come to AA.

After the break we sat down again, and for the remaining forty-five minutes of the session, people spoke spontaneously—about Esther's talk and how closely they had identified with some of her comments, about themselves, about how they were feeling, about what had happened to them that week. Esther replied to each speaker, offering encouragement or practical advice, sometimes using her own experience to show how she'd dealt with a similar problem.

One man seemed to be in serious trouble. He said he'd been on the verge of drinking all week. Esther urged him to keep coming to meetings and to go out for coffee with her and a few of the others after the meeting. "Let's see if you can find a sponsor this evening," she suggested.

The meeting ended with everyone holding hands and reciting the serenity prayer. That was it—no hymns, no uniforms, no coercion. Just a group of people getting together to help one another stay sober.

That night a number of my illusions were shattered—illusions that a lot of people still hold on to and use as barriers to prevent themselves from joining a self-help group. And there are a lot of them to join. In the 1960s, AA was the only anonymous self-help group. Now there are many—Cocaine Anonymous, Narcotics Anonymous, Drugs Anonymous, Gamblers Anonymous, Overeaters Anonymous, and more—organized on the AA model. When I discuss self-help groups, I'm talking about all the groups, not just AA.

More people know about AA now than I did. I don't think many people still believe that it's a branch of the Salvation Army. But many people do assume that the self-help groups have strong religious overtones which they'll find offensive.

Some are also concerned that self-help groups are made up of people with whom they'll have very little in common, or that the members come from a social class other than their own. They're surprised when they attend a meeting, as I did, and discover that this isn't true. Just as I was concerned that the moment I crossed the threshold I'd be forced to confess that I was an alcoholic, many people who aren't yet sure whether they're alcoholics or dependent on drugs stay away from self-help meetings because they're afraid they'll be forced to make a confession. And just as I worried that I'd be coerced into accepting a belief system alien to my own, many people feel that if they go to a self-help meeting, they'll be brainwashed. But none of these things happened to me, and they won't happen to you.

For those who still have doubts and reservations, the following discussion of the most common difficulties people experience—either in going to their first self-help meeting or in continuing to attend—should help. I'd also like to offer some strategies you can use to make the anonymous programs work for you.

Coping with Social Awkwardness

There are some people for whom social gatherings are *agony.* They become extremely apprehensive when they're required to make any kind of personal contact. They're comfortable only when they're alone or perhaps when they're with one other trusted person. But such people are very rare, and the chances are excellent that you're not one of them.

Many newly recovering people do feel socially awkward. "I'm just not good in groups," they tell me, or "I feel so anxious when I'm with a crowd of people that going to a self-help meeting would make me want to drink or use again."

This feeling of being socially inept has certainly led many people to start using alcohol or drugs in the first place. As a result, they enter sobriety with virtually no sense of what it's like to be sober at a social event. Such events can consequently be very frightening.

But you don't see people at self-help meetings sitting alone in a corner with no one to talk to. Not at all. You'll find people grouped around the room, talking to one another, enthusiastically hailing others as they arrive. If you question these apparently gregarious people, most will admit that they were quite anxious before their first sober social gathering. But you wouldn't know it to look at them now. They're confident, calm, at ease, talkative, cheerful, and above all, socially very "ept."

The fact is that it doesn't take very long for human beings to relearn how to behave in a group, and you're no exception. Of course, the first step is always difficult. But many recovering people have found that this step is easier to take in a self-help group where so many others understand and have successfully overcome the same shyness and distress.

Carla is a stellar example of someone who learned to overcome her social fears through her self-help group. Her father had left home when she was four and her mother worked to support Carla and her elderly parents, who were responsible for much of Carla's upbringing. Besides being out of the house much of the time, Carla's mother was also psychologically unavailable because she was dependent on alcohol and tranquilizers.

Carla recalls that as a child and adolescent she lived in a world of her own. She read, daydreamed, helped her grandmother around the house, and went fishing with her grandfather. She had a few girlfriends, but rarely saw them outside of school. Although she was very comfortable with adults—she could talk for hours with her grandmother's friends— she was quite uncomfortable around her peers.

"I felt I was different," she says, "more sensitive than the popular, outgoing girls. I condemned them for being coarse and crude, but secretly I wanted to be just like them."

When Carla was sixteen her mother started to get sober through AA and began to take an interest in her daughter's future. Carla had planned to attend a local junior college. But with her mother's encouragement, she applied to and was accepted by a large university in another part of the state. But she felt terribly ill at ease around her fellow students, and she couldn't bear the thought of making a presentation or even speaking up in class. "I had fantasies of getting appendicitis, being hit by a truck, being summoned home to my grandmother's funeral—anything that would gracefully get me out of having to speak in public."

She even took an incomplete in one course rather than read aloud a paper she'd written. She also got very good at spending Saturday nights in the dorm without a date and became a founding member of "One on the House," a campus drinking club for women. During her last two years of school, as drinking gradually took over her life, the club became her main focus. But thanks largely to the high grades she'd earned as a freshman and sophomore, she graduated with a degree in economics and was hired for an entry-level position as an economics researcher in her state government.

The job was perfect for her. She spent her days poring over statistics and periodically produced a written report of her findings. There were few meetings to attend, and no oral presentations were required. Five years passed, and Carla held on to the same job. She also continued to drink. Finally, with the help of her mother, she found her way to AA. She attended the meetings regularly, but could never bring herself to say a word. She remembers that for nine months, "I sat at the back of the room, saying nothing but, 'My name is Carla and I am an alcoholic. I pass.' "

Then her sponsor, Annette, suggested that Carla chair a meeting. (Chairing a meeting, or qualifying, means telling your drinking story to your group at one of its regular meetings.) Carla was spitting mad at her sponsor for making such a ridiculous suggestion. She'd rather drink than speak in public, she informed Annette. "I suppose you *want* me to drink. That's why you're forcing me to do something you know I can't do."

Annette patiently waited for Carla to cool off. A couple of weeks later she brought the subject up again, this time telling her, "Your story is yours. You own it. You can't get it wrong, and nobody can criticize you for having it. This isn't a performance. Telling your story is showing your commitment to sobriety. Someone out there will be touched by what you say, will identify with and learn from your experience."

It took several more weeks of patient coaxing before Carla actually agreed to set a date to chair a meeting. Then she began to make painstaking preparations. She carefully wrote out her speech, agonizing over every word. She committed it to memory, timing her delivery so that she'd speak for exactly thirty minutes. Every time she sat down to work on her speech, her old fantasies resurfaced. Maybe she'd get appendicitis or be hit by a truck. Her grandmother had already died, but maybe her mother . . .

But now, whenever these thoughts popped into her head, she called her sponsor. When she repeated the words aloud, she started to see how ridiculous they were. She didn't *really* want to spend weeks in the hospital just to avoid speaking to her AA group. And she certainly didn't want to lose her mother, with whom she'd recently become quite close.

Finally the day came. Shaky and trembling, Carla stood up in front of the room. "My name is Carla, and I am an alcoholic," she said. And then something extraordinary happened. Instead of the speech she'd so carefully rehearsed, her story—her real story with all its pain and shame and moments of wry humor—came tumbling out. After what seemed like three or four minutes, Carla looked at the clock on the wall and saw that she'd been speaking for thirty minutes. She abruptly thanked everyone and sat down, the audience's applause ringing in her ears.

During the lively discussion period that followed, many people said they had identified with one part or another of Carla's story. But the most moving moment came when a young woman stood up in the back of the room. She said nothing for several moments and seemed about to sit down again, when in a rush of words she admitted that she was so shy she had never talked at a meeting before. But hearing Carla's story had given her the courage to speak up. She, too, got a round of applause.

Carla left that night feeling dazed and happy. "I learned that I could do something I'd thought was impossible. I didn't die. I didn't even faint!"

Soon Carla was telling her story to many groups. Her humor, her fresh way of looking at a situation, her sense of the absurdities of her self-delusions, and, above all, her sincerity put her in great demand as a speaker. This newly found confidence spilled over into her work. She made occasional forays out of her cubbyhole, seeking more challenging assignments and even making suggestions to her superiors. Several months later she was promoted to a job for which she would have to make oral reports to members of the state legislature.

On the morning of her first presentation, Carla was tempted to call in sick. Instead, she thought about the skills she'd learned from speaking to AA groups. She was honest, straightforward, and funny. Her presentation was not only a great success, but she even drew a smile from a crusty old curmudgeon who, according to rumor, had last smiled in 1967.

Carla's transformation didn't take place overnight. Had she tried to chair a meeting in the first months of her sobriety, her acute anxiety could have caused a relapse. But her attendance at months of meetings had given her a sense of safety which she wasn't even conscious of until she actually got up in front of the group to tell her story. At that moment the mortar that had held together the isolating wall of her social discomfort began to crumble. Over time, the wall which had surrounded her since childhood slowly disintegrated, until Carla was able to function well in any group situation. Slowly but surely, the meetings had helped to change her.

What About Religious Differences?

People tell me, "I am an atheist/Jew/Muslim/Catholic/person who hates religion because I got too much of it as a child, and I couldn't tolerate being forced to conform to another group's religious beliefs." Another excuse I hear a lot is "It would be an offense to my philosophy of life. How will that help me stay sober?"

It's true that God is mentioned in five of the twelve steps practiced by self-help members. But it's *not* true that the self-help groups are religious organizations. I like to think of them as spiritual associations, which is an altogether different matter. Participation in a spiritual association means being dedicated to a process of personal growth, enabling you to reach your full capacity as a human being, and being dedicated to helping others achieve this goal.

When I speak of "full capacity," I mean cultivating your abilities —to do satisfying work, to have close personal relationships, to enjoy nature, music, art, sports, or the company of other people—indeed, all the many wonderful things life offers us. Ultimately, spiritual growth enables us to feel and behave in a truly altruistic way. That means sometimes putting the interests of others ahead of our own. (Of course, the ability to achieve spiritual growth is absolutely alien to anyone who is dependent on any kind of drug.) And it's the replenishment of the spiritual, not the religious, self that is the ultimate goal of a self-help member. This spiritual replenishment enables recovering people to live and enjoy life to its fullest without using any mood-altering substance.

Sometimes their renewed spirituality does draw self-help members to religion. Some find that their religious faith, which had gone by the wayside when they were using, is now restored. Others experience a religious awakening, a new and genuine conversion to religious belief. Occasionally, members may talk about these experiences in meetings, but only as a *part* of the story of their sobriety.

Religious affiliation is neither necessary nor a condition for membership in a self-help group. Many self-help members aren't affiliated with any organized religion; some are atheists or agnostics. But this does not, and should not, infringe on the work of the group, which is helping one another stay sober.

Let me tell you a story I heard about one AA meeting where a participant began to philosophize about the nonexistence of God and got into a heated argument with another member. After a minute or two, the chairperson intervened. "Isn't this the kind of windy philosophizing we all used to do in the bars?" she asked rather wearily. "Let's talk about being sober."

Some self-help members do have trouble with the concept of God, even the "God as we understand him" or the "higher power" that's mentioned in the self-help steps. However, many of these people *are* comfortable with an understanding of the higher power as the power of the group, upon which they call to symbolize the larger collective wisdom of recovering people. They also recognize a person's inability to manage on his or her own with this disease and thus understand the need for help greater than can be provided by any one individual. By reinterpreting statements that make mention of God, atheists and agnostics are also able to enjoy the many benefits of self-help membership without feeling alienated from the group.

Ernie, a forty-seven-year-old recovering alcoholic, is one of the most spiritual people I've ever met. He has the kind of serenity that is fresh and clear. He accepts his own illness and that of others. It's hard to imagine talking to Ernie and not coming away feeling a little better. He has the unique ability to help people help themselves, to show the path without leading. When Ernie is at a meeting, it takes on a different dimension. People stop complaining and whining, and emerge, however briefly, from the fog of their own narcissism. Ernie is also an atheist. "But even from my first AA meetings fifteen years ago, I felt an immense power in the group," he told me. "I could feel it pushing me toward sobriety, toward health and a different, better way of living."

This power supported him through the difficult early days of his sobriety and continued to nurture him as he continued to recover. He calls it his higher power. "It's so sad to see people hung up on the word 'God' in the AA steps. They're dying from their disease, and they're quibbling about the shape of the label on the medicine bottle."

I've known so many people like Ernie, who have been able to use self-help in this way, that I feel confident in saying that a lack of belief in God is not a barrier to self-help membership unless you wish to make it one.

Breaking Through the Stereotypes

Another difficulty many people in early recovery have with self-help groups is that having become isolated by their addiction, they now see themselves as quite unlike anyone else who's ever been chemically dependent. The industrial chemist, a pillar of the community with an expensive house in the suburbs and a lovely family, is certain that no other solvent, respected professional person has ever had a problem with alcohol or drugs. The plumber, the ballet dancer, the telephone operator, and the assembly line worker all share the same conviction.

"*Surely nobody like me would go to a self-help meeting,*" they tell themselves. "*Everybody who goes is uneducated/a college graduate/a blue-collar worker/a professional.*" Or, "*They're just a bunch of lonely bums with nothing better to do with their time."* The stereotypes vary enormously, but who ever "they" are, the speaker is always sure that they're very different from him- or herself.

As far as Clifford was concerned, everyone in AA was a bigot, a prude, and unbelievably smug. The only AA member he had ever known was his Uncle Arthur, a stingy man who Clifford said made Scrooge look like a philanthropist. Uncle Arthur was the publisher of a small New England town newspaper and, as a boy, Clifford had delivered papers for him. At the end of one busy Christmas season when Clifford was about ten, Uncle Arthur asked him if he would like a bonus. "I wouldn't mind," Clifford replied.

"Oh, you wouldn't, would you? Well, I would mind giving you one." Arthur cackled at his superb joke, enjoying Clifford's bewilderment.

Clifford never forgot the incident. "He was in AA too, at the time," he told me. No matter what I said about AA when I treated him at the beginning of his recovery, Clifford resisted going to a meeting. For him, AA was populated only with small-minded, mean, pompous Uncle Arthurs. He couldn't imagine going to such a place, much less getting help there. At this point, I called in a former patient who was willing to accompany newcomers to their first meeting. I explained the situation and asked him to take Clifford to a group where there were no Uncle Arthurs. "So," I asked Clifford when we next met. "Did you meet Uncle Arthur?"

Clifford eyed me rather sheepishly before replying, "Uncle Arthur would have hated every one of the people at the meeting I went to last night. I'm going back tonight. They're a great group!"

Admittedly, there are a few groups in town where Clifford might have met an Uncle Arthur or two. But the reality is that the people in the groups are people like you—of all races, religions, occupations, and genders—drawn together by a desire to stay sober and to help others stay sober. And just as the membership is diverse, so the groups themselves differ one from another. In the five boroughs of New York City, well over seven hundred self-help groups meet every week, and each one has its own unique complexion. In Manhattan's Greenwich Village, for example, you'll meet a lot of artists, writers, and performers, many of whom live in the vicinity. Uptown, near Columbia University, the groups are likely to be made up of students, faculty members, health professionals from the nearby hospitals, and working-class people from the surrounding area.

If you live in a large metropolitan area and go to a meeting near your home, the group will probably reflect the composition of your neighborhood. If you attend a meeting near your office, you'll most likely find people who work close by. One might be a mailroom clerk, another a chief executive officer, but they're all people with a common problem who are there for the very same reason you are. If you live in a more rural area, you may not have as many groups to choose from, but the advantage is that in the ones available, you'll find a mix of people.

But no matter where you attend a meeting, there is one constant, and it's one of the qualities I find most remarkable about the self-help movement. Despite the diversity of people in any one group, and the diversity among the groups themselves, the overall format, the intention, and the philosophy always remain the same.

How Does Anonymity Work?

Anonymity is yet another major concern of many newly sober people. People often tell me, "I can't possibly go to a self-help meeting because I'm a lawyer and one of my clients might see me." Or, "I'm a teacher and a parent of one of my students might be there."

In large urban areas where you can choose from many groups, guarding your privacy isn't a problem. A lawyer can find a group away from where clients work or live. A teacher can attend a meeting outside the school district.

However, in smaller communities where only one self-help group may be available, anonymity may be an issue, particularly when you first come into the program. There are alternatives in all but the rarest instances. You could attend a meeting in a town that's fifty miles away, where you're unlikely to be recognized. When my patients grumble about the inconvenience of having to drive an hour each way to get to a meeting, I always ask how far they would have gone to buy a drink on a Sunday morning when blue laws prevented them from buying beer at their local grocery store. Much further than the next town, they usually admit.

Besides their fear of being found out, many people also doubt that the self-help groups really are anonymous. But your privacy is well-protected. People know each other only by first names. And no one ever need know your occupation or anything else about you, if you don't care to divulge that information. If by chance you do encounter people you know at a meeting, remember that they've joined the group for the same reason you did. They're probably just as concerned about maintaining confidentiality as you are. In my experience, breaches of anonymity are rare. The fear that people have of being exposed is enormously disproportionate to the actual risk.

But if you go to enough self-help meetings, sooner or later you will bump into someone you know. Probably the best way to handle this is to acknowledge the acquaintance with a handshake and a greeting, along the lines of, "Hi, I'm glad to see you here." If the person is new to your group, you could take the opportunity to introduce him or her to some of the other members, using first names only, of course.

You might also one day encounter someone in a business or social setting whom you recognize from a self-help meeting. In the anonymous tradition, you shouldn't indicate in any way that you've previously met at a group. A smile and a warm handshake lets the person know you're happy to see him or her, but if you otherwise make it known that you're acquainted, someone is likely to ask where you've met before. So unless you've both privately agreed on an explanation—you're neighbors, or your children are in the same ballet class—you're better off not advertising your acquaintanceship to the other people in the room.

In large metropolitan areas where you meet many people in the course of the day, you're more likely to come upon someone whose face is familiar. "Haven't we met somewhere before?" you say, groping for the name, only to be greeted by a frozen smile. Too late you realize that the "somewhere" was a self-help meeting. As a member of an anonymous group, you'd be wise to adopt a policy of *never* using that line in a public situation. You should also be prepared for someone to make that mistake with you. You might respond with, "I see more and more people nowadays who remind me of someone I know." Or your answer could be, "I'm sorry, perhaps we've met, but I can't seem to place your face."

There's no doubt that meeting a fellow self-help member in another context can be quite stressful, particularly if you're newly sober. Take the case of John, for example, a real estate lawyer who had been sober for five years. When he arrived at the closing for a large estate, he immediately recognized Rod, who'd been coming to John's group for three or four months. John gave no sign to the others in the office that he already knew Rod, who was representing the sellers of the estate; he merely shook hands warmly when they were introduced. But Rod looked right past him, stared at the wall, and barely twitched a facial muscle as he mumbled a tight hello.

"It was as if I'd slept with his wife or something," John recalled. In fact, the atmosphere between the two lawyers was so tense that during a break in the proceedings, John's client whispered to him, "You two must have had a royal battle in the past. You'll have to tell me about it at lunch."

Hell's bells, thought John. *Not only do I have to sit here calmly while this Rod acts as though I just crawled out from under a stone, but now I have to make up a story about why for my client.*

Later that week, when John saw Rod at a meeting, he muttered the serenity prayer to himself and walked across the room to talk to him. He didn't lash out at Rod and ask him why he'd behaved like such a jerk.

Instead, in the true self-help tradition, he said, "I felt quite upset when you were so cold at our meeting. I was wondering whether you were angry at me for any reason."

Rod immediately apologized for his behavior. "I didn't know what to do," he said. "I'm new to all this, and I was terrified that you were going to give me away. But I learned from your example. I'll know what to do if I ever find myself in that situation again."

Such chance encounters do occur, and you should be prepared for them. On the other hand, when you consider how many people are already aware of your problem, you may be amused by your worries about anonymity. Many newly sober people truly believe that no one ever noticed when they were actively using. Once sober, they go to great lengths to conceal what's already widely known. But your concerns about anonymity will become less pressing the longer you're sober. People have amazingly short memories. Most of us are so involved with our own affairs that, except for family and close friends, we quickly forget much of what we know about the people who pass through our lives. Think about it: How much do you remember about how your acquaintances behaved five years or even five months ago?

We tend to perceive others as however they happen to be at any given moment. If you've been sober for two years, that's how most people will see you. I once had a patient who'd been sober for three years but was very concerned because he was sure people still thought of him as a drunk. Ralph finally stopped worrying when an acquaintance of his who had known about his problem offered him a bottle of beer. When Ralph reminded the man that he didn't drink anymore, his friend was embarrassed and apologetic; he'd completely forgotten about Ralph's days as a boozer.

Helen, another patient, told me she learned this same lesson when she was on her way to an AA meeting and ran into one of her neighbors from down the block. The last time they'd bumped into each other, Helen had been falling down drunk. Betty had helped her across the street, into her apartment, and put her to bed. Now, six months sober, Helen was mortified by the memory of their previous encounter, so she passed Betty with a brief hello. But Betty stopped her to chat for a few minutes, then asked Helen whether she had time for a cup of coffee. No, Helen replied, and explained that she was on her way to an AA meeting.

"AA?" Betty exclaimed. "Why, I didn't know you had a drinking problem."

Helen had stared at the woman in disbelief. What for her had been a painfully embarrassing incident, indelibly etched in her mind, was nothing more than a trivial moment, long since forgotten by Betty.

Newly sober people have their drug-induced or drunken behavior fresh in their memories. They are terrified that their actions, which were often humiliating to themselves and painful to those close to them, are the only things people will remember about them. But the longer you're sober, the more you'll discover that it's your present behavior that counts. Because even if your acquaintances and associates do remember the way you used to be, they won't care much about it now that you're sober and acting altogether different.

I know one man who was so intent on protecting his anonymity that when he first became sober, he'd travel one hundred miles to go to meetings. Now, six years later, he shows up at his local meeting without any qualms at all. Because he's established a strong record of sober behavior, he knows he has nothing to be ashamed of. On the contrary, he's proud of his sobriety. The fact that he used to drink pales in comparison to what he's accomplished and continues to accomplish in staying sober.

The Importance of Slogans

Keep it simple.
Easy does it.
First things first.

You hear these slogans, and many others, time and again at self-help meetings. Some people are put off by them initially, as well as by the fact that some members feel the need to invoke them repeatedly. As one patient (who was headed straight for a relapse) said to me, "Those sayings are boring and simpleminded."

But if you stop to think about it, you'll discover a great deal of wisdom distilled in those seemingly prosaic mottos. For example, what I am saying throughout this book, although in rather great detail, boils down to "Keep it simple." Concentrate on your sobriety by taking care of yourself. Postpone major life changes, defuse negative emotions, eat healthfully, exercise regularly. In short, keep your life as simple and narrowly focused as possible.

You can't memorize this entire book, but you can condense the most important concepts into easily remembered phrases. When your life is on the verge of becoming unnecessarily complicated, you can remind yourself: Keep it simple.

The slogan acts as a trigger, helping you recall all the ways you've learned to simplify your life so that you can take the necessary steps to do so. The sayings you hear at self-help meetings are *not* mindless. The more you use them, the more you'll come to learn how wise and valuable they are.

The Twelve Steps and Sponsorship

Everyone loves to give advice. I should know—I do it for a living. Self-help members love to give advice, too. And when they talk about their sobriety, they should be heeded. When your sponsor or a long-standing fellow member gives you advice about your sobriety, pay close attention. In that area, these people *are* experts. But they are not experts on medical matters or nutrition. Your sobriety will not be served by embarking on bizarre diets, stuffing yourself with expensive vitamin pills, or throwing away all your medications and taking a solemn vow never to enter a pharmacy again, nor by any action that violates the chief principle of this book: moderation.

People in recovery have many reasons, including those I've mentioned above, for not joining a self-help group. Now I'd like to discuss the reasons they do join. First of all, self-help works.

Just look at the numbers. A randomly selected member of the AA population who's been sober less than one year has about a forty percent chance of remaining sober and active in the fellowship for another year. The likelihood rises to about eighty percent for a member with one to four years of sobriety, and ninety percent after five years. This is far better than you can do on your own.

Why do self-help groups work so well? To the newcomer they offer the benefit of the collective wisdom of those who have achieved sobriety over the years. Then, throughout your sobriety, they provide a nonjudgmental and supportive network of people you can turn to twenty-four hours a day. But most important, the groups don't limit their focus to maintaining abstinence. They promote the growth and development of a full, meaningful, and contented life. Participation in the self-help movement lifts the chemically dependent person out of the passive role of "patient" or "problem," and puts him or her into the active role of *doing* something about the addiction, *going* to meetings, *working* the program.

Self-help groups offer the fellowship and understanding of people who have already or are presently experiencing exactly what you're going through. Their specific circumstances may be entirely different from yours, but the process of recovery is the same. You can learn from, take heart from, and be inspired by the example set by others who have been there before, or who are going along with you. Your self-help group can also be your primary source of friendship and companionship. The meetings are a place where you can spend time safely, especially in your first months of recovery when you're trying to fill those non-working hours that you used to waste drinking or drugging.

But the program you learn in a self-help group offers more than example, friendship, and companionship. It ensures that you won't just sit around waiting for sobriety to happen to you. Instead, by working the steps, you create your own sobriety.

The Twelve Steps are as follows:

Step One We admitted that we were powerless over alcohol, that our lives had become unmanageable.

Step Two Came to believe that a power greater than ourselves could restore us to sanity.

Step Three Made a decision to turn our will and our lives over to the care of God as we understood him.

Step Four Made a searching and fearless moral inventory of ourselves.

Step Five Admitted to God, to ourselves and to another human being the exact nature of our wrongs.

Step Six Were entirely ready to have God remove these defects of character.

Step Seven Humbly asked Him to remove our shortcomings.

Step Eight Made a list of all persons we had harmed and became willing to make amends to them all.

Step Nine Made direct amends to such people wherever possible except where to do so would injure them or others.

Step Ten Continued to take personal inventory and when we were wrong promptly admitted it.

Step Eleven Sought through prayer and meditation to improve our conscious contact with God as we understood Him, praying only for knowledge of His will for us and the power to carry that out.

Step Twelve Having had a spiritual awakening as a result of these steps we tried to carry this message to alcoholics and to practice these principles in all our affairs.

The Twelve Steps are a process, a way of increasing self-awareness and at the same time relinquishing that preoccupation with the self which is so engulfing during an active addiction. Gradually, as you work the steps, your focus turns outward toward a power greater than yourself and toward others. This outward turning permits and nourishes an inner spiritual growth, growth that is impossible when you are concerned only with yourself and your substance of choice.

The paradox of the steps is that you have to give up control in order to be free. However, you cannot be truly free when you are full of shame, guilt, and self-hatred. Steps Four through Ten, which are repeated throughout sobriety in increasing depth, are practical guides to relieving yourself of these burdens. But enjoying the spiritual growth that comes from working the steps requires first accepting and then knowing yourself. Being able to say, and mean, "I admit I am powerless over alcohol," is the first step in this process.

And, finally, there is sponsorship. Some self-help members with decades of sobriety have never had a sponsor, even though they may have sponsored many other people. Although it's certainly possible to build a good life in sobriety without one, a sponsor can be helpful in countless ways and on innumerable occasions—when you first come into the program, when you're stuck and seem to be making no progress, when you have a crisis in your life, when you feel despondent, when you feel like using again, and when you want someone special with whom to celebrate your sobriety anniversaries.

Sponsoring relationships get started in many ways. Mel walked into his first Narcotics Anonymous meeting twenty-four hours after his brother-in-law had been shot and killed while sitting in a car with Mel's four-year-old nephew. Mel had been on the street for thirteen of his twenty-six years and had witnessed violence, and even death, on many occasions. But this time, it had a profound impact on him. He decided at that moment that he was going to change his life. He turned over his cocaine supply to a street buddy and told him he wouldn't be around any more. He packed his things and moved in with a married brother. Then he went to an NA meeting.

When the leader asked if there were any newcomers, Mel raised his hand and told his story. He said there was just one thing he wanted to do before he broke completely with the past. He was going to get the guy who murdered his brother-in-law. He knew who he was, and Mel was going to kill him. "That man made my sister a widow. Her two babies got no father now. On the street, the law's an eye for an eye. I'm going to get him."

After the meeting, several members surrounded Mel. "We're going to Jake's place to rap," one said. A huge man laid his hand on Mel's shoulder. "I'm Jake," he said. "And I'm your sponsor now." After two hours at Jake's place, Mel was convinced that going after the guy who murdered his brother-in-law was one of the worst ideas he had ever had.

When the rap session broke up, Jake gave Mel his phone number. "I go to work at seven. I want to hear from you tomorrow morning at six-thirty, and check in again at four, when I get home."

Mel made sure he made those calls the next day, and met Jake again that evening for another meeting. One year later, Jake is still Mel's sponsor. "That man saved my life," Mel told me. "There's no way I'm going to fire him."

Caroline, a twenty-three-year-old recovering alcoholic, had a harder time finding her first sponsor. In the first month of her sobriety, she went to many different meetings and heard many speakers until she picked two groups to attend regularly. Then, each time she thought she had identified a potential sponsor in one of these groups, doubt crept in. She hinted around to one woman, hoping she would volunteer, but she didn't. Instead, she kindly told Caroline that she was already sponsoring five people and that it was a heavy load. After that rejection, Caroline didn't approach anyone else.

She was four months sober and still without a sponsor when her father died suddenly. Returning from three days away at her family's house for the funeral, Caroline went straight to a meeting. She knew she needed to talk to someone. She needed to talk about her anger with her alcoholic father, her mixed feelings of sorrow and relief at his death, her insistence, over her brother's objections, that alcoholism be cited on his death certificate, and above all, her desire to get really drunk and obliterate it all.

Sitting next to her was Valerie, a woman she had spoken to a few times. Valerie was about Caroline's age and had two years of sobriety behind her. Caroline knew very little else about her, except that she seemed reasonably sensible and sensitive. During the coffee break, Caroline turned to her. "Will you be my sponsor?" she asked.

"I'd love to," Valerie responded. "Let's have coffee after the meeting."

A sponsor doesn't have to be perfect. He or she only has to be "good enough," or even "good enough for the time being," and your sponsor must always be of the same sex as you. Anyone who has more than two years of sobriety, common sense, and a balanced attitude can be helpful during your first ninety days of recovery. This person may be your beginning or interim sponsor, if you're not sure you want him or her to be your ultimate sponsor.

Once you've achieved ninety days of sobriety, you may want to choose someone else, or you may want to stick with your present sponsor. But if you do decide to look elsewhere, your standards should be more demanding than they were previously. Now you're looking for someone whose sobriety you admire. This isn't necessarily the funniest speaker, the person who always talks at meetings, or the one in your group with the longest sobriety. Nor must he or she be the most charming, the most popular, or the most brilliant. Your sponsor should be someone who's been able to use the tools of the program to achieve a stable, comfortable sobriety, whose method of solving problems and relating to others you'd like to emulate. This person should be one who is able to listen as well as talk, who can teach by experience and by example.

When you find someone who fits those criteria, approach him or her after a meeting and ask if he or she will be your sponsor. The person has the right to refuse, and you have the right to break off the sponsoring relationship if you feel it's not working well. A member can sponsor more than one person, and your involvement is private, that is, the other group members generally don't know who is sponsoring whom. If you're very shy, or are having trouble identifying a potential sponsor, you might ask another, more experienced member of the group for help. But ultimately, the choice and the responsibility for initiating the relationship rest with you.

With so many self-help organizations available, finding the right one can be confusing. You may find yourself saying, "I've been using cocaine and alcohol. Should I try CA or AA?" or "I was hooked on tranquilizers. Is there the right type of group in my area?" Some people find it helpful to attend more than one group if they have been cross-addicted. Your search can be simplified by consulting a national clearinghouse that keeps a register of self-help groups. You will find its name and address in Appendix C.

Some recovering people can sense the potential benefits of self-help from their very first meeting. They feel immediately comfortable with the format, the intentions, and the philosophy of self-help, the group, and its members. Others come to self-help reluctantly. They feel ill at ease, either because they're shy, or they don't believe in God, or because they're concerned about their privacy. Some find a home group on the first try, others have to shop around until they find the right meeting. But no matter how you come to self-help—whether eagerly or with reservations—come, continue to come, and find yourself a sponsor so that you, too, can enjoy the many advantages offered by this marvelous boon to sobriety.

Chapter Eight
Banking the Home Fires

Rebuilding Your Family Life

No matter how strong your desire to do so, you cannot single-handedly rebuild your family life. Family healing is a family process, which you, your spouse, your children, your parents, and your siblings must undertake together. Just as you are learning new ways of being and behaving in sobriety, so your family members will have to redefine their roles and behavior patterns in the new sober family as well.

Thus far in the book I have largely spoken directly to you, the recovering person, but on this topic I want to address the recovering family as a whole. For the person in the first year of sobriety, this chapter presents an opportunity to gain a better understanding of your family members' needs and wishes for the family in sobriety. It also offers a chance for you to think about how your new sober life affects your family's recovery, and how in turn their recovery affects yours.

Those with a longer sobriety may already have begun the process of building better communication within the family, while others may still be struggling in this area. But whatever the state of your family relations, the principles presented in this chapter are intended not only to help your family heal but to keep it operating as a strong, healthy unit throughout sobriety.

First and foremost, all family members must understand three very important facts about the disease of addiction:

1. You didn't *cause* it.

2. You can't *control* it.

3. You can't *cure* it.

In sobriety, the recovering person is in remission from his or her illness—but the illness exists all the same. He or she must learn to live with it, and so must you. You can accomplish this goal only if you learn to detach yourself from the illness itself, but not at the expense of withdrawing your love and support from your newly sober family member.

You may be among the many people who initially see this principle as contradictory. How can you detach yourself from an illness without simultaneously detaching yourself from the person who has the illness? This is not as difficult as it may seem at first. For example, there are probably very few of you who haven't phoned the employer of your spouse/lover/parent/sibling/child the morning after a drinking or drugging binge to say that he or she was ill and wouldn't be coming in to work. You made that phone call because you desperately wanted to help and be supportive. But were you really being helpful?

No. Even though you honestly and sincerely believed you were acting out of concern and compassion, the reality is that you were supporting the disease and not the person you care about. By picking up the phone, you allowed the user to escape the consequences of his or her using. You made allowances for the *disease*. Such behavior benefits the addiction, but not the addict.

In order to help the person you love, you have to let him or her feel the consequences of the dependency. The user has to be:

• the one to call in sick,

• the one to have the car repaired after trying to drive it into the garage without first opening the door,

• the one to make the phone call to the boss,

• the one to arrange to repay the money stolen for drugs.

Only if the user is forced to do his or her own dirty work can the consequences of using begin to filter into that besotted brain.

Now that your family member is in recovery, and the disease is in remission, you may think that you're past the point of helping the addiction. But that's not necessarily the case. You may continue to nurture the disease:

• by submitting to your perfectly natural fears that something you say or do will drive the recovering person to drink or use again,

• by constantly catering to and treating that person as if he or she were an invalid,

• by being reluctant to discuss what's bothering you about his or her relationship to the family,

• by not participating in the difficult but gratifying work of repairing the family structure,

• by neglecting your own needs.

Lena, a recovering alcoholic, dropped everything when her brother Justin called to say he thought he also had a problem with alcohol. She had long suspected as much, and she was eager to do whatever she could to help him through his first two weeks of sobriety. She flew to Chicago, found an outpatient treatment program, and accompanied him to the intake interview. She took him to AA meetings, made sure he met people, took down their telephone numbers. She scoured the house for hidden liquor bottles and chucked out Justin's hidden stash. She drove him to work in the morning, picked him up in the evening, telephoned him during the day, and planned his free time.

He was barely out of her sight, except to go to the toilet, and she checked the bathroom twice a day or more to make sure he hadn't hidden any booze there. Then she decided it was safe for her to go home. "You have a good routine established now," she told Justin. "You should be fine."

As soon as her plane landed in New York, Lena phoned her brother. And the moment she heard his voice, she knew he'd had a slip. Her next call was to her sponsor. "Why? Why?" she questioned her. "I had everything so well mapped out—treatment, meetings, new routines, the works."

"Sure," said her sponsor. "You had a wonderful plan to keep *you* sober. Justin was only along for the ride. As soon as the car stopped, he got out. You're badly in need of Al-Anon, my friend."

Even Lena, who had more than a passing acquaintance with alcoholism, had put all her attention on the disease, rather than on her brother. Certainly, it may not always be easy to avoid this pitfall and switch your focus, but you can do it. The first step is to acknowledge the tremendous tension that exists within the family during early sobriety. All families experience this tension, and when you think about it, it makes perfect sense. On the one hand, everyone in the family has a great desire to see the recovering person well and abstinent. On the other hand, all of you are also harboring an equally great fear that the person will suffer a relapse.

Moreover, old resentments may still be simmering. Painful memories of angry scenes, disappointments, embarrassments, and humiliations can surface and cause friction. In short, everyone's jittery, wondering how best to behave. No one is sure of what to say or do, or what *not* to say or do. Family members worry about every little thing: "If I yell at her because she came home late for dinner, will that make her want to use?" "If I tell him that he can't wear brown shoes with a black suit, will his self-esteem sink so low he'll reach for the bottle?" "If I ask Dad to raise my allowance will he get so angry that he'll wind up in a bar?" "If I ask Mom to help me shorten this skirt, will she have a tantrum and pop a pill to feel better?"

While you're caught up in trying to figure out how to behave around the newly sober family member, he or she is struggling with other issues, the most basic of which is trust. The recovering person has made a tremendous effort to get sober, and in his or her mind that alone should be enough to earn your trust. But based on past experience, how and why should you put your faith in him or her? This will change, however, as both you and your loved one grow in sobriety.

Angela, whom you met in Chapter 3, couldn't stop checking all her husband's favorite hiding places, even after he had been sober four months. But several months after that, when Vito was still sober, and Angela had come to understand more about the disease and its effect on their family, she was able to give up her searches.

Although understandable, the desire to be trusted is an unreasonable expectation for a recovering person in early sobriety. Family members quite naturally need to proceed with caution and reserve judgment. But their wariness can make the recovering person feel angry, humiliated, and unloved. Here again, you have to distinguish between the disease and the individual. The recovering person is working very hard to stay sober, and that effort deserves your trust. It's the sneaky, unpredictable disease that's fooled you—and the recovering person—so many times in the past that doesn't merit your faith.

I myself have learned not to trust the disease. I can't tell you how many times patients have looked me straight in the eye and lied to me when they said, "I'm not using." I'm often asked to meet with patients because other people—counselors, family members, or employers—have had reason to suspect they were using again. These individuals will sit in my office and so convincingly assure me they're sober and clean that I'm persuaded. Until I get the results of their urine tests, which don't lie. As a result, I've learned always to question, always to remember the power of the disease of addiction—because I can be fooled. Families can be fooled. Sometimes the recovering person can even fool him or herself.

How Family Members Recover Together

So here all of you are—the recovering person and family members—trying to come to terms with a powerful, unstable illness. The family members are walking on eggs, unsure how to behave. The recovering person, still on shaky ground physically and emotionally, wants to be trusted, wants the hurt to be mended as quickly as possible.

With all these conflicting needs, how do you begin to establish a basis for your new sober lives together? How does the family heal itself at the same time the recovering person is healing him- or herself? Here are a few suggestions for what the family as a whole can do to foster the process of recovery.

Open the Lines of Communication

Talk to each other. That may sound simple, but all too often people are afraid to communicate with one another. They don't want to admit that the family has problems. There's a great temptation to say, "Hurrah! Mom/Dad/Sis/Grandpa is sober now! The rest will work itself out." Unfortunately, that's simply not true. But the situation can be improved enormously if everyone is aware of what's going on, knows what the others are thinking about and what they fear.

Early in recovery, family members must get into the habit of having frank, open discussions during which everyone can air his or her fears, anxieties, worries, and concerns. Knowledge and awareness are powerful tools. When you're aware of what other family members are thinking and feeling, you can't project your own feelings onto them, nor can you concoct fantasies about what's going on beneath the surface, to the point where the situation seems hopeless or impossible to solve. When each of you has the opportunity to freely acknowledge problems, the stage is set for open communication throughout recovery. If, however, everyone glosses over the issues and tries to pretend that they no longer exist now that the recovering person is sober, then the stage is set for irritations, misunderstandings, evasions, and eventually some sort of explosion.

Leo's wife Joan had always been famous for saying what was on her mind. She had never minced words, and she was not about to start doing so when Leo became sober. "I worry that I'll scream at you one day for some damn stupid thing, and you'll go out and get drunk and blame me," she told Leo. "I can just hear you—'If I hadn't married that crazy witch, I'd be sober today.' You'll say it, *and* you'll believe it. That's why I want to get things straight now. I'll try to control my temper and not blurt out the first words that pop into my head. But you have to know that if you pick up a drink, it's your choice. If I'm screaming and ranting and raving, you can leave the house and go to a meeting or the gym. Or you can choose to go to a bar. It's up to you. What you *can't* do is blame me."

But very few people are as outspoken as Joan. The day Glenn

came home from the treatment center, everyone sat awkwardly silent at dinner. His wife Meg and their three kids—Shari, fifteen, Greg, ten, and Phyllis, seven—wanted to make his homecoming as normal as possible, but they were all tongue-tied. Finally, avoiding Glenn's eyes and addressing herself to her mother, Shari spoke up. "This reminds me of when Grandpa died and Daddy came to the funeral parlor drunk. We all sat around, pretending it wasn't happening. That felt so weird, and so does tonight. And it's kind of scaring me."

"Yeah, me, too," Greg chimed in softly, staring down at his plate.

Then Phyllis spoke up. "I heard Jill's mom say alcoholics never get better. They're sick all their lives, and anything can make them drunk again. Like if I don't eat my cabbage. Is that true, Mom?"

At this point, Meg had a critical choice. She could have shut down the conversation with a comment like, "That's nonsense," or "Finish your dinner and get started on your homework." Or she could have ignored their questions and started clearing the table. But Meg was courageous. "I feel scared, too," she admitted. "We're all feeling the tension. I think we're all worried that if we say the wrong thing, Daddy will start drinking again. So instead we're saying nothing. Jill's mother is only partly right about alcoholism. How would you explain it, Glenn?"

Glenn was having his own troubles during this exchange. He was feeling ashamed that his family thought he was so weak that he would rush off and take a drink at the slightest provocation. He was also angry that they didn't respect or trust him. His impulse was to get up and stalk out of the room. He thought to himself, *If that's all they think of me, what's the point in sticking around?*

But he knew that walking out would only leave everyone more worried and more determined never to speak up again. So instead, he swallowed his pride and said, "I am an alcoholic. I never intended to be one, and it didn't happen because I'm bad or weak or selfish. I know my drinking has hurt you all a lot, and I'm sorry. Very sorry. I also want you to know that because I'm an alcoholic, I can never again drink anything that has alcohol in it. But as long as I steer clear of it, I'll be perfectly normal. I need your help to stay sober, but if I do drink again, it'll be my responsibility and not yours. You can't make me drunk, and you can't make me sober. Only I can do that." He smiled at Phyllis. "No matter how much cabbage you eat."

Glenn and his family were fortunate in their ability to set aside their feelings of discomfort and keep the lines of communication open. But what about a family that hasn't had open discussions in years, if ever? Open communication is a skill, one that your family can develop if you observe a few simple rules.

1. Set up a regularly scheduled family conference. That way nobody is surprised or inconvenienced by the meeting, and everyone has time to consider what issues he or she wants to raise.

2. Give everyone in the family the opportunity to present his or her views. Some families find it helpful to have an "equal time" policy. They allot each person a certain amount of time to speak (say, five minutes), and keep track with a kitchen timer. During that period no one is allowed to speak except the person who has the floor. The others can respond only when the speaker is finished, or the specified time has elapsed. This rule also extends to nonverbal responses, such as sighing, making faces, or fidgeting.

The point is to provide an open, nonjudgmental forum where all family members can feel free to be candid and say what's really on their minds, no matter how painful or muddled, without fear of being interrupted or ridiculed. This is especially true for children, who are often frightened to speak up.

3. Be specific. When it's your turn to talk, try not to make general statements about another person's behavior. Cite particular incidents, and describe as accurately and honestly as possible how you felt about those events.

Angela, for example, described to her group a family meeting where she'd said to Vito, "When I walked into the garage the other day and saw you rummaging round under the tool cabinet, I got so angry. It brought back all those other times you had 'quit' and still had bottles hidden all over the house."

"After that look you gave me, I felt about two inches tall, as if I should have something to be ashamed of. And all I was doing was looking for a screw I'd dropped," was Vito's reply.

After this exchange, Angela and Vito were able to focus in on the issue of trust. But let's imagine what might have happened if the conversation had instead taken this turn:

"Vito, you're always sneaking around. You're driving me crazy."

"Dammit, Angela, you're always watching me! You make me feel like a criminal in my own house."

Besides being general and ambiguous, these statements are also inflammatory, which brings us to my next point.

4. Discuss feelings and issues without using labels or being accusatory. "You made me feel . . . You never . . . You always . . . You're selfish/lazy/stupid/crazy. . . ." Such charges and name-calling are like a matador's red cape to a bull. They encourage people to charge, attack, or react defensively. All of which gets you nowhere.

5. Listen attentively to what other people have to say. When someone else is speaking, put aside your own thoughts and feelings for the moment, and concentrate on taking in what the speaker is telling you. You'll miss a great deal if you're involved in planning your defense or rebuttal.

6. Talk about what's right as well as what's wrong. This is an obvious but often neglected point. If someone behaved in a way that pleased you or made you happy, say so. If you all agreed upon a plan at the last meeting and it worked well, praise it. The positive steps you're taking to rebuild the family also need reinforcement.

7. Keep a sense of humor and proportion. Yes, what you're doing at these meetings is serious business that requires everyone's full attention and best efforts. But you don't need to put on a grave face or become desperately worried if you can't immediately find a solution to a given problem. Of course, depending on what comes up, some of the meetings simply won't be pleasant or a great deal of fun. Often you'll be discussing painful issues and incidents. But the occasional joke or light hearted comment, when appropriate, will go a long way toward making family meetings not only useful, but enjoyable as well.

Develop a Plan of Action That Addresses Each Concern

Whatever problems your family is having, they won't disappear unless you take steps to deal with them. This is true both of major issues such as getting the family finances in order, or minor ones, like whether you order in Chinese food or pizza after the family meeting. Minor concerns can be easily resolved: You can flip a coin to decide what's on the menu. But no matter how trivial, these questions must be taken care of. You don't have to devote a lot of time or energy to them, but if left untended, they tend to pile up into a logjam that can lead to real trouble.

Planning solutions for major problems requires careful thought and discussion. You may have to consider and talk through any number of alternatives until you find the formula that promises both to solve the problem and address the needs of all the people involved.

Joyce, for example, was a nonaddicted fourteen-year-old member of Alateen who spoke up at a meeting I sat in on. She told her group that even though her mother, Maureen, had been sober for three months, she was still worried about inviting her friends home after school. Would her mom be her usual nice self, or that witchy person who had frightened Joyce so often in the past? Would having a bunch of girls in the house give Mom a headache and make her feel like taking a tranquilizer or a drink?

When Joyce put it to her directly at a family meeting, Maureen admitted that she didn't feel strong enough yet to cope with so much noise in the house. "Why don't you just invite one of your friends home?" she suggested instead. "You could have a snack and visit in your bedroom, as long as you don't get too crazy or play loud music."

Joyce didn't feel comfortable with the idea of having to be on her best behavior, so she told her parents she would rather wait until her mother was feeling better. Then her father came up with another suggestion—that they think about planning some family activities outside the house and have some of Joyce's friends join them. Perhaps in a few weeks, when Maureen thought she was up to it, they could all go roller skating one evening, or take a drive in the country and have lunch at a restaurant some Sunday. That way, Maureen wouldn't have to feel the pressure of providing supervision, snacks, or entertainment for the girls at home.

Joyce was pleased with how she and her parents had worked out a compromise. She appreciated that her mother had been honest with her, rather than blithely saying, "Sure, I'll be okay. You can bring anyone home anytime." On the other hand, Joyce knew she would feel self-conscious about tiptoeing around the house, worrying about disturbing Mom, so she didn't agree to that alternative simply to make her mother feel good. Instead of adopting the first solution that came to mind, she and her parents took the time to find a plan that worked for all of them.

You'll need to be patient, persistent, and willing to participate in a lot of honest give-and-take in order to come up with a viable plan of action. Sometimes the first solution will turn out to be the best. Sometimes the plan you have adopted won't work, so it's back to the drawing board. Other times, it becomes clear that the best solution is to postpone taking any action.

Don't confuse postponement with a refusal to recognize a problem. On the contrary, you're making an active decision that though you're not yet strong enough or don't yet have the resources to tackle a serious issue, you're aware that in three weeks (or three months) your situation will have changed. However, it's important to put a time limit on deferring decisions. If you mark a date on your calender when the problem is to come up again for discussion, you can't "forget" about it. And whatever plan you finally hit upon, carry it out thoroughly until the concern is resolved to everyone's satisfaction.

Maintain Realistic Expectations

Newly sober people have to focus on themselves. This may sound terribly selfish, but your recovery is likely to be unsuccessful unless you put it first, above everything else. Just as people who are convalescing from a serious illness or operation find it hard to be actively interested in anyone's concerns but their own, so people in early recovery have similarly limited emotional resources and energy. And then there's the question of how a recovering person can find the time to carry out all the activities we've been talking about—attending self-help meetings, exercising, eating sensibly, getting enough sleep, relaxing—if he or she is spending a considerable part of the day caring for other people's needs.

Families often become quite upset when they have to face the fact that the recovering person has a very full plate. The reality of early recovery is often at odds with how family members had imagined it would be. Dad is no longer drinking, but he's still not around much because he's out four nights a week at his self-help meetings. He comes home from the office, grabs a quick bite, kisses everyone goodbye, and doesn't get home again until the kids are asleep. Mom has thrown away her pills, but she still isn't cooking breakfast for the kids before they leave for school. It used to be that she lay in bed all morning; now she's up early and working out at the gym three mornings a week, plus she spends Saturday mornings at her painting class.

"First things first," as they say in self-help. Nothing can change the need the recovering person has to take care of him- or herself first. But families who know what to expect and what *not to* expect may have an easier time of it. You've waited and hoped a long while to have your loved one sober and back among you. Now you have to be patient, with the understanding that he or she will be accessible and available at some future point. When Lila's recovery is more stable, she'll happily come and cheer her daughter Amy at her soccer games. Grant will enjoy dinner out and a movie with his wife when he's feeling more secure in his sobriety. But for now, they have to concentrate on what's most important: staying sober one day at a time.

Sometimes people go to extremes, throwing off this crucial balance between self and family. At one end of the spectrum are those individuals who try to compensate for lost family time by spending every free moment caring for or catering to the needs of the family. At the other end are the recovering people who don't recognize that being a part of the family is also an important part of recovery. And so they spend every spare minute at self-help meetings or engaged in activities apart from the family. What often results is a build-up of tension and anger within the family, which the recovering person can ill afford.

To steer a safe course between these two extremes, Glenn and his family worked out the following schedule: On Monday, Wednesday, Thursday, and Sunday, Glenn attended AA meetings. During the week he went straight to AA from the office, which meant he didn't get home until after the kids had already eaten. On Mondays, his wife Meg and the kids got together for dinner with Lois, a single parent with two children. The other two nights, Meg kept a plate of food warm for Glenn.

Tuesday nights were reserved for the weekly family discussion. On Friday evenings, Glenn and Meg went out without the kids, to a movie, concert, or to dinner. Saturday nights they spent as a family, doing something special and relaxing, even if it was simply watching a video and eating popcorn.

With such a schedule, Glenn had time to do whatever he needed to maintain his sobriety without neglecting his family and the work it had to do as a unit. His wife and children knew what to expect in terms of his availability. This gave them the opportunity to plan their own activities—going to the school basketball game, or helping out with the youngest daughter's brownie troop on Saturday morning, giving Glenn a couple of hours at home alone to read, meditate, or nap.

By setting up realistic expectations, Glenn and his family were able to help one another build a new family life in sobriety. And by organizing their own interests independently of Glenn, Meg and the children made a firm step forward in their own recovery.

Make Contracts

Creating a contract may sound like a cold, unfeeling way to interact with members of your own family, but that's not true. It's a smart move, just as it's smart to have a written contract when you enter into a business arrangement, even with family or friends.

Informal business arrangements often fail, resulting in bitterness, family feuds, or ruptured friendships. In the beginning, the partners trust one another, but then the business takes unforeseen twists and turns. Commitments vary and sometimes waver. Unexpected demands may be made on one or another partner's time and energy, so the business falls apart, sometimes with devastating financial and personal consequences.

Similarly, the disease of addiction can take on a life of its own. And informal agreements usually don't work in this case either. For that reason, I tell patients that they must negotiate contracts, especially in those areas that may give them particular problems. I make a lot of contracts with my patients, mostly of the smile and handshake variety. But sometimes we sign written contracts, usually no longer than one page, in which the consequences for specific behaviors are clearly spelled out. These agreements help both of us clarify our thoughts and set our priorities.

Marvin, for instance, was an alcoholic who was prone to ignoring the warning signs of a relapse. He'd had enough slips in the past to know that he was headed for trouble when he started finding excuses not to go to AA meetings. He sometimes had legitimate reasons—an unexpected business trip or the time his wife Julie had to go into the hospital for minor knee surgery, for example. But his normal routine was to attend three meetings a week, so when a month went by and he'd gone to only four meetings, the alarm bells should have gone off.

He had also noticed that when things weren't going well for him, he tended to become withdrawn and isolated, to avoid his family and not call his AA sponsor. He would spend a lot of time in front of the TV, and get very aggravated if anyone dared disturb him. He would become snappish and irritable if one of his family members asked him a question or made a request.

Marvin didn't recognize the familiar danger signals when he was in the midst of an escalating mood. But Julie could see what was happening, even if she couldn't do anything about it. Because Marvin reacted badly to her observations and suggestions, she became terrified of making the situation worse and driving him to drink.

Marvin and Julie solved the problem by drawing up a written contract. They agreed that if Marvin attended fewer than four AA meetings in any two-week period, Julie was authorized to phone his sponsor, something she ordinarily wouldn't do because she didn't want to interfere with Marvin's AA relationships. They also decided that if Marvin spent three nights in a row in front of the TV, he would go out with Julie and their friends the following night. Because of the contract, Marvin could profess neither surprise nor resentment when Julie called his sponsor or when she informed him what time he was expected at the restaurant for dinner.

If the concept of a contract still seems forced or even ruthless, consider the alternatives. Let's say Marvin is headed for a relapse and Julie sees it coming. She gets anxious and worried because she doesn't know what to do. She tries to talk to him, but he gets defensive and lashes out at her. By now Julie has forgotten the lessons she's learned about how she's helped Marvin's addiction in the past. She's flooded with the familiar feeling that she's responsible for Marvin's behavior. She resorts to her old, always counterproductive tactics of pushing, cajoling, and nagging. Marvin starts to feel as he used to before he got sober, that the control of his addiction rests with Julie. He increasingly allows his negative mood to escalate and moves closer and closer to a relapse.

Instead, once the contract was in force, Julie could telephone Marvin's sponsor as soon as he failed to reach his agreed-upon quota of AA meetings. She was able to uphold her end of the agreement without having to nag or feel responsible for his sobriety. How Marvin responded to a call from his sponsor was his business, because he was in charge of his own sobriety. In addition, the contract offered them a simple way to break his pattern of isolation.

Marvin and Julie have used the contract twice in the eight months since they put it into effect, and Marvin hasn't had a relapse in that time. To help you draw up your own contract, here are some examples.

Simon, seventy-five, is a widower living on a modest pension who had fallen into the habit of spending all his money on booze. Then he would rely on his daughter Marie to pay his rent and other expenses. While he was in the hospital recovering from a hip fracture he suffered while drunk, his whole family confronted him about his alcoholism. He also had a visit by an AA member who convinced him to attend meetings. But when his next pension check arrived, he started drinking again. Therefore, Simon and Marie arrived at the following contract:

I, Simon, agree that Marie will handle my finances until I have been sober for six months.

I agree to enter the Billings Rehabilitation Center if I start drinking again.

I understand that if I appear at Marie's house after drinking any alcohol whatsoever, I will be taken home immediately, and an appointment will be made for me to enter Billings as soon as a bed is available.

Tracy is eighteen. Her parents had become increasingly worried about her erratic moods and behavior, and about her consistent violation of her generous 2:00 A.M. weekend curfew. When they realized that two hundred dollars was missing from the top drawer of her father's bureau, they finally confronted her. Tracy admitted that she had taken the money to buy cocaine, which she'd been using regularly with the group of friends she saw every weekend. She agreed to enter a rehabilitation center, where she spent a month being treated as an inpatient. When she was about to be discharged, she and her parents made this contract:

I, Tracy, agree that I will have no further contact of any sort with Melissa, Rachel, Kate, Alex, Jason, or Matthew.

I agree to abide by a midnight curfew on all nights for the next six months.

I agree to follow the plan set out by my counselor, Ms. Simpson.

I agree that if I do not abide by any part of this contract, I will go to a halfway house.

Jean has abused a headache medication called Fiorinal as well as alcohol. In spite of having twice achieved several months of sobriety, she has just had her third relapse. She is a compulsive worker who never refuses an assignment and often stays late at the office. While her husband, Richard, understands and respects her dedication, he sees that overwork and tension contribute to the frequent headaches that trigger Jean's relapses. He's decided that he can't suffer through another of Jean's drinking bouts. Because he also knows that his own anxiety and nagging have frequently made matters worse, he and Jean have arrived at this agreement:

I, Jean, agree that for the next six months I will arrange to leave work at 5:30 P.M.

I agree that I will not bring work home at night or on weekends.

I agree that if I continue to have severe headaches, I will ask Dr. Armitage to refer me to a specialist.

I agree to tell Dr. Armitage that I have been abusing Fiorinal.

I agree to attend three AA meetings a week.

I, Richard, understand that Jean's addiction is not within my control.

I agree to attend Al-Anon once a week.

Decide "Who's on First"

When sobriety hits, the family roles and agreements that were operating before the recovering person became chemically dependent no longer apply. Nobody knows who's on what base because the disease of addiction has totally disrupted the balance of power within the family. This balance must now be redefined, which is often a very tricky process. It requires frank discussions and a willingness on the part of all family members to make a conscientious effort to understand one another's needs and to compromise in order to reach effective solutions. Issues of power often raise strong emotions, so the family should be prepared to be especially thorough, tolerant, and restrained when such matters are being negotiated.

What happened to Jed and Marjorie is typical of many families in which there's been substance abuse. When they got married, Jed and Marjorie decided that since Marjorie was much more organized and knowledgeable about money (she was an accountant), she would handle the family finances. She continued to do so after she left her job to raise a family. But the stress of caring for three babies—a toddler and infant twins—was greater than she had expected. And because she was also concerned about how much weight she had gained during her pregnancies, Marjorie began to take tranquilizers and diet pills. Eventually she became dependent on them.

As her disease progressed, Jed noticed that they were getting frequent delinquency notices along with their bills. But that was Marjorie's department, and easygoing Jed was reluctant to butt in. Then one freezing cold winter day, Jed came home to find the kids wrapped in blankets and shivering because the heat had been turned off.

Marjorie was too out of it to answer his questions, so Jed called the gas company. A customer service representative informed him that their bill hadn't been paid in four months, even though they had sent two warnings and a final notice to disconnect. When Jed confronted Marjorie, she denied that she'd ever received any such notices. She became angry and defensive. How dare the gas company cut off their service? Hadn't she always paid her bills? Couldn't a person make one little mistake?

His eyes opened by this incident, Jed took a close look at the family finances. When he unearthed a whopping bill for delinquent taxes, he reluctantly realized that he had to take over the responsibility. At first he felt incompetent at the task, but his confidence grew until he began actually to enjoy being in control of the family budget. In the meantime, Marjorie's addiction got worse until she finally entered an outpatient treatment program and joined Drugs Anonymous. After she had been clean for one month, she announced she was ready to take on her old job of money manager. Jed flatly refused.

Jed and Marjorie recognized that they had a choice in terms of how they could have resolved their power struggle. They could have slugged it out to see who was stronger. To justify his right to hold on to the family purse strings, Jed could have hit below the belt by pointing out to Marjorie everything she had left undone when she was using. Marjorie could have made her control of the finances a critical sign of Jed's trust in her recovery. She could have subtly threatened to start using again if he didn't relinquish the job to her. The tug-of-war could have gone on indefinitely and become a serious stumbling block to emotionally reuniting the family.

Fortunately, they chose instead to take the other path: a frank discussion that resulted in a plan that was feasible and acceptable to both of them. Jed voiced his concern about letting Marjorie handle the money so early in her recovery. He wasn't so much afraid that she would make mistakes or neglect her responsibilities, but that the sheer amount of work would be too much for her. After all, she had her DA meetings, appointments with her counselor, and her exercise class, not to mention taking care of the kids. How would she find the time to pay the bills and budget the money? And what if she didn't like the way Jed had reorganized the record-keeping?

Jed also reminded Marjorie that stress was one of the reasons she had turned to drugs. Now he felt they should do everything possible to minimize the stress in her life. Marjorie appreciated Jed's concern, but she strongly felt that taking over the finances would help her regain some measure of self-esteem. She was feeling rotten about her past errors and wanted to prove she could once again be a competent, contributing member of the family.

Eventually they arrived at the following compromise: Jed would continue to handle the finances until Marjorie had been abstinent for six months. They wrote up a contract to that effect and marked the date for renegotiation on the kitchen calendar.

Much had changed by the time six months had passed. Marjorie and Jed were able to consider solutions that had seemed out of reach at an earlier stage of Marjorie's recovery. Now she was reluctant to take up the full burden of handling all the money matters. She had found other projects and activities she would rather do. For Jed, meanwhile, the task had become tedious. Although he enjoyed the power, all that responsibility was too much for him.

They resolved the matter by deciding to divvy up the work. Marjorie would pay the bills and prepare the tax returns. Jed would do the banking and check the monthly bank statement. They agreed on a recordkeeping system that was easy for Jed to follow, yet allowed Marjorie to find the information she needed for the tax returns. They also agreed to reevaluate the plan again in another six months.

Of course, husbands and wives aren't the only family members for whom power is an issue. Children also need to understand where they fit within their newly sober family. Take Brian, for example. While his father, Dennis, was out doing cocaine and drinking, Brian, sixteen, learned to take care of his mother and sister. It was Brian who locked up the house at night, who mowed the lawn, who accompanied his mother, Karen, to her doctor's appointments for her severe gastric problems. And it was Brian who helped eleven-year-old Debbie with her homework, who often went to the grocery store, who did the cooking when his parents were fighting and he and Debbie were left without dinner.

But once Dennis became sober, he wanted to be the one to take Karen to the doctor, to help Debbie with her math problems, to cook dinner on the night Karen attended her Al-Anon meeting. Suddenly Brian felt dispossessed, and he began to act out his anger and resentment.

His parents couldn't understand his reaction. What could be better for Brian than Dennis's sobriety? Now that he had been relieved of the responsibilities that shouldn't have been his in the first place, he could have fun with his pals, go out on dates, do all the things that sixteen-year-old boys normally did.

But Brian didn't have any close pals, and he was far from even dreaming of dating. He had been so busy taking care of his family that he hadn't had much time for socializing. A naturally shy child, he had become an even shyer adolescent. He didn't know what to do with his newfound spare time. To his parent's bewilderment, now that Dennis was sober and Karen was happy, Brian was extremely sullen.

I explained to Dennis and Karen that Brian couldn't be expected to change overnight. He needed their help in making the difficult transition from father/perfect son to typical teenager. Their first step was to acknowledge how much he had done for them in the past. Then they had to talk about what Brian's role would be now that his father was sober, and his mother and Debbie no longer needed to rely on him as heavily. What did he want to continue to do for his family? Did he really like taking care of the yard or the car? Would he like to be in charge of dinner once a week?

By addressing these questions, Brian and his family were able to redefine his role so that there was a better balance between his family responsibilities and his need to have a life outside the family. His parents also recognized that he needed some help creating that outside life and becoming reintegrated with his peer group. It had been quite a while since he'd had the time to participate in extracurricular activities, to hang out with the guys. Dennis and Karen suggested that he might be able to meet other kids his age at Alateen meetings, or that perhaps he could join a club at school, try out for the swim team, or go to the next church dance, for example.

I also told Brian's parents that with regular family discussions and a rebuilt family structure, Brian might be able to accept his new role and begin to establish a life for himself independent of his family. And it was possible that he might need some counseling to help him understand the past, mourn the loss of his childhood, and adjust to the changes in his family. In either case, the place for him to begin dealing with his problems was within the family, in the context of honest and open conversations about his feelings and concerns.

Planning a Family Recovery Program

Just as every recovering person has a program for recovery, so should every recovering family. And just as the self-help group is the backbone of many individual recovery programs, so it can be the mainstay of family recovery, as well. Al-Anon, Coke-Anon, and Nar-Anon are groups for the adult family members of recovering people. Alateen is for kids between the ages of thirteen and eighteen, and Alatot is for children younger than thirteen.

With the help of these groups, family members can gain an in-depth understanding of the disease of addiction. They can learn how to live their lives without focusing twenty-four hours a day on the recovering person. And they can have the support of a group of people who understand because they have been through the same experiences themselves. Attending self-help meetings can also end the isolation so many families feel—the isolation that makes it impossible for them to talk about what's happening at home, and that frequently causes them to misjudge what they should do for themselves and the person in recovery.

Marilyn was devastated when her son Adam arrived home from college one day, disheveled and barely coherent because he had been speedballing cocaine and heroin. He had flunked out of school, leaving behind a pile of debts that Marilyn couldn't afford to pay. A divorced working mother, Marilyn received only erratic support from Adam's father. Fortunately, her company health insurance covered most of the cost of the inpatient treatment program that Adam agreed to enter. What Marilyn couldn't cope with as easily were her feelings of turmoil and guilt about why Adam had become an addict.

Marilyn had never known anyone whose child was addicted to heroin, a drug she had always associated with the worst kind of poverty. While there hadn't been much money to spare when Adam was growing up, she had been able to afford a two-bedroom apartment in a good neighborhood, and Adam had done well in school. But now she was ashamed and discouraged. She was a failure as a mother, and she felt she had nowhere to turn. What could she say to her sister, whose family was intact and whose kids had all done well in college? Which of her friends would understand what she was going through?

Although the few people she forced herself to confide in reacted sympathetically, Marilyn avoided them. Depressed and with barely enough energy to get to work every day, she dropped out of her choral group and stopped participating in the adult literacy program in which she was a volunteer tutor.

However, she did manage to drag herself to the family program at Adam's treatment center, where she learned a lot about addiction. And she began to attend Nar-Anon meetings on a regular basis. "It's been wonderful," she told me. "The people there are mostly parents like me. I'm *not* the only mother who's going through this kind of nightmare, and it helps just to know that. We can identify with one another, and I don't feel so ignorant or hopeless anymore."

Nar-Anon also helped after Adam got out of the treatment center and came to live at home for a while, and then later, when he returned to college. And once Marilyn had gotten over the initial shock and disruption of Adam's addiction, her sponsor was able to convince her to resume her after-work activities that she enjoyed so much.

Some of you may have a hard time joining a family self-help group because you can't find a meeting that's close to where you live or work. Or you may be uncomfortable with the idea of airing your most private, painful feelings in front of a group of people you don't know. You may also have some of the same fears about family self-help groups that recovering people have: that the meetings are grim and forbidding, that they're attended by people very different from yourself, that you'll be forced to adopt a system of beliefs that's contrary to your own. If any of these concerns match your own (or if you simply want to read more about the value of self-help groups), I suggest you refer back to Chapter 7, which should allay your fears.

But if you can't join a self-help group, you must still plan a family recovery program. For any family, the first step is to learn as much as possible about the disease of addiction and about the family's involvement in the disease. There is a large and growing body of literature that addresses this subject. Any of the books listed in Appendix A under the heading "The Recovering Family" will help you learn more about what happens to families when someone becomes chemically dependent. You can read about how others feel about what's happened to them, how they've behaved as a consequence of living with a substance abuser, and what they've done to get themselves well. An understanding of the disease and how it affects family life will help you recognize how the addiction has affected your own family. It will also bring you insight and the knowledge that you're not alone.

At the Smithers Center I see family members whose loved ones are in all stages of recovery, as well as those seeking information about what they can do to get a chemically dependent person into treatment. I see mothers, fathers, sisters, and brothers who are depressed and despairing, whose lives are troubled and tense. They want to know how to cope with the recovering person's mood swings, what to do about getting that person to find a self-help sponsor, what to do about the stressful atmosphere at home.

The best answer I can give to all these questions—indeed, to any question a family member asks me—is that the single most important thing you can do for yourself, your family, and the person in recovery is to *take care of yourself.* Not until you begin to fulfill your own needs, not until you become involved in activities you enjoy, not until you stop concentrating all your attention and effort on the recovering person, can you begin to relax and leave the recovering person to take responsibility for his or her own actions. Remember: You didn't cause the disease, you can't control it, and you can't cure it. You can live with it—but only if you stop making it the focus of your life.

Synergy is one of those buzzwords that's now in vogue. Synergy is the act of combining two or more entities to create a new whole that's greater than the sum of its parts. In early sobriety, it may seem as if the demands of individual recovery and family recovery are sometimes at odds. After all, both the individual and the family members have only a finite amount of energy and patience, no matter how hard everyone is trying. But given their proper due, together they can form a synergy: They can feed and enrich each other.

For the recovering family, the route to healing both the family and the individual is found in taking care of the family's needs, while at the same time accepting and accommodating the needs of the recovering person. The road may be bumpy at times, but ultimately it will take you where you want to go.

For the recovering person, resuming a life within the family means initially accepting their lack of trust. Like sobriety, trust is a condition one earns by working at it. In the beginning, your most important task in terms of your family will be to show them that you understand that they're also recovering, and that they need to change as well. This understanding may be all you're able to offer them in the first stages of sobriety.

But you must also keep in mind that you're part of the family, and that family recovery is part of your recovery process, too. This isn't to imply that you should readjust your focus from your recovery to theirs. You must still put yourself at the center of your own life. But the family is the best place to begin to learn and test the new skills—open communication, knowing and stating your own needs, listening to others, working to develop plans to resolve conflicts and solve problems—that will help you to build a comfortable and rich sobriety. As you move through the stages of recovery, the events that precipitate family crises will vary, but these same skills will enable you to solve your problems, whether you have achieved six sober months or twenty sober years.

Chapter Nine
What Is Sober Sex?

How to Improve Your Sex Life

Sex in the First Stages of Recovery

Two people tiptoeing hand-in-hand through a mine field. This is how a patient of mine once aptly described sexual relations during the first six months of sobriety. No matter how careful you try to be in the bedroom, you or your partner can unwittingly detonate some powerful, even frightening scenes, as you will see from the stories in this chapter. But as you will also learn, it is possible to defuse these potential hazards and move ahead to a comfortable, satisfying sex life.

In the first three or four weeks of recovery, overwhelmed as they are by raw, unpredictable, intense emotions, newly sober people often form ardent, all-consuming attachments. In our treatment programs, we frequently find that two people with perhaps ten days of sobriety between them will stick together like silly putty in a passionate, highly-charged relationship. As a result, we have established a strict "no fraternization" rule, a euphemism that refers to any kind of sexual activity between patients, from kissing and petting up to and including intercourse.

The couples who are involved in this type of relationship are experiencing deep and genuine emotions. But they are emotions generated by the disordered brain activity that is a universal part of early recovery, rather than by one person's true response to another. In no way are they based on the factors that underlie all stable, long-term involvements—an intimate awareness of each other's personal qualities, along with shared values and interests.

The real problem with these instant involvements is that the couple becomes totally engulfed by their experience. Because both of them are engaged in an exciting and overpowering affair, neither one can focus on staying sober. The illusion of loving and being loved is very often enough to convince both partners that they don't need to work on their sobriety because their lives are suddenly so wonderful. Wonderful though they may seem, they are really too good to be true. People fall out of such romances as hard as they fall into them—and rarely with their sobriety intact.

Ron, a doctor who specializes in internal medicine, learned this after he had spent a month being treated at Smithers for his alcoholism. Long before he came into treatment, Ron had been having marital problems. When his wife Patti visited him at the center, they had several very disruptive arguments. Our staff felt that Ron and Patti would benefit from couples therapy, but recommended that they postpone seeking help until Ron had achieved three months of sobriety.

I met with Ron about two weeks after he was discharged. He was beaming with happiness and looked pleased with himself. He seemed to ooze self-satisfaction. When I asked him how he was doing, he reported that he had stayed sober and was back at work. Unfortunately, the situation at home was much the same as it had been when we had last spoken. Before I could ask him for more details, Ron launched into a story that explained why he was feeling so great. He had recently reconnected with an old flame and they had slept together. The encounter had been extremely gratifying, he told me, to say the least.

I asked Ron to tell me about the woman. It turned out that the last time he had seen her, she had been hooked on sleeping pills and prescription painkillers. "But she's much better now," Ron assured me. I asked whether she was abstinent. "No," he replied. "But she's cut down a lot."

Before he had finished speaking, I had one of those insights that often occur to people who treat alcoholics and addicts. "Did she ask you for a prescription?" I asked.

Ron looked puzzled. "Why, yes," he answered. "But only to help her taper off." Then it hit him. "I guess I've been had," he admitted.

Based on entirely false assumptions, Ron had been on the verge of embarking on what he had believed was the great romance of his life. Not surprisingly, his judgment had failed him. As we talked further, he agreed that continuing this affair was not going to help his sobriety, and he broke it off very soon after our session. He's now in his ninth month of sobriety, and he's begun to regain his normally sound judgment. I don't think that Ron would be vulnerable again in a similar situation.

Ron's story illustrates the potential dangers of a new or renewed sexual relationship in early sobriety. But even for those of you who are involved in an established relationship, sex can create a great deal of tension and turmoil.

During her inpatient treatment for dependency on alcohol and tranquilizers, Marcia talked a lot about her marriage to Evan. They had been blissfully happy as newlyweds and their very satisfying sex life had continued after the birth of their first child. But gradually Marcia's alcohol and drug use, which had made her more sexually active and adventurous originally, began to interfere with her enjoyment of sex. She found that if she drank enough to get her excited, she would frequently become drowsy even before she and Evan finished making love. She was also having a harder time reaching orgasm, and started faking her climaxes—when she didn't pass out first.

Understandably, Evan was very concerned about Marcia's apparent loss of interest in sex. But whenever he brought up the subject, she would respond defensively. "If you paid more attention to me when we're *not* in bed, maybe I'd get more turned on when we are," she told him.

Evan believed her, and he tried harder to show his love and support. But he was fighting a losing battle against the anesthetizing effects of alcohol and tranquilizers. It almost seemed as if the more he tried to be considerate and kind, the more their sex life deteriorated.

He was also becoming increasingly put off by the powerful odor of alcohol that Marcia always seemed to give off. Although he drank himself, this smell was very unpleasant and quite different from the normal odor of liquor. He also noticed that Marcia had begun to get rather sloppy about her appearance. She would go off to work looking well-groomed, neat, and attractive. But by eleven o'clock at night, after they had both had a few drinks, she would become disheveled and bloated. Her gestures, her whole persona, somehow seemed to become cruder—not at all those of the quiet, elegant woman he had married.

During the last year of Marcia's dependency, when her problem had become too obvious for Evan to ignore, he tried to use sex as a way to control her. On several occasions he refused to make love with her. "You're drunk and you disgust me," he told her bluntly. Finally, he stopped making any sexual overtures at all. By the time Marcia came into treatment, it had been four months since they had made love.

In family program meetings, Evan and Marcia discussed many of their difficulties. They both expressed great sadness and regret that Marcia's addictions had driven them so far apart. During these sessions, they also realized that they still loved each other very much, that they both looked forward to resuming their lovemaking and to being a family again along with their four-year-old son Jeremy.

On Marcia's first night home, they read Jeremy a story and put him to bed. Then Evan prepared Marcia's favorite dinner, which they ate by candlelight, with romantic music playing in the background.

Afterward, they eagerly went upstairs to their bedroom. But despite all Marcia's efforts to arouse him, Evan couldn't get an erection. Evan was shocked and a bit embarrassed. Marcia assured him that she understood, and they fell asleep in each other's arms. But Marcia's already fragile self-esteem had suffered a very damaging blow. She couldn't help telling herself that Evan's inability to get an erection was sure proof that he didn't love her anymore. She had obviously become so unattractive that she couldn't turn him on.

That night she managed to hide her feelings of disappointment and rejection. But when the same scene was played out again and again over the course of the next several weeks, Marcia became increasingly bitter. At first Evan had been apologetic and baffled by his lack of response, but in spite of his good intentions, he began feeling defensive and angry. And in his anger, he lashed out at Marcia with the very words she had been so afraid of hearing: "You were so disgusting when you were drinking. You smelled of vomit. One time you threw up when we were right in the middle of having sex. I'm totally turned off by you."

The memories came flooding back to Marcia, and she was deeply humiliated by her past behavior, as well as deeply hurt by Evan's rejection of her. The two of them had reached a point at which all their attempts to have sexual contact were so permeated by remorse, rejection, anger, humiliation, and frustration—emotions guaranteed to exacerbate any problem—that neither could see how they could save their sex lives and their relationship.

Obviously, the problem wasn't Marcia's alone. Evan also had his part in it, as so many spouses of chemically dependent people do when their partners become sober. Later in the chapter I'll explain how the two of them came to face up to their sexual difficulties and worked out a solution to resolve them. And when they did, they discovered—as you undoubtedly will—that sex in sobriety can be better than it ever was before.

What Is Normal Sex?

What's "normal" for the population at large isn't necessarily the same as what's "normal" for a person in recovery. As you well know and have seen in Chapter 3, the emotional component of your sex life has almost certainly been damaged by your drug dependency or alcoholism. You may also have sustained physical damage to your sexual organs.

Important as these issues are, they aren't the whole story. I have also found that people who are chemically dependent have many more misconceptions about what constitutes normal sexual behavior than their peers who aren't substance abusers. This may be because addicts often aren't privy to those personal and revealing conversations with close friends in which we learn so much about how others behave, both in and out of the bedroom. The pursuit of drugs or alcohol usually prevents the chemically dependent person from building and maintaining intimate friendships. One consequence is that, lacking anyone with whom they can discuss and validate their impressions, they come to have mistaken ideas—let's call them myths—about sexual behavior.

Myth #1: There's a Normal Standard of Sexual Behavior That Everyone Must Abide by.

What's normal in sex, as in any other area of life, applies to a wide spectrum of behavior. Perhaps you remember this scene from Woody Allen's movie *Annie Hall*. Alvy Singer, played by Woody Allen, is visiting his psychiatrist who asks Alvy how often he and Annie Hall have sex. "Hardly ever . . . maybe three times a week," Alvy says sorrowfully. Meanwhile, across town, Annie, played by Diane Keaton, is being asked the same question by *her* psychiatrist. Annie's response is rather different from Alvy's. "Constantly!" she declares, her voice thick with resentment. "I'd say three times a week!"

My point is that whatever feels natural for you is perfectly fine unless you happen to be involved with someone whose needs and desires are very different from yours. If both partners in a relationship are comfortable having intercourse twice a year, they have no reason to be concerned. But if someone whose norm is to have sex three times a week is living with or married to someone whose norm is to have sex three times a year, there's bound to be a problem.

I want to emphasize that while sexual difficulties can contribute to straining a long-term relationship, the roots are much more likely to be based in interpersonal tensions between the partners than in the sexual difficulties themselves.

Myth #2: Sex Should Be Natural.

This may be true for cats, dogs, and earthworms, but humans are far more complicated. Unlike other animals, people have a prolonged childhood and adolescence, as well as a complex sexual behavior that's more learned than instinctive. Because human sexual responses are more flexible and multifaceted, they afford far greater potential for pleasure. But by the same token, they also provide a lot of room for disappointment.

When it comes to sex, as with anything else, both good and bad habits can be learned. Those that are positive promote mutual satisfaction; those that are negative leave both partners unsatisfied. One of your tasks in sobriety may be to learn or relearn good sexual habits, and to replace and unlearn the bad ones you've acquired along the way.

Myth #3: Sexual Abstinence Is Harmful to Your Health.

There's no question that a satisfying sex life can make for great happiness. Doctors often advise their older patients to remain sexually active, if they're so inclined, because sex can improve their psychological and physical well-being. Of course, this is true not just for the elderly, but for all adults.

However, many lifelong celibates lead contented, productive lives. Many other people voluntarily forego sexual activity for months at a time without feeling as if they're suffering or making a sacrifice. The fact is, periods of sexual inactivity are far more common, even in a long-term relationship, than you might suppose. It's not that unusual for a couple to abstain from sex, for one reason or another, for several months. Sexual tension doesn't build up like a volcano under pressure until it explodes in a burst of fury and violence.

Myth #4: Sexual Problems Are a Sign of a Bad Marriage.

People whose relationships are fraught with anger, frustration, and lack of communication often bring those tensions with them into the bedroom. But a couple often experiences sexual difficulties even when other aspects of their relationship are working just fine. They may be having problems because one or both of them are under pressure from emotional factors outside the home, such as job stress, illness, or the death of a loved one.

Among men, the most common and troubling sexual problem is impotence. Though many people are under the mistaken impression that impotence is always psychologically rooted, there are many physical conditions that can cause or contribute to it. Alcohol and/or drug abuse are only two of them. Among the other disorders that can lead to impotence are diabetes, diseases of the spinal cord (including disk problems), heart and kidney diseases, and the use of some medications, such as those taken for high blood pressure. Worrying about impotence can also produce major anxiety, which can make the problem much worse.

A woman's sexual performance is also affected by physical ailments, such as numb nerve endings, decreased vaginal lubrication, or endometriosis (a disease that occurs when the tissue that normally lines the uterus grows into the pelvis and other areas of the body). Women, too, may experience inhibited desire, reduced arousal, and diminished ability or total inability to achieve orgasm.

Myth #5: "Normal" People Don't Have Sexual Difficulties.

My patients are usually surprised to hear that married people and couples who don't abuse drugs or alcohol are frequently prone to some form of sexual dysfunction—whether it is a dissatisfaction with how often they make love, an absence of desire, a lack of arousal, insufficient sexual stimulation, infrequent orgasms, or impotence. However, sexual difficulties are much more common when one or both of the partners are dependent on alcohol or drugs.

People who aren't involved in a long-term relationship may also suffer from sexual problems. These include difficulty being aroused and reaching orgasm, the repeated choice of incompatible or inappropriate partners, or the inability to form a permanent sexual attachment. As is true for long-standing couples, such problems are more likely to occur among substance abusers.

Performance anxiety and depression are also major causes of sexual problems. I know of very few depressed people whose ability to function sexually hasn't been at least somewhat impaired. Even if a depressed person is able to perform in a purely mechanical sense, his or her pervasive lack of joy will surely affect sexual feelings and responses.

Because our sexuality is so wonderfully complicated, calling into play so many physical, emotional, and social factors, it's normal to have sexual difficulties from time to time. In fact, it would be unrealistic for anyone to expect a lifetime of uninterrupted sexual bliss. You can help yourself ride out the rough patches if you remember that having occasional sexual problems does *not* mean you're abnormal.

Myth #6: There's No Relationship Between Sex and Age.

I've heard a lot of different stories from my patients about what they consider to be the normal effects of aging on their sexual behavior. One fifty-year-old man told me that he thought it was perfectly normal that he hadn't had an erection in years. A young woman assured me that her ninety-year-old grandfather had sex every day, and that everyone could be as sexually active at ninety as at nineteen. The truth lies somewhere in between.

Researchers have found that the quickness with which men can achieve an erection and the frequency with which they can experience orgasms seem to peak in late adolescence and early adult life. As they age, men take longer to become erect and need more time after orgasm before they can achieve a second erection. For men over fifty-five, an erection may no longer be a totally spontaneous event; it may require some manual stimulation of the penis. And their recovery period between orgasms may be twenty-four hours, rather than the few minutes it took when they were teenagers. Their erections tend to be less hard, which doesn't necessarily lessen their partners' stimulation or pleasure. It also takes them longer to reach orgasm, a development that's often much appreciated by their partners.

Women, for reasons that aren't clear and may be more cultural than physical, seem to experience their greatest sexual desire in their mid-thirties, when their ability to reach orgasm is at its maximum. Florence, for example, recalled the sexual awakening she experienced twenty years earlier, after her divorce at age thirty.

She had been a virgin when she married Buddy, who was himself barely out of his teens. "He didn't know much, and I knew even less," she said, smiling at the memory. "I had read *Lady Chatterley's Lover* and some other sexy novels, and I had gotten the idea that I was supposed to feel something cataclysmic when we made love. But I could never be sure whether or not I had come. Still, I loved for Buddy to kiss me and hold me, so I didn't really care if I came."

Then, some time after the birth of their first child, Florence experienced her first orgasm during sex. "The earth didn't move, and it wasn't cataclysmic, but it was very, very nice." Unfortunately, she came only a few times during the rest of her ten-year marriage to Buddy.

Florence began to drink regularly after she and Buddy were divorced, partly because she felt so uncomfortable going out on dates and having sex with other men. "I was awkward and restrained. I couldn't let myself go. Then I met Pete and fell in love again."

Pete was a much more experienced and considerate lover than Buddy had been. "I developed an enormous appetite for sex," Florence told her group. "I couldn't get enough. I'd have several orgasms at one sitting, as it were. Pete worried that he couldn't satisfy me, but I was thrilled. I would never have believed that I could enjoy sex so much."

On the other hand, Susan, thirty-one and single, first had sex when she was seventeen. She had her first orgasm after only two or three experiences. "My friends were all sleeping with their boyfriends," she said. "We traded information and tips, and since we all used contraception, we weren't too worried about getting pregnant. I got into sex pretty quickly. Of course, a lot of how I felt depended on the guy I was with. Some guys who turned me on at first would end up being selfish and crude or clumsy in bed. With other guys it would be terrific. Most of the time I got high, either drinking or using drugs—not because I was uptight, but because the stuff was there. Then things started to go downhill. I don't remember exactly when, but I do remember the first time I slept with someone I didn't like because I was too high to think straight. He forced me to have sex with him, and after a while I stopped resisting. Making love was never the same after that."

Susan is now taking a respite from sex while she works on her sobriety, just six months old. "But once I've sorted out how I feel about men and relationships, I'm looking forward to a really satisfying sex life in sobriety. I understand I'm getting to the age when it's supposed to be better than ever for women."

As women approach fifty, the average age of menopause, they generally experience some decline in desire and in their ability to reach orgasms. But their sexual response still remains strong. At menopause, they may notice a dramatic decrease in vaginal lubrication, a result of low estrogen levels. Although this doesn't affect their sexual desire in any way, many women use a lubricant to prevent vaginal tearing. Hormone replacement therapy, which is often prescribed for troubling menopausal symptoms such as flushing, sweating, dizziness, and heart palpitations, also improves vaginal lubrication. But this treatment cannot be used by women with a history of breast cancer.

As couples get older, they tend to have intercourse less frequently, though many continue to make love when they're well into their sixties and seventies. And there's no reason why people in their eighties and nineties shouldn't continue to enjoy sex. Twenty-five percent of men do have significant potency problems by about age seventy. But with proper treatment impotence can often be cured or alleviated.

How to Develop a Satisfying Sex Life

If You Have a Permanent Partner

Talk Frankly with Your Partner About Your Sex Life

Even if you think you don't have any problems, that may not be true for your partner. Although it can be very stressful to initiate a frank discussion about so sensitive a subject, I strongly recommend that you make the effort. This may seem to be contradictory advice, since earlier

I emphasized the importance of avoiding stress as much as possible. But unvoiced sexual resentments can cause far greater tension than an open and honest conversation about how you can resolve your problems.

Let's go back to Florence, whose alcoholism got worse after she married Pete. Eventually her drinking ruined their wonderful sex life. When she was two months sober, she reported to her AA group, "I was usually drunk when we went to bed. I often couldn't have an orgasm, so I'd make Pete try to give me one any way he could, long after he was tired and wanted to go to sleep. I was greedy, demanding, and inconsiderate. I would be angry the whole time we were making love because Pete wasn't getting me excited enough.

"Our fights during the day spilled over into bed, too. Sex was a combat zone when I came into treatment. Now it's more like a demilitarized zone with a UN peacekeeping force in place. We're very polite with each other. You know, 'You go first.' 'Oh, no, please, after you.' We're both so cautious. Neither of us really wants to have sex, but we both feel the other would be offended if we said, 'no thanks.' So we go through the motions. It's such a shame because it used to be so great."

A group member suggested that Florence say exactly that to Pete, and Florence took her advice. She picked a time when they were both relaxed and in a good frame of mind. Then she told him how sorry she was about her behavior when she was drinking, and how she felt about their sexual relationship now. "I'd like for us to get comfortable with each other again, and try to make love when we both want to, not out of a sense of obligation," she said. "My fear is that if we don't make some changes, we'll get more and more turned off."

Pete admitted that he had been feeling the same way. He had come to dread their obligatory weekly sessions in bed, but he hadn't raised the subject for fear of hurting Florence's feelings, possibly even triggering a relapse.

Once they acknowledged their problem, Florence and Pete were able to talk out the bad feelings they had bottled up. Unlike many couples where one partner is newly sober, they didn't need to learn how to make love to each other. They already knew how to communicate in bed, but their fundamentally good sexual relationship had taken a wrong turn. It didn't take long before they were able to get it back on course.

Listen to Your Partner

Communication is a two-way street. A discussion of your sexual needs and fears will lead you down a dead-end alley unless you genuinely listen and try to understand what your partner has to say. Such conversations are probably as difficult for him or her as they are for you. But if you give each other enough time to express yourselves without interrupting or becoming defensive and angry, you'll be promoting a free and frank dialogue that will no doubt prove very enlightening. You're also likely to find yourselves more willing to talk openly about problems in other areas of your relationship as well.

Develop a Plan to Deal with Your Problems

You and your partner will have to spend some time together exploring the various ways your sexual issues can be resolved. The most important criteria should be that you're both comfortable with the solution you arrive at, and that you both see it as the best plan *for now*.

Some couples decide to postpone their discussion of sex for two or three or six months, and agree that during this period they won't have any sexual contact at all. Others choose to kiss and caress each other, stopping short of intercourse for a given period of time. This can give someone a chance to become comfortable with his or her own body, as well as a partner's, before fully beginning a sober sex life. Still others continue to make love and experiment with what each partner believes would make him or her feel better about sex.

You and your partner may hit upon yet a completely different plan that fits your particular needs. But no matter what arrangement you come up with, you'll probably discover that the very act of making plans, awkward though it may be, will improve your relationship.

Remember Marcia, whose rejection by her husband Evan was so hurtful and distressing that she could hardly bear to think about their sexual problems, much less talk about them? One day in her women's therapy group, after another member spoke about a similar situation, Marcia opened up and spoke frankly about her problem. As she listened to the group's comments, she was able to see how her reactions were contributing to the downward spiral in her relationship with Evan. And she liked their suggestion that she sit down with Evan and discuss what had been happening, how they felt, and what they might do about it.

It wasn't easy for Marcia to open such a conversation, especially because of Evan's initial resistance. But Marcia convinced him that the tension between them would only get worse if they didn't talk. "We could try a sex therapist," she offered.

But Evan wasn't ready for that. "I don't feel like going to some professional every time I have a problem. I've already been to the family program. I'd like to believe I can work things out for myself."

"*We*," Marcia quietly reminded him. "This is our problem, *together*."

Evan thought that they should take a vacation together, but

Marcia worried that she wasn't yet ready to be separated even temporarily from her support system—her sponsor, her therapy group, and her AA friends. "Maybe later," she told him. "If we went now and we got tense and angry with each other, I wouldn't have anywhere to go for help."

"That's thinking negatively," Evan countered. "If you expect something to go wrong, it will."

"I don't think I'm being negative," Marcia declared. "I'm trying to be realistic. In my fantasy—projection, we call it in AA—we would have a wonderful week on some sunny island, swimming and snorkeling and playing tennis all day, and having fantastic sex all night. But there's also a possibility that we'd go to bed tired and happy and have perfectly dreadful sex and wake up snapping at each other, the way we've been doing lately. I don't want that to happen, but it might. I've learned at AA that staying sober means learning how to plan, how to look at all the possibilities, and not assuming that things always turn out the way you want them to."

After a long silence, Evan said, "Maybe we should agree not to have sex—not even to try. If I hug you like this"— he reached over and gave her a hug to demonstrate —"it doesn't mean I'm going to carry you off to bed. And if you put your arm around my waist, that doesn't mean you're about to tear off my clothes."

Marcia fought off the old, familiar feeling of rejection. Evan loved her, she reminded herself, and he cared about their marriage. He wasn't discounting or spurning her. He was trying to work with her to resolve their difficulties. "Okay," she agreed. "That's the best idea we've come up with. It feels right." She took his hand and gently kissed his fingertips. "This is okay, but no sex, right?"

Evan leaned over and lightly blew in her ear. "Right. No sex."

"How long do you think we can keep this up?" Marcia giggled.

They agreed to wait until she had been sober for ninety days. When Marcia reported this to her group, several members expressed their surprise because three months sounded like a long time. But everyone congratulated her for having had the courage to confront the problem.

Soon after she had achieved ninety days of sobriety, Marcia came into the meeting smiling from ear to ear. The plan had worked, she reported. She and Evan had recently indulged in a very fine and gratifying session of lovemaking. She acknowledged that they still had a long way to go, but they had begun to build a solid foundation for restoring their sexual relationship.

As you can see, it's not always the chemically dependent person who has difficulties with sex in early sobriety. Very often his or her partner has trouble as well. Simply facing up to the problem and creating a plan for handling it, however, will improve both your sex life and your relationship with your partner outside the bedroom.

Have Nonsexual Physical Contact with Your Partner

I encounter many couples who barely touch each other except when they're having intercourse. The rest of the time they have little or no physical contact. But hugging, holding hands, a kiss on the cheek, and other nonsexual gestures can help you to establish or reestablish a physical relationship.

A comfortable nonsexual physical relationship will carry over into the bedroom and pave the way for more satisfying sex. Far too many couples equate being physical with being sexual. As a result, they miss out on the warmth and comfort that come from simply making physical contact with another human being.

Share Interests and Activities That You Both Enjoy

Your drugging or drinking probably led you to an increasingly solitary life. Even though you've continued to live together, you and your partner may have been going your separate ways for years—you to your addiction, your partner to his or her resentments. Any mutually pleasurable experience outside your normal daily routine that brings you closer to your partner—a visit to a museum, a movie, a drive in the country—will help revitalize your relationship, both in and out of the bedroom. I particularly recommend physical activity, such as walking, cycling, playing tennis, gardening, or any other invigorating outdoor exercise.

Continue to Work on Your Health and Your Sobriety

As your health improves because you're eating properly, getting enough sleep, and exercising regularly, you'll also see an improvement in how you feel about yourself sexually. But none of this happens overnight, and in the meantime, your task is to focus on strengthening your sobriety. Don't postpone the other requirements of your sobriety while you repair your sex life. Remember: Your sobriety *always* takes priority over everything else. Satisfying sex will follow.

If You Don't Have an Ongoing Sexual Relationship

Nobody ever died of masturbation. No matter what stories you heard as a child, you won't be struck by lightning, or become deaf or blind because you give yourself pleasure by masturbating. Many people believe that masturbation is somehow wrong or shameful. It is neither. Masturbation is a perfectly healthy, natural, and legitimate way to release sexual tension and obtain pleasure.

Nobody ever died of celibacy either. It's perfectly all right not to have sex if you don't choose to. In fact, many newly sober people feel the need to be at least temporarily celibate—and then harbor suspicions that they're not "normal."

I was present at a women's discussion group when Ellen, who had been sober for four months, said with some embarrassment, "When I was using cocaine, I was forever hopping in and out of different beds. Now that I'm sober, I want nothing to do with sex. I'm quite comfortable not being in a sexual relationship, which I never expected to happen. But I also feel like I'm weird, like there's something wrong with me."

As Ellen spoke, I saw several heads nodding around the room. "I had exactly the same experience," Sharon spoke up. "I felt totally turned off sex when I first got sober. After about six or eight months, I started feeling sexual stirrings again, but I wasn't ready to get involved with anyone. So I didn't, until three months ago. Just as I was about to celebrate my second anniversary in recovery, I made love with a wonderful man I'd known for six months. We have a terrific relationship, and not only in bed. I think this just might work out."

I have been told that similar stories emerge in men's groups, too, although usually only after the men have been working together for a long time. Men seem much more reluctant than women to admit that they're not interested in sex. But whether or not you want to discuss such feelings, my message to you is that it's okay *not* to have sex. You'll not only survive a period of celibacy, you're much more likely to stay sober.

I'd like to add a word here about single-sex discussion groups. They can be enormously helpful for some people, in that you can talk about a wide range of issues that you may not feel comfortable discussing in a mixed group. Sex itself is only one of these issues. The opposite sex in general, and how gender affects your sobriety and your role in society, are other topics that are frequently raised in single-sex groups. You can find such groups through treatment centers and programs, and in some locations, AA offers single-sex meetings.

Everything I've said thus far in this chapter applies to anyone, no matter what your sexual preference, or whether or not you have a permanent partner. But male homosexual contacts, perhaps more so than lesbian or heterosexual encounters, have traditionally occurred in bars or other milieus where alcohol and drugs play a prominent role. If you're a gay man and in early recovery, it's very important that you avoid such places, as well as the casual sexual involvements that are often begun there. This may not always be easy, but it could save your sobriety.

One of my patients, a thirty-five-year-old gay man named Jack, faced this issue when he was two months sober. Charles, his lover of six years, had broken up with him four months before Jack came into treatment. Charles had watched Jack's life disintegrate into a chaotic mess of daily cocaine use and round-the-clock drinking. Charles was responsible for getting Jack into treatment, and he wanted to be involved in Jack's recovery. But he was adamant that they were finished as lovers. Jack had agreed to Charles' condition, and at the end of his month-long, intensive outpatient treatment, they had reaffirmed their friendship.

Then, two months into recovery, Jack felt his sexual urges reawakening. In the past, he had gone to bars in search of sex, but he realized that as an alcoholic, he couldn't do that. How, then, was he to find himself a sexual partner? He came to me because he didn't know what to do.

During the course of our discussion, we explored why he so urgently needed to have sex. Jack admitted that in the past he had had periods of several months when he had gone without sex. It occurred to him that his present intense sexual desire came from having been rejected by Charles. He was feeling worthless and unattractive. He was hoping that a sexual conquest would make him feel better about himself and affirm his sexuality.

Luckily, Jack agreed to my suggestion that he put off his search for a sexual partner while he worked on his self-image. He began working out at a gym and became more involved in his self-help group. He applied for and won a promotion at his job. He started eating sensibly, and in the following six months lost thirty pounds. He also found that his need for sex had ceased to be so overwhelming. When I saw him recently, after two years in sobriety, he had just begun a new relationship, his first since giving up cocaine and alcohol. He was feeling happy and excited about the future.

Jack's extreme need for sex early in sobriety could have been his undoing. But instead of dropping by a bar, he was able to talk about his problem and understand what was really troubling him. With his sobriety on a more secure footing and his self-esteem bolstered, Jack was finally able to get involved with a man with whom he now hopes to share his new life.

Eventually, like Jack and Susan, most people decide they would like to resume an active sex life. Here are some suggestions to prepare you for this next step.

Begin to Develop Nonsexual Friendships

The impulse to leap into bed first and allow the relationship to develop afterward is particularly strong when you're under the influence. As a result, few chemically dependent people have nonsexual friendships—either with members of the opposite sex if they're heterosexual, or with members of the same sex if they're homosexual. Learning to be friendly and caring without being sexual is an important first step for unattached people in sobriety.

Begin to Get Involved in Activities You Enjoy, and Share Them with Someone Else When Possible

If that other person is someone to whom you might be sexually attracted, fine. If not, that's fine, too. Sobriety is the most important priority for people who aren't in a long-term relationship, as well as for those with permanent partners. Improving one's self-esteem comes a close second. Sexual conquests won't restore self-respect. Staying sober will. When the time is right, as it was for Sharon, you'll recommence your sexually active life. Until then, you can apply the same philosophy to your sexuality as you do to your sobriety—take it one day at a time.

When to Seek Professional Help

Impotence

Men who have been abstinent for three to six months and still can't achieve a full erection or masturbate to orgasm, or never have an erection when they wake up in the morning, should first ask their primary care physician—most of whom are specialists in internal medicine or general or family practitioners—to do a medical workup. If no immediate physical cause can be found, the doctor may recommend treatment with a sex therapist or at a sex clinic, or the patient may be referred for further testing to a urologist who specializes in potency problems. Impotence is sometimes the result of medication, or hormonal or neurological disorders that can be corrected. In other cases, erections can be artificially produced so that satisfactory intercourse can occur.

Lack of Desire

If your internal plumbing is working—you are able to be aroused, have an erection and ejaculate if you are a man or lubricate and come to orgasm if you are a woman—but you're just not very interested in sex, you may have what is called lack of desire or lack of libido. Just as hair color varies from one person to the next and changes with age, so does sexual desire. Your life circumstances, some of which may be the result of your addiction, can also affect sexual desire in early sobriety.

Think back to the recovering people you read about earlier in this chapter. Susan, who was forced into an unwanted sexual act because she was too high to resist, had no desire for sex for many months after she became sober. The rape altered the way she felt about men, about sex, and about herself. Until she was able to accept herself, improve her self-esteem, and begin to trust other people, especially men, she couldn't allow herself to feel desire. It was simply too threatening.

Ron, on the other hand, was easily aroused during early sobriety. But his relationship with his wife was so bad that he unwisely sought sex elsewhere, in the arms of his old girlfriend who was using him.

For Florence and Pete, on the other hand, lack of desire was a passing stage, brought about by unsatisfactory sexual experiences during the last phase of Florence's drinking and the first phase of her recovery.

Of course, it's perfectly normal to be occasionally uninterested in sex—after a hard day at work, for example, or if you're feeling particularly stressed. But if you've been sober for a year and continue to experience a lack of desire, if this is a change from your previous pattern of sexual behavior, and if your feelings bother you or your partner, then you should certainly seek help from a sex clinic or a sex therapist.

Victims of Childhood Sexual Abuse

Another patient of mine, Cassie, aged twenty, still had no interest at all in sex more than a year after she became sober. Cassie had been a heavy alcohol and drug abuser; she had tried every substance she could get her hands on in every combination she could think of. I recommended that she see a psychotherapist with experience in sexual difficulties. In the course of her treatment Cassie was able to recall a number of long-buried incidents. Between the ages of nine and twelve she had been sexually abused by an uncle who was then living with her family. These episodes had left her feeling confused about her sexual identity and conflicted about sex in general. All of her subsequent sexual activities had occurred while under the influence of some sort of drug. Cassie continued in individual therapy. Over the next two years she was able to sort out her feelings and work through the trauma of her childhood experience and finally to feel and acknowledge sexual desire.

Unfortunately, a proportionately high number of people addicted to alcohol or drugs have been sexually abused as children. The abuse may have been perpetrated by immediate family members, by a more distant relative (an uncle or a cousin, for instance) or by a trusted family friend. While women are the more frequent victims of childhood sexual abuse by trusted male figures, some men have also been abused, predominantly by adult males.

Sexual abuse in childhood always leaves a mark on the adult. The symptoms that may be experienced are exceedingly variable and complex and beyond the scope of this book, but they can include lack of desire, a confused sexual identity, and promiscuity. Many people become aware for the first time when they get sober that they had been abused as children. Others feel in sobriety the full impact of their emotions surrounding these incidents.

Just as the symptoms of childhood sexual abuse are widely variable, so are the courses of action people need to take to come to terms with past abuse. Some are able to deal with this issue with the help of their recovery program, friends, and families. Others need to seek professional help. This may mean a long-term commitment to individual psychotherapy. Or briefer, crisis-oriented therapy or participation in a therapy group for victims of childhood sexual abuse may be adequate to discuss and resolve the issue.

Frigidity

Frigidity is an unpleasant label that doesn't accurately describe the condition it represents. Nevertheless, it's the commonly accepted term to denote a woman's inability to come to orgasm even though she very much wants to.

Some women may have experienced this problem before they began using alcohol or drugs. Indeed, I know of many instances in which women began taking mood-altering drugs for the very purpose of overcoming frigidity. Some can masturbate to orgasm, but can't achieve a climax with their partners, in which case the cause is emotional rather than physical. Time and a sense of mutual understanding and concern will usually resolve it. However, women who have painful vaginal spasms during intercourse or who have been sober for a year and still can't have orgasms might arrange an appointment with their partners at a sex clinic or with a sex therapist.

Sexual Addiction

The compulsive use of sex to achieve feelings of well-being and to bolster self-esteem has been labeled an addiction by some. While this is indeed a serious problem, it is different from a pharmacological addiction to alcohol or drugs. Although you may have done a lot of indiscriminate bed-hopping while you were drinking or drugging, I caution any recovering person against leaping to the conclusion that he or she is a sex addict, based on this past performance. Indiscriminate sexual behavior is frequently a symptom of drug and alcohol abuse. Until you've been abstinent for at least six months, you can't have an accurate picture of what basic sexual difficulties you do or do not have. Deciding that you're a sex addict will only serve to shift your focus away from your primary task—recovery from your dependency on alcohol or drugs. If you continue to be bothered by compulsive sexual urges after six months of solid sobriety, you should consult a sex therapist. You may also find it useful to attend meetings of Sex Anonymous or Sexaholics Anonymous.

If, despite your best efforts, you can't make any progress with your sexual problems on your own, seek help from a qualified professional. There's no one answer to the question of when you should seek help; that varies depending on your circumstances. But generally speaking, if you've been sober from six to twelve months and your sexual difficulties are so worrisome or disruptive that they're threatening your recovery, you can probably benefit from professional help.

Depending on the nature of your problem, you may be able to get the help you need from a medical doctor, at a clinic that specializes in sexual dysfunction, or from a sex therapist, that is, a psychotherapist who's specifically trained to treat sexual problems. Unfortunately, not all people who call themselves sex therapists are genuinely deserving of the title. Should you decide to go to a sex therapist, make sure you get a reliable referral from a physician or another health professional, preferably one with experience in addiction medicine. If there's no one you feel you can trust, get in touch with the American Association of Sex Educators, Counselors, and Therapists, an organization that certifies and refers qualified sex therapists. You can find this organization's address in Appendix C.

This chapter wasn't intended to be a complete guide to all the sexual wonders and woes that a recovering person can encounter. But I do hope it's given you a realistic sense of what sober sex is all about. Unfortunately, people who have been substance abusers have suffered a greater-than-average incidence of sexual abuse, incest, and rape. Those of you who have experienced such traumas may need to seek professional help to come to terms with these problems. Most of you, however, will find that after two or three years of sobriety, your sex life has improved enormously without your doing much more than staying sober and rebuilding the rest of your life.

Chapter Ten
Reaching Out

Making Sober Friendships

Friendships, both the new ones you make in sobriety and the old relationships you "recycle" to fit your new sober life, play an important role in your recovery. As I mentioned earlier, it is through friendships that you lose the feeling of uniqueness and isolation that all too often beleaguers newly sober people, and you also expand your capacity to participate in all types of intimate human relationships.

Chances are very good that whatever friends you had during your final days of drinking or drugging were mostly users themselves. In the first six months of sobriety, you simply cannot afford to pal around with people who are either drinking or using. Included in this category are the people with whom you went on binges, *as well as* those you spent time with while drinking or drugging, even if your primary connection with them wasn't getting high.

If you want to be able to see friends who are users when your sobriety is on a firmer footing, you'll have to make a plan to inform them about your commitment to sobriety. And you'll want to consider how to reestablish contact with people whom you alienated by your addictive behavior.

One of the many wonderful aspects of sobriety is that it affords you the opportunity to get to know a lot of different people. Of course, that's not so easy at first. You probably feel unsure of yourself and a bit tentative with strangers. But give yourself time. Eventually you'll find people to connect with now that you have a positive central focus, namely sobriety.

Because recovery is the single most important theme in your life, for the first three to six months you're very likely to find most of your new relationships at your self-help meetings. The longer you're sober, the more involved you'll become in other activities outside of your self-help meetings, and these developing interests will lead you to further friendships. You can broaden your social circle at the gym, at your job, at your adult education class, or at the volunteer program in which you participate. But you should also be aware that getting to know new people brings with it the possibility of rejection, particularly if you rush head-long into a new friendship.

Time and again I've heard stories from patients who were so impatient to make new friends to replace the close friends they once had that they poured their hearts out, revealing intimate secrets to people they had met only once or twice. Hoping for a deep and long-lasting friendship, they felt terribly hurt when the relationship didn't pan out, when the precious gift of their friendship was turned away. In some instances, the rejection may be felt as such a severe blow to self-esteem that it can even trigger a relapse.

Take Al, for example. The last months of his cocaine addiction had been a nightmare. He got fired from his job after he was caught stealing money from his boss. Then he started selling crack, but he smoked up his entire inventory so that the dealer he was working for came gunning for him. Desperate and penniless, Al turned to prostitution. He was good-looking enough that at first he had an upscale clientele, but his physical condition quickly deteriorated. He lost so much weight that he looked ill and haggard and he became dirty and unkempt. Soon he was selling himself to whatever takers he could find, for any amount of money—sometimes even a single hit on a crack pipe. He hit bottom the night he appeared wild-eyed at his mother's apartment and forced her at knife-point to give him all her money.

Al had been clean for two months when he met Ray at a CA meeting. Like Al, Ray was in his early twenties, and he had been off cocaine for four months. The two men liked each other immediately, and one evening after a meeting, Ray invited Al over to his apartment for a chat. Al was still having nightmares about the scene with his mother, who had cut off all contact with him. Guilt-ridden and desperately ashamed, he longed to unburden himself to someone. It wasn't long before he was telling Ray everything.

Listening to one sordid incident after another, Ray became in-creasingly perturbed. Al's experience was so completely different from his own that he found it impossible to follow the advice he had so often heard at CA: identify, don't compare. There was nothing in Al's bizarre and frightening story with which he could identify. Moreover, he felt helpless and put off by the intensity of Al's remorse and self-revulsion.

He wished he could somehow comfort Al, but he was so appalled that really all he wanted was for Al to leave the apartment as quickly as possible.

But Al wasn't going anywhere. He poured out all the horror that he had kept bottled up for so long, painting graphic pictures of scenes so grotesque that Ray began having thoughts that he recognized were dangerous: *If this is what cocaine addiction is really about, my habit was pretty mild.* Soon, he felt his sobriety being threatened.

Finally, at 3:00 A.M., too exhausted to continue talking, Al told Ray he needed to go home and get some sleep. Almost euphoric with the relief of having confessed, he was oblivious to Ray's distress and the restraint with which he responded to Al's emotional goodbyes. Alone at last, Ray immediately phoned his sponsor, who told him emphatically not to see Al again. "You're not ready to handle this now," said his sponsor.

At their next meeting, Ray very awkwardly told Al that they couldn't continue their friendship because his sponsor felt that spending time with Al would jeopardize his sobriety. Convinced that he would never be accepted by another human being, that night Al tried to kill himself.

He didn't succeed, and eventually Al did pick up the pieces of his life. He's been sober for three years now and is studying to be a family therapist. Recalling that evening with Ray, he told me, "Of course I should have found a sponsor, someone whose sobriety was stable enough not to be threatened by the feelings my story inevitably would have raised. I should have been talking to someone who might have been objective enough to recommend professional help.

"But I was desperate, and Ray seemed so warm and decent. Sure I knew that Ray's experience had been limited to snorting cocaine at his office. I also knew that his family had intervened and gotten him into treatment before his addiction took him as far down as mine did. And I knew he hadn't been sober very long, but he seemed so stable and together. I guess I almost blew us both apart."

One way to avoid this kind of premature soul-baring is to find yourself a self-help sponsor. In early recovery, people have an enormous need to talk about the most personal details of their drinking or drugging life. They're aching to tell someone those things that can't be said to their spouse, parents, or best friends, much less in public. But a sponsor has heard it all. He or she won't be shocked or turned off, but rather will listen compassionately and provide a lot of sound, experienced advice.

You can tell your sponsor anything, without fearing that you'll be rejected later on. Thus your new and old friendships, which may still be on shaky ground, don't have to bear the brunt of your need to "tell all." Over time, your sponsor may also become your friend, but friendship isn't a necessary component of a successful sponsoring relationship.

Dealing with Your Drinking or Drugging Buddies

You won't have too much difficulty severing your ties to people whose only connection to you was a bottle or a joint or a snort. Because you're no longer hanging around your old haunts, you won't have much occasion to see your former drug or booze buddies. But you may very well have friends with whom you've been accustomed to drinking or using. These are people you have a lot in common with; perhaps you've grown up with them, gone to school or worked together, or lived on the same block. Whatever the connection, your shared relationship is valuable both to you and to them. You'll have to tell them about your recovery and put them on notice that your friendship has to change—because it can't continue on its former basis.

For the time being, while you're struggling to stay sober, you're better off avoiding these friends because seeing them may revive old memories, and perhaps trigger your desire to start drinking or using. However, do let them know how much they mean to you. Tell them that when you feel your sobriety is stable, say in six months, you'd love to get together with them again—on a non-using basis, of course. Also assure them that you still care about them, but that for now your sobriety has to take precedence over everything else.

If they are truly caring and concerned friends, they'll have no problem accepting what you have to tell them. But be prepared for the comments that can come from even your most well-meaning friends: "Surely, *you* couldn't be an alcoholic. You must be kidding! Who brainwashed you? Where the hell did you get that crazy idea? Why, you don't drink any more than I do. Sure, we all do a lot of drugs, but that doesn't make us *addicts*." In early recovery, such remarks can be very seductive, and can lead you to challenge your still shaky perception of yourself as an abstainer.

Ever since they had graduated together from law school, Irene and Tess had met once or twice a month for a three-martini lunch. After Irene got sober, she was caught unprepared by a phone call from Tess, who wanted to schedule their next date. "I have someone in my office," Irene improvised. "I'll call you back." After she put down the phone, she picked up her pen and made a list of the different ways she could handle the situation.

1. Lunch with Tess, no booze for me. Say nothing. Dangerous.

2. Lunch with Tess, no booze for me. Tell her I'm an alcoholic while she socks back her martinis. Tough.

3. No lunch. Make excuses. Tess may be hurt. I can't make excuses forever.

4. No lunch. Tell Tess why. I'll have to call her at home.

Irene decided on the last option. She called Tess, said she needed to discuss a personal matter, and that she would phone her at home that evening. But before they spoke again, Irene jotted down what she wanted to say to Tess about becoming sober, and why she felt they should postpone their lunches until she had been sober for six months. She thought she was prepared when she made the call, but her friend's reaction shocked her.

Tess was furious. "You're no alcoholic," she raved. "You've let that namby-pamby husband of yours brainwash you. You don't get drunk at lunch. Neither of us do. We can't afford to show up bombed at our offices. But hell, if you're so determined to make a big deal of this nonsense, why don't you meet me and order a delicious ginger ale?"

Irene explained that she was afraid of exposing herself too soon to situations in which she was used to drinking. "The smell of your martini could make me want to drink, and I can't ever drink again, Tess. I have a disease. I could die from it."

"Give me a break," Tess said acidly. "Next you'll be telling me you're into megavitamins and macrobiotic foods. You're not going to live forever, Irene. You might as well have some good food and drink while you're around."

It occurred to Irene that Tess had already put away a few drinks that evening. "Maybe we could meet one night after work at that new café on the corner of Broadway and Eighty-fourth Street," Irene suggested. "The food's terrific."

"You mean that place that doesn't have a liquor license? Forget it," Tess hooted. "But if you ever come to your senses, Irene, give me a call."

Most of your conversations with your friends aren't likely to end as this one did. But if you know someone like Tess, who may be secretly worried about her drinking, your commitment to sobriety can be very threatening. It is wise then to plan what you'll say when you call your friends, and how you'll react if they are skeptical or defensive. If this does happen, you should firmly avoid getting into a discussion of why you became sober. You don't want to give friends any opportunity to refute your reasoning, so that you wind up convinced that they're right—your decision *was* unwarranted.

Tell them instead that your alcohol or drug use is out of control for you, that right now you don't want to discuss the reasons for your decision, but that in order to stay sober you have to stay away from anyone who uses, at least for the time being. You should also further protect yourself by planning to be busy, preferably with a self-help meeting, on the day you make your calls. You may want to postpone getting in touch with your friends until you feel more secure in your sobriety. However, then you have to be prepared for the fact that they may call you. This is one very good reason to take the initiative yourself, so they don't catch you off-guard.

Your understanding friends are likely to be concerned, warm, and eager to get together with you. You may feel uncomfortable about saying you can't see them, and even when you do, they may continue to press you. You can forestall their efforts by saying immediately, "I have something very important to tell you, and I need your help with it." Follow that up with the points I made above.

It's entirely possible that one or more of your friends may have a drinking or a drug problem. And now that you're sober, it can be trying, even painful, to see what the substance abuse is doing to someone you care about. But you have your hands full coping with your own recovery. In early recovery you can endanger your sobriety by trying to resolve your friends's problems with drinking or drugging.

That's what happened to Margaret, who was involved in a near-fatal automobile accident while driving under the influence. During her recuperation in the hospital, she came to recognize that she was both an alcoholic and dependent on cocaine. She was visited by two women who were AA members, and she began to attend meetings at the hospital. She was quickly sold on sobriety and AA as the most wonderful things that had ever happened to her.

When Margaret came home she was not only determined to stay sober, but she was also eager to share her new found sobriety and her discovery of AA with her former drinking and drugging buddies. She was especially close to and concerned about one of her friends. The more she thought about Sheila, the more determined Margaret was to enlighten her.

Margaret didn't discuss her decision with any of her new friends in AA. Instead, she arrived unannounced at Sheila's apartment, where she found that Sheila had already made a good-sized dent in a quart of vodka. "Great to see you," Sheila said happily. "What good timing! Robert's due here any minute. Then we can really party."

Ignoring Sheila's obvious drunken state, Margaret began telling

Sheila about her own alcoholism, and about her discovery of sobriety and AA. But Sheila wasn't paying any attention because she was already high, and she had no interest in hearing about someone who wasn't using. Margaret faltered. This wasn't at all what she had fantasized.

She had pictured Sheila listening attentively and admitting to her drinking problem. Then the two of them would go off hand-in-hand to an AA meeting. Instead the doorbell rang and in walked Robert, providing immediate reinforcement for Sheila. They told Margaret she was understandably overreacting to her accident. That could happen to anyone, but she was no more an alcoholic than they were. Why was she being such a drag when all they wanted was to have a good time?

Little by little, they wore down Margaret's determination. She still didn't have much faith in the image of herself as an abstainer. By the end of the evening Margaret was as drunk as her friends. And she continued to get drunk for quite some time after that.

The impulse to rescue people you care about is natural and noble, but it also places an often intolerable strain on your own sobriety. Perhaps when you've been sober for a year or longer, you'll be able to confront your friends about their chemical dependencies. But if you undertake to do such Twelfth Step work, as it's called in the self-help groups, I suggest you join forces with a sober friend who's also working a Twelve Step program. Anyone who has done Twelve Stepping will tell you that as difficult as it is to undertake with a total stranger, it's that much harder with your own friends, because you can inadvertently set off distressing mental tapes of your own past drinking or drugging.

Reestablishing Lapsed Friendships

Now that you're sober, you may want to contact friends with whom you've long been out of touch because of your addiction. While some of these people may be thrilled to hear from you, you should be prepared for the painful possibility that others may slam the door in your face. They may have established new friendships and no longer have time for you in their lives. Or they may still be angry with you for past instances when you hurt or took advantage of them.

Their rejection and criticism are quite likely to threaten your still shaky self-esteem and perhaps trigger a relapse. It is a good idea, therefore, to wait until you've achieved at least three months of sobriety before you attempt to renew lapsed friendships. And in case your friends make it clear that they're *not* happy to hear from you, you should further protect your recovery by scheduling in advance some sort of activity to take place after you've made your calls. You might plan to go to a self-help meeting or a concert with one of your new sober friends. If your old pal sounded happy to hear from you, you can share the news. If, on the other hand, you got a chilly reception, you won't have to spend the evening alone, dwelling on your hurt.

Some recovering people prefer to get back in touch with old friends by writing rather than telephoning. You can write any time of the year, but Christmas, Chanukah, and the New Year provide wonderful opportunities to drop them a note. Letters have their advantages: They don't demand an immediate response the way a phone call does. They afford recipients the chance to get over their initial reactions, and consider the sincerity of your message. Letters or cards also allow your friends time to think about what happened between you, and decide whether they can find it in their hearts to accept your apology. They may be impressed by your commitment to sobriety and your efforts to put things right again. Or your friends may still decide not to renew their contact with you because they feel that your behavior was too horrendous to forgive. But a polite note to that effect is generally much easier on both of you than strained silence or an angry rebuff on the phone.

The last time Tim had seen Keith was in the hospital emergency room where Keith had turned him over to the medical staff. Then Keith had stalked off, thus ending a fifteen-year friendship that, as far as Keith was concerned, Tim had singlehandedly destroyed over the years.

Keith, a real estate developer, had given a cocktail party, to which he'd invited many prominent business people and politicians, in order to garner support for a new project. He hadn't invited Tim because past experience had taught him that Tim's presence was unlikely to be an asset at such a gathering. But because they were still friends, he had made the mistake of telling Tim about the project and the gathering.

That evening, Tim happened to be drinking in a bar near the restaurant where the party was being held. Awash in booze and sentiment, he thought of Keith and how important this venture was to him. He could just imagine the invitees looking solemn and stiff in their business suits, making dull small talk. What Keith needed, Tim realized, was someone who could liven up the scene. So he rustled up a couple of his drinking cronies and crashed the restaurant.

As expected, the party was a total bore, and Keith was behaving like an uptight stuffed shirt. All the more reason, Tim told his pals, for them to stir things up. But the harder they tried to have fun, the colder the atmosphere became. Finally Tim decided to entertain the guests with his guaranteed-good-for-laughs Russian folk dancing show. Unfortunately, he lost his balance in midstep, slid into a table laden with hors d'oeuvres, and gashed himself in the head. Keith's final act of friendship was to deliver Tim, bleeding profusely, to the hospital.

When Christmas rolled around, Tim had been sober for three months and he hadn't seen Keith in over a year. Sadly recalling the friends he had lost, Tim especially missed Keith, so he decided to send him a Christmas card with a note inside. The note read:

Dear Keith,

I am an alcoholic. I'm telling you this not to excuse my past behavior but to explain it. I've been sober now for three months and I'm in AA. Getting sober has been the most wonderful experience of my life. I can't make any guarantees, but I believe that I can stay sober a day at a time.

I'm writing you now because I miss you. I miss the fun we used to have together, and the discussions we had before alcohol got in the way. I miss your humor, your wit, and your solid good sense. I also know that you're thoroughly fed up with me and my promises. I can even see your skeptical smile as you read this note, but I promise, this time *is* different. I can feel it.

I'd love to see you again. I've written my new address and phone number on the back of the card. Unless you've decided that it's too late to repair the damage, give me another three months to see if my sobriety sticks, then please get in touch.

All the best,
Tim

Keith never answered his letter. Tim was disappointed but not crushed. He had allowed himself, as well as Keith, three months breathing space. During that time he had made some new friends. None of them could replace Keith, of course, but Tim felt less lonely and vulnerable than he had at Christmas. He also felt good about having put to use the advice he had often heard in AA. He had taken responsibility for contacting Keith, but he had recognized that he couldn't control Keith's response.

Telling Close Friends

Your close friends, those who weren't your drinking or drugging pals, do need to know about your commitment to sobriety. They will be your support in sobriety, and they deserve your honesty as you begin your new, honest life. They also won't want to do anything that might endanger your recovery. Out of ignorance, they might insist you take a hit of a joint even after you've already twice refused, or they might hand you an open bottle of beer and tell you to loosen up. But no truly concerned friend will push you toward using if he or she is aware of your problem, unless that person is in such serious denial about his or her own problem with alcohol or drugs that your recovery is intolerable.

Nancy, whose disastrous one-night stand you read about earlier, prepared a speech for her close friends that went something like this: "I am an alcoholic. I don't want to discuss that fact—I've decided I am, and that's all there is to it. My priority now is to stay sober. I know I can't have even one drink. I don't know why, but one drink often sets off a desire for more. I've tried to control my drinking, and I've tried having just one drink. But that doesn't work, at least not for long.

"For now, I need to stay away from the sight and the smell and the sound of the stuff. Even ice cubes clinking in a glass of water make me salivate. I'm told that in time I'll be able to be around alcohol quite comfortably, but in the meanwhile I need your help."

All of Nancy's close friends to whom she gave her speech received it well. Several people asked if she were going to AA because they had heard it was so helpful. One woman asked how she had come to her decision, and another confided that she was worried about how much her sister drank. But everyone was supportive and respectful of her commitment to sobriety.

I suggest that you be as direct as possible with your good friends and tell them face-to-face. Get together with them at a quiet place where you can talk, where you'll have some privacy and you know that liquor or drugs won't be available. They are very likely to ask for details, and you'll have to decide in advance how much you want to tell them. If you're reluctant to discuss more than the fact of your sobriety, be candid. You might say, "I don't feel I can get into this subject right now." Your friends will also want to know how they can help. I recommend you tell them, "By *never* trying to convince me that I don't have a drug problem. By not believing me if I say I can have 'just one.' By encouraging me to go to my self-help meetings. And by including me in the fun, as you did in the past, but without any alcohol or drugs around."

Telling Acquaintances

Your acquaintances—coworkers with whom you have a casual social relationship, the people with whom you play sports, your neighbors, members of the clubs you belong to—don't need to know about your addiction. They may notice that you're not drinking, but they don't have to know why if you don't want to tell them. The longer you're sober, the less ashamed you'll be of having an addictive disease, and the easier it usually becomes to tell other people that you're alcoholic or have been addicted. However, many people in recovery simply don't wish to reveal the details of their private life to acquaintances, no matter how cordial. This is perfectly acceptable, and should have no impact on your sobriety.

Stu, for example, was by nature a reserved man who was an avid golfer and an active member at his country club. Before he got sober he had done some drinking at the club, but the men he golfed with weren't his drinking buddies. The club's unspoken rule was that a couple of drinks were okay, but drunkenness was definitely unacceptable.

Once he began his recovery, Stu spent even more time playing golf. After his games, he often relaxed in the clubhouse, chatting with his fellow players. Some of them would have a beer or a drink; others, including Stu, would drink juice or soda. But drinking—or not drinking —was never an issue there. In six years of sobriety Stu never mentioned either his alcoholism or his sobriety to his golf chums.

Then one day at an AA meeting he bumped into Vince, another golfer. It turned out that Vince had been sober for almost four years. The two men became closer friends because of their shared experiences. But both had already achieved a very solid sobriety without in any way indicating to each other or their other golfing pals that they had a drinking problem.

A good rule to follow for friendships in early sobriety is that less is often more. This applies to quantity as well as to quality. You'll benefit much more from a few good friends, old or new, who can encourage you in sobriety, than from an extensive social network in which you have no one to whom you can talk candidly.

You should also realize that your friendships may not be the two-way street you'd prefer them to be. You must—first and always—put your focus on yourself and your sobriety in the first year of your recovery. So you may not be able to meet some of your friends' needs without endangering your sobriety. You can't stay up all night hearing about Sylvia's latest heartbreak. Nor can you attend Burt's silver wedding anniversary party because he's having an open bar. As much as you'd like to be available for your friends, you can't afford to miss a night's sleep or expose yourself to people who are drinking or drugging. That's just the way it is for now . . . the way it has to be.

As you move beyond the first year of sobriety, it becomes easier to make friends outside the recovery network. Your recovery is well on its way to being an integral part of who you are, and so it becomes possible to form new friendships based on other common interests. However, the principles for safeguarding your sobriety with friends and for telling friends about your recovery continue to apply.

In the long run, the experience, strength, and hope you gain from your recovery will help you not only to make new friends, but also to be a better friend to everyone with whom you share the bond of friendship.

Chapter Eleven
Getting Down to Work

How to Sustain Sobriety on the Job

Just as your friendships change in sobriety, so does your work life. You may find a new enthusiasm for your job, or you may decide that you have invested too much energy in your career, to the detriment of other aspects of your life. With the clarity that accompanies abstinence, you may discover a new vocation. Or you may be faced with overcoming a record of poor performance in the past, or with being unemployed. Whatever your situation, you will have to make some adjustments, possibly some difficult ones, to being sober on the job.

Job performance is often the last area to be affected by chemical dependency. I can't begin to count the number of people who have come into my office with their lives in a shambles—they've been thrown out of the house, they've been left by their spouse, they're deeply in debt, they're in poor health, they're psychologically unstable—but they proudly declare, "I can't be an alcoholic. I haven't missed a day at work for fifteen years," or "I can't be addicted to cocaine. I just got a promotion." Such people hang on to their continuing good—or good enough—performance at work as if it were the last lifeline that's saving them from being towed under by alcohol or drugs.

You may recall from Chapter 3 the story of Ken, the young surgeon who was so involved with cocaine that he missed the birth of his first child. After I had spoken with his wife Emily, I went out into the hall to ask Ken to step back into my office. But Ken was gone. He didn't resurface for two weeks, until late one afternoon when he showed up at my office without an appointment, looking haggard and uncharacteristically unkempt.

He told me he had been high most of the time since I'd last seen him. But now he had run out of cash. Emily had canceled his credit cards and his checks were bouncing. He hadn't been able to buy any cocaine for twenty-four hours. Although Ken could hardly think clearly, and he bounced from one topic to another, he kept returning to one theme—how much he loved being a surgeon. But he knew he was on the verge of throwing away all his years of training and hard work if he didn't get straight and stay straight. I had to agree with him.

Most people don't get as close to the edge as Ken did before they realize that the situation at work isn't as rosy as they had been telling themselves. They come to see much sooner that their drinking and drugging has affected their work. The consequences may be more or less subtle, but they are present.

Many others who come into recovery have allowed their dependency to affect their jobs visibly. They have established a pattern of lateness and absenteeism, particularly on Mondays and Fridays, and their deteriorating performance has brought them to the attention of their supervisors. Sometimes, faced with a warning or the threat of being fired, or because an employee assistance counselor intervenes, they seek treatment and/or join a self-help group.

Whether your career seems to have been unaffected or whether your work-related problems have brought you to recovery, you'll have to face certain issues when you're sober and back on the job.

Telling Your Supervisor and Coworkers

Here are some of the questions my patients frequently worry about: How many people know that I have a problem with alcohol or drugs? How obvious has my behavior been? Are people talking about me? Do people know I've been in treatment? Do they know I go to self-help meetings? How much should I tell them?

The curiosity, the disbelief, the intrusive personal questions, the sometimes almost prurient interest in what's happened to you, is always difficult to face. But you have to be prepared to encounter such behavior, and you have to plan ahead to cope with it when it occurs.

In the first six to twelve months of your recovery, you'll want to limit your work hours so that you'll have time to devote to your sobriety. This means no working overtime, weekends, or night shifts. You may also need to take time off for medical or therapy appointments. You might therefore consider telling your supervisor or whoever is in a position to help you arrange these absences, *but only if that person can be counted on to be discreet*. If you feel that you can't trust him or her, you'll have to find other ways to readjust your schedule.

I recommend that you not tell anyone at work about your addiction unless that person needs to know. If you've been away at a treatment center for several weeks, your co-workers will naturally be concerned and curious when you return. You should, of course, acknowledge their concern, and also indicate that your circumstances have changed. But you don't have to reveal where you've been or exactly what's happened. You might say, "I've been sick, but I'm better now, thank you." Or, "I was having a problem, but it's been straightened out."

If people press you for details, you can tell them firmly but politely that you don't care to discuss the matter further. Even if you haven't been away, your fellow employees may notice a change and remark on your new behavior and appearance. In that case, you could say, "You're right. I was under the weather for a while. Thank goodness these things don't last forever."

But isn't that dishonest, you may ask. And isn't honesty an important part of recovery? Yes, a searching personal honesty *is* essential for sobriety. But some people mistakenly believe that personal honesty means telling all to anyone who will listen. Unfortunately, this assumption is sometimes reinforced by well-meaning but misinformed counselors and other people in recovery. And sometimes it can prove to be a costly error, as Gordon discovered.

A vice president for sales, he had been a valued member of his clothing manufacturing firm for over fifteen years. His efficiency on the job had been declining for a couple of years before he voluntarily sought treatment for his alcoholism. But he was so good at what he did, so personable and well-liked, that his diminished performance didn't receive the attention it otherwise might have from senior management. The fact that sales were down in his division was attributed to a number of factors: overseas competition, a tougher business environment, the failure of a particular line.

His secretary, who had been with the firm even longer than Gordon, knew that something was amiss. Phone calls were going unanswered, and customers had been lost because of poor follow-up. She suspected that Gordon might have a problem with alcohol, but she said nothing.

Gordon was drinking about a quart of hard liquor a day, and most days he was also taking several tranquilizers. His first three days at the hospital detoxification unit were physically uncomfortable. But once he had made it through withdrawal, he began to feel far better than he had in years. His head felt clear, he started eating normally again, he slept well, and he was attending the group and AA meetings on the unit. He was so astonished that such a miraculous transformation could have occurred simply because he had stopped drinking and using drugs that he wanted to share the wonderful news with everyone.

On his fourth day in the hospital, without telling anyone, Gordon picked up the phone and made one call after another. He spoke to the president of his company, to the other vice presidents, to some of his long-standing customers, to his friends and relatives. He told them all about how marvelous sobriety was, and he even suggested to a couple of people that they check themselves into the detox unit.

He was back at work two weeks later, and energetically made the rounds, greeting his colleagues. Then he dialed his way through his Rolodex, getting in touch with all his customers. It didn't take long for him to notice that people were quite cool to him, and that they continued to be distant as the days passed.

The following week Gordon came into my office, shaking with anxiety and anger. "Why did you let me do it?" he railed. "Why did you put a phone in my room? Why did you let me call those people?"

The results of his phone calls had been disastrous. His two biggest customers had canceled their accounts. The president had seriously considered firing him and had been restrained from doing so only by the efforts of his closest associates. Nobody wanted to trust him with any new business. He had virtually nothing to do all day.

"My secretary is right," he said sullenly. "She told me I wasn't as bad as everyone is now saying I was, and that I should never have opened my mouth."

Gordon was feeling very sorry for himself, almost sorry enough to take a drink. Fortunately, he didn't give in to the urge, and eventually the situation at work was restored to normal. He regained the confidence of his associates and his customers. He rebuilt his reputation and is once again a valued member of his company. And most important, he remained sober.

Because of the poor judgment that's so common in early sobriety, Gordon overestimated people's capacity to be compassionate. He expected everyone to sympathize with his problem and share his elation. But it's one thing to talk to counselors and other recovering people about your addiction, and quite another matter to discuss it with people who have had no experience, or only negative associations, with the disease of addiction. You can't expect to get deep understanding from people who may be terrified at the mere thought of entrusting any decision, much less important business matters, to someone who is an alcoholic or addicted.

Who should Gordon have told about his alcoholism? Perhaps the president of the company and the person responsible for processing his insurance reimbursement. Perhaps one associate, someone who was as much a friend as a colleague. And because of his long and close relationship with his secretary, it was appropriate to tell her, but no one else need have known. And he should have waited until he returned to work, until he could make an appointment with the president and tell him calmly, and in private, using a script he had carefully prepared and thoroughly rehearsed.

Don't make Gordon's mistake of indiscriminately talking about your recovery with people who may not know how to handle the information. Discuss your problem *only* with the people at work who must know. If no one has to know, then discuss it with *no one*.

Dealing with a Reputation for Poor Job Performance

If you've had problems on the job—poor performance reviews or warnings because you've taken too many sick days, for example—you may have to contend with increased vigilance on the part of your supervisors when you return to work. As necessary as this may be from their point of view, it can be very difficult for you, especially in the first two or three months when you tend to see their skepticism as a form of criticism and a lack of trust in your capabilities.

Think of it instead as your employer's way of ensuring that you're doing what you're getting paid for. Just as you can't expect your family to forget about your past behavior and trust you implicitly from Day One of your sobriety, so you can't expect to regain your employer's lost faith in you immediately. You simply have to do your work to the best of your ability in spite of the scrutiny. As you rebuild your record of performing well, the close supervision will become a thing of the past.

Barry, a graphic artist for a large publishing company and a recovering alcoholic, described his experience to his sponsor. On a recent morning his art director, Fran, had seemed to be hovering over his worktable, checking on his progress. When she asked him for the fourth time that day, "How's it going?", Barry replied as politely as he could manage, then got up from his stool and headed down the hall to grab a cup of coffee.

Cynthia, who sat at the next desk over, followed him into the kitchenette and held out her mug for Barry to fill. Aside from Fran, Cynthia was one of the few people at the office who knew about Barry's recovery. In fact, she had been instrumental in getting him to make an appointment with the employee assistance program coordinator. She knew about alcoholism because her older brother was also in recovery, and from her own involvement in Al-Anon.

"Fran's been on my back, too, all morning. You shouldn't let her get to you," she told Barry.

"That's easy for you to say, Cyn," Barry shot back. "But your job isn't at stake. I'm scared that if I make the slightest mistake, if I draw a single line that isn't perfectly straight, she'll think I'm drunk. Sometimes my hands shake more than they did when I was putting down a quart a day."

"I know it's tough, but you've got to hang in there," Cynthia said sympathetically. Then she suggested he discuss the situation with his sponsor, Alec.

Barry took her advice and called Alec as soon as he got home from work. "And why shouldn't the art director watch you?" asked Alec. "I'd worry if she didn't. Your job is to stay sober. Hers is to check up on you. You do your job, and let her get on with hers. You can't afford to build up resentments the way you're doing. They eat away at you, and you start to want to drink. You better stop feeling sorry for yourself, or you're headed for a slip. The next time this comes up, give me a call from work. I'll straighten you out."

Barry realized Alec was right. The more he had replayed his fantasy of being fired by Fran for drawing a crooked line, the more he had begun to pity himself, and the greater his urge to grab a quick beer. In the end, he didn't have to call Alec at his office, nor did he have a slip. He was too busy—doing a good job and letting Fran do hers.

Of course, it will take time for your boss to forget the reports you didn't deliver that resulted in her looking foolish and unprepared at an important meeting. You may have to turn in several excellent reports exactly when they're due before your boss can forget about your having missed the earlier deadline. It will take time before your foreman forgets the shoddy work you did last summer on the company's biggest project. You may have to prove yourself on two or three jobs before he stops double-checking your work. But gradually, as your boss sees that you can be relied upon, as your foreman notices that your work is up to par, they'll stop peering over your shoulder at your every move.

You'll also find that as your recovery progresses, you'll be able to do your job more smoothly and efficiently, without so many of the hassles you used to have with your coworkers. You won't have to make any extraordinary efforts to put things right; you merely need to stay sober and do your work competently. You don't have to overcompensate, be perfect, take on too many assignments, or fall all over yourself to be nice and cordial. Indeed, such measures are likely to head you straight for a relapse.

Ian was a recovering alcoholic who had been a "star" since childhood. His parents glowed with pride whenever they spoke of his achievements. Growing up, his bedroom was always immaculate, his desk so neat that he even lined up his colored pens according to the colors of the spectrum. His academic record was also exemplary. He graduated from high school with excellent grades, as well as a special attendance certificate for having never missed a day of school in four years.

Then off he went to a prestigious university, where he was introduced to a new endeavor—the art of drinking. Ian excelled at this activity as he had at everything else in life. When he got high, he could be completely irresponsible for a few glorious hours. When he wasn't high, he always had something to do, some task to complete, some nagging duty to perform. But when he was drunk, he could forget that he had to be perfect.

After college, Ian went to graduate school to study architecture, a field for which he was well-suited because of his perfectionism and his obsession with detail. He continued to drink as a way to relax and perform even better under the considerable pressures of his job. But about five years into a successful career with a respected architecture firm, his drinking began to get out of control. He missed deadlines, lost blueprints, and made careless, avoidable mistakes. And he turned into a slob. His apartment eventually became so filthy and disgusting that Ian himself hated to spend time there.

He hit bottom one Sunday morning. Awakening from a stuporous sleep, he watched a beam of sunshine pierce through a hole in the window shade and play on the speckled bronze carpet. *What a lovely carpet*, thought Ian. But why didn't he recognize it as one that belonged to him? Then he sat up. The carpet broke up into hundreds of cockroaches running in every direction. Ian's screams of terror woke a neighbor who called the police.

The police took Ian to the nearest emergency room, from which he was immediately admitted to the hospital's detoxification unit. He stayed there five days and began attending AA meetings. Two weeks later, Ian returned to his firm. He worked feverishly to rectify all his mistakes on the few minor projects he'd been allowed to handle in recent months. When he asked to be allowed to be given a new project, he was assigned some work that normally would have been handed to someone fresh out of graduate school. Ian was stung, but was nonetheless determined to complete the job perfectly. He had to show his colleagues that he could perform better than he ever had.

He attacked the assignment with his usual meticulous attention to detail. But his hands were still a bit shaky, which made drafting difficult. His thinking wasn't as sharp as it should have been. His photographic memory was unaccountably and unpredictably faulty. He had to repeat his calculations again and again because he reversed numbers and misplaced decimal points. But he persisted, working twelve hours a day, including weekends, until he finished the job on time and without a single mistake.

Once his colleagues noticed how well he was now functioning, they started dumping work on his desk in ever-growing piles. Suddenly Ian had deadlines he could barely stick to, and more work than he could hope to finish. But because he feared that he'd be suspected of drinking again, he never turned down a request. Instead he smiled heartily and said, "Certainly, I can do it."

He arrived at the office early and left late. When he wasn't actually working, he worried about what he'd already finished and what he still had to get done. Perfection was his relentless master, and it gave him no respite. He didn't even think about drinking because he was too preoccupied with work. But his tension was mounting. He longed for release, to feel free and irresponsible, to throw off the dead weight of duty.

One Sunday evening, Ian was sitting in his spotless apartment, worrying about all the work that awaited him the next day. The thought of setting his alarm for four A.M. so that he could get to the office by five was suddenly too much for him to bear. Minutes later he found himself in a liquor store. When the alarm rang at four o'clock, Ian didn't hear it. He had found his release.

Avoid risking your sobriety by striving for perfection as Ian did. You can, and should, set reasonable and realistic limits for what you can and cannot accomplish at work. But beyond that, it's enough—more than enough—to be competent, pleasant, and above all, sober.

Dealing with a Reputation for Moodiness and Unpredictable Behavior

The mood swings and erratic behavior that are part of an active addiction have inevitably affected your relationships with your coworkers. Probably they've learned to be rather wary of you, to test the waters before talking to you because they don't quite know how you'll respond today or this hour or this minute. They steer clear of you whenever they can. Or perhaps you had an enabler right there on the job—someone who made excuses, explained your absences, maybe even took over some of the work you didn't do. Now you no longer need that person, so he or she may be disappointed, resentful, or angry.

Bertram was a fifty-five-year-old executive who had been protected while he was drinking by his superefficient secretary, Norma. She wrote his letters, made his phone calls, kept him from going to meetings when he was too high, and came up with all the right excuses for his absences. When he got sober, Bertram wanted to run his own office, but Norma continued to take care of his business as she always had. Tension mounted between them.

Bertram recognized that though Norma was bright and talented, her resentment of his sobriety was hindering him greatly, both in his work and in his recovery. He suggested that she apply for a promotion that had been posted on the office bulletin board. He wrote her a glowing recommendation and made several calls on her behalf. Norma was thrilled when she got the job, and Bertram was then free to hire and train a new secretary.

You know that your behavior in sobriety will be very different from how you behaved in the past. But your fellow employees will need some time to realize that you're no longer so touchy. Your enabler will take time to accept that you can be relied on to do your job without his or her help. Again, you don't have to do anything special to replace your record of addictive behavior with one of sober conduct. If you're amiable and courteous, people will begin to notice. And one day you'll have a particularly pleasant and productive meeting, or someone will do something especially considerate for you, and you'll think, *Aha! I'm finally being treated like a person, not a porcupine.*

Avoiding Relapse Triggers in Your Work Environment

Conditions at work can contribute directly or indirectly to your having a relapse. Perhaps several people at your office drink heavily or abuse drugs. Perhaps there are frequent Friday afternoon booze-ups, or lots of drinking or pot smoking at lunch. Or perhaps everyone in your profession seems to be doing cocaine, so that you can't go to a meeting or a business meal where coke isn't a significant item on the agenda.

If you're at a job with built-in relapse triggers, you'll have to change your routine. If lots of people drink at lunch, go to an AA meeting instead, take a brown bag lunch to the park, or find a nearby coffee shop. If you've always left with the five o'clock crowd to go to the bar down the street, see if you can arrange to come in to work an hour earlier so you can leave at four. Whatever it is that might set off a relapse, find a way to avoid that stimulus. Don't slide back into the old routine on the assumption that you can hang out with the gang without drinking or using drugs. If alcohol or drugs seem to be an inescapable part of doing business, then perhaps you're in the wrong field.

But if you're committed to and substantially invested in your work, then you owe it to yourself to undertake a thorough exploration of how to continue in that same environment without succumbing to the familiar temptations of drugging or drinking.

Finding Time to Do It All

How do you hold down a job, go to treatment sessions and self-help meetings, exercise regularly, eat sensibly, plus find time for yourself, especially if you commute and have family responsibilities as well? Can you fit so many activities and commitments into a day? Yes, but only with careful planning.

Your first step is to develop a *written* daily plan for the week ahead. Decide what's essential and what's optional for each day. Then, as the week goes by, make a note of how much you actually accomplish. What worked out well? Which activities were rewarding or pleasurable? When did you feel hurried, harried, or tired? Next, when you draw up your schedule for the week after that, cut out some of the optional items, especially those that caused you more stress than enjoyment. But as you scale down your schedule, remember that you *don't* have a choice in terms of setting aside time for eating, sleeping, and relaxation. You can, however, eliminate items such as extra work assignments, bringing work home with you, and overtime.

To create a sensible schedule that works for you and your sobriety, you may have to talk to your employer about whether you can rearrange your hours to accommodate counseling or exercise sessions. You can investigate opportunities for part-time work or job-sharing until your sobriety is on firmer footing. If you're used to making your career your first priority, you'll have to readjust your outlook so that your sobriety moves to the top of the list. As we saw earlier with Ian, taking on too much work can be a powerful trigger for relapse and isn't compatible with building a comfortable, stable sobriety.

Changing Jobs

Some recovering people find that as they begin to enjoy their sobriety, they want to change the entire direction of their life. They feel capable of doing things that never before seemed possible, or they realize that the job at which they have been working more or less automatically for years isn't at all satisfying, and they're feeling bored and restless. Sometimes a change means applying for a more responsible position with another employer. But it can also entail going back to school and starting an entirely new career, or pursuing neglected job-related avenues, or resuming a profession or trade that had been abandoned because of your addiction. These new beginnings can be very exciting. But they can also be hazardous to sobriety if undertaken too soon and without extremely careful consideration of the time and energy involved in pursuing new and demanding goals.

As I've said before, it's best not to make any major life changes until you've achieved a full year of sound sobriety. My recommendation especially applies to career changes that involve going back to school, which is best postponed until you're once again in command of your full intellectual abilities. However, when you do feel well enough to make a start, you should first take the time to investigate fully whatever you're planning to get into. Discuss all the aspects of your proposed life change with people whose opinion and judgment you respect.

Having so often suggested that you postpone major life changes, I have to add a qualifier here. Some life situations simply aren't conducive to sobriety, and have to be altered as soon as possible. But you shouldn't charge ahead without first talking about your situation with your self-help sponsor, your family, your counselor, or your trusted friends.

Suzanne, for example, found herself in just such an untenable position. She was married, had a four-year-old daughter, as well as a high-pressure job as director of marketing for a prestigious museum. She lived in a large house in the suburbs and commuted into New York City for work, a ninety-minute trip each way. Her marriage was under considerable strain, not only because of her drinking and dependency on tranquilizers, but also because her husband Gary had been out of work for three months and couldn't find a new job. Suzanne was the sole financial support of the family, and her salary alone wasn't adequate to meet their monthly expenses.

The first time I saw her, she was using three times the recommended dose of tranquilizers in an attempt to control her nightly drinking. She had recognized for some months that her drinking and drug use were getting seriously out of hand, which was why she had finally decided to come for help. She entered an intensive outpatient treatment program, and I saw her again two weeks later when she was clean and sober.

As we discussed her jam-packed schedule, we both realized that it left her with no time to focus on her sobriety. She was constantly in motion, from 6:00 A.M., when she rolled out of bed to get herself and her daughter ready for the day, to 11:00 P.M., when she finally sank back into bed. Her husband, who was depressed over his career problems, was unable to be of much help. We agreed that her priority was to rearrange her life in such a way that she would have time for herself and her sobriety. But unless she made some major changes, her chances for remaining sober seemed slim indeed.

Suzanne didn't rush out and leave her husband or quit her job. Instead, she talked about possible solutions, not only with me and her counselor, but also with her husband, her mother, her sponsor, and the woman who had been her best friend since high school. She convinced Gary to attend the family counseling program; in the course of these sessions he agreed that the family should move to less expensive housing. He also agreed to pick up their daughter from nursery school three evenings a week and take care of her while Suzanne was at her self-help meeting. Next, Suzanne agreed to give up her job and look for work closer to home, even though it would mean taking a cut in salary. Her new position wasn't as exciting or prestigious as her old one. But it was much less stressful, and the salary was sufficient to cover her now reduced expenses.

In the first three months of recovery, Suzanne made two major life changes: she moved, and she looked for and found a new job. Those first ninety days were very difficult and demanding, but with thorough and prudent discussion each step of the way, she was able to do what she had to, *and* maintain her sobriety.

Looking for a Job

Some newly sober people don't have the choices that Suzanne did. They have to cope with the additional stress of finding a new job because they were fired, resigned under pressure, or have been unemployed for some time because of their drinking or drugging. The following questions then arise: What information do they include on their resumes? How do they account for the gaps in their employment history? Whom do they have to tell about their recovery? How do they deal with job interviews? And how do they deal with *not* getting the job?

Given that everyone in early sobriety is exquisitely sensitive to rejection, it's not surprising that looking for a job, with its built-in potential for rejection, can be very hazardous to sobriety. If you're unemployed, first ask yourself, do I absolutely have to get a job now? Many of my patients have taken time off from work as they begin their recovery. They've lived on savings, on unemployment, on public assistance, or on the generosity of friends and relatives. Some have gone to halfway houses where they found that living in a safe, nurturing atmosphere alleviated some of the stress of looking for work.

But if your answer is yes, you do need to find a job, then you have to prepare for job-hunting. You may need to write a resume, and you'll certainly have to think about what you want to say at interviews. By all means, get all the help you can from your sponsor and friends, particularly from other recovering people who have been through this same experience.

Your resume is your foot in the door, and as such it has to be attractive and interesting. It should state your goals, achievements, educational qualifications, and any other relevant interests or assets. It must be written in straightforward, grammatical prose, correctly spelled and neatly reproduced on good paper. You don't have to lie about anything, but you can arrange the information so that any gaps in your employment history are less apparent. (Keep in mind that many people, not only those who are in recovery, have had periods when they've been unemployed for one reason or another.) You'll find many books full of helpful tips about resume-writing in the business section of your library or bookstore. If you can afford the expense, you may want to hire a resume-writing service, available in most larger cities, to help you create, format, and reproduce your resume.

What you most certainly should not do is adopt a defeatist attitude about your resume. I once supervised a recovering medical resident, Charlotte, who asked me to write a recommendation for her, adding that she didn't think she had a chance of getting the job for which she was applying. I asked Charlotte to bring me a copy of her resume, and she came in the next day with a tattered sheet of paper. Her resume listed only the barest facts of her education and training; it was also poorly typed and contained two spelling errors.

Charlotte's resume was a dramatic metaphor for how she viewed herself. Anyone reading it would jump to the conclusion that she had nothing to offer either as a doctor or as a human being. In fact, she was a responsible, concerned, and compassionate physician who had been highly rated by all her supervisors. I told her that I wouldn't write a reference for her until she had put together a resume that reflected her true abilities, because the one she had showed me would negate whatever good I had to say about her. Charlotte enlisted the help of a friend, and with her assistance compiled a resume that presented her as a valuable job candidate.

Few people, whether in recovery or not, enjoy interviewing for jobs. But poor self-esteem, lack of assertion, and the belief that they have nothing to offer can make job interviews especially stressful for those who are newly sober. They think they have to defend themselves against an interviewer who's out to discover just how worthless they are. Instead of cultivating an open, frank attitude, they adopt a cringing, "guilty until proven innocent" stance that's indicative of their conviction that only the most desperate employer would hire them.

When you first start going on job interviews, you may actually believe that you have little or nothing to offer. But you have to make an effort not to act that way. You might want to rehearse what you're planning to say at the interview with a friend. Practice your dialogue over and over again until you're comfortable with it, until you begin to see and believe that you *do* have a great deal to offer.

Your recovery isn't relevant to what you have to offer a prospective employer, so you don't have to discuss it unless you're asked a direct question. In that case, answer truthfully, because a lie will only lead to anxiety and further deception, both of which can be a threat to your sobriety. Some interviewers may coldly and abruptly end your appointment when you're honest about your recovery. Others will be more informed about the disease of addiction, but you still may not get the job.

You may not get *several* jobs, and you may have more than one interview that goes badly. To protect your sobriety, you have to make plans for after every interview—self-help meetings, lunch with a sober friend, a cup of coffee with your sponsor, any contact with people who can help you maintain your perspective.

Many books have been written on the subject of job hunting, and you'll find a partial listing in Appendix A. Help is also available specifically for recovering people. In New York State, the government-sponsored Employment Program for Recovered Alcoholics (EPRA) offers a structured approach to determining what jobs might be appropriate for you and preparing yourself to enter the job market. Unfortunately, I know of no other program like EPRA in the United States. Your local chapter of the National Council on Alcoholism also provides guidance to job-seekers. Services vary, but in many locations the Council offers counseling and referrals. You can find the addresses of these organizations in Appendix C. Some alcohol and drug treatment programs also offer vocational guidance to their patients. However, no directory of treatment programs includes this information, so inquiries should be made directly to the individual facilities.

Work is important to most of us, not only as a source of money, power, praise or recognition, but for other, less tangible reasons as well, such as the fact that it can give us a sense of mastery and competence, the ability to solve problems, improve skills, and work well with others, to name just a few. Unfortunately, many people in early recovery think so little of themselves that they're overly dependent on the obvious external rewards of work. They're crushed when they don't get that raise or promotion or the award they had hoped for.

Among the many other wonderful opportunities it offers, sobriety is also a chance to reassess one's attitude toward work. I recall Lucille, forty, a patient of mine who was a salesperson in a large department store. She had worked at the store for fifteen years and clearly loved her job. She described with evident pride her techniques for dealing with difficult customers during the Christmas rush, how she sorted out those whose feet were hurting from those who were feeling overwhelmed and those who by nature felt they were entitled to immediate service. She had developed ways to soothe each type—providing a chair for the foot-sore, a rapid transaction for the hurried, and flattering attention for the egocentric.

About a year after she became sober, Lucille was offered and accepted a promotion to be a floor supervisor of her department. The position included a pay raise, more vacation time, and a better choice of hours. But after six months, Lucille stepped down. "I wasn't good at it, and I didn't enjoy it," she explained. She happily returned to her sales job. For Lucille, feeling good about her work wasn't contingent on tangible demonstrations of approval. The satisfaction she derived from performing well and enjoying herself in the process was more important than the money, power, and other perks that went along with her promotion.

One of the many joys of sobriety is learning to take pleasure in the less tangible—and indeed, the more spiritual—rewards of work. It's also gratifying to learn that you're not what you *do*, that a whole person is more than a police officer or a banker or a musician or an electrician. Your other roles are also important parts of you—being a parent, a sibling, a spouse or a friend, helping others who are struggling with their sobriety. Satisfying work can be a substantial aspect of being a whole, sober person, but by no means does it tell the whole story of your sobriety.

Chapter Twelve
Relapse

In the self-help groups, it's called "having a slip." Among medical and health professionals who treat patients with addictive disorders, it's called a relapse. Whatever you call it, it means that, despite your best intentions and all you've learned, you drink or use drugs again.

Relapses are common to many chronic diseases. People who have arthritis and follow a particular treatment regimen may be virtually symptom-free until they unexpectedly have a flare-up of joint pain. Diabetics who keep their condition well controlled by regulating their diets may suddenly begin to develop high blood sugar again. Those who are successfully coping with their epilepsy may have a seizure without any prior warning. Afterward, when the patient and his or her physician look closely at the potential causes, they very often find some change in the patient's routine that explains why the relapse occurred.

Virtually everyone who suffers a chronic medical condition will have relapses throughout his or her life. Only among people with addictive disorders do you find those who have been free of relapses for ten or twenty, even forty or fifty years, and who may well live the rest of their lives without any further relapses. In fact, that's one reason I am so glad I changed my specialty from neurology, where so often the best I could do was keep my patients from getting worse, to addiction medicine, where many of my patients improve and may never again have another bout of the disease.

Among addictive diseases, the highest risk of relapse comes in the early stages of recovery. The longer you remain abstinent, the greater the chances you'll continue to remain alcohol- and/or drug-free. The patterns of relapse among those in recovery from alcohol, cocaine, or even nicotine are very similar. About seventy percent of relapses occur in the first six months of abstinence. Some continue to take place over the next six months, but the incidence drops off as people approach one year of sobriety. And once they've remained abstinent for two years, they have only a *five percent* chance of relapse during the third year.

When you consider the condition you're in during the first six to twelve months of recovery, these statistics make sense. Your body is still convalescing from the prolonged effects of physical withdrawal; your behavior, habits, and thinking are only just beginning to change. Your emotions are still unstable. These are some of the reasons why "one day at a time" is such a marvelous slogan. Because if you can stay sober one day at a time, one hour at a time, or even one minute at a time, the next day or hour or minute is that much easier. When people who are two weeks into recovery contemplate a lifetime of feeling as they do—overwhelmed by cravings and extremely uncomfortable physically and psychologically, it's small wonder that they find it incredibly difficult to imagine remaining abstinent for the rest of their lives. By contrast, the thought of remaining sober and clean for a short period of time usually doesn't seem as daunting.

About one-third of the people treated at Smithers remain successfully abstinent on their first attempt at recovery. That is, as far as we know, they don't have any relapses and stay sober forever. The remaining two-thirds have one or more relapses, which vary enormously —from one drink downed or drug taken in a fit of anger and repented immediately, to a binge that lasts several weeks or months. What I most often see among those people who eventually succeed at maintaining abstinence is a pattern of recovery that shows steady, if sometimes shaky progress toward a lifelong sobriety.

The Pattern of Recovery

Terry, a businessman in his late twenties, followed a typical recovery pattern. He came into our inpatient treatment center largely due to the intervention of Roger, his partner. Following his release after three weeks in treatment, Terry maintained a two-month abstinence, during which time he and Roger put together a very lucrative deal. When they went to sign the final papers, one of the other people involved in the deal passed around some cocaine, and Terry couldn't resist taking "just one line. How could it hurt?" Two days later, he bought some cocaine from his old dealer. Before long he was using both cocaine and alcohol on a regular basis.

Roger was once again concerned by Terry's frequent absences and unreliability, and intervened again. This time, Terry agreed to participate in an intensive outpatient program where his urine was tested each week. He also sporadically attended CA and AA, but he didn't find himself either a home group or a sponsor. He continued to remain abstinent as long as he was participating in the outpatient program. However, shortly after he left the program, he had another relapse; on this occasion he went back to drinking only.

Terry had been using the outpatient program and the urine tests as a way to control himself, which was perfectly acceptable. But he hadn't worked very hard on developing alternative patterns of behavior. He had also allowed himself to become caught up in working very hard to rebuild the business that had been jeopardized by his addiction. For about three or four months, although he didn't use cocaine again and drank only sparingly during the week, he drank heavily on weekends. One Monday when he was due to attend an important meeting, he couldn't even go to the office because he was so badly hung over. The deal fell through.

Terry was devastated. After all the time and effort he had lately devoted to the company, it was now in danger of collapsing again. This time, he took a hard look at his situation. In the past, he had done so because of pressure from his business partner; this time he scrutinized himself because he needed and wanted to do so.

He decided that he was going to change his ways. He started going to AA meetings regularly, joined a home group, and got himself a sponsor. During the first few months at his home group, Terry, the businessman who was unused to performing menial tasks, came in early before meetings to make the coffee. Six months later he became secretary of the group. With his newfound motivation and the continuous support of his sponsor and AA friends, he remained abstinent for a full year.

And then he had one more relapse. Bursting with confidence in himself and his sobriety, he went on vacation alone to a Caribbean resort. There he met Allison, a bright, attractive woman who also owned a successful business. Terry and Allison spent a lot of time together—playing tennis, swimming, talking, and sharing long, leisurely meals. One evening at dinner, Allison suggested they order a bottle of wine. Terry worried that if he told her he was an alcoholic, he would ruin what seemed to be a promising relationship. So he agreed to the wine and drank two glasses.

The next morning, he became very frightened when he realized how close he had come once again to destroying the life he had so carefully put together. He made up his mind to be honest with Allison. He told her he was a recovering alcoholic, and that in drinking the wine, he had made a mistake. He also told her he would very much like to spend that evening with her, but he would have to ask her not to order any alcohol. To his surprise and delight, Allison agreed. In the two years since his Caribbean vacation, Terry hasn't had another drink or taken any drugs.

With each relapse, Terry learned more and more about himself, and about what triggered his drug or alcohol use. He also learned new ways to think about himself and new ways of living. At the beginning of his recovery, he certainly couldn't have been so candid with Allison, because he didn't yet have the tools. There is no question that had this event taken place two and a half years earlier, it would have been the occasion for a full-blown binge, rather than two glasses of wine and some sober reflection by the light of day.

Terry doesn't assume that he "got away with something" that night. Nor does he think that because he didn't go off on a blind drunk, he can safely drink again. He realizes that he has a chronic, incurable disease, but he also believes and hopes that his Caribbean relapse was its final kick.

What Triggers a Relapse

Some valuable systematic studies have been done, most outstandingly by Dr. Alan Marlatt of the University of Washington, of large numbers of people who have had relapses. These studies have clearly identified the stimuli that typically trigger relapses. The research has also demystified the subject. A slip is no longer viewed as a banana peel that unexpectedly appears in your path to trip you up, but rather as a phenomenon with *definite antecedents* that you can be aware of and avoid.

Relapse triggers may be divided into three main groups:
• people, places and things,
• negative moods,
• loss of self-esteem.

I will also talk about a fourth, much smaller group of miscellaneous triggers.

People, Places, and Things

About thirty percent of all relapses are related to exposing yourself to risky situations, such as the following:
• stopping by the bar where you used to go drinking or the place where you often used to do drugs,

• hanging out with people who were your drinking or drugging buddies,

• going to parties, clubs, discos, or rock concerts where alcohol or drugs are heavily used,

• keeping drugs or alcohol around the house,

• passing by the liquor stores where you used to buy your supply or the places where you used to score.

In short, a risky situation is one that's likely to bring back physical memories of alcohol and/or drug use.

Negative Moods

About twenty percent of relapses are the result of not taking care of yourself properly when you're feeling bad—anxious, depressed, panicky, tired. Anxiety that's been allowed to build can become so intolerable that you seek relief in a drug or drink. Depression often leads to the belief that sobriety is too painful a condition to maintain. A dry drunk —a period of time when you feel tense and irritable, as if you have a hangover—can make you think that the only way to feel better is to use.

Antoine reached this conclusion on a gray Saturday in February when he was stuck alone in Manhattan with no plans for the day except doing his laundry and feeling sorry for himself. His lover Marc was in Vermont for a weekend of skiing, a sport that Antoine hated. Marc had invited him to come along, but Antoine couldn't understand how anyone could enjoy an activity that was cold and uncomfortable, not to mention dangerous. Besides, he was sure that Marc's invitation had been half-hearted at best. Probably, he was hoping to meet someone new on the slopes—someone handsomer, younger, and richer.

As he sorted through his dirty clothes, Antoine thought about how his life hadn't gone the way he had planned. He had come to New York hoping to be an actor. He had snared a few parts, but nothing major, nothing that paid the rent. At thirty, he was getting past the age when he could hope for a big break. His cocaine habit had lost him his job waiting tables at Charlie's, an "in" spot in the theater district. Now he was working Sundays through Tuesdays, the worst nights for tips, at a tacky Italian tourist trap in Greenwich Village. He hated the noise, the rush, the way the owner ordered him around as if he were an army recruit. He even hated the smell of tomato sauce.

Antoine was feeling desperately sorry for himself and on the verge of tears when the phone rang. It was his friend Chuck. "All alone?" he asked sympathetically. "Why don't you come on over? I have some terrific blow."

"You know I'm off that stuff," Antoine said without much conviction.

"Yeah, sure," said Chuck. "You don't have to do any. We could just talk. I can tell from your voice that you need some cheering up."

Antoine didn't need much more convincing. He grabbed his jacket and was on his way. Of course, he ended up using that afternoon.

Loss of Self-Esteem

It is not difficult to see why self-esteem is so low in the early stages of recovery. Not only are you still very close to the often personally degrading episodes you experienced when you were using, but you haven't yet been sober long enough to see sobriety itself as an achievement. Any event that damages your fragile self-esteem is likely to make you feel angry, impotent, or out of control—and so you feel even worse about yourself than you already did. But even after a year or more of sobriety, when you have done much to rebuild your self-esteem, your sense of self may still be vulnerable and may continue to be throughout sobriety.

Blows to your self-esteem can be serious, such as losing a lover or a job, or minor, such as being criticized for incorrectly filling out a form, or losing a game of Scrabble or tennis. But any event that makes you see yourself as less than competent, attractive, desirable, well thought of, or capable may set you thinking about a drug or a drink. Such loss of self-esteem is so dangerous that it accounts for some forty percent of relapses.

Other Triggers

The remaining ten percent of relapses are related to a variety of causes. These include what is called "testing"—drinking or using again to see whether you can get away with it—as well as using again during an illness or when physical pain provides an excuse. Relapses also occur among that small group of people who can't tolerate success, and who therefore slip when they are feeling especially positive or happy about some event in their life.

Clark, a veterinarian by training, was the owner of Pregnant Paws, a pet-breeding establishment that provided everything from fertilization to neonatal care. The people who had laughed when Clark had first thought of the idea had stopped laughing because Pregnant Paws was an unqualified success. Clark was well on his way to becoming a very rich young man. His pride and joy was his shining, clean, up-to-date clinic. But Pregnant Paws had also spawned other lucrative enterprises —a line of puppy and kitten food and accessories; comprehensive mother/puppy or kitten health care by a staff of veterinarians; an obedience training center; and pet psychology services.

Pregnant Paws and all its spinoffs had kept Clark so busy that he hadn't had much time to work on his sobriety. He took it so much for granted that on the day he was elected state president of the California Junior Chamber of Commerce, he celebrated with a glass of champagne. Riding on a crest of euphoria, he drank it thoughtlessly, then threw back several more drinks that evening, all with the same unthinking abandon.

In the morning, Clark assessed the situation. He felt great, no hangover, no guilt, no blackout. He remembered every glorious moment of the night before, which led him to conclude that he must be one of those exceptional alcoholics who can control his drinking. There was obviously no harm in taking a drink whenever he wanted, he decided. Within six months Pregnant Paws was in a shambles, and Clark was forced to make a new start, both with his sobriety and his business.

Clark *was* exceptional in that no clear-cut cause pointed to his slip. He wasn't ambivalent about success; he had no secret agenda setting himself up for failure. But he had become lax about his recovery. He hadn't kept fresh the memory of his previous drinking disasters by attending self-help meetings. So when the opportunity presented itself, his disease was ready to move front and center.

Besides such events or situations, two additional factors, also identified by Alan Marlatt, can contribute to a relapse. The first, which is called the *abstinence violation effect*, happens to a lot of people when they use again after a period of abstinence. They don't stop with one drink or one pill—they get plastered, perhaps even pass out, because once they've taken that first drink or pill or hit, they figure that they might as well be hung for a sheep as for a lamb.

If you do use again after a period of sobriety, no law says you have to continue to drink or use until you're completely intoxicated. Indeed, you yourself know that isn't so. Weren't there times when you were using heavily when you stopped after just one snort, or one or two drinks? But very often, when people break their abstinences, they begin to believe that the game is lost for good. They might as well go on and get sky high, not just today, but tomorrow and the day after as well. They forget that if they do have a slip, they can, of course, immediately renew their commitment to sobriety. Instead, they get caught up in the abstinence violation effect.

One reason this happens is because they don't yet see themselves as abstainers. In early recovery, they have only a tentative self-image of themselves as nondrinkers or nonusers. As soon as they pick up that first drink or drug, they're no longer abstainers. They're users again in their own eyes. And so they may as well go all the way.

It is difficult to alter that self-image, to stop thinking of yourself as a user and a jolly good fellow, and to start seeing yourself as someone who's sober. (And also to accept the negative labels that our society often places on such a person—party pooper, uptight, wet blanket, etc.) But the longer you abstain, and the harder you work at your sobriety, the stronger your self-image as an abstainer becomes.

Think back to Terry. His first relapse, when he couldn't pass up that celebratory snort of cocaine, occurred when he had only a very weak sense of himself as a nonuser. Within a short period of time, he was using heavily again, and making no attempt to stop the process. Compare that initial slip with his last relapse. After he had shared the bottle of wine with Allison, he managed not to be engulfed by the abstinence violation effect. He didn't say, "I've had some wine, so now I'm going to get good and drunk." Instead, he told himself, "I've had the wine, but I also have the tools to prevent this from becoming a full-scale disaster." His image of himself as someone who was sober, and his self-esteem in general, were strong enough to bring him back to sobriety.

The second factor that can also contribute to relapse is what Marlatt calls *apparently irrelevant decisions*. Most relapses don't occur out of the clear blue sky with no warning whatsoever. Choices you make along the way can lead you ever closer to a slip, even if those choices superficially appear to have no connection with your taking the first drug or drink.

Here's a typical sequence of apparently irrelevant decisions that caused one of my patients to start drinking again. Mike was a welder who was having trouble with Fred, one of the other workers at the shop. In the heat of an argument, Fred told Mike that he was a lousy welder, and that the only reason their boss hadn't fired a drunk like him was out of kindness. This wasn't the first time that Fred had made such cracks, and Mike knew that Fred's constant criticisms were unfounded. He did good work and he had been sober for three months. But rather than defend himself, he decided not to waste good breath on someone so nasty and narrow-minded. So he walked away from the fight feeling hurt and angry, wishing his old friend, Phil, still worked at the shop instead of Fred.

On his way home that evening, Mike thought about how long it had been since he had last seen Phil, who now had his own shop in a nearby town. True, they had spent a lot of their time together drinking at a local bar, but their friendship went beyond that. Phil knew what a good worker Mike was; in fact, Mike had taught Phil a trick or two on the job. And when Mike called Phil, Phil immediately said, "Hey, great to hear from you! What've you been up to?"

"Been busy," Mike replied, not wanting to discuss his recovery with Phil over the phone. "But it sure would be nice to see you."

"Sure," said Phil. "How about right now at the usual place?"

Against his better judgment, and because he was already feeling shaky after his fight with Fred, Mike agreed to meet Phil at the bar. He would order ginger ale, he told himself. No alcohol.

When he arrived at their familiar haunt, he and Phil greeted each other with hearty handshakes and much backslapping, then grabbed seats at the bar. "What'll you have? Let's celebrate, on me," Phil offered.

Mike tried to ask for a ginger ale, but the words wouldn't come out.

"Two of the usual," Phil ordered on their behalf.

Now let's look at the apparently irrelevant decisions Mike made once he had left the shop that evening. First, he thought about the good old days, when he had friends around who appreciated him. Second, he phoned Phil, a decision that he didn't consciously connect with Phil's predictable invitation that they meet at their old watering hole. His final and most costly decision was to go to the bar while he was feeling lousy, and without a well-rehearsed plan for maintaining his sobriety.

Mike could have taken other steps that would not so surely have led him to drinking that night. If he had spoken his mind to Fred instead of swallowing his anger, he might not have felt so bad about himself. If he had stopped to consider why he suddenly wanted to talk to Phil, he might not have made the phone call. He might instead have called his sponsor or an AA friend.

But once he phoned Phil, he placed himself in a risky position. He exposed himself to two environmental triggers—the bar where he had done so much of his drinking, and his old drinking buddy. One could argue that Fred's nasty remarks caused Mike's relapse, but it's not that simple. All along the way, Mike could have made choices to make himself feel better. But in each instance, he decided on solutions that increased rather than decreased his chance of having a relapse.

How to Prevent Relapses

Preventing relapses and making choices is really what sobriety is all about. Not only must you avoid your particular relapse triggers, but you also have to keep an eye on the choices you make every day. If you do have a slip, if you take that first drink or that first pill—and many people do—you still have a choice about taking the second, third, or fourth. You don't have to turn a slip into a fall from a fifth-story window. You can choose to avoid the abstinence violation effect.

You can also carefully consider the options that may push you toward taking that first drink or drug. After a bad day at work, should you call an old drinking or drugging pal, or a friend from your self-help group? If you've had a fight with your spouse or lover, you may well want to go out for a walk to cool off, but should your route take you past the bar where you used to drink, or should you head in the other direction toward the park? You can help maintain your sobriety one day, indeed, one choice at a time if you keep in mind that *you always have a choice*. But I'd like to offer some other suggestions as well for how to decrease your chance of relapse.

Take Your Relapse Risk Assessment

Now that you're familiar with what kinds of stimuli can set off a relapse, you should take your own relapse risk assessment. Be as honest as you can with yourself as you go through the checklist. Think hard about *exactly* what makes you feel bad and what makes you flirt with the idea of drinking or using. Also think about the specific situations in your life right now that might accidentally lead you to a trigger. Then go beyond the list. Can you come up with anything that's specific to your life circumstances that could be a trigger for you?

Some triggers are obvious: accepting an invitation to a party where you know liquor or cocaine will be available, for example. A less obvious trigger might be deciding to walk home past the liquor store you occasionally patronized, even though it wasn't the one where you regularly bought your supply. An example of an even less apparent trigger would be putting on a record you always used to listen to when you were drinking or using.

Listed below are some of the most common situations that precede relapses. Think carefully about each one. Did you use alcohol or drugs in the past when this happened? If it happened now, would you be tempted to use? Based on your answers to these questions, rate each situation on a scale of 1 to 4. A rating of 1 means there is no risk of relapse for you in this situation; 4 means your risk is high. For each rating of 3 or 4, write out the specifics of the situation as it applies to you, and your plan for coping with it should it occur.

Situation	*1*	*2*	*3*	*4*

1. I had a problem at work.

2. Someone criticized me.

3. I felt tense or uptight.

4. My plans didn't work out.

5. I felt frustrated.

6. I was treated unfairly.

7. Someone didn't like me.

8. Someone made me angry.

9. I felt put down.

10. My supervisor demanded too much.

11. I quarreled with a family member or a friend.

12. I felt uncomfortable in a social situation.

13. I didn't get along with someone.

14. My family pressured me.

15. I felt I had behaved badly.

16. I didn't know what to do.

17. I felt bored.

18. I had trouble sleeping.

19. I had trouble staying awake.

20. My stomach was tied in knots.

21. I felt nauseous.

22. I was in pain.

23. I had a bad headache.

24. I felt anxious or panicky.

25. I wanted more fulfilling sex.

26. I felt anxious about having sex without my drug.

Situation	*1*	*2*	*3*	*4*
27. I felt confident.				
28. I was feeling good and wanted to feel even better.				
29. I wanted to have a good time.				
30. Everyone was celebrating and I wanted to celebrate too.				
31. I remembered how good it felt to be high.				
32. I went to a bar with a friend.				
33. I went to a place where I had used.				
34. I met a friend I had used with in the past.				
35. I passed by a liquor store.				
36. I passed by the place where I used to buy my drugs.				
37. I accidentally came upon a bottle of liquor.				
38. I accidentally found a small quantity of my drug.				
39. I saw somebody getting high.				
40. I wanted to prove that one drink wouldn't hurt.				
41. I wanted to prove I could use a little and walk away.				
42. I wanted to prove that just enough to make me more relaxed/alert wouldn't hurt.				
43. I had a sudden urge to use.				
44. I felt cravings all day.				
45. I had a dream in which I got high.				
46. List your special situations.				

To help you get started, here are some examples of plans two of my patients made for situations they rated 3 or 4.

Jocelyn gave #6, I was treated unfairly, a rating of 4.

"When I was drinking, my supervisor, at a department meeting, praised a coworker for his terrific efforts in getting the annual report out. He didn't even mention me, and I had worked just as hard as my coworker. I got plastered that night.

"If something like that happened now, I would talk to my sponsor and go to a meeting that night. The next day, if the situation warranted it, I would make an appointment with my supervisor to discuss my role in the work that had been done."

Alonso rated #44, I felt cravings all day, a 4.

"I had been off cocaine for five weeks. I was doing okay, not great, but I was getting along. Then I had this day when I couldn't think of anything but getting high. As soon as my shift was over my feet just took me to my dealer's place, and I used. It took me three months to get straight again.

"If I felt like that now, I would do several things. First, I'd call my friend Juan, from my CA group, and ask him to meet me at work so that we could go to the gym together. Working out helps when I'm having cravings. Then we would have a good dinner together and go to a meeting afterwards."

Leslie took her relapse risk assessment and did very well in recovery for nine months. She avoided the people, places, and things that could tempt her to drink again; she avoided potential blows to her self-esteem and frustrating situations; she learned to defuse her negative moods. And she accomplished all of this while she was supervising a particularly complicated and worrisome project at work. When the project was finally completed, she decided to take a well-earned vacation, her first in sobriety. But vacations were one item she hadn't considered when she had taken her relapse risk assessment.

Because she had once spent a memorable week in Cancun, Mexico, she arranged to go back to there. But she didn't stop to think about why that week had been so memorable. She also didn't think about what vacations had always meant to her—freedom from her heavy work-related responsibilities, exciting no-strings-attached affairs, and lots of drinking. She never considered that without the alcohol, she might not be able to abandon herself as she had in the past. Not surprisingly, she had a relapse while she was in Cancun.

Eventually she became sober again. On her next holiday, she was careful to choose the more structured environment of a tennis camp. Her week there was relaxing, satisfying, and enjoyable. She returned to work rested, refreshed, and sober—and with a mean backhand.

The point of this story is, of course, that triggers can surprise you

228 RESTORE YOUR LIFE
in the oddest places, when you're least expecting them. That's why it's so important that you come up with as many of your own special situations as you can when you take your relapse risk assessment.

Make a Plan

The essence of relapse prevention is to plan ahead very carefully. The converse is to act impulsively. Spontaneous behavior can sometimes be wonderful because it gets us to try things that are new and exciting. But in early recovery, it's very likely to lead to a relapse, so you have to arm yourself by preparing for every item on your relapse risk assessment. You also have to rehearse your planned responses until they become second nature to you.

Let me give you an example of successful planning on the part of a newly recovering alcoholic. Frank was an advertising executive who frequently had to entertain clients at lunches where a lot of alcohol was usually consumed. Frank had always done his heavy drinking at night. Though he had looked forward to his two noontime drinks, he had never allowed himself more than that for fear that it would interfere with his work. Now that he was sober, those business lunches were high on his list of relapse triggers. He could entertain less frequently, but he couldn't avoid the lunches entirely without losing his clients. What was he to do?

Before his first lunch date in sobriety, Frank carefully rehearsed the exact sequence of events that was likely to occur. He wrote down precisely what he would say when the waiter asked what he wanted to drink: "Club soda with a twist of lime, please." He also decided how to respond if his business associates asked why he was drinking club soda: "I find I work better in the afternoon." He practiced this routine with an AA friend at a coffee shop where no alcohol was available.

When it came time to sit down to lunch with his client, Frank had no difficulty ordering the soda with lime. And when his client asked why he wasn't having his usual scotch, Frank calmly repeated the line he had planned. The words tripped easily off his tongue. He didn't stutter, stammer, blush, fall off his chair, or in any way embarrass himself.

Such careful preparation for something as simple as ordering a drink at lunchtime may strike you as excessive. But for years, Frank's regular order had been scotch on the rocks. He recognized that old ways die hard, and that it takes practice to alter ingrained habits.

Whatever plan you make must be appropriate to the situation. Frank quite appropriately explained his order of club soda in terms of wanting to protect his efficiency at the office. It would have been inappropriate for him to launch into the long and depressing tale of his alcoholism—or worse yet, try to get his long-time client, whom he now perceives to have a drinking problem, to accompany him to AA meetings.

Here are some other useful answers to the question of why you're not drinking: "It's better for my health" or "I find I feel better if I don't drink."

However, I *don't* recommend either of the following: "I'm on an alcohol-free diet" or "doctor's orders." These statements imply a temporary situation, the terms of which have been dictated by someone else, rather than your having made the decision for yourself. Likewise, "I'm on the wagon" suggests that you'll soon be off the wagon. On the other hand, if you truthfully state, "I'm alcoholic and I can't drink," you're likely to cause embarrassment all around, except in the most intimate personal situations. The response many recovering people find most helpful as well as appropriate to most situations is, "I'm not drinking today." These words remind people that they are committed to staying sober one day at a time and that they have the support of the AA fellowship.

Whatever plans you make for dealing with your particular triggers, try to involve someone who will be supportive and helpful as much as possible. For example, if your monthly departmental review is always stressful, plan to go to an AA meeting after work that day. If a visit to your father at his nursing home always upsets you, plan to meet a sober friend or perhaps your AA sponsor afterward. Even if you ultimately have to carry out your plan alone (for example, Frank couldn't very well bring his AA pal to lunch), asking a friend to help you formulate and practice what you want to say can greatly contribute to a positive outcome in any given situation. In any case, one of the best insurance policies for your sobriety is talking about your feelings instead of acting on them.

Of course, sometimes the best form of relapse prevention is personal time spent alone. If anxiety is one of your triggers, you may decide to listen to a meditation tape in a quiet room, or take a long soak in a hot tub, go for a run, or bake a loaf of bread.

However, no matter how carefully devised your plans may be, they will do you no good at all if you don't follow them. Maybe all you want to do after your departmental review is go home and collapse in front of the TV set. But the danger here is that you might collapse with a beer in your hand. If, instead, you attend an AA meeting, you may still be tired and cross, but you'll have reinforced your commitment to sobriety by doing what you promised yourself you would. If your kids are clamoring for dinner but you're feeling anxious and need fifteen minutes to meditate, take the time. Your kids won't starve just because they have to wait a few minutes to eat.

Relieve Unpleasant Feelings

In Chapter 5 I discussed at length the steps you can take to defuse your negative moods. Using those techniques can help you prevent a relapse due to unpleasant feelings. But there is one more circumstance I want to talk about here—the dry drunk.

You may recall from Chapter 1 the story of Clara, who was perplexed because her husband Herb was acting as if he'd been drinking, even though she was reasonably sure he was not. When she brought this up at her therapy group, she learned about the phenomenon of the dry drunk.

You may be told, perhaps in your self-help group or by another recovering person, that dry drunks occur only at specific times. After four months, after eleven months, after eighteen months, and after three years of sobriety are the times I have heard most often. But my experience tells me that a dry drunk can occur at any time. Saying to yourself, "I'm twenty-five months sober, so this low, irritable mood can't be a dry drunk," is dangerous.

It is difficult to say what brings on a dry drunk. Certainly these moods occur more frequently in the first year of sobriety because of the convalescent state of the brain. But there may be contributing factors at any stage of recovery. Fatigue is one, as are stress and disappointment. In women the premenstrual period may set off a dry drunk. For some the season—especially short, dark, winter days—can be a trigger. So can a low-grade viral infection, something you don't even realize you have.

People who are not recovering frequently experience mood shifts due to such factors. For them, these feelings are disagreeable, but not dangerous. But for a recovering person, a low, irritable mood state can give rise to a set of reactions that are risky to sobriety. Shame, guilt, remorse, self-pity, and resentment are only a few of the feelings that can emerge during a dry drunk. Because these particular feelings are so reminiscent of having a hangover, they can have a powerful effect in a recovering person. And if allowed to gather momentum unchecked, these feelings can turn a dry drunk into a real drunk.

When you recognize a dry drunk, take action immediately. I have found that the best course is to be especially good to yourself. First, establish your priorities and take care of what must be done. Then let go of the rest. Set aside time in the day only for you, and do something you enjoy. Or do something that will bring pleasure to someone else. Above all, tell yourself that your dry drunk will pass. It will.

Change Your Environment

Some environmental triggers are relatively easy to avoid. You can take a different route home from work to avoid passing the liquor store. You can turn down invitations from your old drinking or drugging friends. But sometimes the triggers are right there in front of you at home or at your job, and you can't move or switch jobs simply to escape a trigger. The stress of such enormous life changes may be more hazardous than the trigger itself. You can and should alter the triggering environment as much as possible, however.

Lorraine, a former cocaine addict, was having a very hard time at home after she got clean. When we met for the first time after she left our inpatient treatment center, she told me that every corner of her apartment held associations of her former habit. She had gotten high in the bathroom, the bedroom, and the living room. She had hidden her supplies in various drawers and closets all over the place. Moving was out of the question, not only because of the stress involved, but because the acute housing shortage in New York City made finding a new apartment a daunting task.

Lorraine's solution was to redecorate her home. Her financial resources were limited, so she couldn't toss everything out and start from scratch. But she could rearrange the furniture, buy paint and fabric, and scout the thrift shops. Over a long weekend, with the help of some friends from CA, she transformed her apartment so it was virtually unrecognizable. Her "new" place had none of the old, negative associations, and now she felt both comfortable and at home there.

Lorraine's redecoration scheme may seem excessive. But Lorraine is straight and sober today, and she's convinced that she wouldn't be if she had continued to live in her "old" apartment. You may not need to go to such great lengths, but you do have to make whatever changes are necessary to defuse your environmental triggers.

Build Your Self-Esteem

I know I've talked a lot about the importance of self-esteem, but I want to reemphasize how important it is in terms of preventing relapses. Low self-esteem is responsible for about forty percent of relapses, so building it up is obviously crucial to preventing relapses. I have yet to meet a chemically dependent person who didn't feel terrible about him- or herself in early sobriety. I've also seen that many of the people who celebrate their first anniversary of sobriety and beyond are those who came to feel much better about themselves.

How do you build self-esteem? How do you come to like yourself more? By creating a different life for yourself. One way is by taking care of your body, getting into shape through regular exercise and good nutrition. Another way is by regularly attending self-help meetings, and beginning to contribute to the group by making the coffee, cleaning up after the meeting, or becoming the secretary. You can also start to help others. Take a friend to dinner to thank her for standing by you when you needed her, lend an ear or offer advice to another substance abuser.

Self-esteem also comes from participating in the world around you, by leaving behind the very limited world that was comprised of you and your bottle or line of coke or handful of pills. The more you participate in activities that give you pleasure, the better you'll feel about yourself. The more you grow and develop spiritually, the more your self-esteem will grow and develop, too.

Many, many recovering people have mentioned to me their memories of the day they first experienced a turning point in how they viewed themselves. That was when they became aware that no matter how rotten they might be feeling at that moment, a few months or weeks or days down the line, they would be feeling much better. They had come to know and accept that their lives would improve—indeed, must improve. You can't predict exactly when that day will come for you, but if you're committed to sobriety and to your plans for sober living, I promise, it *will* come.

This happened for Sophie the day she ran into Dick, whom she had met on the detox unit. After several slips, he had finally achieved ninety days of sobriety, he told her. When she remarked that she'd been sober for a year, he exclaimed, "How did you do it? When we were in detox, I always thought you were a lot sicker than I was because you seemed to be holding on so stubbornly to your addiction. But you made it! That's terrific! Would you come and qualify at my home group?"

Sophie said she'd be happy to come to one of his meetings and tell her story. She walked away from the encounter feeling wonderful. "I realized that staying sober for a year, the first time, without a slip, was really quite wonderful and unusual. I had been so busy beating myself up for all the little things I still hadn't done that I'd overlooked the one big thing I had done," she said.

It took a chance meeting for Sophie to recognize her sobriety for the achievement it was. She was among the approximately one in three recovering people who accomplish what she had. Unfortunately, many recovering people allow their sense of guilt to keep them from acknowledging how well they've done in sobriety. After all, they reason, if they hadn't been addicted in the first place, they wouldn't have to be working so hard to stay clean and sober. But such thinking is counterproductive because by taking pride in the achievement of your sobriety, you can continue to build up and strengthen it.

Practice Asserting Yourself

Many people have trouble asserting themselves because of that very same problem we discussed above—low self-esteem. Like so many behavior problems, assertiveness (or the lack thereof) tends to feed on itself: The less assertive you are, the worse you feel, which makes you even less able to ask for what you want or need, and so you like yourself even less. But the recognition that you're entitled to assert yourself calmly and firmly, without provoking the other person, is part of recognizing that, as a human being, you have every right to be treated fairly, a right you haven't forfeited because you have an addictive disease.

Several pages back I told you the story of Mike, the welder. When confronted with Fred's unfair accusations, he could have said something like, "Fred, it's true I used to be a drunk, but I'm sober now. And I don't agree with you about my work. I do good work here, and I also know that the boss wouldn't keep me on if I didn't." But Mike didn't feel good enough about himself to make such a statement to Fred, and instead he ended up in a bar.

Assertiveness is something that needs to be practiced. You have to anticipate situations in which you might need to speak up for your rights, and rehearse what you'll say on such occasions. For example, let's say you know you're underpaid but you've ignored the inequity because you felt ashamed of your drinking. But now you're sober, and you're more than pulling your weight on the job. So every Friday when you look at your paycheck, you get so angry that sometimes you feel like stopping for a martini on the way to deposit the check at the bank.

You know you should ask for a raise, but you keep putting it off. This is an uncomfortable and difficult situation for *anyone* who has problems with self-assertion. But if you rehearse your "script" beforehand, you'll have an easier time asking for more money. Enlist the help of a friend who can play the role of your supervisor. Write down what you want to say, whatever you think your supervisor's responses may be, and how you could reply to his or her comments. Then think about what you're going to wear, and when would be the best time to approach him or her. Try to anticipate every possible outcome so you're as well-prepared as possible. You may not succeed in getting the raise, but you'll feel much better about yourself for having tried.

Or perhaps you work with someone like Fred, a fellow employee who puts you down a lot. You can either sit there and take it, or you can lose your temper and feel terrible. But as a recovering person, you can't live with situations that make you feel bad about yourself. Since your persecutor isn't about to change, you'll have to alter your behavior. Again, write down what you want to say the next time he or she insults you, and practice your comeback with a friend until you're sure you can deliver it no matter how nasty or hurtful the other person's put-down.

In a way, recovery *is* change. And your willingness and ability to change is yet another critical factor in your recovery. *You are the only person who can change your behavior, and yours is the only behavior you can change.* Other people aren't going to act different because you want them to, but you *can* modify how you react to what they're doing—and thereby save your life.

If you feel you need help becoming more self-assertive, assertiveness training workshops are readily available through adult education programs, many corporations, hospital education departments, and community service organizations.

Reward Yourself

When you've had a hard day, when you've survived a difficult period, when you've succeeded at something, or even tried something and failed, you should reward yourself. But the question then arises: how to do that without turning to the familiar rewards of a drink, a snort, a joint? People in recovery aren't the only ones who have trouble giving themselves a treat. Many individuals who've never been chemically dependent drag themselves through their mundane existences without ever allowing themselves to celebrate. You can't afford to do that. Your sober life has to have its celebratory moments, and you have to arrange them for yourself. Because if you don't, your well-conditioned mind will arrange them for you—and they will involve some chemical.

Take some time now to make a list of the kinds of things you enjoy, and the occasions when you might avail yourself of these pleasures. If you get that raise, for example, you might want to treat your spouse or lover to dinner and a concert. If you meet your exercise goals every week for a month, you might buy yourself some new clothes to show off your newly fit physique. If you're feeling tired, you might want to pamper yourself by getting a massage or a facial. If you get a B on an exam when you were sure you'd get a C, you might take the night off from studying and go to the movies. Rewards come in many varieties and flavors, from a crisp, tart apple to a trip to the zoo. One person's treat might be someone else's nightmare. What's important is that you know what pleases you.

If you can't think of anything you really enjoy, don't be alarmed. After all, it's been a while since you've taken pleasure in anything besides a drink or a drug. Do some exploring. Talk to friends, especially non-drinking or nonusing friends, and find out what special treats they like to give themselves. Experiment with whatever sounds interesting or intriguing. But start to build your list of rewards as soon as you can, and begin to put it into practice.

Many of my patients have found the acronym RELAPSE a handy device for remembering what to do to avoid those situations that leave them vulnerable to relapse.

Relieve unpleasant feelings.

Eliminate environmental triggers.

Let self-esteem grow.

Avoid the abstinence violation effect and apparently irrelevant decisions.

Put people in your life.

Sidestep social pressures.

Enhance positive moods.

Try to remember the dos and don'ts of how to prevent relapse, but also work on your attitude. If you think of a slip as a great black cloud hovering over your head, ready to burst without a moment's notice, then you'll feel helpless and frightened. But if you recognize that slips don't just happen, that they have prior causes that can be identified, then you'll be able to identify your triggers, make plans, consider your choices, build self-esteem, and assert yourself and thus take charge of your sobriety. Taking charge of your sobriety is very different from controlling your drinking or drugging. When you take charge of your sobriety, you must change your behavior and your thinking. Those changes are the foundation of your sober life; they *are* your relapse prevention program.

Recently I met with some doctors from the Soviet Union who were studying the treatment of alcoholism in the United States. At first they found it hard to understand the concept of addiction as disease. "But if it's a disease over which one has no control, then the individual will feel no responsibility and will just go on drinking or taking drugs," they protested.

Paradoxically, it's the admission of powerlessness—taking the First Step—that allows people with the disease of addiction to take responsibility for their own recovery. Having admitted your powerlessness over your disease, you can then take whatever steps you must to stay sober. But if you're fighting the disease and blaming yourself for having it, you can't take responsibility for staying sober. And staying sober means preventing relapse, one action at a time, one choice at a time, one day at a time.

Chapter Thirteen
Your Physical Health

Taking Care of Aches and Pains
While Being Cautious About Medications

Sobriety is not only an emotional and spiritual state, it is a physical state. Now that you are sober and in charge of your life you have a responsibility to care for and protect your body. In the last seven chapters I have concentrated on the pressing concerns of your emotional, interpersonal, and spiritual growth in sobriety. Now I want to return to the physical aspects of the living plan that I introduced in Chapter 4—getting adequate rest, eating properly, exercising regularly, giving up your cigarettes, and generally caring for your health.

Most people who aren't chemically dependent regularly visit their doctor and dentist both for regular checkups and when they have a specific health problem. But as a recovering drug abuser or alcoholic, you're likely to have an altogether different approach to medical care.

Perhaps you're like Doug, who hadn't seen a doctor in fifteen years when he came into treatment at the age of fifty-five. Now that he was sober, he told me that he had no intention of going for a physical. He already knew he was in terrible shape from drinking and smoking. He certainly didn't need a doctor to tell him that. Doug also knew that a doctor would urge him to give up his cigarettes, and he didn't need to pay good money to get advice that would go unheeded.

Cora also resisted going to the doctor when she got sober. She had stopped going for her annual Pap smear and mammogram some years earlier when her drinking had gotten out of hand, even though she knew she was at risk of breast cancer. Her mother had died of the disease at fifty-two, just two years older than Cora was now. But every time she received a reminder in the mail from her gynecologist, she would toss it in the garbage without a second glance. When her daughter finally convinced her to have a checkup, Cora arrived for her examination on the wrong day. She didn't bother to reschedule the appointment.

Jessie, on the other hand, had made frequent visits to doctors' offices while she was using, conning them into giving her prescriptions for sleeping pills, tranquilizers, and headache remedies. Some of the pills she used herself; the rest she sold to her addicted friends so she'd have the money to buy cocaine. When she got straight at twenty-five, she was determined never to see another doctor for the rest of her life.

These attitudes are typical of people in early recovery. But they're not beneficial to either your sobriety or your physical well-being. A regular program of preventive medical and dental care is essential to both.

Because you haven't gone for a checkup, you may be unaware that you have high blood pressure, and you therefore don't limit your salt intake. Or let's say you start an exercise routine and hurt your shoulder. Because you decide you're too busy to see your doctor, you run the risk of permanent damage, especially if you continue exercising and the injury is exacerbated. You refuse to visit the dentist because you hate the drill so much. That slightly bothersome cavity goes uncared for and you wind up with a king-sized toothache.

Now that you're mentally awake and aware, free of the drugs and alcohol that dulled your senses and occupied all your waking hours, it's time you put aside your negative feelings about doctors and dentists, and adopted a health maintenance routine. But first I'd like to offer a few simple rules that will help safeguard your sobriety when you seek medical or dental care or take any medication.

What to Do About Medication

For our purposes, I will define medication as any substance that a doctor or dentist prescribes or that you purchase legally to relieve your symptoms. Any medication—in fact, any non-food substance that you introduce into your body—is likely to produce not only the desired effect, but also some unwelcome side effects.

Of course, you're familiar with the side effects of the mood-altering chemicals you've been using. Indeed, the main reason you used alcohol or drugs was to get high and feel good. But you also got dizzy, sleepy, or nauseated. Or perhaps you passed out and woke up the next morning with a hangover.

But even simple, useful, nonaddictive medicines have side effects. Aspirin is a perfect example. It has been proven over years of use to be both very safe and very effective. When you have a high fever, aspirin will help lower your temperature. When you're feeling sore and achy, especially from any kind of inflammation, aspirin will reduce the pain. Aspirin also thins the blood, and thus can help prevent clogging of the arteries. In short, it's a wonderful medication, useful for treating headaches, fevers, and arthritis, and for preventing heart attacks.

However, aspirin also has its drawbacks, foremost among them being gastritis, an irritation of the stomach lining. For some people this amounts to nothing more than an upset stomach; for others, who have a tendency toward gastric ulcers, it can aggravate the condition. In fact, the combination of aspirin's irritating effect on the stomach lining and its tendency to thin the blood can cause serious gastric bleeding among some ulcer patients. As with any drug, the more you take, the more likely it is that you'll suffer side effects. Very high doses of aspirin can cause ringing in the ears, nausea, or dizziness.

I don't mean to imply that you should avoid aspirin. My point is that what holds true of aspirin is valid for *all* medicine: It should be used in the minimum quantity necessary to achieve relief, and it shouldn't be taken unless you actually need it. All too often, people reach for the aspirin bottle and swallow three or four the instant they feel the slightest twinge of pain.

One of my patients, Ginger, did this—and more. During the period when she had been addicted to alcohol and painkillers, she had been unable to tolerate any physical distress whatsoever. If she thought that she felt a headache coming on, she'd start with four aspirins, and if she didn't get instant relief, she'd take four more. She'd even chew the pills in an attempt to get them to work faster. On a bad day, she'd eat twenty or thirty tablets. The combination of her considerable alcohol intake and her misuse of aspirin eventually caused the erosion of a blood vessel in her stomach. She ended up in the hospital emergency room, in serious condition after having vomited a considerable quantity of blood.

One of the points we stress to patients at the Smithers inpatient treatment center is that they shouldn't reach into the medicine chest, even for something as relatively harmless as aspirin, every time they feel the slightest degree of discomfort. When patients ask for aspirin (or any other medication that hasn't specifically been prescribed for them), the nurses tell them to wait a bit to see whether the ache disappears by itself.

If the twinge actually develops into a bad headache, the staff suggests a short rest and one or two aspirins taken with some food to protect the stomach. Again, there is no evidence at all that three or four or nine or ten aspirins are more effective than one or two. Nor will they act more effectively if you increase the frequency of the dose. Aspirin, like most other medications, stays in the body for a limited period of time. If the pain doesn't subside after four hours, you can take two more aspirin—but you don't benefit by taking them any sooner than that.

Before you use any medication, whether you purchased it over-the-counter or it's been prescribed for you, here are five simple questions to ask yourself or your doctor:

- What are the risks?
- What are the benefits?
- What are the potential side effects?
- What would happen if I didn't take this medicine at all?
- What's likely to happen if I do take it?

Your answers will enable you to decide whether you really need and want to take that medication for your condition.

According to an old joke that's popular in the medical profession, most illnesses are either self-limiting or fatal. In other words, either you get better—or you die. Another joke has it that medicine is what doctors give patients to keep them happy while the disease heals itself. Both these one-liners serve to remind doctors that no matter whether or not they treat them, most ailments will eventually go away. Medication may shorten the course of the illness, alleviate discomfort, and prevent further complications, but time and the body's own restorative powers remain our most powerful cures for most diseases.

Of course, some conditions are fatal, and there are also some for which medication may indeed be life-saving. But many people mistakenly believe that *every* medical complaint can be remedied by a pill. Take the common cold, for example. You can take decongestants to clear a stuffy nose, cough syrup to temporarily halt a cough, and aspirins to relieve a headache and bring down the fever. The medicines may make you feel more comfortable, but they do not affect the course of your cold. Despite the efforts of scientists to provide one, no medication yet exists that can kill the viruses that cause the common cold. So when you come down with one, first remind yourself: *I will get better within seven to ten days no matter what I take.* Next, ask yourself the five questions above for *each* of the medications you think you might want to use, so that you can assess the potential risks and benefits. You can (and should) apply this same process to all self-limiting illnesses, not simply colds.

Now let's take a look at those cold remedies. Medicines that un-block the nasal passages fall into two major categories, both of which can alter your mood and level of alertness. Antihistamines, such as Benadryl, generally make you feel mildly sedated and drowsy, whereas adrenaline-like substances, such as Actifed and Sudafed, can make you feel jittery and tense. Because of these side effects, even people who have never been substance abusers must make a risk/benefit determination before using one of these medications.

Victor's cold reached its peak the day he had to talk about cost overruns on the building to which he was relocating his growing company. The meeting was being held at the office of the construction company, a two-hour drive from his home. Victor is a recovering alcoholic, four years sober. He's aware of how some non-addicting drugs can affect his mood and is therefore very cautious about using them. He decided not to take an antihistamine because he didn't want to be drowsy, either while he was driving or during the negotiations. Nor did he choose to take an Actifed, which he thought would make him irritable. Victor knew that even if a drug itself is not addictive, *any medication* that produces a mood change can be a hazard to sobriety, because it can trigger memories of and induce a craving for the formerly abused substance.

If you think Victor sounds overly careful, let me tell you about George. At fifty-two, George was a partner in a large insurance firm. His alcoholism had become so disruptive that his three partners finally confronted him with the choice of losing his position or getting treatment. He chose to become an outpatient at our clinic. George had never even experimented with drugs other than alcohol, so he found it hard to believe that he was susceptible to any other mood-altering substances. He told me that he could understand why some of the younger people in his therapy group, who had used every drug known to humankind, should be warned against accidental relapse caused by seemingly "harmless" over-the-counter medications. But surely this caveat did not apply to him.

After seven solid months of sobriety, George caught a very bad cold. Like many former abusers, he couldn't tolerate even mild pain, and he was also a bit of a hypochondriac. In the past he'd treated his colds and flus with liberal doses of alcohol, as well as antihistamines, cough syrups, and aspirins. This time George didn't reach for the brandy bottle, but because he felt so miserable, he bought a package of antihistamines.

The first pill made him feel much better—pleasantly sleepy and a little woozy. His brain somewhat addled because of the medicine, he decided he should take a nice, warm bath. As he lay in the tub, soothed by the antihistamine, he couldn't help but remember his favorite cold remedy—a special hot toddy made of brandy, honey, and lemon. The more he thought about it, the more medicinal his concoction seemed. Why, it wouldn't be at all like drinking, he assured himself. With that in mind, he picked himself up and went to fix one. Fortunately, he was thinking more clearly by the next morning. When he realized what he'd done, he renewed his commitment to sobriety and saved his slip from turning into a disastrous binge.

George hadn't become addicted to the couple of antihistamines he'd taken. Nor did the antihistamines make him high. But they did produce a sedated, foggy sensation that evoked memories of his drinking. Those feelings so interfered with his judgment that he was able to convince himself that brandy mixed with honey was medicine, not alcohol.

This is not to say that as a recovering person you should never take any medicine. If you suffer from a severe asthmatic condition, your medicine may save your life. If you have very bad hay fever with such uncontrollable sneezing that you can't function normally, the benefits of taking an antihistamine may well outweigh the risks. I have no one, simple response to the question of whether or not you should use a medication. You will have to answer that question each and every time you are confronted with the issue.

If you do decide that the pluses outweigh the negatives, try to choose the remedy that has the fewest harmful effects. For example, if antihistamines make you sleepy, try to find the one that's the least sedating. Or you may decide that you can put up with a runny nose, but you need aspirins, which won't affect your mood, to relieve your headache. Of course, if you have an ulcer, the risks of taking aspirin may considerably overshadow the advantages.

What I'm trying to illustrate here is the process of *thinking about medication*, of asking yourself, *do I really need it?* If you consider every pill before you pop it in your mouth, you can help safeguard your sobriety. This applies not only to medicine you purchase over-the-counter, but to prescription drugs as well. Be sure you always ask your doctor about a medication's side effects, so you can make an informed decision about whether or not you want to take it.

Let me give you an example. Many high blood pressure medicines cause temporary impotence in men. Some men continue to be impotent even after they've gone off the medication. Allen, a fifty-five-year-old patient of mine who'd been sober for six years, had high blood pressure that was being treated with a beta blocker. A few days after he started taking the medicine, he lost his erection while he and his wife were making love. He'd been working particularly long hours and was feeling generally fatigued, so he dismissed the episode without another thought.

Though Allen functioned perfectly normally when they next had sex several days later, the week after that he began experiencing increasing difficulties, and by the end of the month he couldn't get an erection at all. He was sufficiently alarmed to consult his internist, who immediately took him off the beta blocker. Within a week Allen was able to have intercourse again, but unfortunately, his blood pressure had also shot up. He and his doctor then embarked on an ultimately successful search for a medication that could both control his blood pressure and enable him to function sexually.

Andrew, forty-three, was not as fortunate as Allen. For several months after he began taking a diuretic to control his high blood pressure, Andrew experienced progressive impotence. Too angry and embarrassed to discuss his condition with anyone, he announced to his wife that their sex life was finished. His drinking, which had been heavy but controlled, escalated, and three years later he entered alcoholism treatment.

Both men had a medical condition which required treatment with medications that have side effects. But Allen, together with his doctor, was able to find a workable solution, while Andrew, because he refused to confront his problem, only exacerbated the situation and ultimately found himself in very bad shape indeed.

Each time a medication is prescribed, you have to decide whether it's in your best interests to take it. This includes medicines you've taken safely in the past—your circumstances may be different now. In order to make an informed decision, you must have all the facts. Of course, your doctor is the best person to provide that information, but don't shy away from asking the questions and getting the answers you need.

In Appendix B you'll find lists of three types of medications to avoid: those which contain alcohol, those which may make you drowsy and those which may make you jittery. Because there are so many medications available, these lists are not all-inclusive, but they will help you to avoid the most commonly used preparations which can threaten your sobriety. If you have any questions about a medication, either prescription or over-the-counter, check with your physician and/or your pharmacist.

Medications That Alter Your Mood

Mood-altering drugs carry a particular risk for recovering substance abusers. Generally speaking, medications that have mood-altering properties fall into three major categories:

- tranquilizers (anti-anxiety medications)
- hypnotics (sedatives, sleeping drugs)
- narcotics (painkillers)

Many medications, though they aren't primarily meant to be mood-altering, may have this side effect. This doesn't pose much of a problem for the nonaddict, but as a person in recovery, you have to factor it into your risk/benefit equation.

Dinah had been sober six months when she was hit with a bad bout of rheumatoid arthritis. She knew that her drug addiction and her arthritis were two entirely separate ailments. But she secretly had hoped that when she stopped using heroin and alcohol, her arthritis would magically disappear, as a special reward for being clean and sober. So when her condition flared up again, she was not only in terrible pain, but also badly disappointed.

She was also very worried that the arthritis would jeopardize her new job at a day care center. The steady income had enabled Dinah to reunite her family for the first time in three years. Her husband had long since abandoned them, and her four children had been living with relatives or in foster homes because she hadn't been able to care for or support them while she was using. Now they were enjoying being together again, and Dinah was feeling good about herself for the first time in years. But her work involved a lot of writing, and when her fingers ached, pushing a pen became an agony.

The doctor she saw at an arthritis clinic was very sympathetic to her situation. He not only outlined a course of treatment for her condition, but also said that because she seemed so tense, he would prescribe a drug called diazepam. It would help her relax and ease the stiffness in her joints, he said. Dinah hesitantly told the doctor that she'd been addicted and wanted to be sure this particular drug was safe for her to take. It was then that the doctor's tone became noticeably cooler. "This is very safe medicine," he insisted. "You have four children and a job, and you need something to help you cope." With that he hurried her out of the examining room.

Dinah wasn't convinced. What concerned her was that the doctor had said the diazepam would relax her. She remembered hearing that tranquilizers or relaxing drugs could be a problem for recovering addicts. At her self-help meeting that night, she discussed the question with her sponsor. Frances was a sensible, down-to-earth woman who didn't make decisions without first getting as many facts as possible.

"I'm an alcoholic," she said. "And I don't know anything about drugs. But the way I see it, you won't die if you don't get that prescription filled tonight. Let's wait until we can talk to LuAnn. She's a nurse, and she may know more about this stuff."

That was good advice—because LuAnn told them that diazepam was the same as Valium. "The doctor was right," she said. "It's not a dangerous medication. In fact, for most people it's very safe. But not for us."

LuAnn also suggested Dinah check with a doctor she knew who was an addiction specialist. The specialist confirmed that Dinah shouldn't take diazepam, but that she could take the other medications prescribed by the arthritis doctor. The specialist then called her colleague and discussed the special needs of recovering people, information he didn't have and was happy to get.

As a recovering person you should never take medicines designed to make you sleep. There are much better ways to handle insomnia. Nor should you ever take tranquilizers. As you now know, there are many healthier methods for coping with stress and reducing anxiety.

Sometimes drugs that are primarily tranquilizers may be prescribed as muscle relaxants for conditions such as bursitis, tendinitis, back strain, and muscle spasms, soreness, tenderness, or arthritis, as in Dinah's case. Tranquilizers are quite effective as muscle relaxants, just as alcohol is. However, they can be every bit as addictive when prescribed for that purpose as for any other. So when your doctor hands you a prescription for those conditions, be sure to check (and double-check) whether the medication is a tranquilizer. As Dinah found out, you have alternatives. There are a number of non-addictive medications (aspirin-like substances) that can be safely used for the above conditions. If you have any doubt about a prescription, do seek a second opinion from a doctor with experience in addiction medicine.

As far as the third category of mood-altering drugs—narcotics or painkillers—you should take a different but still very cautious approach. You may use painkillers when absolutely necessary, *but only under tightly controlled circumstances*.

When You Must Have Relief for Pain

It's very easy to be dogmatic about sedatives or tranquilizers, declaring that the risks for a chemically dependent person always outweigh the benefits and that no recovering person should ever take them. Unfortunately, the same statement cannot be made about painkillers, which are also known as analgesics.

All currently available painkilling drugs are potentially addictive. However, circumstances may arise when you have to take these medications. Indeed, there may be occasions when an effective analgesic could save your life. But there may also be many occasions when the pain will be minor and will abate of its own accord, so that you have no need to use a risky drug. As a general rule, the risk of addiction is much lower when the analgesic drug is taken over a short period of time for severe pain than when it's used over a long period for a chronic condition.

For example, if you take painkillers for a condition such as lower back pain, which may continue indefinitely, you run a high risk of becoming addicted, even if you're not in recovery. On the other hand, if you've just had surgery and you're being treated with painkillers for a short time while you're in the hospital, your chances of becoming addicted are very low.

Painkillers pose the greatest danger when you're responsible for administering the medication yourself. Even if you've never abused any other drug but alcohol, even if you've taken painkillers in the past and not become addicted to them, now that you're sober you'll experience a lift from any painkilling medication. Your mood will be affected. You may not like the feeling as much as you enjoyed the effects of alcohol or whatever your drug of choice was—but your altered state of mind may either persuade you to take more pills than you need, or trigger the urge to get high with the substance that you really used to like.

So how can you best protect yourself from potential addiction, and at the same time prevent unnecessary suffering? Connie's story may help you understand the process. Connie was a twenty-five-year-old teacher who was recovering from dependency on nitrous oxide, or laughing gas, as it is sometimes called. Because her father was an alcoholic, Connie never drank. But when her boyfriend, Gerry, who was a dentist, introduced her to laughing gas, she took to it the way an alcoholic takes to liquor.

When it became clear to Gerry that Connie was more interested in the nitrous oxide than she was in him, he broke up with her. He asked her to return his keys, which she did—but not before she'd made copies of the ones to Gerry's office doors. One night, about a week after they'd split up, Connie was so desperate to get high that she sneaked into his office. Gerry found her there the next morning, passed out on the floor beside the gas canister. She came into treatment shortly afterwards.

After six months of sobriety, Connie began having some trouble with a wisdom tooth, and her new dentist told her he would have to remove it. Connie carefully made plans for the day of her dental surgery. She asked her roommate Joy to come with her and help her get back to their apartment. She discussed her problem with the dentist, and he agreed to use only a local anesthetic for the extraction. She also planned to meet her sponsor and attend a self-help meeting that evening. Connie was sure that she had covered all her bases, but the one detail she hadn't thought about was whether she'd be in a lot of pain after the procedure.

Sitting in the dentist's waiting room, she was reminded of her gas-sniffing days, but she was too apprehensive about the operation to get caught up in her memories. After the surgery, which wasn't as bad as she'd expected, the dentist gave her two prescriptions—one for an antibiotic, the other for a painkiller called Percodan. Connie wasn't thinking too clearly after the operation, so she meekly accepted the slips and listened to the dentist's instructions without asking any questions.

She and Joy stopped at the pharmacy on the way home to have the prescriptions filled. By the time they got back to the apartment, most of the anesthetic had worn off and Connie was beginning to feel a lot of pain. Joy suggested she take her pills right away. "That way, the painkiller can start working before it gets much worse," she said, doling out one of each and putting the vials in the bathroom cabinet. Then she tucked Connie into bed.

In about ten minutes Connie's spirits began to lift. She became rather talkative, but at the same time she felt very calm and peaceful. She felt as if she was drifting off and asked Joy to leave because she wanted to sleep. Actually, she wanted to be alone to enjoy her high. She finally fell asleep for about half an hour, but when she woke up, her first thought was that she needed another pill. The pain wasn't all that intense, but she wanted to recapture that lovely, floating feeling. And she did— again and again all afternoon.

Joy assumed that Connie was knocked out from the surgery, so she wasn't concerned that she spent the afternoon in her room. But she was surprised when Linda, Connie's sponsor, came by to pick her up and Connie said she was feeling too rotten to go to their meeting. Linda promised to drop by afterwards to see how she was doing. "Don't bother," said Connie. "I'll probably be asleep."

"We'll see," Linda said suspiciously.

As soon as Linda left, Connie rushed to the bathroom to take another pill. To her horror, she discovered she had only three left. She frantically searched the cabinet. There had been twelve to start with. She knew she'd taken one at noon, another at about one, and a couple more at two. Could she possibly have swallowed *five* since then? Beginning to panic, she became nauseated and broke out in a sweat. She was almost too dizzy to make it back to her bedroom where she collapsed on her bed.

When she came to, she found Linda and Joy anxiously peering down at her. "Okay, what did you take?" Linda demanded.

Joy retrieved the bottle of Percodan. "The prescription was for twelve pills, enough for three days, one every six hours," she said. "And I only saw Connie take one."

Linda inspected the vial. "Three left. I don't know what Percodan is, Connie, but I do know you've had a slip." She stuck the bottle in her purse and said, "I'm confiscating these. I hope you have some aspirin, because that's what you should take if you have any pain. I'll call you in the morning."

"Who does she think she is? A doctor?" Joy said indignantly after Linda had gone. " 'Take two aspirin, and I'll call you in the morning'? When we were trying to get you to wake up, Linda said that when she came by earlier she thought you were high. Boy, you were really out cold! Did it feel like that gas you used to sniff?"

"Sort of," Connie said. "But I didn't think about that until it was too late."

Even with the best intentions and good precautions, Connie had a slip because of a prescribed pain medication. Should you find yourself in a similar situation, you don't want to deny yourself the benefit of being pain-free. On the other hand, you also don't want to expose yourself to the danger either of abusing the analgesic or of using another substance while you're under the influence. Here's how you can prevent this from happening:

1. Use every method of non-narcotic pain relief first, including:

• Ice packs for swelling;
• Heat if you have muscle or joint pain;
• Non-narcotic analgesics such as aspirin, acetaminophen (Tylenol), ibuprofen (Nuprin, Advil), or non-steroidal anti-inflammatory medications (Motrin, Naprosyn) which must be prescribed by a physician;
• Local anesthetics (Anbesol);
• Diversion;
• Human comfort.

Only if all these measures are ineffective should you proceed to steps two through five.

2. Get a prescription for only enough painkilling medication to last until your next visit to the doctor or dentist. *Never* leave the office with a prescription for more than a three or four days' supply of a potentially addictive medicine.

3. Tell your family or close friends that the medication has been prescribed, so that they're not alarmed to see you taking it.

4. If possible, ask someone else to give you the medicine as prescribed. If you have to take the medicine with you when you leave the house, take only what you'll need during that time period. Leave the rest in someone else's care.

5. While you're using painkilling medication, plan to be in close contact with your sponsor or a sober friend. If your condition permits, attend a self-help meeting. Otherwise, try to find some reading material that will reinforce your commitment to sobriety.

What About Stimulants?

In the United States it's now against the law for doctors to prescribe amphetamines for the purpose of weight loss or to prevent sleep. Although some people still believe to the contrary, no one—most especially a person in recovery—needs to take stimulants, including over-the-counter preparations, in order to shed unwanted pounds or stay awake.

Amphetamines, as well as cocaine, over-the-counter diet pills, or pills designed to keep you up (which frequently contain phenylpropanolamine, a relatively mild stimulant), do make people lose their appetite or remain alert for a short period of time. However, if taken long-term, these drugs not only become ineffective, they may also be addictive. Sustained weight loss requires more than popping a pill: You have to change your eating and exercise habits permanently.

When You're in the Hospital

If you've been admitted to the hospital because you've had an accident or you're being operated on, you should certainly get the medication you need to feel comfortable. Generally speaking, it's extremely rare for people to become addicted while they're under appropriate hospital supervision for serious or acute conditions. However, you don't want to leave the hospital with a pocketful of painkillers. *That is dangerous.*

People in recovery sometimes ask for a lot more painkillers than other hospital patients. This is the addiction rearing its ugly head. Unfortunately, if you ask, you may be given more than you actually need, and for longer than you need it. Then, when you're ready to leave the hospital, because you're still dependent on the painkiller, you may be given a prescription to take home with you. So you have to take steps to make sure it doesn't become a threat to your sobriety.

Of course, you'll have told your personal physician about your addiction. But many other people, doctors as well as nurses, will be caring for you while you're in the hospital. Anyone who prescribes or administers your medicines must be informed of your addiction. To ensure this, ask your doctor to write a note on your chart.

At first, Leo was skeptical about taking precautions with medication when he entered the hospital for knee surgery. He'd had a bad knee ever since he'd torn the ligaments in it while playing college football. When he was nine months sober, he dashed to his car one winter morning and slipped on a patch of ice, reinjuring the knee. By lunchtime, the knee had blown up like a balloon and Leo was in excruciating pain.

When ice packs and aspirin didn't help, his doctor referred him to an orthopedic surgeon, who recommended the operation, especially if Leo wanted to continue with his exercise program. Leo felt that his workouts had greatly contributed to his sobriety—and his trimmer waistline—so he said yes to the surgery.

His wife Joan, though, was worried about the anesthesia. "Won't it be like getting drunk?" she asked.

Leo had already told Dr. Shepherd, the specialist, that he was a recovering alcoholic, but to allay Joan's fears he agreed to ask the doctor about possible side effects of the anesthetic. "You won't be going anywhere for a few days afterwards, certainly not the bar around the corner," Dr. Shepherd reassured him. "But you could be in a lot of pain after the operation. And painkillers are addictive."

"I never had a pill problem," Leo boasted. "I even took codeine once when my knee was acting up. I hated the stuff. It made me sick."

He went on to tell the doctor that after he'd fallen down drunk and hurt himself, he'd gone to bed with ice packs, aspirin, and codeine, prescribed by his internist. He'd also drunk a quart of whiskey for good measure. Joan found him later, passed out in their sodden bed—the ice packs had melted—with the empty whiskey bottle in an ice bucket next to the bed. Leo had taken only two codeine pills, but he woke up feeling very nauseated, which he never had felt when he was drinking, no matter how much he'd put away. "I don't imagine that I'd take to codeine any better now than I did then," he assured Dr. Shepherd.

Dr. Shepherd was still wary, so he insisted that though Leo could have analgesics during his hospital stay, he wouldn't be given any to take home. Leo scoffed that he could handle any medicine the doctor could dish out. But Dr. Shepherd held firm.

His first two days after surgery, Leo took the painkillers as prescribed. But by the third day, when he was beginning to feel better, he realized that he was getting a little high from the pill he took just before bedtime. "I was in a dreamy, fantasy state," was how he described it to Joan. "I could bring myself down or let myself drift off. I guess that's how junkies feel. I can't say I didn't like it, but when the nurse came around with the painkillers the next morning I didn't take any. I didn't need them that badly, and that floating sensation scared me! I thought Shepherd was going way overboard about this, but now I'm glad he was so careful."

On the rare chance you could someday be admitted to the hospital in an emergency when you can't speak for yourself, it's a good idea to ask the person most likely to be notified—your spouse, lover, parents, brother or sister—to alert hospital personnel, so that you can be treated appropriately.

Anesthesia

When people are hospitalized, their conditions frequently require that they be anesthetized. Anesthetics are drugs that can be abused, but that doesn't mean you shouldn't be anesthetized under medical supervision. However, do be sure to inform the anesthesiologist of your addiction. As we discussed earlier, a substance abuser's liver becomes highly efficient at ridding the body of drugs, so your anesthetic requirements may be affected by your having been chemically dependent.

What to Do About Chronic Pain

If you're among the unfortunate people who suffer constant pain—or experience regular periods of intense pain—from such ailments as arthritis, a lower back condition, colitis, headaches (including migraines), and extremely severe menstruation, you're faced with a serious dilemma, whether or not you're in recovery.

You already know that painkilling medications are potentially addictive. What you may not realize is that the body also learns to tolerate these analgesics, so that even a non-addicted person has to increase the dose in order to maintain the painkilling effect. I've treated many people for what's known as "iatrogenic addiction," meaning an addiction that's caused by medical treatment. This may occur when a well-intentioned physician, in an attempt to ease a chronic condition, prescribes large quantities of analgesics and the patient becomes addicted to them.

In fact, many alternative treatments exist that can enable the vast majority of chronic pain sufferers to lead comfortable lives without relying on painkilling medications. Physical therapy, exercise regimens, stress reduction techniques (such as meditation, self-hypnosis, and biofeedback), electrical muscle stimulation, massage, hydrotherapy, and the use of other kinds of medicines have all been shown to be successful. Of course, one person may respond very differently from the next, and what works for Harold may not work for Hilda. But *something* will prove effective for Hilda, if only she continues to search for a remedy. Unfortunately, too many people give up after experimenting with—and not getting satisfaction from—only one alternative. Though it may take a while before you find a treatment that satisfies your needs, you should continue to consult with your doctor until you find a suitable therapy that doesn't involve painkilling drugs.

Visiting the Doctor

The American Medical Association first recognized alcoholism as a disease in 1956, and the International Classification of Diseases, a reference book used by physicians throughout the world, also lists alcoholism and drug dependency. But unlike many illnesses, alcoholism and drug dependency—when they're in remission—have no distinctive physical signs. In other words, a physician can't tell just by looking at you, or even by examining you, that you're in recovery. It is therefore up to you to tell your doctor that you have been addicted.

When you go for your first appointment, you'll be asked for a medical history of all the illnesses, operations, and allergies you've ever had. A doctor can't evaluate your condition or treat you unless he or she knows about your chemical dependency, even if it's not related to the specific reason that brings you to the doctor's office. Just as you would report the tonsillectomy you had when you were seven, so you must mention that you're now recovering from substance abuse.

In the early 1970s, a woman friend of mine made a first visit to an internist, a young man fresh out of his residency. When he queried her about past illnesses, she answered appropriately, "I had pneumonia when I was twelve, hepatitis at twenty-two, an appendectomy at thirty, and alcoholism. I've been sober five years."

"But that's not a . . ." the doctor began.

"A disease?" she finished for him.

"Well, no . . ." he stammered. "I mean, yes, of course it is. You just caught me by surprise. I've never had a patient come right out with it like that."

Fortunately, times have changed. People now routinely list addictive disorders as part of their medical history, and doctors are no longer taken aback when they do.

If the condition for which you are seeking treatment can be alleviated through medication, your doctor will probably give you a prescription before you leave the office. But don't assume that because you've told the doctor about your addiction, he or she will have prescribed a medicine that's safe for you. You'll still have to ask the five questions on page 240. Not only do you have to reassure yourself that the medicine won't put you in any danger, but you also have to remind the doctor to double-check that the medication is safe for you. You're much better off asking a few seemingly unnecessary questions than putting your sobriety at risk.

When I went to medical school in the 1950s, we received no information whatsoever on alcoholism or drug dependency. At that time, and for many years after, substance abuse wasn't considered a topic worthy of inclusion in an already heavily laden medical school curriculum, nor was much then known about the subject. I've already described how, when I was in training in the neurology department at Bellevue Hospital, we learned how to treat only the head injuries and nerve damage of patients who were also addicted to alcohol. Their alcoholism—which had been the cause of their ailments—was not thought to be treatable, and was therefore largely ignored by teachers and trainees alike.

It wasn't until the late 1970s that alcohol and drug addiction began to be discussed in medical schools and specialty training programs. Although the disease now garners far more attention, it still isn't granted the time it deserves to be taught in the classroom. Consequently, far too many doctors don't know a whole lot about your addiction. Although they keep up by reading their journals in cardiology, dermatology, internal medicine, or whatever their specialty happens to be, they don't often have the opportunity or the time to read very much about alcoholism or drug dependency. Thus, as a recovering person, you may know more about your disease than your physician does. You may have to be the instructor. At any rate, *you* are certainly responsible for making sure you don't take any medicine that's hazardous for you.

The good news is that a growing number of physicians are knowledgeable about addiction medicine. The American Society of Addiction Medicine, listed in Appendix C, can help you find a doctor who practices in your area.

Visiting the Dentist

All the points I made above about your dealings with doctors hold equally true of dentists. However, because most dentists don't take a detailed medical history, you may have to make the extra effort to inform your dentist that you're in recovery. You also have to take the same precautions regarding prescriptions from your dentist as you would from your doctor, especially since dentists often prescribe painkillers.

Dental Anesthesia

Many of my patients are concerned about taking a local anesthetic when they go to the dentist. After all, novocaine *sounds* very much like cocaine, and in fact, they are chemically related. But they are different in one important aspect: novocaine doesn't get into the brain, which is why it's referred to as a "local" anesthetic. It remains in—and numbs only—the tissues around the gum where it's been injected. I know of some stoic souls who choose to undergo dental procedures without a local anesthetic, but there's absolutely no reason why you shouldn't opt to have relief from the pain. It's easier on you, as well as on your dentist, and it doesn't pose any threat to your sobriety.

But what about nitrous oxide, which dentists frequently use as an anesthetic? As Connie's story shows, people can and do become addicted to it. I don't expect that once you've been exposed to it, you'll run out and buy yourself a couple of canisters. That would be both difficult and impractical. The real danger lies in the fact that the experience of getting high from the nitrous oxide can spark a craving for your drug of choice. As you leave the dentist's office feeling rotten, the taste of your recent high, which is still lingering in your system, may propel you to the nearest bar or drug dealer.

Except in the case of extremely difficult extractions, you should absolutely avoid using nitrous oxide or any other anesthetic used in dentistry. A local works very well for virtually all dental work, including root canal. If you do need to have a difficult extraction, and an anesthetic has to be administered, ask a friend to come along with you, and make sure he or she accompanies you home afterward. It's also smart to schedule an activity afterwards, or plan to spend the evening with someone, so that you're not sitting home alone thinking about how nice it felt to be high.

Starting Your Program of Regular Preventive Medical and Dental Care

Preventive medicine is good medicine. The major reason that life expectancy has increased so remarkably in this century is not so much because of expensive medical technology or sophisticated surgical techniques. Our longevity can be attributed to the vast improvement in public health practices along with the advent of preventive medicine.

Although there's some disagreement as to how often you should have a physical examination, a reasonable guideline to follow is once every five years up to age thirty-five; every two years from age thirty-five to fifty; and annually thereafter. If you're a woman, you should have an annual Pap smear to detect early cancerous changes in the cervix. Learn how to do a breast self-examination as well, so you can examine your breasts for lumps every month to detect early signs of cancer. The American Cancer Society also recommends that you get a baseline mammogram (breast X-ray) at age thirty-five, then an annual mammogram once you turn forty-five. Visit your dentist annually for an oral checkup and cleaning; this will keep your mouth free of damaging tartar and plaque buildup, and will enable your dentist to identify tooth and gum problems early, so that you may be spared pain (and expense) later on.

Remember that these are only *guidelines*. Your family history and your individual condition may prompt you to seek more frequent check-ups. For example, a man whose father had a fatal heart attack before the age of forty might be wise to see his doctor annually beginning at age thirty-five. A woman whose Pap smear showed abnormalities caused by an infection that's since been treated may be told by her gynecologist to come back for the test every six months instead of every twelve.

As your sound health practices take hold and your body—including your immune system—gets stronger, you'll probably find that you get sick less often than you did when you were drinking or using. But when you do get laid up, whether because of a wretched case of the flu or a throbbing sprained ankle, one medicine that's always safe to take in liberal doses is TLC—tender loving care. When you're feeling less than your best—pamper yourself. Better yet, ask someone to provide the TLC. You can always return the favor.

By now it should be clear that taking care of your health doesn't mean loading yourself up with over-the-counter medications at the slightest sign of the sniffles, rushing to your doctor every time you have a sore throat, or buying out the health food store. Nor should you be listening anxiously for every skipped heartbeat, or diagnosing cancer every time you get a pimple or a skin rash. What your good health requires is a moderate, balanced regimen of regular exercise, nutritious food, having fun, making friends, practicing prevention, thinking twice before you take any kind of medication, and getting as much sleep as your body needs.

Chapter Fourteen
Nature's Sweet Restorer

How to Get a Good Night's Sleep

For some people, sleep is quite a simple matter. You feel tired, you get into bed, you turn out the light, and you fall asleep. The next morning you awake, refreshed and rested. Jerry was one of the fortunate, a rare breed in early sobriety.

"I don't even need to lie down. I can drop off standing up, like a cow," he said at an outpatient meeting. "Once I fell asleep standing in a packed subway. When the crowds piled out at Times Square, I fell over, flat on my face. Missed my stop."

His story got appreciative laughs from everyone except Randy. "I should have your problems," he said with genuine longing in his voice. "I haven't once slept through the night since I got sober three months ago. Some nights I go to bed at eleven, and I'm awake again by one or two. Sometimes I get up, other nights I lie in bed and watch the clock. Maybe I drift off around five or so, then the alarm goes off at seven. The trouble is, I feel lousy. I don't know how Churchill did it, never going to bed, taking twenty-minute catnaps through the day and waking up ready to plan an invasion. When I nap during the day I wake up feeling like I'm hung over. I can't plan a trip to the supermarket, much less an invasion."

"As far as I'm concerned, an invasion's easier," quipped Wilma, a mother of five. "But don't worry, it'll get better. When I first got sober I never knew whether or not I would be able to sleep. Sometimes I'd be out like a light. Other nights I'd toss and turn. All I could think of were the awful things I'd done when I was drinking. I'd get so embarrassed I'd blush, right there in bed. Can you imagine anything sillier?"

"Sure. Being thirty-four and afraid to be alone in the dark." Lorna was obviously upset, and talking was an effort. "Since my boyfriend moved out, I can't get to sleep until I see the early morning light through the windows. I don't want him back. He's still drinking, and besides, it was over a long time ago. It's not as if I'm frightened of anything specific—like burglars or the apartment catching on fire. I'm just filled with this nameless dread. When my sister stays over, it's all right, but I can't ask her to stay every night. I'm so ashamed of being such a coward."

"I stayed with my brother for three months when I first got sober," Woody offered encouragingly. "Forget about sleeping alone in my apartment—I was afraid to walk in there by myself. And I'm fifty years old and six feet tall. You're not a coward. You're just suffering the aftereffects of the chemicals."

The fears and complaints voiced in this group meeting are typical of those experienced in early recovery, when sleep disturbances are quite common. However, there is no evidence that sleep problems caused by alcohol or drug addiction persist beyond the first year of recovery. If you have been sober for more than a year and continue to sleep poorly, the chances are that the cause of your difficulty is unrelated to your addiction. Still, following the guidelines in this chapter can be helpful. If your sleep disturbances persist, you may wish to seek treatment at a sleep clinic, as I describe on page 264.

What Is Sleep?

Normal sleep has several stages, the first of which is the ritual of going to bed. Most people follow more or less the same routine every night. They brush their teeth, perhaps take a shower, read for a few minutes or watch the news, check the locks on the doors, or have a hot drink. Perhaps they always sleep on the same side of the bed, resting their head on the same number of pillows.

This ritual, whatever it may be, is the first signal you send to your body that you're preparing yourself for sleep. Though you may not be consciously aware of it, like most people, you're probably sensitive to disruptions in your bedtime routine. Some people are so sensitive that they can't sleep at all when they're away from home and deprived of their special pillow, their own mattress, or the hum of the refrigerator in the kitchen.

This bedtime routine is followed by a period of time between turning off the light and falling asleep, which sleep researchers call "sleep onset latency." Most people take the same amount of time to fall asleep every night; the norm is between ten and thirty minutes. Studies have shown that people with sleep problems seriously overestimate how long it takes them to get to sleep. What seems like hours is often not much more than the average thirty-minute period.

When you first fall asleep, you enter what's known as stage one, or alpha sleep, a semiwakeful state from which you can be easily aroused. Everyone has had the experience of being awakened by a cough, a car honking outside, or some other noise just as they were peacefully drifting off. Most people go right back to sleep when this happens, but problem sleepers may lie awake afterwards for what can seem like hours.

If uninterrupted, the sleep cycle then progresses through stages two and three, which are deeper, and completes itself in stage four, a very deep state also known as delta or slow-wave sleep. The average person spends about one-fifth of the night in this satisfying, restorative sleep. When people are in this state, it is very difficult to wake them.

In addition, every ninety minutes, usually beginning a couple of hours after you drop off, you experience periods called rapid eye movement (REM) or dreaming sleep. REM periods last for about fifteen minutes and can occur during any stage of the sleep cycle. If you are awakened during REM sleep, you are usually aware that you are in the middle of a dream. The dreams you tend to remember are those that are so frightening that you force yourself to wake up, dreams that occur when you have to get up to use the toilet, or dreams that you have early in the morning just before the alarm clock rings. Everyone has dreams. People who claim they don't dream simply never wake up soon enough after a REM period to remember their dreams.

During dreaming sleep, your body is very relaxed. Your eyes move back and forth under your closed eyelids, and men often experience erections. Both dreaming and slow-wave sleep seem necessary for the brain and body to recuperate and function at optimal levels the next day.

The circadian, or sleep, rhythm also affects sleep. This twenty-four-hour cycle is what makes you feel sleepy at about the same time each evening, and wake up at approximately the same hour every morning. Body temperatures and certain body hormones also rise and fall during this cycle. For most people, the body temperature is usually at its lowest ebb at about three or four in the morning, which is why it is so difficult to be awakened or forced to stay awake at that hour. When your temperature is low, your body is biologically set for the low-level activity of sleep; if you keep yourself awake, your body will respond sluggishly and reluctantly.

People who work evenings and night shifts frequently experience maladjustments of their circadian rhythm, as do most long-distance travelers from jet lag. These disruptions can cause difficulties with concentration, attention span, and mood.

How Alcohol and Drugs Disturb Your Sleep Cycle

Alcohol and drugs interfere with both your sleep pattern and circadian rhythm. When you're taking sedative drugs or drinking alcoholically, you pass out rather than fall asleep naturally. When that happens, your brain is in a state that's more akin to being anesthetized than being asleep. You miss the normal stages of sleep, as well as those periods of REM sleep that are so essential. It is only after the drug or alcohol wears off that your brain rhythms begin to return to those of normal sleep.

Sometimes, early in the morning after a night of heavy drinking, people go through a compensatory REM period of frequent and especially vivid dreams. These are often very frightening, and may involve images of distorted body parts or of the entire body rotting away. This catch-up dreaming can occur when you're almost awake, so that you drift into a peculiar waking dream condition, known as the hypnagogic state. You're still asleep, still dreaming, but on some level you're also awake and aware of sounds and sensations intruding from the outside world.

Woody, who admitted to his group that he'd been afraid to stay alone in his apartment when he first got sober, often experienced these hypnagogic states. "After a booze-up, I'd be lying in bed asleep. I knew I was asleep, but I could hear the alarm clock ticking and the traffic noises outside my window. I felt like I was under some kind of spell. I couldn't move my legs, no matter how hard I tried, but at the same time I felt I could break the spell and wake up, if only I made the right move. Then I'd sense that there was a gaping hole in my belly that had started as a small ulcer and kept getting bigger. I *knew* the hole was there, but I kept trying to tell myself it wasn't. I was afraid that if I stood up, my guts would fall out and I'd have to push them back in. So I'd lie there, afraid the hole would get even bigger than it already was.

"Then I'd wake up in a sweat, my heart pounding like a jackhammer. I continued having these nightmares for about two weeks after I stopped drinking. Now that I can think about them calmly, I know that I was really dreaming about my alcoholism, the way it was eating me up from the inside. But at the time, they scared the hell out of me. I think that was one of the reasons why I didn't want to go home alone. It was a month before I trusted that they were gone forever."

Many people who have experienced these disturbing hypnagogic states see an end to them more quickly than Woody did—often as soon as four or five days after they stop drinking. Others continue to slip into them for two or three weeks. They rarely persist for longer than a month.

If you've been using stimulant drugs such as cocaine, you'll experience a loss of sleep while you're using, and abnormally heavy sleep when you crash. As a result, you may find yourself sleeping much more than usual for the first week of your sobriety, while still feeling drained and exhausted.

While alcohol, sedatives, and cocaine have the greatest impact on sleep, most drug abuse disturbs your circadian rhythm because the natural cycle has been taken over by the drug. It is then the drug that determines when and how you fall asleep.

Sleep Problems in Sobriety

During the first weeks of sobriety, your sleep pattern will continue to be abnormal, and one or *all* of the following problems may occur.

It may take you longer than the normal thirty minutes to get to sleep. Because the twenty-four-hour cycle of your circadian rhythm has been disrupted, you may be going to bed before your body is ready for sleep. For the same reason, you may also feel sleepy in the middle of the afternoon.

When you do finally fall asleep, your sleep may be punctuated by clear, often horrifying nightmares. Gail, the paralegal who saw leering men imprinted on her eyelids, spent two nights dreaming fearful, anxious dreams, even after her perceptual distortion had resolved itself. One dream was especially scary, the more so because it occurred several times both nights. She dreamed that while she was sitting in on a meeting with a number of clients, they suddenly became a tribunal with sneering, hairy, monkey-like faces. They pelted her with angry accusations and rotten food, then built a pyre of office furniture and tied her on top of it. Just as they were about to set it on fire, she would wake up, shaking and drenched with sweat.

Gail's brain was trying to make up for past losses of REM sleep. REM sleep is suppressed by chemical abuse, but it returns after you stop drinking or using, and you are likely to have more REM periods in the first weeks of sobriety. The quality of your sleep may also be poor. Instead of spending part of the night in a deep, refreshing sleep, you spend all the night in a shallow sleep. In fact, whereas the average person wakes up briefly four or five times a night, someone who's just stopped using mood-altering drugs may wake up *one hundred* times a night. In addition, you may wake up in the early morning hours and not be able to get back to sleep at all.

You may have nights when you don't get a wink of sleep, and toss and turn for what seem like endless hours. These are often the moments when you're most vulnerable to the humiliating memories of everything that happened to you during your addiction.

Any or all of these sleep problems will affect how you feel and behave the next day. Although you may have been in bed for eight hours, and asleep for seven and a half of those hours, the actual sleep you got hasn't revitalized you. In the morning you feel tired, out of sorts, and irritable. If you've been up the entire night agonizing about the past, you're very likely to get out of bed feeling tense and exhausted. Needless to say, neither situation gets your day off to a good start.

Getting a Good Night's Sleep

You *can* get a good night's sleep on a regular basis, but first you have to allow your body to reestablish its normal rhythms. It is most important that you neither do anything nor take any substance that will disturb your internal balance.

Sleeping medications, whether prescription or over-the-counter, do *not* promote normal sleep; they change sleep patterns and interfere with dreaming sleep. They also cause a rebound effect, so that in all likelihood you'll have an even harder time falling and staying asleep the following night.

Sleep experts agree that sleeping pills are not only ineffective for chronic insomnia, but they can also be addictive. Neither prescription nor over-the-counter sleep preparations should be used by anyone on a daily basis. People who are recovering from drug or alcohol abuse should avoid them altogether. Having said this, I must make an exception. There are rare occasions when you have an acute and specific need for sleep —when you're in the hospital the night before or after an operation, or when you are facing a grave life crisis. Should such a need arise, the benefits of taking sleeping medication for one or two nights may outweigh the risks. In that case, you should discuss your decision with your physician and follow the guidelines I outlined in Chapter 13.

When you establish a normal sleeping routine you help your circadian rhythm to regulate itself so that you feel sleepy at a time that's convenient for you to go to bed, and you wake up having slept long enough that you feel refreshed and alert. Though some people are comfortable with as few as four or five hours of sleep a night, most require between seven and eight hours, although that number often decreases as people reach their sixties and seventies.

The point is that there's no such thing as a "normal" daily sleeping requirement. If you feel rested and energized after five hours sleep, count yourself fortunate to have a few extra hours in your day. If you need eight hours sleep each night, get it. In any case, pay attention to your body's signals in order to determine what's normal for you.

Remember that it's also natural for you to spend a restless night occasionally, when you get only an uneasy hour or two of sleep, or maybe no sleep at all. Often, though not always, the reason is obvious—an emotional upset, a crucial presentation coming up the next day at work, a queasy stomach, a bad cold. Worrying about not having slept can be even more debilitating than the loss of sleep itself, so learn to accept those once-in-a-while nights when not even a glass of warm milk or a few pages of the most boring book can help you doze off.

Over time, your body will adjust itself so that you get the amount of sleep you need. Most recovering people find that their sleep patterns gradually become normal; it may take weeks or months, but eventually a regular routine and abstinence from alcohol or drugs allows the body's natural healing process to work on the sleep cycle.

How to Establish a Regular Sleeping Pattern and a Normal Circadian Rhythm

1. Go to bed and get up at regular times.

In early recovery, when your body rhythms are still disturbed, you may have trouble falling asleep. But by settling down to relax at the same hour every evening, you'll begin to reestablish your regular biological rhythm.

2. Avoid activities or substances that may delay you from falling asleep.

You should avoid any kind of stimulant within four hours of your set bedtime. This includes nicotine and caffeine, both of which can delay the onset of sleep. However, since more than eighty percent of people with alcohol and drug problems are also hooked on nicotine, and many on caffeine as well, this may not be realistic advice—yet. Do try, though, to drink only decaffeinated coffee or tea after 5:00 P.M., and to reduce your evening cigarette use as well.

Events and conversations can be stimulating too. It is unwise to expect yourself to rush home after a lively meeting or an entertaining movie, throw off your clothes, jump into bed, and immediately fall asleep. Allow yourself time to wind down and relax before you begin your bedtime routine.

3. Take a warm bath or shower.

If you're having difficulty falling asleep, this can be very soothing. The relaxing combination of heat and water can induce sleep rhythms in the brain and promote drowsiness. It can also help prevent muscle cramps that may interfere with falling asleep.

4. Exercise regularly.

Exercise is an excellent sleep-inducer, although not right before bedtime. Get your exercise at least four hours before you retire. Studies have shown that regular exercise performed in the morning or afternoon can reduce the sleep onset latency period, and can also increase the amount of time spent asleep. Researchers have also found that insomniacs generally exercise less than people who sleep soundly.

5. Spend time during the day interacting with other people.

According to sleep researchers, people who suffer chronic insomnia tend to be more isolated and have fewer personal encounters than people who sleep well. If you spend a lot of time alone and are sleeping poorly, make an effort to get out and see people more during the day.

6. Establish a bedtime routine.

If you are in the earliest stages of recovery, chances are you haven't had much of a routine lately, which means you've been missing out on an important aspect of the sleep process. Your routine should include whatever physical preparations you need to make at bedtime— changing into your pajamas, setting out your clothes for the next day, brushing your teeth, and so on. But you should also give yourself a period of personal time during which you can relax and get some distance from the events of the day, whether they were enjoyable, exciting, or demanding. You might choose to meditate, read, listen to music, or watch a TV program, but try to do the same things every night.

One of my patients had passed out drunk every night for years until he became sober. He told me that he felt as though he were reliving one of the best parts of his childhood when he recently established a bedtime routine for himself. He takes a warm bath, puts on his pajamas, and prepares a cup of hot cocoa before he climbs into bed and reads one short story each night. "The only thing that might improve my bedtime," he said, "would be to have someone read me the story aloud. But even so, I sleep like a baby now."

7. If you can't sleep, get up and do something useful.

One of the worst things you can do to yourself when you can't sleep is to lie in bed worrying about how terrible you'll feel in the morning. Try not to let your bed become associated with insomnia. Get up and do something—read a book, write a letter, finish the ironing, fix your daughter's broken doll, listen to music, draw up the plans for your dream house. You can accomplish a great deal with these extra hours —so much that people who sleep eight or nine hours may feel envious of the extra time you have.

8. Always get up at your usual time, even if you've had a sleepless night.

Don't stay in bed longer in the morning to catch up on your sleep and don't take naps during the day. If you always get up on time after a sleepless night, you'll be surprised at how soon you begin to feel genuinely sleepy at bedtime.

Chronic Insomnia

Approximately eleven percent of the population has chronic (long-term or frequently recurring) insomnia. If you're one of these people, you're likely to have had sleep problems whether or not you used alcohol or drugs. Indeed, you may have used alcohol or drugs to help yourself fall asleep. Your sleep patterns may improve when you stop drinking or using, but they probably will never become what's generally considered normal.

I know many insomniacs who have made splendid adaptations to their sleep problems; they are able to accept the difficulties they have and have come to know that they'll be able to function the next day in spite of not getting a solid night's sleep. One insomniac acquaintance of mine, a medical school professor, prepares all his lectures on nights when he can't sleep. He comforts himself with the fact that he never has to spend weekends catching up with work, as so many sound sleepers must do.

Other chronic insomniacs have sought help from sleep clinics, where doctors and researchers analyze their sleep patterns to determine whether the problem can be corrected. If you're interested in such an evaluation, consult your physician, who will refer you to a clinic. But wait until you've been sober and/or drug-free for at least one year. And do be aware that some sleep clinics may prescribe medications that you, as a recovering person, *cannot* take.

Relaxation training, meditation, self-hypnosis, and biofeedback techniques can also help promote sleep, as I mentioned in Chapter 6. (Because it is a physical discipline, yoga should not be practiced within four hours of your bedtime.) If you haven't already begun to investigate these methods of stress reduction, and you're having trouble sleeping, I suggest you reconsider trying one (or more) of them. The list of books and tapes in Appendix A can help you get started.

Mary found relaxation training, as well as other recommendations in this chapter, quite useful. "I think I was born sleepless," she once told me. She'd been a restless infant, and even as a child (when insomnia is unusual) she remembers the many nights she spent lying in bed and worrying. Sometimes she crawled into her parents' bed to be comforted. They weren't exactly pleased, she recalls.

When she started drinking in her early twenties, she noticed that she always slept well on the nights she partied. But it wasn't until she was twenty-five and having a particularly bad period of insomnia after an ended love affair that she consciously began to take a drink or two before she went to bed. By this time her drinking was already causing her problems. She was getting drunk, even though she kept vowing not to, and was also having blackouts. Her nightcaps only accelerated the progress of her disease.

She came into treatment when she was in her early thirties. By then she was drinking around the clock, and she hadn't had a normal night's sleep in about four years. She had a difficult time withdrawing from alcohol and barely slept for three days. Then she finally had a wonderful night's sleep and woke up the next morning feeling refreshed and optimistic.

Though she did have other good nights over the next four weeks, Mary continued to have trouble falling asleep. Or she would fall asleep at first, only to awaken and not be able to sleep again. Even worse than not sleeping was her dread of insomnia, and her fear that she wouldn't be able to function in her demanding job as a systems analyst without adequate rest. I pointed out to her that in the past she had somehow managed to operate on a quart of vodka a day. Insomnia couldn't possibly be more disruptive than her drinking had been.

The other members of her self-help group counseled her to be patient. "Stay sober and it will get better," they said. They were right. She made some progress, but nowhere near as much as she desired. Then Mary began a regular exercise program for the first time in her life. She also saw a therapist for six sessions of relaxation training and bought a series of relaxation tapes. As a result, her sleep improved dramatically.

Most important, she no longer worries that she won't be able to get to sleep. "Of course, I have my nights when I don't sleep, more than the average person does, I expect. But that's hardly surprising, when you consider my history. The difference is that now when I'm awake most of the night, I know that I won't be at my best the next day. But I also know I'll be able to manage, so I don't lie in bed fretting about whether I'm ever going to fall asleep. The tapes are very helpful, so helpful that I also use them during the day if I'm feeling overwhelmed. I think the nicest part of all is how much I get done in the middle of the night when I'm wide awake."

The techniques Mary uses have improved her sleep patterns and significantly lessened her anxiety about her insomnia. She'll never be a "perfect sleeper," but her life is no longer disrupted by her sleep problems.

I have noticed that people who focus on their sleep problems have the hardest time changing their patterns. They become obsessed, worry about every aspect of sleeping, and adopt a defeatist attitude about any advice they're offered.

"I've tried exercising," Brandon, a recovering alcoholic, told me. "It made my muscles so sore that I couldn't find a comfortable position to lie in. It's no good for me."

I finally pried out of him the exact nature of his exercise. On two occasions he'd jogged around the boating pond in Central Park, a distance of perhaps a quarter of a mile.

Brandon, a brilliant trial lawyer who had been arguing cases for twenty years, insisted that he would never make it through his next court appearance if he didn't sleep the night before. I asked him whether he had ever had to appear in court after staying up late, even most of the night, preparing a case.

"Of course, but that's different. I *had* to stay awake then. What I'm talking about is when I don't want to," he replied.

But as I pointed out to him, there really is no difference. You *can* function well if you miss a night of sleep, but not if you become preoccupied with your lack of sleep.

If you focus on your sobriety and on leading a healthy life instead of dwelling on your sleep problems, your sleep *will* improve. Your expectations about sleep will also become more realistic. But if you're constantly anxious about not sleeping, you may get yourself into a mindset in which anything—even taking a drink or a pill to help you nod off—seems better than another night without sleep. And you may make yourself vulnerable to a relapse.

You can't allow yourself the luxury of indulging in this cycle of insomnia, worry, and defeatism. Instead, cultivate a healthy lifestyle and some satisfying hobbies for those nights when you can't fall asleep, and you'll be taking great strides towards protecting your sobriety.

Chapter Fifteen
Eating for Sobriety

Most people would readily agree that they feel less than their best, physically and mentally, after a poor night's sleep. The connection is easy to make. But the relationship between your diet and your physical and mental states is not so apparent. Only when you are unwell—with an upset stomach, for example—do you think: Oh, it must have been something I ate. However, the food you eat directly affects the way your body and brain function. Your diet also has an impact on your sobriety.

A lot of my patients hold the mistaken belief that wholesome, nutritious food is tasteless and drab. If it's good for you, they argue, it has to be boring. In fact, nothing could be further from the truth. But if you still associate a nourishing diet with what's served up in hospital or school cafeterias, you'll probably be tempted to skip this chapter. Keep reading and you'll soon discover that healthy eating is much more than a way to regain or maintain your physical well-being. It can be a source of great pleasure—and taking pleasure in your newly awakened senses, especially your senses of taste and smell, is an important part of recovery.

Avoiding Foods That May Be Hazardous to Your Sobriety

Before I go on to talk about how to eat well and enjoyably, let's spend a few minutes on the subject of what you *shouldn't* be eating. As a recovering alcoholic or addict, you should be aware that some foods may actually trigger your urge to drink or use drugs again. In the interests of your sobriety, you'll have to stay away from the following foods.

Foods Cooked with Alcohol

Many fine cooks use wine, liqueurs, or even beer in everything from sauces to desserts. If the dish is properly prepared, the alcohol will evaporate as it's being cooked. But unfortunately, some chefs aren't as careful as they might be about cooking off the alcohol. Sauces are often concocted at the last minute, and some cooks add a finishing splash of wine to such entrees as coq au vin or beef Bourguignon to achieve a distinctive wine flavor.

Even if the dish has been properly cooked, eliminating the effects of the alcohol, just the flavor of the wine may be enough to trigger your desire to drink, especially during the early stages of recovery. I know people who have been sober for years and are still reluctant to eat food to which wine or hard liquor has been added. Others, after two or three years of sobriety, feel they can safely enjoy a wine-based sauce or dish and even cook with spirits themselves.

Foods Soaked in Alcohol

It should come as no surprise to you that the alcohol in desserts such as brandied apple pudding, rum cake, and strawberries soaked in champagne has not been evaporated, not even partially. You'll have to say no to these delicacies not only in early sobriety, but for the rest of your life, as they could trigger a relapse. In fact, if you find yourself fantasizing about desserts that contain alcohol, be alert for signs of a possibly impending relapse.

Gavin, an actor, rushed into his AA meeting and announced, "I've had a slip. I've had a slip!"

This drew the usual concerned response and he was asked to tell the whole story. Gavin told all, missing no opportunity for embellishments. He had just come from a charity fund-raising dinner. Everything was "too divine"—until dessert. The fruit in the compote had been marinated in liqueur, and Gavin had taken a few spoonfuls before realizing it.

"As soon as I tasted it, I dashed from the room and ran to the loo. I stuck my finger down my throat, hoping to bring up the liquor before it got into my system. But I couldn't. I didn't know what to do then, so I left and came here. Three years of sobriety lost," he wailed.

He was inconsolable. His sponsor took him aside. "If you carry on like this," he told him, "you're going to have a real slip. Maybe that's what you're working yourself up to," he suggested.

If you do inadvertently eat a bite or two of food that contains alcohol, you don't have to work yourself up into a froth over it, the way Gavin did. That could be even more dangerous than what you just ate. Instead, simply push the dish away and remind yourself to be more careful in the future.

Near-Beer and Nonalcoholic Wine

Stay away from drinks that are meant to taste like wine or beer, even if they don't actually contain any alcohol. I've treated several patients whose relapses were touched off by soft drinks because the flavors were reminiscent of their favorite alcoholic drink. It may be that they were setting themselves up for a relapse by choosing the near-beer or nonalcoholic wine, but the fact remains that those beverages provoked their urge to drink. Why tempt fate when there are so many alternatives to quench your thirst?

Caffeine

Caffeine is a stimulant drug. It's milder, but it is in the same general category as cocaine or amphetamines. While the caffeine itself may not trigger a craving, it can increase your tension and anxiety, and may also make it harder for you to fall asleep. And like any stimulant drug, caffeine increases your heart rate and constricts your blood vessels.

Because you don't want to increase the stress on your already irritable nervous system, especially during the early weeks of sobriety, you should cut down as much as possible on caffeine-rich beverages and foods, such as coffee, tea, colas, and chocolate. If you can eliminate caffeine altogether, so much the better. But do try to drink no more than two caffeinated drinks a day, and never within two hours of bedtime.

You'll be surprised by how much better you'll feel without the heart-racing, nerve-jangling effects of "real" coffee or cola. There was a remarkable change in the behavior and anxiety level of patients at our inpatient treatment center when we switched to decaffeinated coffee, tea, and colas. Most restaurants now serve brewed decaffeinated coffee, and many also offer herbal or decaffeinated teas. Again, while abstaining or limiting your caffeine intake is most important in the early weeks and months of recovery, it can be a boon to your emotional state and your health throughout sobriety, and I recommend it to everyone.

But beware that reducing or eliminating the amount of caffeine in your diet can make for a difficult initial twenty-four to forty-eight hours while your system goes through withdrawal. As with other drugs, over time the body becomes tolerant to caffeine. If you're used to drinking three or more caffeinated drinks a day and you stop abruptly, you may go through a period of feeling fatigued, depressed, irritable, or headachy. Not everyone experiences these symptoms, but if you do, you'll be uncomfortable for a day or two after you quit. If your normal intake of caffeine is five or more doses a day, I recommend that you cut down gradually—by two drinks a day, for example—rather than stopping all at once. And if you do suffer any of the side effects I mentioned above, it's important that you not try to relieve them with medication. They will go away in a short time on their own.

Eating Well and Wisely

Switching to a well-balanced diet can help you in every stage of recovery on several fronts. Eating properly can reduce your cravings for alcohol and drugs, improve your energy level, promote a stable mood, and increase your opportunities for enjoyment and relaxation. These great benefits can be derived with relatively little time and effort. Changing your eating habits isn't difficult if you understand a few simple principles and the components of a sensible diet.

But first it is useful to see what you are actually eating. When I talk to patients about improving their health and nutrition, I also ask them to keep a weekly log. That way, I can point out how their choice of foods may be hindering their recovery. A food log can be helpful for you, too.

Laura is a very slim, attractive thirty-one-year-old account executive at a New York brokerage firm. Formerly one of the company's star performers, her productivity declined precipitously when she became addicted to alcohol and cocaine. Through an employee-assistance program, Laura was referred to our inpatient treatment program. She had been sober for six weeks when she completed her diet sheet. It was full of blanks and listed many meals that consisted of nothing but black coffee. Laura reluctantly admitted that she was "sort of" dieting—not strictly, just trying to limit her calories. Here is a typical day's menu:

Breakfast	Black coffee
Lunch	Half bagel with cream cheese
	Black coffee
Dinner	Scoop of tuna salad with lettuce and tomatoes
	Black coffee
Snack	Vanilla ice cream

Certainly Laura didn't seem to be eating very much. But despite the fact that she was trying to be diet-conscious, the food she *was* eating derived half its calories from fat. Moreover, she was not only taking in less than half her recommended daily requirement of calories, she was also cheating herself of vital nutrients like vitamins, fiber, iron, and calcium. I explained to Laura that if she didn't change her eating habits, she could develop serious nutritional problems.

At the other end of the dietary spectrum is Tom, a thirty-five-year-old police officer and self-described junk-food king. Tom is separated from his wife, who forced him to go into treatment after she awoke one morning to find their four-year-old daughter pointing Tom's loaded service revolver at her younger brother, saying, "Hands up or I'll shoot." The little girl had found the gun on the living room floor, where Tom had left it before he passed out.

Tom had been sober for three months when I spoke to him about his diet. He was living alone in a studio apartment and eating most of his meals out, so I wasn't surprised to see the following list of foods on his weekly record:

Breakfast	Fast-food biscuit, with bacon, egg, and cheese
	Sixteen ounces of apple juice
Lunch	Two cheeseburgers
	French fries
	Twelve-ounce cola
Dinner	Spaghetti and meatballs
	Garlic bread
	Sixteen ounces of orange juice

Tom's diet was extremely high in saturated fat, cholesterol, and salt. Though he was getting adequate amounts of vitamins and minerals, he was eating almost no fresh vegetables or fruit, both excellent sources of fiber. It was no wonder that Tom listed frequent constipation among his health complaints now that he had stopped drinking.

In contrast to both Tom and Laura, Anna was a frail-looking fifty-four-year-old widow whose adult children had arranged an intervention to force her into treatment. They had become increasingly concerned about her failing health and her tendency to pick up undesirable characters in the bars she frequented. When I first spoke to Anna, she was four months sober and trying to stick to the low-fat, low-salt diet prescribed by her doctor because of a heart condition. Here's a typical day's fare:

Breakfast	Oatmeal
	Tea
Lunch	Water-packed tuna
	Lettuce, radishes, and cucumber
	Low-fat salad dressing
	One slice of pumpernickel bread
	Tea
Dinner	Broiled chicken breast
	Rice
	Broccoli
Snack	Twelve ounces of grapefruit juice

Perhaps because she was following her doctor's orders, or because he'd given her a list of permitted foods and sample menus, Anna was eating much more healthfully than either Laura or Tom. Her calorie intake was adequate for her age and weight of 110 pounds. Moreover, her diet was low in fat and included adequate fiber and vitamins. But I felt that she could be eating a little more, especially because her regimen was low in calcium, a particularly important mineral for a woman in her mid-fifties. I suggested she drink one cup of skim milk a day, which would provide her with more calcium as well as the additional calories she needed.

Of the three, only Anna's diet was conducive to recovery, though it called for some improvement. Laura and Tom, however, were not only harming their health, they were also possibly hindering their recovery by depriving themselves of nutritious food.

The Principles of Good Eating

Variety

Where eating is concerned, variety is more than simply the spice of life—it's the most important element to keep in mind when you plan your meals. A healthy diet has to include the right proportion of carbohydrates, fats, protein, vitamins, minerals, and fiber. A well-balanced eating plan which includes the right variety of foods should provide all these substances in the amounts you need to function well.

People who stick to the same few foods day after day—whether they're "bad" foods like hot dogs and French fries or "good" foods like brown rice and alfalfa sprouts—are the ones who find themselves with nutritional deficiencies.

Regular Mealtimes and Planned Snacking

People who skip meals tend to substitute high-calorie, low-nutrition snacks. This is certainly true for most of my patients, even Laura, who said she was dieting but snacked on vanilla ice cream. I rarely meet anyone who snacks on apples, pears, oranges, or raw vegetables.

If you can't skip the cake, cookies, candy, or chips entirely at snack time, you should make the effort to keep them at a minimum. This is easier to do if you eat three *nutritious* meals a day, at more or less set hours. Allowing yourself the time to dine in a leisurely fashion means you can relax and enjoy yourself while you're eating. If you find that you're frequently hungry between meals, learn to bring along a nutritious snack to tide you over until your next meal. A few crackers and a small chunk of cheese or a piece of fruit will help you resist the sugary treats on the coffee wagon at break time. When your energy takes a dip in the late afternoon, try an apple or raw carrot sticks instead of a candy bar. Of course, if you're not hungry, you don't have to eat anything at all. But being prepared is far preferable to fighting off a craving.

Moderation and Balance

Eating three meals a day doesn't mean eating three *huge* meals a day. Nor does it mean consuming more than you really want because you're worried that you haven't taken in enough B vitamins that day. Eat what you need to satisfy your hunger. If you learn to pay attention to the signals your body sends you, you'll begin to have a sense of how much of which foods are right for your diet.

Work on developing a balanced attitude about what you eat. If one morning you wake up ravenously hungry and decide to treat yourself to a high-calorie breakfast of bacon, eggs, home fries with ketchup, and buttered toast, keep in mind that you've consumed more than your fair share of fat, cholesterol, and salt for the day—possibly for two days. Your next several meals should include foods that are much lower in those three elements.

No Bad Foods

You can hardly turn on the TV or pick up a newspaper these days without having someone tell you what you can and cannot eat. Consequently, you may have gotten the impression that certain foods are "bad" and must be avoided at all costs. Many of these maligned foods *are* hazardous to your health if consumed in large quantities. However, when eaten in moderation, they can be a positive addition to your diet.

The egg, for example, has all but disappeared from many menus because of its high cholesterol content. But it remains a valuable and concentrated source of many nutrients. For those who aren't at risk for coronary artery disease, one or two eggs a week can be beneficial. The reputation of milk and milk products has also become somewhat tarnished. There's no question that a steady diet of high-fat dairy products is bad for your health, but an occasional ice cream cone on a hot summer day can be a delicious treat. As long as you practice moderation and restraint, there are no such things as good and bad foods—except, of course, for those I mentioned earlier that can trigger a relapse because of their alcohol content. For the most part, you can safely eat just about anything you choose.

The Components of a Sensible Diet

Carbohydrates

The one high you *should not* avoid in sobriety is a diet that's *high in complex carbohydrates*. Such stick-to-your-ribs foods as oatmeal, pasta, and lentils, as well as fruits and vegetables, are complex carbohydrates and supply you with a steady stream of energy. These foods not only provide the fuel that keeps you going, they also help you avoid the cravings for a drink or drug that may come from being hungry.

Carbohydrates also occur in another form, simple sugars, which can be found in fruits and in most vegetables to some extent. They are also found in refined sugar, and in products made with refined sugar. Refined sugar has come to have a bad nutritional reputation, mostly because the typical American diet contains far too much of it. Eating large quantities of sugar can contribute to weight gain, and if you have a tendency toward diabetes, sugar-laden foods can present a serious health hazard. But if you're not significantly overweight or diabetic, there's no evidence that some sugar in your diet is harmful. I emphasize the word *some*. A daily menu that relies heavily on cakes, cookies, and soda is neither well-balanced nor healthy. But an occasional sweet treat won't harm you, especially if you have it as dessert, rather than as a snack without any other food.

Unfortunately, my advice may be contradicted by a well-meaning, but misinformed, member of your self-help group, who tells you to eat something sweet whenever you have a craving for alcohol. Skip, a thirty-two-year-old plumber, was told this by another alcoholic whose sobriety he respected. Never one to do things halfway, Skip gorged himself on cakes, pie, and ice cream.

I asked him if his cravings for alcohol lasted the entire time he was eating the ice cream. "No," he replied, "after a while, it has nothing to do with craving alcohol. It's a way of being nice to myself now that I can no longer get drunk. But I've noticed I feel rotten a couple of hours later, sometimes even the next morning."

I explained to Skip, as I will to you in the next pages, how his nightly sugar binges were affecting his body and his mood. With this new knowledge, he cut them out immediately.

You should be getting most of your carbohydrates in the form of naturally occurring complex carbohydrates, which are broken down by the liver over many hours. In the process, your body is well supplied with energy as well as nutrients from the vitamins and minerals in these foods. Refined sugar, by contrast, gives you only a quick spurt of energy; it contains no other nutrients. Because it's so easily processed by the liver, it causes your blood sugar—and your mood—to spike upward, then dip down and adversely affect your mood, which is already quite precarious in early recovery.

To better understand how this works, let's imagine that at noon you ate a lunch that was low in complex carbohydrates. Four hours later you indulge in a sundae that's loaded with refined sugar—in the ice cream, the hot fudge, and the sweetened whipped cream on top. The sugar from the sundae hits your now-idle liver, which rushes to process it, causing your blood sugar to rise sharply and quickly. You walk away from the table feeling happy, warm, and satisfied—the so-called sugar high.

However, nature abhors extremes and struggles always to maintain its internal balance. In response to your suddenly high blood sugar level, your pancreas secretes a large amount of insulin. This, in turn, causes a sharp, rapid decline in your blood sugar level, so that within a short time your pleasurable feelings have faded and instead you're feeling tense, tired, possibly even headachy.

On the other hand, if you replace the sundae with an apple, pear, or any other fruit that contains both simple sugars and complex carbohydrates, the liver is asked to perform a far more complicated task. Your blood sugar rises gradually, without provoking an extreme response from the pancreas. You don't get the high, but you're also spared the low. Your body's equilibrium is maintained.

Nutritionists now agree that complex carbohydrates should supply at least fifty-five to sixty percent of your daily calories. This is quite a change from previous decades when the normal American diet consisted largely of fat and protein in the form of red meat and milk products. Today, we know that while fat and protein are part of our dietary needs, they shouldn't account for the majority of our daily caloric intake.

One more word about complex carbohydrates: They are excellent foods indeed, but that doesn't give you license to eat more than you need. You may have heard stories about runners who "load carbohydrates," that is, consume enormous bowls of pasta the night before a big race. Carbohydrates taken in excess of your daily requirement can be stored in the muscles and later converted to energy when your body needs it. This is fine if you're running a long race or doing some other strenuous physical exercise or labor. But if you are only moderately active, the unused stored carbohydrates will soon be converted into unwanted fat.

Fat

Fats and fatty acids are essential components of your body's cells. Fatty acids are depleted each day as the body expends energy. They can't be manufactured by the body, so they must be replenished through your diet. Your body also needs some stored fat—under the skin to provide warmth, in the muscles, and in the abdominal cavity where it insulates and protects the body's organs. Even the leanest, best-conditioned athletes need some stored fat. But too much fat can not only make you gain unwanted weight, it can also clog your arteries and lead to heart disease.

Animals store fat just as we do, both in their muscles and in the fatty deposits surrounding the muscle. (This is the fat you see and can cut away from your meat before you cook it.) Because of the fat that's embedded in the muscle, even trimmed meats may be high in fat. Hamburger can be approximately forty percent fat, and spareribs may be more than seventy-five percent fat. Poultry, fish, eggs, milk and milk products, oil, butter, and margarine also contain fat at varying levels.

Fat is not only an essential nutrient, it also contains much of the flavor in food. Because so many people are accustomed to a diet that consists of forty percent fat (and in many cases even more than that), they have acquired a palate that favors fatty foods. Nutritionists agree that forty percent is much too high, and recommend taking in no more than thirty percent—and preferably as low as twenty to twenty-five percent—of your daily calories in the form of fat. If you've never paid attention before to your nutritional needs, it may take several weeks for you to adjust to menus with a reduced fat content. But I promise that once you get used to this new regimen, you'll find that the food you eat tastes lighter, fresher, and better.

Cholesterol is an organic fat-like substance found in all animal fats and oils. An integral part of cell membranes and nerve sheaths, cholesterol is also necessary for the production of sex hormones. After the age of about six months, however, the liver produces enough cholesterol to meet that requirement. You don't actually need to take in extra cholesterol through your food, but a diet that has a bit of cholesterol won't harm you.

Trouble can start, however, if there's too much cholesterol in your blood. Fatty deposits can build up on the walls of your arteries and restrict the smooth passage of blood to the heart, in much the same way that corrosion hinders the flow of water in a pipe. This curtailed movement of blood contributes to heart attacks, strokes, and other circulatory ailments.

High cholesterol levels are related in part to genetic makeup. Some susceptible people, in spite of rigorous low-fat diets, still have higher than normal cholesterol levels and may be candidates for cholesterol-lowering medications. Others with no genetic predisposition to high cholesterol may have normal levels despite eating eggs, red meat, and cream daily. Even if you are one of these fortunate people, a diet containing thirty percent or less fat is still healthier for you.

A diet that's too rich in cholesterol can raise the blood cholesterol levels. So can eating too much saturated fat, which is found in meat, egg yolks, and full-fat dairy products, as well as in palm oil, coconut oil, and cocoa butter, an ingredient of chocolate.

You can reduce the amount of saturated fat in your diet, and actually lower your cholesterol, by switching to foods that are high in *un*saturated fat. Unsaturated fats are found in some fish, as well as in nuts and seeds, olive, corn, peanut, safflower, and soybean oils, and margarine. The easiest way to differentiate between saturated and unsaturated fat is to look at its state at room temperature. Saturated fats are solid at room temperature; unsaturated fats are liquid. The obvious exception is margarine, which has been hydrogenated; that is, it's been processed so that the unsaturated oils remain solid even when not refrigerated. Though margarine is less healthy than the unsaturated oils, it's still preferable to butter.

When you plan your meals, try to limit the saturated fats to one-third of the calories you take in from fat. For example, if you take in thirty percent of your calories in fat, only ten percent of your total calorie intake should be from saturated fat.

Protein

Protein is an important component of many parts of the body, including the skin, bones, blood, and muscles. In fact, half your body weight (excluding water, which accounts for fifty-five to sixty-five percent in women and sixty-five to seventy-five percent in men) is made up of protein. Protein consists of strings of amino acids, which are the chemical building blocks of the body. Some of these amino acids can't be manufactured by the body itself, so you need to take them in through your diet.

Animal products—meat, poultry, fish, milk, and eggs—are the most complete sources of protein because they contain all the amino acids your body needs. Protein is also present in many vegetable sources, especially legumes, grains, nuts, and seeds. It's possible to combine or complement these vegetable proteins, as many vegetarians do, in ways that provide all the amino acids. For example, lentil soup (a legume) eaten with a whole wheat roll (a grain) gives you a complete source of protein. So does eating a peanut butter sandwich—make sure it's "natural" or "old-fashioned" peanut butter with no sugar, salt, or saturated fats added—on whole wheat bread (a nut and a grain) along with a glass of low-fat or skim milk (dairy product). Another benefit of deriving some of your protein from vegetable sources is that they don't contain any cholesterol and most contain no saturated fat.

Just as the average American diet is too high in sugar and fat, it's also too high in protein. When you consume more protein than you need, some of it will be converted to stored fat and the rest will be excreted in your urine. No more than 10 to 15 percent of your daily calories should be provided by protein. For most adults (weighing between 110 and 180 pounds), daily protein requirements range from forty to sixty-five grams or 1.4 to 2.3 ounces of pure protein—not very much at all when compared to the amounts many of us eat. Flounder, for example, is an excellent, low-fat source of protein. Six ounces contain fifty grams (1.8 ounces) of pure protein—enough to meet the daily protein requirement of a 140-pound adult. The same adult could meet his or her protein needs by eating *all* of the following over the course of one day:

1 slice pizza (7.8 g)
3 oz. tuna (24.4 g)
½ cup broccoli (2.4 g)
½ cup kidney beans (7.2 g)
1 cup unpolished rice (4.1 g)
½ cup milk (4.5 g)

This varied diet would provide greater overall nutritional value from the vitamins, minerals, and fibers it contains than would the six-ounce slice of flounder.

Vitamins

Vitamins are organic substances that act as catalysts for the many chemical reactions that take place in the body. There are thirteen known vitamins: eight B vitamins and C (all of which are water-soluble) and vitamins A, D, E, and K (which are fat-soluble). The body requires only very small amounts of any of these vitamins, and people who eat a varied diet that includes fresh vegetables and fruit, whole grains, legumes, meat, poultry, fish, and dairy products will take in *all* the vitamins they need.

Unfortunately, the all-too-human search for an easy route to health, happiness, and longevity, combined with market greed, has produced a billion-dollar industry that at best has given Americans the most expensive urine in the world, and at worst has caused serious illness and even death from vitamin megadosing. Despite arguments to the contrary by some nutritional researchers, including Nobel Prize winner Dr. Linus Pauling, many scientists still believe there's no evidence that taking vitamins in excess of the Recommended Daily Allowance (RDA) established by the National Academy of Sciences is in any way beneficial for normal, healthy people. In my opinion, higher doses, including shots of vitamin B12 and megadoses of vitamin C, do not promote well-being nor do they ward off disease. In fact, doses above the RDA, especially of the fat-soluble vitamins A, D, E, and K, can be quite detrimental to your health. Because unused quantities of these particular vitamins aren't flushed out of the system, they can build up in the fatty tissue, perhaps reaching toxic levels. Even the B vitamins and vitamin C, which are water-soluble, aren't entirely safe in large doses. Regular doses of more than 200 milligrams per day of B6 have been associated with nerve damage and impaired brain function.

Rudy began taking megadoses of all the vitamins soon after he became sober, only to become seriously ill from them within four months. He became jaundiced, which turned the whites of his eyes and his skin yellow, and, because his blood levels of vitamin A were excessively high, he developed liver damage as well. I visited him in the hospital while he was recuperating. "I was still looking for a magic pill to fix everything," he admitted. "I know now that excess is dangerous. To feel good, I have to change me. There's no pill in the universe that can do that—only I can do it."

Your best source of vitamins are fresh, unprocessed foods (foods that are overcooked or boiled too long lose vitamins). Of course, I'm not suggesting that you eat raw meat or drink unpasteurized milk, but I do recommend eating at least some of your vegetables raw, and steaming instead of boiling the ones you eat cooked. The husks of grains contain many of their vitamins, so whole grains and flours are preferable to processed grain products, such as white bread or white flour.

Most people get a perfectly adequate supply of vitamins from the food they eat, but there are some exceptions. Heavy smokers have between thirty and fifty percent less vitamin C in their blood than non-smokers, which is one of many excellent reasons why you should stop smoking. But if you're not ready to quit, make sure that you get extra vitamin C to bring you up to the required levels. That doesn't mean you should stock up on vitamin C pills; one eight-ounce glass of orange juice a day will correct the deficit.

Elderly people, women who take birth control pills, and dieters —even if their diet is appropriately varied—also may not be getting their proper doses of vitamins, particularly B-complex and C. The same is true of people who, for one reason or another, eat mostly processed foods. If you fall into one of these categories, you should invest in a multivitamin supplement to be taken daily.

Minerals

Minerals, like vitamins, are essential catalysts for many of the body's chemical reactions. Trace minerals such as copper, chromium, selenium, zinc, and others are needed in only very small daily doses, whereas the macro-minerals, such as calcium, chloride, magnesium, phosphorus, potassium, sulfur, and sodium, are needed in greater amounts. If you stick to a nutritious, varied diet, you'll get adequate amounts of most of the essential minerals. Mineral supplements are, for the most part, unnecessary and in some cases may actually be hazardous to your health. But there are four minerals that some people need be concerned about: calcium, iron, sodium, and chloride.

Calcium

The mineral most likely to be lacking in your diet is calcium, which is needed for strong bones and teeth. During childhood and early adulthood plenty of calcium is required to build dense, strong bones, but even with a good foundation, the need continues throughout life.

After age thirty-five, both men and women begin to lose calcium from the bones, a process that is accelerated in women at the onset of the menopause. Severe loss of calcium can result in osteoporosis, a painful degenerative bone disease that can lead to fractured bones and collapsed spinal vertebrae. You can help prevent osteoporosis, which is most common among postmenopausal women but can affect men as well, by getting enough calcium in your diet. Regular exercise is also beneficial because, in a process that's not yet fully understood, it increases the amount of calcium deposited in the bones. Smoking, caffeine, high fat foods, stress, and alcohol all increase the risk of osteoporosis.

The combination of early menopause at age forty-three, heavy alcohol intake, a sedentary life, a poor diet, and a family history of osteoporosis made Bertha a prime candidate for the disease. When she came into treatment at seventy-two, she had a humped back (what used to be called a widow's or dowager's hump) as a result of collapsed vertebrae and a limp from a previous fracture of her hip. While she was in the hospital, she also developed a spontaneous rib fracture, simply from turning over suddenly in bed.

As you can see, drinking and fragile bones are a dangerous combination. But "little old ladies" with poor health habits, such as Bertha, are not the only candidates for bone loss and osteoporosis. All alcoholics, even young men, can suffer dramatic bone loss and osteoporosis, like Aileen, the nurse from Chapter 2 who suffered a "little old lady" fractured wrist at the age of forty-one. That's why, if you're a recovering alcoholic, it's essential that you take enough calcium to correct any deficiencies you may have developed. The RDA for calcium is 1000 milligrams daily. Calcium-rich foods include milk and milk products (such as cheese and yogurt), canned sardines and salmon, collard greens, broccoli, oats, and bean curd (tofu). Choosing low-fat milk products will enable you to get your calcium without exceeding your fat allowance. You could be supplied with your daily 1,000 milligrams of calcium by eating *all* of the following at some time during the day:

1½ cups skim milk	474 mg
2 ounces Edam cheese	410 mg
½ cup broccoli	83 mg
1 packet plain instant fortified oats	164 mg

Calcium carbonate supplements have recently been touted in the popular media as a good way to supply your body with the calcium it needs. Researchers, however, are currently debating the usefulness of these supplements. It is much better to get your calcium from food than from tablets. With careful planning, you can get all the calcium you require from your diet alone.

Iron

We need iron in our diet in order for the red blood cells, which carry oxygen through the body, to function properly. Many people, especially women, don't get enough iron; an estimated 10 to 15 percent of Americans are iron-deficient, and 8.5 percent of women between the ages of twelve and fifty are actually anemic. The elderly of both sexes are also likely to be iron-deficient, and menstruating women who have been using alcohol or drugs to excess are likely to have diminished iron stores that must be replenished.

Iron is readily available in foods such as liver, kidneys, spinach, wheat germ, brewer's yeast, oysters, clams, soybeans, nuts, and dried fruit. Many breakfast cereals are fortified with iron, and some provide 100 percent of the 18-milligram RDA. Vitamin C, supplied by fruit, can increase the absorption of iron. A breakfast of half a grapefruit, iron-fortified cereal, and low-fat milk is an excellent first step to meeting your daily iron and calcium requirements.

If you take care to eat properly, you can get all the iron you need from your diet. Although some people do require iron supplements, don't assume that just because you're frequently tired, it means that you're anemic. Iron supplements should *never* be taken without first consulting your doctor. Even at the recommended doses, iron can cause gastrointestinal upset and constipation, and excess iron can be toxic to your system.

When Sally came into treatment for using alcohol and crack, she looked deathly pale and said she felt tired all the time. At thirty-three, she looked well into her forties. She told me that she could not remember the last time she had eaten a proper meal, and I didn't find that statement surprising, since Sally was at least twenty-five pounds underweight. The only foods she could tolerate were sweets and milk. She had also been having heavy periods until they stopped entirely a few months before she entered treatment. Sally's condition was so extreme that her doctor prescribed iron supplements to replenish her iron stores, along with a balanced, high-calorie diet to bring her weight up to normal.

Sodium and Chloride

When chemically combined, sodium and chloride form salt, a mineral that's essential for maintaining the body's proper cell function and fluid balance. Most Americans, however, eat far more salt than they actually need. The average consumption is about 6600 milligrams or three teaspoons a day—that's two to six times more than the 1100 to 3300 milligrams generally deemed safe.

Excessive salt intake has been tied to high blood pressure. The Japanese, whose consumption of salt is the highest in the world, have the greatest incidence of high blood pressure—and Americans aren't far behind. In countries and cultures that don't make a practice of adding salt to food, blood pressure is much lower. The message is clear: *Reduce your salt intake.* Unless you're working or exercising strenuously in hot weather and sweating a lot, there's absolutely no reason to season your food with salt. The salt that's naturally present in your food is more than enough to meet your body's needs for it.

You can reduce salt intake by not adding salt to food, either at the table or while you're cooking. Familiarize yourself and experiment with other spices that can enhance the flavor of soups, salads, and main dishes. But more important, you can choose to eat fewer processed or prepared foods. Learn to read the labels carefully. Salt is added to enhance flavor and as a preservative, and much of what you find on the supermarket shelves contains enough salt for the entire day in a single serving. Canned goods, cold cuts or luncheon meats, bacon, frankfurters, such snacks as pretzels, potato chips and crackers, pickles, and condiments should be eaten sparingly. The same is true for prepackaged meal mixes and frozen dinners. Cheese also has a high-salt content, but it's a valuable source of both protein and calcium, so it shouldn't be completely eliminated from your diet unless you're seriously concerned about cholesterol. Rather, on the days that you eat cheese, be more careful about your overall salt intake.

Fiber

Fiber is a term that identifies a group of mostly complex carbohydrates found in the cell walls of plants. There are two types of fiber, soluble and insoluble. Both kinds have beneficial dietary properties, but insoluble fiber is particularly good because it creates bulk in the digestive tract without adding calories, binds up cancer-causing agents, and hastens the movement of fecal matter through the colon, thus facilitating excretion. Diets high in fiber may decrease your chances of getting hemorrhoids and have also been shown to decrease the risk of colorectal cancer. (Both the American Cancer Society and the National Cancer Institute recommend a high-fiber diet for the prevention of colon cancer.) Some types of fiber—particularly those found in oats, carrots, and dried beans such as kidney, black, and navy—have also been associated with lowering cholesterol levels. Other good sources of fiber include whole grains, bran, raw fruits, and vegetables.

The many benefits of fiber make it a desirable component to your diet. If you eat too much fiber, however, you may lose essential minerals or experience bloating, gas, and frequent bulky stools. And there's no need to invest in over-the-counter fiber preparations. Naturally occurring fiber is better for you, not to mention much cheaper.

To give you an idea of how much total fiber is found in various foods, here are some examples:

1 ounce (⅓ cup) All-Bran cereal	10 g
1 ounce (⅓ cup) rolled oats (dry)	3 g
1 medium carrot	3.2 g
1 slice whole wheat bread	2.4 g

Nutritionists are still debating the optimum quantity of fiber in the diet—a debate that's complicated by variations in methods of measurement. The older method measures crude dietary fiber; the more recent system measures total dietary fiber, which includes both soluble and insoluble fiber. But thirty grams of total dietary fiber a day is generally considered adequate.

Planning Your Diet

Reversing the Nutritional Effects of Your Addiction

Now that you're more familiar with the principles of healthful eating and the components of a sensible diet, you're ready to set up your own plan for eating well in sobriety. As we've seen from the descriptions of Laura's, Tom's, and Anna's diets, many drug addicts and alcoholics who enter recovery are stuck in a rut of poor eating habits.

Now that you're sober, you need to take only two simple steps in order to correct your nutritional problems: Eat a sensible, varied diet, and take one—and only one—multivitamin supplement each day for the first three to four weeks of sobriety. This regimen will promptly reverse any deficiencies that may have resulted from eating poorly in the past. But don't fool yourself into thinking that vitamin supplements are a substitute for nutritious food. The supplement is merely an insurance policy. If you've already been sober for more than three months, you don't need to take any supplements at all. It's far more important to evaluate your eating habits to ensure that your diet promotes your physical health, your emotional well-being, and, of course, your sobriety.

Eating What Counts Without Counting Calories

Food, when it's broken down in the body, provides energy. And calories are simply a measure of this energy. How many calories you require depends on how much energy it takes to run your body. In Table

1 you will find your daily calorie requirements, as recommended by the Food and Nutrition Board of the National Academy of Sciences–National Research Council.

As you can see, the recommended ranges are quite wide. Your daily calorie intake will depend not only on your age and sex, but also on your weight and how active you are. If you are small and inactive, your calorie requirements will be at the lower end of the range for your sex and age group; at the higher end if you are large and very active. One constant applies, however: If you take in more calories than you use, you will store the excess energy in the form of fat. Conversely, if you take in fewer calories than you need, stored fat is converted to energy and you will lose weight.

You should also note that the lowest recommended daily intake is 1,200 calories. Even if you are dieting, you should never eat fewer than 1,200 calories per day. Otherwise you will seriously compromise your nutrition.

As I've said, early sobriety is not a time for stringent eating plans. Many newly sober people, however, are justifiably concerned about their weight. Whether you are too heavy or too thin, reaching your ideal weight through a sensible nutrition regimen can improve your appearance and your self-esteem. Table 2 (page 286) will help you determine your best weight.

Whether your goal is to lose, gain, or maintain your weight, you need a simple, easy-to-follow method of planning your meals. An "exchange program" offers just that. Using the four basic food groups and standard serving sizes, you choose a certain number of servings, or exchanges, from each food group. In this way you get all the vitamins and

Table 1

Age	Daily Calorie Needs
MALES	
19–22	2,500–3,300
23–50	2,300–3,100
51–75	2,000–2,800
Over 75	1,650–2,450
FEMALES	
19–22	1,700–2,500
23–50	1,600–2,400
51–75	1,400–2,200
Over 75	1,200–2,000
Pregnant	+300
Nursing	+500

Table 2
Ideal Weight in Pounds

			Age		
Height	20–29	30–39	40–49	50–59	60–69
MEN					
5'3"	125	129	130	131	130
5'6"	135	240	142	143	142
5'9"	149	153	155	156	155
6'0"	161	166	167	168	167
6'3"	176	181	183	184	180
WOMEN					
4'10"	97	102	106	109	111
5'1"	106	109	114	118	120
5'4"	114	118	122	127	129
5'7"	123	127	132	137	140
5'10"	134	138	142	146	147

minerals you need, as well as the proper proportions of carbohydrates, proteins, and fats that I talked about earlier in the chapter. You can eat well without having to count calories, add up milligrams of iron or vitamin C, or worry about your ratio of saturated to unsaturated fats.

Each day you should try to eat the following:

Fruits and Vegetables—4 or more servings
Breads and Cereals—4 or more servings
Milk Products—2 servings
Meat/Poultry/Fish/Other Protein Sources—2 servings

Table 3, adapted from the *New American Eating Guide* developed by the Center for Science in the Public Interest, explains standard serving sizes and how often you may choose various foods within each group.

To use Table 3 first find the number of servings you should have each day of a particular food group. Then look at the "Serving" listing to find out how much of a food constitutes one serving. Then make your choices from the three categories within each food group. You can have the foods marked "Every Day" as often as you like. Other foods should be restricted according to their category headings. Your selections of fruits and vegetables for one day might then be as follows:

Breakfast: 1 banana
Lunch: 1 small salad

Dinner: 6 oz. tomato juice
½ cup steamed spinach

Having chosen the tomato juice from the "One to Three Times per Week" category, you would then be careful for the next couple of days to choose your fruits and vegetables only from the "Every Day" category.

Table 3
Fruits and Vegetables

(4 or more servings per day, including one vitamin C source and one green leafy vegetable)

Serving = 1 orange or banana; or 1 medium apple or pear; or ½ grapefruit; or ½ cantaloupe; or 1 cup raw vegetables; or ½ cup cooked vegetables; or a small salad; or 1 medium potato; or 6 oz. juice.

EVERY DAY:
Most fruits and vegetables: raw, unseasoned frozen, or steamed without added fat or salt, especially dark green and yellow vegetables (spinach, kale, carrots, squash, etc.); or cruciferous vegetables (broccoli, cauliflower, brussels sprouts, cabbage); or melons; or citrus fruits.

ONE TO THREE TIMES PER WEEK:
Unsweetened fruit juices or sauces; or unsalted vegetable juices; or frozen seasoned vegetables; or canned fruit in light syrup or own fruit juice; or avocados; or olives.

ONCE A WEEK OR LESS:
Vegetable or fruit products prepared with fat, salt, or sugar, such as pickles; or sweetened canned fruit or fruit juices; or potato chips; or french fries.

Breads and Cereals

(4 or more servings per day)

Serving = 1 slice bread; or ½–¾ cup rice or pasta; or ½–¾ cup cooked cereal; or 1 oz. dry cereal.

EVERY DAY:
Whole grain products such as whole wheat bread; or brown rice; or whole wheat pasta; or whole grain, unsweetened hot or cold cereals; or

oatmeal; or pancakes made with whole grains; or rye or pumpernickel bread.

ONE TO THREE TIMES PER WEEK:
Lower fiber grain products such as white bread or rolls, rice, or pasta; or waffles or pancakes made with white flour; or corn bread; or flour tortillas.

ONCE A WEEK OR LESS:
Grain products low in fiber and high in salt, fat, and/or sugar, such as pastries, doughnuts, cookies, cake, sweetened breakfast cereals, pretzels, salted crackers; or sweet condiments such as jam, jelly, or maple syrup.

Milk Products

(2 servings per day)

Serving = 1 cup milk or yogurt; or 2 cups cottage cheese; or 1⅓ ounces hard cheese (cheddar, Swiss, blue); or 1½ cups ice cream.

EVERY DAY:
Skim milk; or low-fat plain yogurt; or low-fat cottage cheese; or 1% low-fat milk.

ONE TO THREE TIMES PER WEEK:
Low-fat cheeses such as part-skim mozzarella or Swiss, sapsago, or farmer; or buttermilk (made from skim milk); or 2% low-fat milk; or regular cottage cheese (4% milk fat); or frozen low-fat yogurt; or ice milk; or sweetened low-fat yogurt.

ONCE A WEEK OR LESS:
Processed cheese and cheese foods; or salty natural cheeses such as blue; Camembert, cream cheese, cheddar, Swiss; or sour cream; or whole milk; or ice cream; or cheese soufflé; or cheesecake; or puddings made with milk.

Meat/Poultry/Fish/Other Protein Sources

(2 servings per day)

Serving = 3 oz. meat, poultry, or fish; or 1½ cups cooked dry beans; or 2 eggs; or 4 tbsp. peanut butter; or ½–1 cup nuts, sesame or sunflower seeds.

EVERY DAY:
Dried beans and peas such as lentils, chick-peas (garbanzos) or soybeans; or egg whites; or poultry (boiled, roasted, broiled, or baked without skin); or broiled or baked fish; or tuna packed in water.

ONE TO THREE TIMES PER WEEK:
Nuts; or sunflower seeds; or tofu; or peanut butter; or canned beans; or shellfish; or lightly sautéed poultry or fish; or lean, well-trimmed cuts of meat.

ONCE A WEEK OR LESS:
Fried chicken; or frozen fish sticks; or egg dishes; or bacon; or organ meats; or cold cuts; or corned beef; or ground beef; or ham; or frankfurters; or spareribs; or sirloin steak; or veal; or pork; or sausage.

When planning your menus, you should also be careful about added fat. This includes the oils you use in salad dressings and in cooking, as well as any butter, or preferably margarine, you use in cooking or as a spread. Limit yourself to two servings, two teaspoons each, of added fat each day.

As you can see from Table 3, you don't have to give up any of your favorite foods, as long as you eat those that are high in fat, salt, or sugar in moderation. If you want a handful of potato chips with your turkey on whole wheat sandwich while you're watching the game on Saturday afternoon, fine. But don't eat the whole bag, and don't eat a handful every day. Treat yourself to a six-ounce sirloin once in a while, but eat no other meat, fish, or poultry that day.

One of the beauties of the exchange program is that it allows you to eat everything. It encourages variety, which I consider the cornerstone of a healthy eating plan. If you are accustomed to eating mostly the foods listed in the "Once a Week or Less" category, you can easily change your habits by learning to choose your foods primarily from the "Every Day" category. Pick half a grapefruit instead of sweetened, canned grapefruit juice; tuna packed in water on pumpernickel instead of the oil-packed kind on white bread; broiled flounder instead of lamb chops. These are small changes, but they give a big boost to better eating.

Harvey, Carl, and Dolores had widely different nutritional goals in recovery, but they were all able to use the exchange program successfully.

Harvey

At twenty-eight, Harvey is six feet tall and weighs 150 pounds, down from the 165 pounds he weighed before he began doing a gram or more of cocaine two or three times a week. During the last months of his addiction he regularly drank a pint or more of whiskey to come down from his cocaine highs, but the calories from the liquor neither provided him with nutrients nor compensated for his poor appetite.

The dinnertime manager of a small restaurant, Harvey is on his feet most of the day. While he is not sedentary, he gets no other exercise, as he is still too shaky after one sober month to begin a regular fitness program. To gain the eleven pounds that would put him at his ideal weight of 161 pounds, Harvey requires about 3,000 calories per day. His appetite has returned with a vengeance, and he has easy access to well-prepared food, so it is unlikely he will have any difficulty gaining the additional weight.

However, he does have two problems he must solve in developing his plan for eating in sobriety. His first challenge is organizing regular mealtimes, instead of continuing his habit of picking on a bit of this and a bit of that as he goes about his long workday. He has hit on the plan of a substantial breakfast when he gets up, about ten o'clock, before his noontime CA meeting. When he arrives at the restaurant, about half past one, he has a snack. Then at four o'clock he sits down with the rest of his staff for a meal before the dinner rush begins. When the last diners have been served, usually about eleven, he has his own dinner, then locks up the restaurant and returns home to relax and unwind until about three in the morning.

Harvey's second hurdle in planning his meals, as it was in getting straight and sober, is letting go of his uniqueness. As a knowledgeable food professional, he is well aware of the hazards of saturated fats, but he has always eaten exactly what he wanted because he felt, as he put it, "none of the rules really applied to me." Now Harvey has decided to watch his fat intake by keeping his meat, milk, and fat servings close to the two standard-size servings recommended in the exchange program. Because Harvey's cholesterol level and blood pressure are normal, he can afford to be occasionally liberal with his meat and fat servings, and, while his calorie requirements are still higher than usual, to choose full-fat dairy products. However, he plans to get most of the extra calories he needs by adding exchanges of fruits and vegetables and breads and cereals. By planning menus much like the one below, Harvey rapidly gained the eleven pounds he needed, in about six weeks. By then he also felt strong enough to begin a walking program. At that time, to maintain

Harvey's Sample Menu

Meal	Calories	Food Group	Number of Exchanges
BREAKFAST			
Grapefruit, ½	38	Fruit/Veg	1
Whole wheat pancakes, 3	519	Bread/Cereal	3
Margarine, 2 tsp.	68	Fat	1
Maple syrup, 2 tbsp.	98	Bread/Cereal	1
Milk, 1 cup	157	Milk/Cheese	1
Coffee, decaffeinated, black	—	—	
SNACK			
Cinnamon bun, 1	185	Bread/Cereal	1
Herbal tea	—	—	
LUNCH			
Minestrone, 1 cup	83	Fruit/Veg	1
Pork chop, 1 lean	166	Meat	1
Spaghetti, 1 cup	120	Bread/Cereal	2
Marinara sauce, ½ cup	85	Fruit/Veg	1
Lettuce, 1 wedge	10	Fruit/Veg	1
Salad dressing, 2 tsp.	68	Fat	1
Whole wheat bread, 2 slices	126	Bread/Cereal	2
Margarine, 2 tsp.	68	Fat	1
Fruit salad, 1 cup	74	Fruit/Veg	2
DINNER			
Roast chicken, 2 thighs	306	Meat	1½
Baked potato, 1	220	Fruit/Veg	1
Sour cream, 2 tbsp.	52	Fat	1
Green peas, 1 cup	134	Fruit/Veg	2
Hard roll, 1	157	Bread/Cereal	1
Margarine, 1 tsp.	34	Fat	½
Vanilla yogurt, 1 cup	194	Milk/Cheese	1
Total Calories:	2,962		
Total Exchanges:		Fruit/Veg	9
		Bread/Cereal	10
		Meat	2½
		Milk/Cheese	2
		Fat	3½

his weight, he eliminated one fat serving and one bread and cereal serving from his meals.

Carl

Carl is sixty-four and has been drinking since he was eighteen. He's done virtually no exercise in his adult life and is in poor physical condition. For the last ten years, he had been putting away two drinks at lunch, then six or more in the evening. But in the past year or so he found himself increasingly affected by alcohol. He was becoming easily intoxicated and was nauseated, headachy, irritable, and frequently had trouble concentrating. When he went for a checkup, his doctor told him his blood pressure was high, that his liver was enlarged and functioning poorly, and that he must stop drinking.

Carl didn't feel he could do so on his own, so he entered a hospital. He spent a week in a detoxification unit and is now attending daily AA meetings. At 5' 10", Carl weighs a normal 155 pounds, but his arms and legs are very thin, and most of his weight appears to be concentrated in his abdomen. His blood pressure is 150/95 (it should be 120/80), his cholesterol level is too high, and his liver enzymes are still abnormal. Tests have also shown him to be deficient in thiamine and folic acid, so his doctor recommended that he take a multivitamin supplement for three weeks.

Carl will need about 2,300 calories a day. Given his age, his high blood pressure and cholesterol level, and a family history of heart disease, Carl must be especially careful when choosing his proteins. Even though he does need to build up muscle, he must do this by exercising and not by adding unnecessary protein to his diet. Carl should get the bulk of his protein from fish, poultry, and vegetable sources, and from low- or non-fat milk products. He will also need to avoid processed foods containing high levels of salt and fat. As he suffers from constipation, he requires a diet high in fiber, with lots of fresh fruit and vegetables.

A widower living alone, Carl had been accustomed, since his wife's death, to eating mostly convenience foods. When he returned from the hospital with his doctor's dietary recommendations, he decided to try his hand at cooking for himself. His daughter-in-law helped him get started, and he found that he quite enjoys planning and preparing his meals. Now one month sober, he has added a daily walk, during which he shops for fresh provisions, to his routine. Carl cooked everything on his sample menu himself, including the soups and the chili, which he prepares once a week and freezes in single-portion servings. He has become an inveterate label reader and has learned how high in salt and

Carl's Sample Menu

Meal	Calories	Food Group	Number of Exchanges
BREAKFAST			
Orange juice, ¾ cup	84	Fruit/Veg	1
Raisin Bran, 1 cup	174	Bread/Cereal	2
Milk, skim, 1 cup	90	Milk	1
Prunes, 5	90	Fruit/Veg	1
Coffee, black, decaffeinated	—	—	
LUNCH			
Mushroom barley soup, 1 cup	153	Bread/Cereal	1
		Fruit/Veg	1
Whole wheat bread, 2 slices	126	Bread/Cereal	2
Flounder, 3 oz. broiled	101	Meat	1
Carrots, steamed with dill, 1 cup	70	Fruit/Veg	2
Potatoes, boiled with parsley, 1 cup	136	Fruit/Veg	2
Spinach, steamed, ½ cup	21	Fruit/Veg	1
Fresh fruit salad, ¾ cup	93	Fruit/Veg	1½
DINNER			
Tomato rice soup, 1½ cups	180	Bread/Cereal	1
		Fruit/Veg	1
Bread sticks, 2	86	Bread/Cereal	1
Chili, 1 cup	311	Meat	1
		Fruit/Veg	1
Bulgur wheat, 1 cup	225	Bread/Cereal	2
Tossed salad	10	Fruit/Veg	1
French dressing, 2 tsp.	68	Fat	1
Vanilla low-fat yogurt, 1 cup	194	Milk	1
Corn oil for cooking, 2 tsp.	80	Fat	1
Total Calories:	2,292		
Total Exchanges:		Fruit/Veg	10½
		Bread/Cereal	9
		Meat	2
		Milk	2
		Fat	2⅓

fat commercially prepared foods can be. Carl's homemade chili, his own special recipe, contains mostly kidney beans and vegetables (onions, garlic, tomatoes, and mushrooms) and a small amount of ground turkey. He has also been experimenting with grains, and has found that his chili is delicious over bulgur (whole grain cracked wheat) instead of rice.

Dolores

When Dolores, thirty-five, became sober six months ago, she weighed 145 pounds. Much of this was retained water, and within three months on a nutritious but unrestricted eating plan, she lost ten pounds. Then she began a regular exercise program of fast walking for thirty minutes three times a week and dropped an additional five pounds over the next three months. At 5' 4", Dolores's ideal weight is 118 pounds, a goal she would like to achieve now that her sobriety is well established.

Dolores was smart to wait until she felt solidly sober to begin a weight loss program. She was also wise to restrict her calories on the exchange program, rather than opting for a fad diet. Eccentric eating schemes are not good for anyone, chemically dependent or not. While they may help you to lose weight initially, they do not allow you to keep it off. You gain the pounds back and then try to lose them again when the next gimmick appears, a phenomenon sometimes referred to as the rhythm method of girth control. Following fad diets not only keeps you fat, it prevents you from developing the good eating habits that will serve your health—and your figure—for the rest of your life.

Dolores knew that sensible weight loss means no more than three to four pounds a month, and that it would take her at least three months to lose the twelve pounds. There are about 3,500 calories in a pound, so to lose weight prudently, she had to cut her calorie intake by 300 to 500 calories per day. She had been eating about 1,700 calories per day, and set a 1,200-calorie-per-day limit for her reducing diet. While she was drinking, Dolores's menstrual periods had been erratic. Now they are regular, but quite heavy. Like many women, she must be careful to include enough iron, as well as calcium, in her meals.

It is relatively easy to get adequate calcium while on a weight reduction diet, because low- or non-fat dairy products offer as much calcium as the full fat varieties. Green leafy vegetables and citrus fruits are also good sources of calcium. With two low-fat milk servings, two portions of leafy green vegetables, and a citrus fruit each day, Dolores will meet her calcium requirements. She should also avoid carbonated beverages—even the "no-cal" sort—as their high phosphorus content increases the body's need for calcium.

Unfortunately, getting enough iron from a calorie-restricted diet can be tricky. Green leafy vegetables are an excellent source, but you will absorb their iron better if you eat them with meat or fish or with a vitamin C source, such as citrus fruit or tomatoes. You can also increase your iron intake by cooking in cast-iron skillets or pots. Another tactic

Dolores's Sample Menu

Meal	Calories	Food Group	Number of Exchanges
BREAKFAST			
Grapefruit, ½	38	Fruit/Veg	1
Bran flakes, ⅔ cup	82	Bread/Cereal	1
Skim milk, 1 cup	90	Milk	1
Black coffee, decaffeinated	—	—	
LUNCH			
Chicken livers, 3 oz.	219	Meat	1
Rice, ⅔ cup	156	Bread/Cereal	1
Spinach, ½ cup	21	Fruit/Veg	1
Tomato, 1 sliced and lettuce	40	Fruit/Veg	1
Oil and vinegar dressing, 2 tsp.	68	Fat	1
DINNER			
Spaghetti with clam sauce, 1 cup	226	Bread/Cereal	1
		Meat	½
Breadstick, 1	43	Bread/Cereal	1
Broccoli, ½ cup	21	Fruit/Veg	1
Fresh fruit salad, ½ cup	62	Fruit/Veg	1
Nonfat yogurt, 8 oz.	126	Milk	1
Total Calories:	1,192		
Total Exchanges:		Fruit/Veg	5
		Bread/Cereal	4
		Meat	1½
		Milk	2
		Fat	1

is to avoid tea, because the tannic acid it contains interferes with iron absorption.

Dolores stuck to her diet conscientiously, taking particular care not to exceed the standard serving sizes. In just under four months she had reached her goal weight and began a program to maintain herself at that level. She increased her bread and cereal and fruit and vegetable servings to five or six per day and allowed herself an occasional indulgence in desserts, higher-fat meats, and hard cheese. She also added one more walking session to her weekly exercise regimen and began to carry hand weights on her walks. With the added exertion, she was able to take in about 1,800 calories per day and remain at 118 pounds.

Choosing Healthy Food

My hope is that the two most important things you learn from this chapter are why you should eat sensibly and how to go about it. You should now be able to get all the healthful food you need to maintain or reach your ideal weight, and to foster your sobriety by using an exchange program. But I'd like to leave you with a few reminders and tips for making healthy choices.

Vary Your Diet

This is the single most important concept for eating well. There are many delicious foods, so why limit yourself to the same few over and over? Try foods that you haven't liked in the past. Your tastes may have changed now that your palate is no longer clouded by alcohol or drugs.

Be Flexible

Becoming compulsive about what you eat won't help your sobriety. A healthy attitude allows for give-and-take: If you take too much fat at one meal, make sure you eat low-fat, lighter foods at the next. Did you grab lunch on the run from the corner hot dog stand? Then have a salad, fresh vegetables, and fruit for dinner. Once in a while, when the opportunity for a delectable feast presents itself, go ahead and splurge. But for the next day or two after your high-calorie meal, cut back and eat less than you normally do.

Eat Breakfast

To maintain your energy and a balanced mood throughout the day, it's important that you fuel your body first thing in the morning. Breakfast doesn't have to be elaborate. Cereal and low-fat milk, whole grain toast with low-fat cottage cheese, or yogurt with fruit and a few spoonfuls of granola or a bran muffin are examples of quick meals. If you're used to skipping breakfast, you'll soon notice the difference. You'll work better and play better if you start the day with a nutritious meal.

Stick Close to Nature

Fresh foods are healthier than processed foods. They contain fewer additives, less salt, and in general, less fat. There is certainly no need to become a health food fanatic and go over budget to buy expensive organically grown produce, or go overboard and pursue a macrobiotic diet. But when you are planning your meals, remember that fresh fruits are more wholesome than canned, leftover sliced chicken makes a more healthful sandwich than bologna, and baked potatoes beat potato chips hands down for nutrition.

Choose Foods Which Are Less Calorically Dense

Caloric density is the ratio of calories to weight in a particular food. Calorically dense foods such as cheesecake, chocolate bars, and salami contain a great deal of fat and/or sugar. A small portion provides you with a heap of calories, but leaves you feeling hungry after a short time. On the other hand, foods which are less calorically dense, like bananas, whole grain bread, or roast turkey, contain more water, fiber, and/or complex carbohydrates. Even though they have fewer calories they will keep you satisfied for a longer time.

Avoid Unplanned Snacks

Snacks aren't particularly harmful, but they can wreak havoc with your attempts to set up a regular eating schedule. If you find that you're hungry between meals, include a nutritious snack as part of your routine. But don't let that sugar doughnut on the coffee cart spoil your appetite for lunch, or a sandwich wolfed down between phone calls rob you of a relaxed break in the middle of the day.

Eat Meat Only Once a Day

And favor chicken, turkey, and lean beef when you do eat meat. When you simply can't resist fatty meats such as hamburger, pork, or cold cuts, eliminate saturated fats from the rest of your day's meals. As you now know, there are many low-fat and non-fat protein sources other than meat.

Plan an Occasional Vegetarian Main Meal

You can easily combine vegetable protein sources for complete nutrition. Split pea soup, whole grain bread, and a salad with yogurt or buttermilk dressing makes a well-balanced, low-fat meal. Many ethnic dishes naturally combine proteins. For example, there's Southern red beans and rice, Mexican pinto beans wrapped in corn tortillas, Indian vegetable curry with chick-peas served over rice, and Italian *pasta fagiola*, a macaroni and bean soup.

Eat More Fish

Fish is an excellent low-fat source of protein that too many people either overlook completely or eat only heavily breaded and deep-fried. Bake or broil your fish for a delicious, light, nutritious meal.

Use Eggs Sparingly

One or two each week is plenty. A single egg will use up your entire cholesterol allotment for the day. Remember, however, that it's the egg yolks that contain cholesterol. An omelette made with one whole egg and one egg white will keep you within your daily allowance. If you like to bake, you can easily find low-cholesterol recipes that call for egg whites only.

Choose Low-fat Dairy Products

Milk products are your best source of calcium, but they can add unwanted fat unless you opt for low-fat varieties of milk, yogurt, and cottage cheese. If you can't live without sour cream on your baked potato, try plain, nonfat yogurt instead.

Substitute Vegetable Oils or Margarine for Butter or Lard

You can eat fried foods very occasionally if you make sure that they have been fried in oils—such as corn, safflower, sunflower, peanut, sesame, soybean, or vegetable oil—that contain no cholesterol. You can include lightly sauteed foods more often in your diet, but again be sure to use vegetable oils rather than butter or lard for cooking them. For eating and baking, choose margarine rather than butter.

Emulate Popeye

He was strong to the finish 'cuz he ate his spinach . . . and probably his beets, turnips, carrots, cauliflower, apples, and bananas as well. Reacquaint yourself with fresh vegetables and fruit. You'll quickly discover that they're not only good for you, but that they taste good, too.

Avoid Sugar

During early sobriety it is especially important that you eliminate sweets from your diet as much as possible. Your new diet and your life plan in general is geared to restoring the natural balances in your body. Sending yourself into sugar highs and lows will only hinder your recovery. But again, an occasional sweet treat is fine, especially if it's part of a well-balanced meal.

Gradually Cut Back on Salt

If you're used to heavily salted food, unsalted food may initially seem bland and unpalatable. Eating food you don't enjoy will only undermine your attempts to establish new eating patterns. But if you gradually reduce your salt intake, your taste buds will have a chance to adjust. You'll begin to recognize the true flavors of food, so that eventually heavily salted food will be unpalatable.

Season Your Food with Herbs

Plain steamed carrots don't taste very exciting. But you can easily perk them up with a sprinkling of thyme, marjoram, basil, or dill. Fresh or dried herbs add zest to food without adding fat, calories, or salt. You can make up your own combinations or try one of the many no-salt herb mixtures available on supermarket spice shelves.

Drink Plenty of Water

Now is the time for you to discover water as something other than a handy substance for diluting whiskey or making ice cubes. Water supplies your body's needs for fluids without adding caffeine, calories, sugar, or fats. When you get a craving, when you're thirsty, or when you're hungry and eating isn't convenient, a glass of water can fill you up and make you feel more comfortable without any side effects. Try to drink six to eight glasses a day.

Use Your Freezer

If your schedule doesn't give you much time to shop or cook, a well-stocked freezer ensures that you'll have nutritious meals even when you're running late. When you have a few free hours to cook, make a double or triple batch and freeze what you don't use immediately in meal-sized portions. Or set aside a weekend day every now and then to stock the freezer with soups, stews, pasta sauces, or casseroles.

Read Labels

Once you get to know what's actually in all those processed and convenience foods you've been buying, you'll be less likely to pile them into your shopping cart. Be especially aware of the sugar, salt, and fat content in processed foods.

Beware of Fad Diets

Most fad diets are the brainchildren of untrained enthusiasts and enterprising marketers. Their theories are unlikely to be based on sound scientific research and are even more unlikely to "revolutionize" your life, despite all their promises to do so. What they will do, however, is make you poorer, possibly even sick, and distract you from focusing on your sobriety.

Read About Nutrition and How to Prepare Healthy Meals

In Appendix A, I've included a list of books that explain in greater detail the principles of good nutrition, as well as cookbooks to help you plan wholesome, easy-to-prepare meals.

The choice is yours as far as eating is concerned. You won't necessarily drink, or use again, or get sick if you don't eat properly. But you'll feel so much better physically and mentally if you do choose to eat sensibly. Poor eating patterns are yet another habit to change at the same time you're trying to change so many habits, and it may seem like too much trouble and bother. But the rewards can be great for what's actually very little expended effort—improved health, greater energy, increased concentration and endurance, and more opportunities for pleasure and relaxation. Most important, when you feed yourself well, you feed and nurture your sobriety.

Chapter Sixteen
A Natural High

Starting an Exercise Program

Like good nutrition, regular exercise can be a tremendous boon to sobriety. By now you've heard most of the answers I give my patients when they ask me why they should exercise. But let's recap them here:
- You'll feel better, physically and mentally.
- You'll look better.
- You'll be healthier.
- You'll have more energy.
- You'll sleep better.
- You'll enhance your self-esteem.
- And you may even live longer.

As a physician, I have been convinced by a number of studies that have determined conclusively that people who exercise regularly get sick less often and frequently live longer. Other studies have shown that people who exercise also have a more desirable body weight and report that they feel greater satisfaction with their lives than before they began exercising.

Certainly these are valuable benefits, but for people in recovery, exercise has an important additional benefit: It's a way to feel good without pills, pot, coke, or booze. Exercise stimulates the body to produce endorphins, its own natural "feel-good" substances. The chemicals on which you had become dependent may have suppressed your normal endorphin production system, but with regular exercise you can get that system working again. You can feel good—and still be completely sober.

But you won't feel good if you don't do it. If you are in the first three months of your recovery, you may not feel strong enough to go to the gym three times a week. But there is no reason why you should not start to take a five- or ten-minute walk each day. If you have passed the three-month mark, now is the time to assess your fitness level and begin to plan an exercise program.

You also won't feel good if you overdo it. The key principles as far as exercise is concerned are moderation and gradual progression. Moderate levels of exercise—about twenty minutes a day—do carry some minimal risk of physical injury, but the benefits far outweigh the risks. The likelihood of your getting hurt rises as you increase the level of activity, but even too much exercise has a better risk/benefit ratio than no exercise. If you start slowly and build gradually, you'll have a much better chance of avoiding injuries. You'll reap all the many benefits of exercise with one big bonus—a healthier, more stable, and more plea-surable sobriety.

Three Ways to Succeed With Your Exercise Program

We'll get into the specifics later in this chapter, but first I'd like to talk about three general rules that will help you develop a plan that works for you.

Enjoy Yourself

Finding the activity that best suits your personality is perhaps the single most important step in formulating a program that you can con-tinue to follow. This is an obvious but important point that bears re-peating: If you don't enjoy doing whatever it is you're involved in, the chances are high you won't be doing it for very long.

If you've always been active and participated in one sport or another, the memories of your past pleasure will help motivate you to start and maintain a regular exercise program in sobriety. However, if you're one of those people who has always found exercise boring, tedious, and unrewarding, then you'll have to learn by doing that it can be a source of great satisfaction. Forget about the endless jumping jacks you were forced to do in high school. Ignore the grim faces of the runners you see in the park. Focus instead on finding the regular physical activity that would make *you* happy.

Priscilla, age thirty-one, had been off alcohol and tranquilizers for three months when she enrolled in an hour-long aerobics class that met Monday, Wednesday, and Friday at five-thirty at a community center downtown. To make the class she had to leave work on the dot of five.

Afterwards, she had to hit the deck running the second the instructor turned off the music to get to her seven o'clock AA meeting at a church across town. More often than not she arrived at the meeting still panting and damp from the shower. She kept this up for about two weeks, her zeal for aerobics waning with each class. Then one night she had to stay at work until ten past five. She missed the warm-up exercises and pulled a muscle in her calf. She couldn't exercise for two weeks.

When she realized she couldn't sandwich in her exercise class between work and AA, Priscilla took another approach. She bought an expensive membership at a health club, thinking that if she could plan her workouts at her own convenience she would avoid having to rush from one place to another. But she was bored by the club's facilities—stationary bikes, rowing machines and complicated weight-resistance systems—not to mention the singles-bar atmosphere of the place. After a month of trying to whip up enthusiasm for the club she sold her membership at a loss. Five months sober, she still wasn't exercising regularly, even though she wanted to very much. During a break at an AA meeting she happened to mention this to Doreen, who said she was having similar troubles. The two went out for coffee afterwards. As they chatted, they learned that they were both early risers, they both hated exercising alone, and they were neighbors. They made a date to meet for a walk in the park the following morning, which they both enjoyed immensely. After walking for five or six weeks, they changed their regimen to a combination of walking and running, and two months after that graduated to all running. Now six months later, Priscilla and Doreen get together three mornings a week for a three-mile run.

The desire to exercise isn't always enough to ensure that you will do it. As Priscilla learned, your program must also suit your schedule, your temperament, and your pocketbook. You must take these factors into consideration, as well as your physical capabilities and your fitness goals, when you plan your exercise regimen.

Once You Choose It, Use It

Between thirty and seventy percent of the people who begin exercise programs drop out within the first three months. Obviously, it's relatively easy to summon the enthusiasm to sign up for an aerobics class or to buy a pair of running shoes. But actually attending the classes or putting those shoes to use is a different matter. Even the most carefully conceived fitness plan is useless unless you stick to it. Building your workout into your daily schedule, rather than trying to fit it in if you can, will help.

"I'd been going to the pool after work three times a week for about six weeks," Kay told me. "I hadn't missed a session, but then one night I walked out of the office, and it was pelting with rain, windy, and cold—the kind of cold that seeps right into your bones. Swimming was the last thing I felt like doing. So I didn't. But I was left with a spare hour and a half on my hands. It was about the time of day I'd have been heading to the bar too, and for the first time in a long time I really wanted to drop into the old place. It would be cozy, with lots of laughter and friendly faces, not to mention a warming scotch or two. When I go to the pool I don't pass the bar on my way home, but the direct route from the office to my apartment goes right by there. You know, I actually pulled into the parking lot. And pulled right out again, thank God. I went back to the pool. The water was cold, but it sure felt good."

Of course there will be times when you have the flu and can't get to the gym or you miss an aerobics class to celebrate your wedding anniversary. Your exercise program should be flexible enough to accommodate such infrequent disruptions. There will also be days, however, when you just don't feel up to making the effort to exercise. On these occasions, you will have to muster the determination, as Kay did, to put your plan into action. Honoring your commitment to exercise at these times can only confirm and strengthen your commitment to sobriety.

Don't Do Anything That Can Injure You

Most people who have been actively drinking or taking drugs haven't been exercising at all. If they have engaged in some physical activity, it's usually in the form of sporadic bursts of exertion followed by weeks of inertia. A recent survey of health habits found a strong correlation among heavy drinking, heavy smoking, and lack of exercise —a conclusion that wasn't in the least surprising.

You'll probably embark on your exercise routine in a weakened physical condition. Thanks to the combined effects of drinking or drugging and the lack of exercise, your heart and lungs have to work overtime to provide enough oxygen if you suddenly exert yourself more than usual. Your muscles are flabby, and your ligaments are tight. In such a state, you can easily hurt yourself, so it's crucial that you learn to listen to what your body is telling you.

No doubt you've heard the popular exercise maxim: No pain, no gain. I absolutely don't agree with this at all. Pain is the body's signal that something is wrong. If you feel an ache or a cramp—whether it's in your foot, knee, heart, or chest—stop exercising. Don't ignore it; it may mean you have put a strain on your heart or your muscles. At best, you may sustain injuries from which it can take several weeks to recuperate. At worst, you can cause yourself serious harm.

Carol, a fifty-five-year-old housewife who had been addicted to Valium and sleeping pills, had just such an experience after she launched herself headlong into a running program early in her recovery. She had been something of an athlete in her youth, but as an adult she had never exercised systematically, and she was slightly overweight. Her daughter, a fitness enthusiast, encouraged her to become active again and bought her a colorful sweatsuit for motivation.

One Saturday Carol got dressed, went out to the park, and proceeded to run five miles, despite shortness of breath and pain in her lower legs. By the time she got back home she could barely walk up the steps to her front door. The next day her feet and ankles were grotesquely swollen and she couldn't walk at all. A visit to the doctor determined that she had torn the ligaments around both her ankles. It took almost a month for the pain and swelling to subside, and for the ligaments and surrounding muscles to repair themselves. During that time, she had to rely on crutches and couldn't get up and down stairs at all. As a result, Carol decided that exercise was dangerous to her health, and she never tried it again!

When I tell people about Carol, I sometimes see a sly grin sneak across their faces. I can hear them thinking, *Aha! The perfect excuse not to exercise. I might get hurt.* But they've missed the point. Exercise, even in moderation, hurts a little. That's inevitable. Your muscles *will* ache after twenty-four leg lifts, and you'll have to endure the ache to get to twenty-five. Your muscles *will* sometimes feel stiff, especially if you're over forty, and you'll have to work out that stiffness with careful stretching. But I'm talking about discomfort, not pain—and without some discomfort you won't improve your physical condition.

You shouldn't be aiming to prove how many times you can run around the track, or how many push-ups you can do. Your goal is to condition yourself so that your body is fit and healthy, so that your muscles are functioning at their optimum capacity, so that your heart and lungs are working well, and above all, so that you feel good. Yes, you should stop exercising if you have severe, persistent pain, particularly at a joint or in your back. But please don't avoid exercise on the grounds that you *might* get hurt. The self-help groups have a saying that perfectly sums up the best approach: *Easy does it—but do it.*

Planning Your Exercise Program

Assessing Your Fitness Level

In order to assess your fitness level you first have to learn how to monitor your heart rate. You do this by taking your pulse, a simple procedure once you've practiced a bit. You can most easily feel the pulse beats at your wrist and neck.

Put two fingers over either of the areas highlighted in the diagrams, and at regular intervals you'll feel a slight change in pressure. If you're having trouble finding your pulse, enlist the help of a health professional or a friend who has learned how to do this in an exercise or first-aid class. When you can clearly feel the beats, start to count them and continue counting for a full sixty seconds. The number of pulsations you count is your *resting heart rate.*

Your resting heart rate is a very good indicator of how fit your heart and lungs are. It will tell you not only at what level of difficulty to begin your exercise program, but also when you've improved enough to increase the duration and intensity of your activity. Here are the norms for resting heart rates in beats per minute:

	Males	*Females*
Excellent	52–65	59–68
Average	72–84	73–85
Poor	93	92

You should always take your resting heart rate before you begin to exercise and continue to monitor your heart rate throughout the session. What you want to determine is that you're reaching your *target heart rate*, the point at which you'll achieve a conditioning effect.

You also want to be sure that you're not exceeding that target rate, or approaching your *maximum heart rate*, the point at which your heart can no longer get enough oxygen to continue pumping. To find your maximum heart rate, subtract your age from 220. If you're forty-five, for example, you have a maximum heart rate of 175.

Your target heart rate depends on both your maximum heart rate and your resting heart rate. It's determined by the following criteria.

• If your resting rate is in the poor range on the chart above, your target heart rate during exercise should be at least, but no more than, 60 percent of your maximum.

• If your resting rate is average, your initial target can be 60 to 70 percent of your maximum.

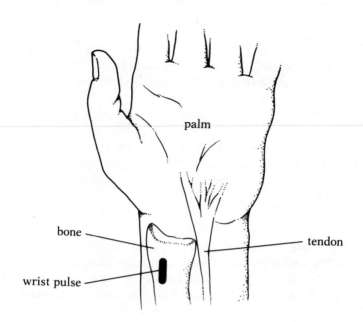

palm

bone

tendon

wrist pulse

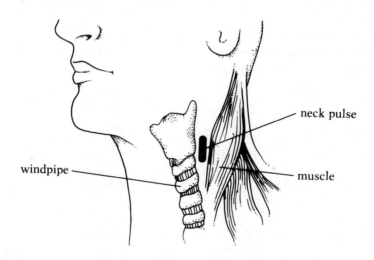

neck pulse

windpipe

muscle

• If your resting rate is excellent, your initial target can be 70 to 75 percent of your maximum.

As your resting heart rate indicates that your fitness level is improving, you can gradually increase your target heart rate. But no matter how fit you eventually become, you should NEVER exceed 85 percent of your maximum heart rate.

People in recovery are generally in poor physical condition and must therefore take extra care when they exercise, especially because they may not realize how weak they are. Therefore, I strongly recommend that when you first begin your program, you take your pulse not only before every session, but also every five minutes while you're engaged in aerobic exercise.

To get an accurate count, wind down your activity, and count your pulse for sixty seconds. When you're sure that you're getting a good count, you can begin to take your heart rate over a shorter period of time. The most convenient way is to count the pulses for six seconds, then multiply the number of pulses by ten. In time you'll become proficient enough so that you won't have to slow down your movement.

As you build up your endurance and strength, you'll need to take your pulse much less frequently. Taking it once near the start of your aerobic activity and once toward the end will be sufficient. With practice you'll come to know, without actually taking your pulse, whether you're meeting your target heart rate or whether your heart rate is too high. Still, it's a good idea to check your target rate at least once during an exercise session.

You should also assess your overall muscular fitness before beginning an exercise program by counting the number of bent-knee sit-ups you can do in sixty seconds.

Table 4
Bent Knee Sit-ups in 60 Seconds

Age	Males				Females			
	20–29	30–39	40–49	50–59	20–29	30–39	40–49	50–59
Good to excellent More than	40	34	29	25	31	24	20	14
Average	30–39	25–33	20–28	16–24	21–30	15–23	12–19	6–13
Poor Less than	29	24	19	15	20	14	12	6

If your muscular fitness is poor, start rebuilding your muscles with two to four minutes of gentle toning exercises and increase the length and intensity of your routine very slowly. If your muscular fitness is in the average or excellent range, you can begin with a more ambitious muscle toning routine of five to ten minutes or more, and increase the range of difficulty more rapidly.

Developing Your Program

Your exercise program includes three variables: frequency, duration, and intensity. You need a minimum *frequency* of three times a week in order to achieve conditioning. You can best maintain that conditioning by exercising every other day, and missing no more than two consecutive days. *Duration* and *intensity* are interdependent to some extent. In other words, you can get similar results from exercising at a lower intensity over a longer period of time as you can from a higher intensity over a shorter period.

If you're in very poor shape, you may be able to achieve a conditioning effect with fewer than twenty minutes of aerobic exercise, but for improvement or maintenance conditioning, you'll need a minimum of twenty minutes. Your target heart rate must be at least 60 percent of maximum to realize a conditioning effect.

Initial Conditioning
Your start-up exercise program should last four to six weeks. During this period you should be exercising three times a week, and your workout should consist of two to five minutes of warmup and stretching exercises (see page 313); twelve to twenty minutes of aerobic exercises (see page 316); two to ten minutes of toning exercises (see page 314); and two to five minutes of cool-down and stretching exercises (see page 314). Your target heart rate should be at least 60 percent of your maximum. If your resting heart rate indicates that you can safely aim for a higher target rate, do so.

Improvement Conditioning
After you've completed your initial conditioning, you can move on to the next stage, improvement conditioning, which should last from twelve to twenty weeks. Continue working out at least three times a week during this period, with the option to add more sessions if you'd like. You can also extend the duration of both your aerobic and your toning routines, and gradually build the intensity of your aerobic exercise by raising your target heart rate from your starting level to as high as 85 percent of maximum.

Maintenance Conditioning

Approximately four to six months after you begin your initial conditioning, you'll probably be ready to think about a maintenance program. This means that you'll continue to be involved in some form of physical activity at least three times a week, at the duration and intensity that maintains your desired level of fitness.

If for some reason—holidays, illness, a family crisis—you don't exercise for more than two weeks in a row, you shouldn't immediately resume your maintenance level program. You'll save yourself a lot of muscular wear and tear if you start out with an easier routine and slowly work your way back up to your previous level.

If you take a break of longer than four weeks, your best bet is to assume that you've lost most of your conditioning and start from scratch. It may not take as long for you to return to your maintenance level program as it did to reach that plateau in the first place, but you're still better off beginning slowly and building gradually.

Sample Exercise Programs

At age fifty-five, Karl is a busy executive who hadn't exercised regularly in at least fifteen years, although he had been quite fit before he started drinking heavily in his thirties. When he was still drinking, he would usually put away ten to twelve drinks a day. He was twenty pounds overweight when he became sober, and his blood pressure was high. His resting heart rate was 82, which is on the high end of average.

Karl was in his third month of sobriety when he felt ready to begin a physical fitness program, but first he went for a comprehensive physical exam. His doctor gave him the go-ahead, and recommended that he safely target his heart rate at 70 percent of maximum.

Karl figured out that his maximum heart rate was 165 (220 minus his age of 55). His target heart rate, 70 percent of 165, was 115 beats per minute. His initial routine, which he completed before work on Mondays, Wednesdays, and Fridays, consisted of a two-minute warm-up of moderate walking with arm swings; two minutes of stretching; fifteen minutes of brisk walking to bring his heart rate to 115; two minutes of cool-down walking; four minutes of abdominal and upper torso toning exercises; and two minutes of stretching and cool-down exercises at the end of the session.

After six weeks on this regimen, Karl moved on to improvement conditioning. For the next sixteen weeks, he gradually upped the duration and intensity of his walking until he was doing it for thirty minutes, three times a week, at 80 percent (132 beats per minute) of his maximum heart rate. He also increased his toning routine to seven minutes, so that with warm-up, cool-down, and stretching, his sessions are now forty-five minutes long. His resting pulse has declined to a much healthier 64 beats per minute, and he maintains an acceptable blood pressure without medication.

"Once I made the effort and put exercise on my daily schedule," he said, "it was easy. I don't worry the way I used to about where and how and when and how long. I just do it. I took out my calculator one day and figured out that the total time I spend exercising is only one-sixth of the time I used to spend drinking. Not to mention how much better I feel and can work."

Karl is now fifty-eight, but he looks years younger than he did in the photograph taken when he entered treatment three years ago.

Barbara, a forty-year-old secretary, is a mother of two and a self-described couch potato. She had been smoking pot and drinking since high school, and was putting away a daily fifth of hard liquor in her last year of drinking. After six months of sobriety, she had lost twenty-five pounds, and her weight was back to normal. Like Karl, she went to see her doctor before starting her exercise plan and was told that she had no medical problems.

Barbara's resting heart rate is seventy-four, which is average. She set her initial target heart rate at 70 percent of her maximum of 180, or 126 beats per minute. Because she has always loved music and dancing, she enrolled in a beginning aerobic exercise class at her local YWCA. Here's how the hour-long class is structured: ten minutes of gentle warm-ups; ten minutes of stretching; fifteen minutes of low-impact aerobics; five minutes of cool-down and stretching exercises; ten minutes of muscle-toning floor exercises; and a final ten minutes of stretching and re-laxation.

Barbara attends the class on Tuesdays and Thursdays after work. To meet her goal of exercising three times a week, she also takes a brisk twenty-minute walk with her husband every Sunday, making sure that she reaches and maintains her target heart rate of 126.

Jeff is a twenty-eight-year-old firefighter. He has always been in-terested in keeping physically fit and had actively participated in the fire department's intensive fitness program until his involvement with co-caine began to consume all his leisure time. By the end of his six-month infatuation with the drug, he was using two grams a week, as well as drinking large quantities of beer and whiskey to bring him down from his highs. Two weeks into abstinence, when Jeff was experiencing intense cravings, his sponsor suggested that exercise could help to divert his mind from the drug. Because of the nature of his work and the relatively short duration of his addiction, his physical condition hadn't seriously deteriorated. In fact, his resting heart rate was still an excellent 63.

Jeff set his target heart rate at 75 percent of maximum, 144 beats per minute. He joined a health club, where he worked out in the gym four days a week. He warmed up by walking briskly on the track. Then he did some stretches and rode the stationary bicycle for twenty minutes. After a couple of cool-down laps around the tracks and more stretching, he put himself through a twenty-minute routine of sit-ups, push-ups, and supervised weight training. (Jeff already had experience with weight training thanks to the fire department's fitness program. But he realized that his coordination wasn't up to par and that he needed the supervision until he regained his former proficiency.) On days when he wasn't working out at the gym, he swam for twenty to thirty minutes in the club's pool, and afterwards took a relaxing whirlpool bath.

Jeff realized that his routine was more than he necessarily had to do, but he found that the exercise helped enormously to reduce his cravings for cocaine. After four weeks he was feeling much better and cut out the swimming. But he continued to work out at the gym four times a week and also rejoined his Saturday afternoon basketball game, which had always been one of the highlights of his week.

Jeff's exercise program does disregard some of the guidelines I offer later in this chapter, but Jeff was much fitter and far more knowledgeable than the majority of people with drug or alcohol problems. He knew how much he could safely do without hurting himself, and what precautions he had to take because he was still in early sobriety. Most important, the exercise plan he designed for himself helped keep him clean and sober during a very difficult period.

The Five Types of Exercise

Before you begin to plan your personal program, let's spend some time talking about the five basic varieties of exercise, each of which benefits your body in a different way. Your workout should certainly include at least the first four of the five categories:

1. Exercises that stretch your muscles.

2. Exercises that tone your muscles.

3. Exercises that condition your heart and lungs.

4. Exercises that improve your coordination.

5. Exercises that build your muscles.

The last type of exercise is an optional activity, suitable only if you've attained a high level of general fitness.

But before you undertake any fitness regimen—and especially if you're over thirty-five, haven't exercised recently, or have a family history of heart attacks—consult your doctor and have a medical checkup first.

Stretching Your Muscles

Muscles are attached to bones by tendons, which are rather like rubber bands. Optimally, they should be elastic and flexible, but if they're in poor condition, they can snap or tear from excessive strain. The same holds true of the muscles themselves.

Newborn babies have very flexible tendons, which is why they can easily put their toes in their mouths, a posture very few adults can achieve. As we age, our tendons lose this flexibility to one degree or another. I've seen adolescents who couldn't even touch their toes, and I know adults in their sixties who can bend from the waist and place their hands palms-down on the floor. But whatever your natural degree of flexibility, if you lead a mostly sedentary life your tendons will gradually tighten up.

This is why it's so essential to warm up and stretch each time *before* you exercise. Even professional athletes at the peak of their physical prowess have to spend some time stretching, and it's absolutely crucial for anyone in a weakened condition who's just beginning an exercise program after a period of inactivity. Just as your car won't serve you very well or long if you make a practice of revving up from zero to fifty-five miles per hour in two seconds flat, neither will your body if you run out the door at full speed or charge onto the basketball court without first properly warming up and stretching.

Your warm-up should consist of two to five minutes of undemanding exercise—walking at a moderate pace, slow running, doing arm circles or any similar activity that eases you into your routine. When you start slowly, you raise your heart rate gradually, instead of jolting it into action. You also increase the flow of blood to the muscles, which increases both their flexibility as well as that of the tendons.

After you've warmed up, spend the next two to five minutes stretching. Move slowly and easily—never bounce or push. Brief, rapid movements send the wrong signals to your muscles, and shorten rather than lengthen them. Simply hold the stretching position and allow gravity or the weight of your body do the work. Be sure to continue breathing normally as you stretch.

Just as each of your exercise sessions should begin with a period of warming up and stretching, it is essential that each session end with a period of cooling down and stretching once again. The cool-down should consist of two to five minutes of gentle activity, followed by two to five minutes of stretching. Stopping abruptly is as bad for your heart as starting suddenly; the cool-down allows your heart rate to return to normal gradually. And stretching relaxes the muscles that have contracted as you were working out, thus lessening the strain on your tendons.

A good stretching routine involves all the major muscle groups. People often forget to stretch the head, neck, and upper torso, but the muscles and ligaments in these areas can get as tight as the ones around the hip and knee joints.

I realize that warming up, cooling down, and stretching may seem boring and unnecessary, but think of them as an insurance policy against injury, one that must be renewed every time you exercise, no matter how fit you may become or how eager you are to get to the fun part of your workout.

Toning Your Muscles

Muscle-toning exercises are not only relatively easy to do, but they're also the best starting point for anyone in the early stages of recovery who's just beginning to get into shape. They help prepare your body for vigorous aerobic exercise and for playing sports.

Your muscles work by alternately contracting and releasing. You contract a muscle to engage it, and you release that same muscle when you stop working it. Muscles that aren't frequently used are flabby; they tend to be less responsive and to have weaker contractions. Your goal should be firm, responsive muscles that are capable of strong contractions. Muscle toners include sit-ups, push-ups, leg lifts, and arm circles, all of which work one particular muscle or muscle group at a time.

Conditioning your muscles also helps prevent injuries. Flabby muscles give poor protection to your joints and ligaments, and leave you more prone to suffer strains, sprains, and joint inflammations such as bursitis and tendinitis. Such ailments may be caused by exercise, but they also often plague people as they age because their muscles lose tone and deteriorate through lack of use. These complaints can be avoided, however, if muscles are properly conditioned.

Aerobic exercises (see page 316) do strengthen the muscles, but the effects are largely limited to those of the lower torso, if you're bicycling, walking, or running. Unless you swim, participate in a comprehensive aerobic exercise/dance class, row, or cross-country ski, be sure to include a muscle-specific workout for the upper torso in your program.

Even if your upper torso muscles were once in good shape, over the years they've probably lost strength and power. They may not be able to support the weight or perform the same movements that gave you no trouble when you were younger or before you started drinking or drugging. Women are particularly prone to muscle-related problems of the upper torso, and should take special care to strengthen this area.

During her first trip to England, Millicent had reason to wish she had done just that. At forty-two, she was celebrating her second anniversary of sobriety. En route from London to Cornwall, she discovered that she had to change platforms in Woking to make her train connection. With not a porter in sight, she gamely set out to get herself, her large suitcase, and her crammed overnight case up a flight of stairs, across a bridge, down the stairs, and onto the next train.

Halfway up the stairs she stopped to rest, puffing heavily. An elderly man walked past her, then retraced his steps and said, "Need a hand, do you? Let me take that for you." Then he picked up her suitcase and carried it easily to the top of the stairs, where he waited with exaggerated patience for her to catch up with him.

"You seemed to be having a bit of a struggle," he said smugly and signaled her to follow him to the next platform. As he helped her aboard the train and stowed her suitcase in the overhead rack, Millicent murmured her thanks as graciously as she could.

"Always a pleasure to come to the aid of the weaker sex," he said with a patronizing tip of his hat.

On the long train trip to Cornwall, Millicent vowed to add upper torso exercises to her bike-riding regimen. With all the traveling she had planned now that she wasn't spending her money on liquor, she wasn't about to crisscross Europe at the mercy of a string of self-satisfied men thirty years her senior.

The thatched cottage she'd rented in Cornwall was as charming and picturesque as she had hoped, but she quickly learned another lesson about the gaps in her exercise program. No sooner had Millicent arrived when she strained her back lugging her cases up the narrow, winding stairs to the bedroom. Now she wished she had spent more time doing sit-ups and strengthening her abdominal muscles, which provide the best possible protection against back strain and pain. (They also help flatten your stomach, which is a great boon to your appearance and how you feel about your body.)

Many of the books and videocassettes cited in Appendix A offer muscle-toning programs, but the list is by no means all-inclusive. With so many programs available, through books and on videocassettes, in health clubs and adult education centers, how can you tell whether a routine is good and right for you? All well-designed programs will:

• Include exercises for all of the body's major muscle groups— neck and shoulders; arms and chest; abdominals; thighs and lower legs; and ankles and feet.

• Match your ability.

• Encourage you to do only as much as is safe for you.

• Include warm-up and cool-down stretching.

• Be enjoyable and easy to follow.

Conditioning Your Heart and Lungs

When you exercise vigorously and without interruption, your heart rate is elevated and you breathe more quickly. The increased activity conditions, or trains, your heart and lungs (the cardiopulmonary system). The more you exercise, the more efficient your heart and lungs become, so that you're then able to exercise for longer periods at a higher level of activity. Also, because your heart is more efficient, your resting heart rate decreases, proof that the heart doesn't have to work as hard to circulate your blood. Karl, the executive I mentioned some pages back, is a perfect example of how cardiopulmonary conditioning can improve health.

Aerobic exercise—any strenuous activity continuously performed for at least twenty minutes—is the best way to get this kind of conditioning. Walking briskly, running, bicycling, swimming, aerobic exercise/ dance classes, rowing, and cross-country skiing are all forms of aerobic exercise.

Most sports, including golf, racquet sports, baseball, and basketball are not aerobic, because they only give you short spurts of exercise. In fact, if you haven't properly conditioned your heart, taking up a sport like tennis can be dangerous, especially for people over forty, because it subjects an untrained heart to sudden strain.

Aerobic exercise, specifically running, got something of a bad name when one of its best-known advocates, runner and author Jim Fixx, was found dead in 1984 on a Vermont road. Although Fixx died during a run, it wasn't the exercise itself that killed him. Unfortunately, he had violated the principles of moderation and prudence that should govern a healthy approach to working out. His father had died of a heart attack at age forty-three, and in spite of his family history and such warning signals as chest tightness and throat pain, Fixx hadn't consulted a doctor. Sure that running eighty miles a week would be his salvation, he had become an exercise addict.

The lesson of Jim Fixx's death is one that you, as a person with an addictive disease, have already learned the hard way: Healthy living isn't achieved by performing any one activity to excess. On the contrary, a plan for ongoing good health combines an aerobic workout and/or other forms of exercise, a wholesome diet, reduced stress, no smoking, and regular preventive medical care.

Improving Your Coordination

Being coordinated means you have the ability to integrate the movements of your various muscle groups. Ballet dancers, champion ice skaters, and world-class tennis players exemplify this facility at its peak. An alcoholic's staggering gait and slurred speech represent it at its worst, with the muscle groups acting independently of one another.

Many people in early sobriety have very poor body coordination. Although there's a tremendous degree of variation in terms of natural abilities, anyone can improve or regain the coordination he or she once had. Certainly if you were always a bit of a klutz, you're not going to turn into a Baryshnikov or a Chris Evert now that you're sober. But any exercise that promotes coordination can help restore the control over your body movements that you lost during your years of drinking or drugging.

Lisa, an accountant recovering from cocaine addiction, told me that when she first started attending an aerobics class, "everyone there was in step except me. They went right, I went left. They hopped twice, I hopped once. After a while I got the legs straight, but it took ages before I got my arms and legs moving together. I felt like one of those dinosaurs that became extinct because it took so long for messages to get from their tiny brains to the end of their tails. They didn't know they were being eaten until it was too late. I wasn't *quite* that bad—at least I knew I was sending signals to my feet. But they trickled down so slowly, and they didn't always get where they were supposed to. I'd feel really stupid and angry. But luckily, instead of getting extinct, I got better."

The best types of exercise for improving coordination are those that require you to move several parts of your body at the same time, such as aerobic exercise or dance. If there's musical accompaniment, you'll probably have an easier time of it, because the body unconsciously responds to rhythm. Racquet games and such sports as baseball, volleyball, or basketball, all of which require hand, eye, and foot coordination, are also very helpful.

I've seen some rather dramatic cases of improved coordination among people in recovery. Ted, for example, was 6'3" but weighed only 150 pounds when he came into treatment for his addiction to alcohol and cocaine. He had played varsity tennis doubles in college and had even spent several months on the pro circuit before deciding to go for a graduate degree in business administration.

He continued to play tennis regularly up until two years before he came into treatment. His long-standing doubles game had finally broken up because as his addiction worsened, Ted—or Ted the Temper, as he'd come to be known—had been throwing increasingly violent tantrums on the court. On one occasion he threw his racquet so hard against the wall of an indoor tennis center that he caused $200 worth of damage. Another time he almost came to blows with his partner when they collided in mid-court after Ted had called "Yours!" and then ran for the ball himself.

"It was very hard hitting the ball when I was seeing *two* of them," Ted confessed. "Most of the time I was so edgy, tense, and hung over that I couldn't get the ball in focus . . . couldn't seem to hit it where I wanted to. I kept wondering what I was doing there."

His partners wondered, too. Playing with Ted the Temper had lost its appeal, so they broke up the foursome.

When he got sober, Ted realized he was in terrible shape. The alcohol and cocaine had reduced his once muscular frame to "skin and flab," as he put it. He was very eager to start playing tennis again, but knew he could injure himself if he picked up a racquet before he'd improved his physical condition. He therefore began a graduated program of aerobic exercise and toning, starting with daily fifteen-minute walks, followed by five minutes of muscle-toning exercises. He also started eating well in order to gain back the weight he had lost.

About two months later, when he could walk briskly for three miles, he started a combined program of walking and running three times a week, and slowly increased his toning routine to ten minutes. Two months after that, when he was up to running three miles three times a week and a full fifteen-minute routine of toning exercises, he got out his racquet and began hitting against the backboard at the local high school courts. A month later he found himself a new doubles partner. Just after the first anniversary of his sobriety, he and his partner won their club's over-forty championship.

In sobriety, Ted was able to recover not only his ability to play tennis, but his enjoyment of the game as well. But if he had jumped right in and tried to play while still debilitated from the effects of his dual dependency, he might have hurt himself and become discouraged about ever regaining his previous expertise. By checking his impatience and building up gradually, he was able to play well again—perhaps even better than he had before his addiction had taken hold of him.

Building Your Muscles

Weight-resistance training involves repeatedly working a particular muscle or muscle group against the resistance of a weight. Body-builders, who carefully work each muscle group to produce the well-defined torsos we see in the body-building magazines, practice this activity in its most extreme form.

Weight-training is optional to your fitness program; it doesn't suit everyone. For people in recovery who do decide to incorporate it into their routines, it should come only—if at all—after a full year of sobriety, when there's been a general improvement in your health, your cardio-pulmonary conditioning, and your muscle tone. Premature and unsupervised use of either free weights or weight-lifting machines is extremely hazardous in early sobriety, when both coordination and muscle strength are poor.

Supervised and careful use of machines and free weights, when your level of fitness warrants it, can, however, help to strengthen your muscles, protect them against injury, and improve your appearance. And not only for men. Too many women worry that if they work out with weights they will suddenly wake up one morning looking like Sylvester Stallone. As increasing muscle bulk is a gradual process, especially for women, such a transformation is highly unlikely. Unless you spend hours each day in the gym, as body-builders do, assigning a few minutes of your weekly exercise sessions to working out with relatively light weights can firm and strengthen your muscles without adding to their mass. And many people enjoy the sense of achievement that comes from adding five more reps or five more pounds to their weight-lifting routine.

Some fanatic body-builders take drugs, such as steroids, to increase muscle bulk. These drugs can be very dangerous, even for people who aren't recovering from an addiction. Of course, you must *never* take any drug for the purpose of building up your muscles.

Benefits and Risks of the Most Popular Forms of Aerobic Exercise

Because the main component of your program will be aerobic exercise, I want to mention the pros and cons of the most popular aerobic activities.

Walking

Walking is the best aerobic exercise for early sobriety. It has very little potential for injury, it requires no equipment other than a sturdy, comfortable pair of shoes, and it can be done almost anywhere at almost any hour. Many people find it so pleasurable, especially if they have access to a park or other scenic route, that it becomes their only form of aerobic exercise. Others find that after four to six weeks of walking, they feel strong enough to try some other aerobic activity. Dedicated walkers who are past the initial phase of conditioning and who have already begun to tone their upper torso muscles may wish to carry hand weights to increase the intensity of their walking workout.

Ruth and Edgar, for example, spent the first forty years of their marriage drinking together. Then they got sober together after an intervention planned by their three children. Both in their mid-sixties, overweight, and in poor physical condition, they pooh-poohed the idea of regular exercise; that was for young people, not them.

But one balmy spring evening, at about the hour that Ruth formerly would have been mixing the first batch of martinis, she suggested that she and Edgar take a stroll around the block. As they walked, they admired their neighbors' azaleas and chatted about the upcoming visit of their grandchildren. A couple of days later, they went out again, but this time they walked around the block twice. They worked their way up to four, then six blocks. Before long they were taking an evening constitutional of twenty-five to thirty minutes every night that they didn't attend an AA meeting, as well as on most weekends.

They began to notice that their clothes were fitting better, too, but they still didn't think of their walks as *exercise*. Then, browsing in the library's video collection, Ruth noticed a tape touting a walking program for folks over fifty. She borrowed it, and she and Edgar learned about stretching, toning exercises, and target heart rates. Now, a year after the intervention, they are familiar figures in the neighborhood, walking briskly in their snazzy sneakers and bright-colored sweats. They've recently added hand weights to their regimen and are "training" for a summer walking trip in Switzerland.

Running

Running is an excellent aerobic exercise, but it's *not* for everyone. Not only do some people find it excruciatingly boring, but it also carries a high risk of injury. The average fifteen-mile-per-week runner can expect one injury every two years. Even with good running shoes to cushion the shock (and no one should ever run without making that investment), your body takes quite a pounding with every step, especially if you're running on roads or pavements. For anyone with chronic hip, knee, or ankle problems, running will only worsen these conditions.

Beginning runners are especially prone to injury, because they're not in good enough condition and/or because they fail to warm up and stretch before they take off. If you've never run before and think you'd like to give it a try, or if you used to run but haven't in some time, do as Ted did. Begin by walking briskly for twenty to thirty minutes three times a week. After four to six weeks of walking, you can begin a routine that combines walking and running, and continue for at least two to four weeks before you embark on a full running program. Since the risk of injury is so high, warming up, stretching, and cooling down are especially important for runners, whether you're a beginner or a marathoner.

Swimming

Swimming is probably the best all-around exercise both for conditioning the heart and lungs, and for toning all of the body's major muscle groups. Because the water bears your body weight while you're active, it's also especially good if you have joint problems.

Many people find that swimming provides additional psychological benefits. Some feel particularly soothed and relaxed by immersing themselves in the water; others find it tremendously invigorating. Kurt, a recovering alcoholic who lives near the beach, swims in the Atlantic Ocean every day from spring until well into December! He enjoys the ocean so much that when the water finally gets too cold even for him, he exercises by taking long walks on the beach every day.

If you like the water, but don't particularly care for swimming laps, you may be able to find a pool that offers aerobics classes in the water. These are very good for cardiopulmonary conditioning, toning muscles, and improving coordination. They're also a good alternative for people whose joint problems prevent them from taking aerobic exercise classes.

Aerobic Exercise/Dance Classes

Aerobic exercise classes—forty-five to sixty minutes of combined stretching, heart and lung conditioning, and toning exercises—can be a lot of fun, especially if you like to exercise in a group and enjoy moving to music. It's also a good way to meet people, an important benefit if you're newly sober.

But before you go out and look for an aerobic exercise class, let me give you a couple of pointers. There are two styles of aerobics: high impact and low impact. In high impact classes, you'll find a great deal of jumping, which can lead to joint and ligament problems, notably painful shin splints. You should avoid these classes and choose instead a low impact class, where you always keep one foot on the floor. That way, you're less vulnerable to injury because your body isn't being jarred.

You should make sure that the class routines are sensibly structured. They should begin with a warm-up, followed by gentle and steady stretching. There should be at least fifteen to twenty minutes of aerobic activity, followed by toning exercises (also performed slowly and smoothly). Each muscle group should be stretched after it's been worked. The class should end with a cool-down and more stretching. A few minutes of quiet relaxation at the very end is desirable, but not essential.

The expertise and ability of the instructor are also important criteria when you're choosing a class. Some health clubs and programs require their instructors to be certified exercise physiologists. Certainly there are some very good instructors who haven't taken the certification exam, but passing one does ensure that the instructor has achieved a basic competence.

Good instructors, whether or not they're certified, are familiar with the potential hazards of exercise. They not only teach you how to monitor your heart rate, but make time during the class for you to do so. They also instruct you on how to protect your back, and make sure you're not pushing yourself too hard.

I've seen some poor instructors who could have doubled for Marine drill sergeants, shouting contemptuously at the laggards and rushing their "recruits" through heroic bouts of exercise. This approach is highly detrimental, even for people in peak condition. It's surely not acceptable for you as a recovering person.

To avoid strained muscles and torn ligaments, be cautious. Before you sign up, spend some time observing the class. Ask friends and acquaintances for recommendations. Talk to the instructor about his or her goals for the class.

Jazz dance, ballet, and even tap dancing classes also provide a good workout that also brings with it the pleasure of moving to music.

Many dance schools and adult education programs are geared for beginners. Ballroom and folk dancing can be fun, too, but more as social activities than as real exercise because they offer little in the way of aerobic conditioning or overall muscle toning.

Bicycling

Bicycling is also good aerobic exercise. Many people complain that riding a stationary bike is about as stimulating as watching grass grow, but if you prefer an activity that's convenient and private, this may perfectly suit your needs. A stationary bike doesn't take up much room, and the weather need never interrupt your exercise schedule. While you ride you can watch the news, listen to the radio, or even read a book by resting it on a rack that's attached to the handlebars. (These racks are sold at sporting goods shops.)

No matter where you're doing your cycling, indoors or out, take care to include plenty of upper torso exercises in your toning program. While walking and running provide some minimal use of the upper body because we naturally swing our arms as we move, cycling doesn't call for any of this type of movement.

Some health clubs also have rowing machines and machines that simulate cross-country skiing. These are also available for home use, but they're expensive, so you may want to think twice before making the investment. Such machines have all the benefits and drawbacks of a stationary bike, but they also exercise the upper body.

Things to Keep in Mind

At the beginning of this chapter I said that choosing an exercise program you enjoy is the single most important factor in making it a success. Now, as you begin to plan your program, I'd like you to take several other factors into consideration.

Schedule your workout at a regular, convenient hour and location. If getting to the pool or your aerobics class is a chore because of rush-hour traffic, you'll soon stop going. If you have to rush to get to the gym before it closes, you'll be more likely to skip it. If you're worried about getting home in time to relieve the babysitter, you won't relish your bike ride.

Some people are invigorated by bounding out of bed and going for an early morning run. Some find that exercising after work is a great way to wind down from their workday. Others prefer to take a long lunch break two or three times a week to attend an aerobic exercise class near the office. Whatever works for you is fine. Just remember to schedule your exercise sessions at least four hours before you go to sleep.

Consider your budget. You may love to swim, but if membership at the only decent pool in town strains your wallet, you may come to resent your exercise program and ultimately give it up. The same holds true for credit card payments for an expensive stationary bike. If money's tight, a better choice might be a relatively modest investment in a pair of walking or running shoes.

Supplement your regular routine whenever you have the opportunity. You can certainly get *more* exercise than you planned for, as long as you don't injure or overtire yourself. So go ahead and play left field at the company picnic softball game. Join your kids for an afternoon at the skating rink. Take a walk with your spouse or a friend after dinner. Not only will you benefit from the extra activity, you'll also have fun, relax, and have more time with your family or friends.

Take your temperament into account. Choose a form of exercise that suits your personality. If you hate other people seeing you sweaty and with your hair in a mess, it probably isn't a good idea to sign up for an aerobic exercise class just because it's held in the basement of your church. You might do better with a solitary pursuit such as walking or running. On the other hand, these are poor options if you need to be inspired by the company of others, unless you can persuade a friend to join you. If you thrive on competition, think about adding a competitive sport to your routine once you're fit enough. But no matter what you do, always remember that accommodating your personal tastes will help you accomplish the goals of your program.

I have often been impressed by the transformations I've seen in my patients as a result of exercising. But Peggy stands out in my mind. When I first saw her she was fair, fat and forty. Years of drinking had muddied her once-translucent skin. Her flesh sagged. There were dark patches under her eyes and the skin around her nose was coarse and threaded with a network of tiny red capillaries. Her blue eyes were dull, the whites yellowish and bloodshot, and her blond hair was overbleached and lifeless. She was wearing a pink track suit at least one size too small and had a cigarette dangling from her lips. Her whole appearance declared that the only exercise she ever got was bending her elbow.

After her first visit, I saw Peggy once a week for six months in group therapy. Her appearance improved rapidly in the first two months of her sobriety until she looked well and passably attractive. Four months after Peggy stopped group therapy I saw her at one of the picnics we have for our former patients. Actually, I didn't see *her*. I saw a slim, attractive woman with bright blue eyes and a wide smile. Her skin shone and her hair gleamed. She bounced up to me, radiating health and energy. "You don't know who I am, do you?" she asked in response to my puzzled look. Fearing early senility, I admitted I did not. When she told me she was Peggy, I tried to visualize the defeated, sagging woman in the tight pink sweat suit, but I couldn't.

The transformation in Peggy had begun when she threw away her cigarettes and started a daily walking program soon after completing group therapy. She had been determined to make it a part of her schedule. Each morning, she got up an hour earlier to take a brisk walk in the park. She could only manage fifteen minutes at first, but as her physical condition improved she increased her walking time by five minutes every two weeks until she was doing thirty minutes a day. After three months she bought a pair of hand weights and added ten minutes of arm exercises during her walk. The first few weeks she had to force herself to get up and out to the park every morning, but now she looks forward to her exercise and actually misses it when bad weather makes walking unsafe and keeps her indoors.

Peggy's metamorphosis was dramatic but not difficult. It took some determination at first, but the result has been a startling change in appearance, one which came from both her improved physical condition and the psychological lift that followed close behind it. Exercise may not be a magical cure for all your problems, but it does produce remarkable results. It did for Peggy and it can for you, too.

Chapter Seventeen
Smoke Free

Giving Up Cigarettes

If you are among the many recovering people who are still smoking, sobriety holds an additional challenge for you: breaking your addiction to nicotine, a step that will also facilitate your exercise program.

Nicotine is a drug that falls into the same pharmacological category as amphetamines and cocaine. The amount of nicotine that's contained in a single cigarette can raise your blood pressure and increase both your heart and breathing rates.

All smokers—except for people who have just taken up the habit and a few individuals who smoke only occasionally—are addicted to cigarettes. There is virtually no such thing as a social smoker, in the sense that there are social drinkers. Most individuals who drink (about 85 percent, in fact) do so socially, one or two drinks at a time. They may not drink again for several days, or even several weeks. It's just not that important to them. Very few smokers feel that way about cigarettes. The majority of them are like the 15 percent of drinkers who need a drink to get through the day and can never stop at just one.

Thanks to all the information about smoking that's been disseminated in recent years, most of you are aware that smoking is very bad for your health. Many people who smoke even go so far as saying they would like to break the habit. So why can't they? Because, like cocaine, nicotine increases the availability of neurotransmitters in the brain—particularly dopamine, which is thought to promote feelings of pleasure and well-being. Nicotine also increases alertness, improves the memory, and reduces irritability and anxiety. And like other stimulants, it reduces the appetite and can help maintain a desirable weight. Moreover, it allows the smoker to enjoy all these reinforcing effects in a socially acceptable manner, by simply lighting up. Is it any wonder, then, that it's so addictive? On the other hand, people who try to kick the habit must endure not only pharmacological withdrawal from the drug, but also psychological withdrawal from the many activities that they have always associated with smoking.

Let's look more carefully at the health hazards caused by smoking. Lung cancer and chronic lung conditions such as bronchitis and emphysema are far more common among smokers than among nonsmokers.

Smoking is also a serious risk factor in coronary artery disease, high blood pressure, and arterial disease elsewhere in the body. Smokers suffer more frequently from chronic respiratory infections such as sinusitis, as well as from peptic ulcers. Studies have shown that women who smoke during pregnancy are more likely to miscarry, deliver prematurely, and give birth to babies with low birth weight. Smokers also experience a variety of discomforts, including shortness of breath, heart palpitations when they exert themselves, dizziness, headaches, muscles spasms, cramps, and gastrointestinal irritation. As if that weren't enough, cigarette smoke has now been shown to affect nonsmokers who are exposed to it. In other words, when you light up a cigarette, you may be endangering not only your own health but that of your family and friends as well.

If you're a smoker, one of the goals of your recovery should be to give up cigarettes. You can't derive the full benefits of good nutrition and regular exercise if you continue to smoke. Thus, the next question —which I hear so often from my patients—is *when* to quit.

An oft-quoted belief among many self-help members is that you're putting your sobriety at risk if you try to stop smoking before you've been in recovery for at least a year. But no evidence exists to indicate that this is true. I don't know of a single study that has proven that the incidence of relapses is higher among smokers who quit before they achieve a year of sobriety than among those who continue to smoke.

Marion, only one month sober, had never considered tackling her nicotine addiction until she came down with severe bronchitis. She was so sick that, for the first time in twenty years, she didn't even think about lighting up. After a couple of weeks in bed, when she was feeling better, she started craving cigarettes again. But when she really thought about taking smoke into her still-aching lungs, she decided that this might be a good time for her to quit. That way, by the time she went back to work, she would have three smoke-free weeks behind her.

She kept her decision to herself, mulling it over until the night before she was set to go back to the office. Then she told her husband and kids. Since none of them smoked, it was easy for her to abstain at home. She managed at work by telling her coworkers, avoiding the lunchroom, and sipping water whenever she wanted a cigarette. But she was concerned about what would happen at her AA meetings. No non-smoking groups existed in her area, so she asked Dorothy, an AA friend who had visited her during her illness, to find out whether there were any other nonsmokers at her meeting.

Dorothy came up with two names, both of whom Marion called. Together the three of them formed a no-smoking section which they later nicknamed the "Survivors Corner for Twin Winners." They let it be known that anyone who was willing to deal with both alcohol and nic-otine addiction was welcome to join them. Gradually several others, including Dorothy, came over to sit in the Survivors Corner.

Earlier, when she had visited Marion during her illness, Dorothy had had to excuse herself several times to go to the bathroom so she could quickly smoke half a cigarette. She began connecting the way she was sneaking cigarettes with the way she had sneaked vodka during her drinking days.

Since becoming sober, she had rationalized her smoking by say-ing she didn't want to jeopardize her recovery by quitting. She was alarmed when Marion stopped smoking after only a month's sobriety. But as the weeks went by and Marion remained sober as well as smoke-free, Dorothy no longer had an excuse not to stop smoking herself. So, she tossed out her last pack of cigarettes and joined Marion and the others at their end of the meeting room, saying, "You forced me into your corner."

Ideally, it would make sense for someone to deal with *all* of his or her addictions at once—just as most people stop using alcohol when they give up cocaine. But almost all of the 80 percent of my patients who smoke tell me they would find it too difficult to give up cigarettes along with the alcohol and other drugs. And given the mood swings of early recovery, the physical and mental disruptions, the need to rees-tablish relationships with family, friends, and colleagues, you may well be right to avoid taking on yet another challenge. It may take three to six months, or even a year, before your life becomes stable and calm—but once it does, you no longer have a reason not to stop smoking.

If you don't, the consequences can be serious. On more than one sad occasion I've had to watch a sober alcoholic or drug addict die of lung cancer. My friend Irving was one. As the director of the employee assistance program at a large corporation, he had helped many people get and stay sober. Irving was himself a recovering alcoholic who had been sober five or six years when we first met at a business meeting. Over the next seven years I came to know him as a valued colleague.

Irving was also a chain smoker who adamantly believed that no one should try to stop smoking until he or she had achieved a stable sobriety, no matter how long this might take. "It's just not worth the risk," he maintained. Irving had fifteen years of good sobriety—until he died of lung cancer. I often wonder how many more he might have had if he had been able to give up cigarettes.

So, let's go back to the question of when you should stop smoking. The answer is: AS SOON AS POSSIBLE.

How to Stop

At your self-help meetings you learn to abstain from alcohol one day at a time. But when you stop smoking, you have to abstain one *minute* at a time.

Physical withdrawal from nicotine generally lasts from three to five days. You may experience such symptoms as irritability, poor concentration, sleep disturbance, fatigue, or headaches. These ailments can be uncomfortable, but they are really quite mild compared to physical withdrawal from alcohol or drugs.

On the other hand, the psychological withdrawal is very intense because most smokers repeat the many acts they associate with the habit—buying cigarettes, removing one from the pack, lighting up, inhaling, flicking the ash, stubbing out the butt—at least twenty times a day. If you've been smoking for many years, these cigarette-related activities have become firmly established rituals, so much so that it may seem odd or unsettling to drink a cup of coffee or pick up the phone without first reaching for your pack. If lighting up is synonymous with a moment's relaxation, disrupting your routine can make you feel tense and jumpy. Something old and familiar is missing.

A colleague of mine said he felt completely disoriented when he stopped smoking. "I kept feeling as if I'd forgotten something. I'd lose track of what I was saying or doing because I couldn't concentrate without a cigarette. And I couldn't spell, or at least I thought I couldn't. When I had to write reports, I'd find myself looking up a word every three lines. Usually I had spelled it correctly, but it just didn't look right on the page. After years of performing well at my job, I lost my confidence. I think it was because my world *was* different for a while without my cigarettes."

The first three to five days are the hardest. After that, you're no longer physically dependent on nicotine, just as you're no longer physically dependent on alcohol if you can get through the first few days of sobriety. Then the major part of your effort will be to cope with your desire for the effects produced by nicotine, and to change those habits that you've come to associate with smoking.

Getting Help

Smokers Anonymous is a Twelve Step program open to anyone who wants to quit smoking. Their headquarters, listed in Appendix C, can help you find a group in your area. Or you may want to find a smoke-free meeting of the twelve-step program you are already attending. As more and more sober people discover the benefits of giving up cigarettes, these meetings are becoming easier to find. Phone your local contact number for help with locating a smoke-free meeting in your area.

The American Cancer Society and the American Lung Association both sponsor behavioral modification programs for would-be ex-smokers, and many programs (often free or low-cost) are also available through hospitals, employers, churches, and community organizations.

In addition, any number of private organizations offer smoke-ending programs. These can be expensive, however, so be sure to investigate their success rates and the credentials of their instructors before you enroll. You can get a recommendation from your doctor, friends who have quit, or by checking the yellow pages of your telephone book. With a few phone calls you should be able to find a suitable program in your area.

If you've never tried to quit smoking before, or if you've made a couple of unsuccessful attempts over the last several years, then self-help or behavioral modification programs are still your best bet. But if you've tried repeatedly over three or four years, or you've been unable to abstain from cigarettes for more than a day or two at a time because of intense physical discomfort, you might want to consider a program that uses nicotine-containing gum. Bear in mind, however, that the gum is available by prescription only, and such programs may be expensive.

Helping Yourself

Like any other, nicotine addiction has a high relapse rate. So don't be discouraged by failures. As you already know from getting sober, you can learn from setbacks. Nevertheless, here are a few simple steps to help you succeed:

Throw Away All Your Cigarettes

You have to get rid of all your drug supplies, just as you did when you decided to stop using or drinking. This includes the almost-empty pack in the glove compartment of your car, those stale cigarettes in the quaint old cigarette box on the coffee table, and any stubs that happen to be lying around. Collect the ashtrays in your home and office and put them away in a cupboard, and empty and clean the ashtray in your car, as well. Throw away your matches, lighters, and any other paraphernalia you associate with smoking.

Avoid and/or Change Routines That You Associate with Smoking

As you go through your first few smoke-free days you'll become aware—sometimes painfully so—of the many rituals you've created around smoking. Try to refrain from as many of these familiar routines as you can.

If you're like most smokers, for example, you probably light up your first cigarette just after you get out of bed. Try taking a shower and drinking a glass of orange juice instead. If your favorite cigarette of the morning is the one you smoke with that first cup of coffee, switch to some other drink—tea, hot chocolate, warm milk—that you don't associate with smoking. For the first few days after you've quit, don't linger over breakfast. Leave the table quickly—before you give in to the urge to smoke "just one."

Many people smoke their second or third cigarette as soon as they get to work. This makes for a nice break between the often hectic commute to the job and the business of the workday. But you can't afford to take such a break. Force yourself instead to jump right into whatever awaits you.

If you work in an environment that has designated smoking areas, avoid them. Plan to go elsewhere during your break: get some fresh air, do a few stretching exercises, take a few minutes to meditate or to do some deep breathing. Eat lunch in the non-smoking area of the cafeteria, if there is one; otherwise, try to sit well away from tables where people are smoking.

When Eileen, who had been addicted to tranquilizers, decided to give up smoking, I asked her to make a list of high-risk situations for cigarettes, just as she had learned to do in her relapse prevention group. Her list included: while drinking coffee, after sex, while waiting in line —and after feeding the snakes.

"What snakes are you feeding?" I asked her. "Why is that high risk?"

"They're my son's boa constrictors," she explained. "They eat live mice, and somehow, because Jamie is so busy with his schoolwork and sports, I've fallen into the role of snake feeder. And I hate it." She shuddered. "I buy these tiny, defenseless baby mice and hold them by the tail over the cage. As they struggle and squeak horribly, the snake opens its mouth and swallows them. You can see them still wriggling inside and"— she paused— "and their little tails hang out of the snake's mouth like a strand of spaghetti. Ugh!"

I suggested to Eileen that perhaps she smoked a cigarette afterwards as a way of consoling herself. "Isn't feeding the snakes carrying maternal love too far?" I asked.

"Of course it is," she answered, "and I intend to tell Jamie he has to take care of his own snakes or sell them."

Drink Six to Eight Glasses of Water a Day

Many people find that drinking water helps fill the void left by cigarettes. True, it's not nearly as rewarding, but it does give you something to do with your hands and mouth. Also, if you drink water instead of eating candies or cookies as a cigarette-substitute, you won't gain weight. Not to mention that some of the time you used to devote to your cigarette rituals will now be taken up with frequent trips to the bathroom!

Tell Everyone You're Quitting

Enlist the encouragement and support of your family, friends, and coworkers by telling them that you've stopped smoking. Going public will help keep you honest.

Paul, six months sober, had been off cigarettes for seven weeks when I spoke to him. "I found out that I could use the same safeguards to stay off cigarettes as I did to stay off the booze. The first, second, and third times I quit, I didn't tell anyone except my doctor. And I only told her because she said she wouldn't treat my asthma if I kept on smoking. I used to think that if I made a strong, silent resolution, later on I could surprise everybody with the results. 'Hey, whaddaya know? I haven't had a smoke in six months.' Then there would be a big celebration, and I'd be the center of attention. Of course, the addict in me knew that if you don't tell anyone, you don't get any support. No one's watching either, so if you fail, so what? It's no big deal.

"So this time I spread the good news around. Most people don't want to see you die from an addiction. The only ones who get upset when you quit are other addicts. I know how I used to feel when people told me they were going to stop smoking. I'd wait around for them to light that first cigarette. Then I'd be ready to welcome them back into the fold with open arms. Now I know to stay away from smokers—the way I stay away from drinkers."

Plan Enough Activities to Fill Your Days and Evenings

Don't leave yourself with nothing to do. How often have you spent an evening sitting around and smoking? Maybe you watched some TV or chatted with a friend, but think about it: Wasn't smoking the major business of the evening? Just as when you first became sober, when you first stop smoking you can't afford to spend your free time "hanging out," thinking about how much you'd love to have a smoke. Go to the movies. Take a class, preferably one in which you have to use your hands. Learn to knit or do macrame. If you enjoy cooking, chop vegetables or make bread. Find something to keep yourself occupied.

As Marion told me, "One of the advantages of quitting smoking and drinking almost simultaneously, the way I did, is that you've already planned your free time so that you're not lounging around, thinking how much you'd like to have a drink. My evenings and weekends were booked, but it was those little snippets of time that gave me trouble when I first stopped smoking—coffee breaks, the ten minutes at lunch after I'd finished eating, waiting to get the last load out of the washing machine. Then I discovered needlepoint. I take my bag with me everywhere, and whenever I have a few minutes, I pick up my work. I've needlepointed the whole house, so now I'm starting on hooked rugs."

I've known a number of people, some of them men, who've become interested in needlework as a way to keep their hands busy. In fact, I have a beautiful hand-hooked rug in my bedroom, a gift from a recovering alcoholic and smoker.

Exercise Regularly

You're giving up cigarettes because of your concern for your health, as well as the health of others. Now is therefore a very good time to review your exercise program or to begin one if you haven't already done so. There's nothing like a vigorous workout to reinforce your desire to quit. The exercise both calms and energizes you, and takes up some of those hours when you might otherwise feel at loose ends.

Avoid Friends Who Smoke, and Don't Let Anyone Smoke Around You

As a recovering person, this should be obvious to you. You know not to hang out in bars or with people who are doing drugs. Similarly, if you've stopped smoking, you don't pal around with people who are still lighting up.

Odd as it may seem to nonsmokers, I've heard people say that they're still turned on by the smell of cigarette smoke, even years after they've quit. If you allow someone to smoke in your vicinity when you first stop smoking, the temptation to take a puff may be too great to resist.

Alice, one of my former patients, had been sober for four years before she decided to stop smoking. Though she was initially successful, she developed a recurring relapse pattern. She'd quit for a month or sometimes six weeks, and then she'd start again. I suggested that we examine her daily routine to figure out what the problem might be.

It turned out that Alice ate lunch in the smoking section of the cafeteria with her friend Pamela, who was a chain smoker. Day after day, Alice would sit across the table and watch Pam light up after the meal. On one occasion, when Alice was especially nervous about a presentation she had to make that afternoon, she bummed a cigarette from her friend. She bummed another when she was upset because she was anticipating a difficult parent-teacher meeting about her daughter who was doing poorly in school. In each instance, it took a few days before Alice bought her own pack of cigarettes and resumed smoking.

Unfortunately for Alice, even after she'd pinpointed the trigger for her relapses, she wasn't ready to give up her lunches with Pamela. It wasn't until Pamela went to work for another firm that Alice was finally able to quit for good.

As a recovering person, you have the tools to stop smoking at your fingertips. You recognize that it's necessary for your good health. You understand the importance of sound nutrition and regular exercise in fighting an addiction. But most of all, you're familiar with what it means to give up an addiction. You're learning how to change your habits and thought patterns so that you can successfully abstain from addictive substances. In short, you know how to stop smoking. Now all that remains is for you to do it.

Afterword

by Anne Geller, M.D.

I am a recovering alcoholic and addict. Those words can be said with pride or with bravado, with humility or with shame. They can be given as simple information or issued as a warning. They can also be used as I am using them now, to give you confidence and hope.

Throughout this book I have spoken mainly about your recovery, but now I want to say a bit more about my own experiences. Were it not for my recovery, I could not have written this book. Had recovery not provided the impetus to change my medical specialty, I would not have had the rewards of treating thousands of addicted people over the years, which has made it possible to gather together all the information for you to use. Nor would I have had the pleasure of working with patients who recover as neurological patients seldom do, of teaching my fellow medical professionals about addiction, or of working to increase awareness of addiction in the medical profession.

The course of my recovery was not entirely smooth. Over a chaotic three-year period, I had several relapses. Intervals of sobriety lasting for several months were followed by inexplicable bouts of drinking again. I was confused by what was happening to me and could make no sense of the bewildering changes in my emotions, my thinking, and my physical reactions. It seemed that I was a different person from day to day, often not recognizable to myself.

Each of my several relapses had its own antecedents. There were parts of my life which were not in order, steps which I had failed to take, moods and emotions for which I was unprepared. Recovery is a learning process, but recovery through relapse is a dangerous way to learn. During one of my relapses I endangered the life of another person, who escaped harm only by an incredible piece of luck. On at least two other occasions

I placed myself at great risk. You do not have to do this. You can learn from my experience and the experience of all the other people you have met on these pages. Relapses can be prevented, and the keys to prevention are knowledge and a commitment to change.

My sobriety began in earnest only when I stopped waiting for it to happen and started making it happen. Much later, after I had achieved a stable sobriety of four or five years, I began, as part of my new work in addiction medicine, to read what little had been written about recovery and to talk to my colleagues about the process of living a sober life. Above all, I began to listen more closely than ever to my patients, and to think about what they were saying in a way I had not done before. From them I learned that what I had experienced was *not* unique and unusual. Their stories both corroborated my experiences and increased my awareness of the wide variety of things that happen to people when they become addicted.

I have written the book I would have liked to have read while I was struggling through the first three years of my recovery. In these pages I have tried to make sense of the chaos, and to keep it simple, straightforward, and clear. Above all I have tried to avoid excesses—of medical dogmatism on the one hand and of unscientific enthusiasms on the other. I embrace moderation. We addicts are people of excess. In our recovery we must change our image of ourselves from that of wild, unconventional free spirits liberated by alcohol or drugs to that of people who value straightness and sobriety. We do this in order to attain true freedom: freedom of the spirit.

What I have offered in this book is a program for change, a way of ridding yourself of your rigid, repetitive, and destructive habits and replacing them with fresh, flexible, and balanced behavior. By embracing change, you give yourself a unique opportunity to make a new beginning in life. Few people are so fortunate. Sobriety was forced upon you, but it is a gift. Use it well.

Appendix A
Suggested Reading

1. Addiction and Recovery

Books

Alcoholics Anonymous World Services, Inc. Staff. *Alcoholics Anonymous* (the big book). New York: Alcoholics Anonymous World Services, 1986.

FitzGerald, Kathleen. *Alcoholism: The Genetic Inheritance.* New York: Doubleday, 1988.

Ford, Betty, and Chris Chase. *Betty: A Glad Awakening.* Garden City, NY: Doubleday, 1987.

Johnson, Vernon E. *I'll Quit Tomorrow.* New York: Harper & Row, 1980.

Milam, Dr. James R., and Katherine Ketcham. *Under the Influence.* New York: Bantam Books, 1988.

Mueller, L. Ann, and Katherine Ketcham. *Recovering: How to Get and Stay Sober.* New York: Bantam Books, 1987.

Robertson, Nan. *Getting Better.* New York: William Morrow & Co., 1988.

Sandmaier, Marian. *The Invisible Alcoholics: Women and Alcohol Abuse in America.* New York: McGraw-Hill, 1981.

Twelve Steps and Twelve Traditions. New York: Alcoholics Anonymous World Services, 1965.

Weiss, Roger D., and Steven M. Mirin. *Cocaine.* New York: Ballantine Books, 1988.

Wholey, Dennis. *The Courage to Change.* New York: Warner Books, 1986.

2. Spriritual Growth and Stress Reduction

Books

Benson, Herbert, and Miriam Z. Klipper. *The Relaxation Response.* New York: Avon Books, 1976.

Benson, Herbert, and William Proctor. *Beyond the Relaxation Response.* New York: Berkley, 1985.

Borysenko, Joan. *Minding the Body, Mending the Mind.* New York: Bantam Books, 1988.

Carr, Rachel. *Yoga for All Ages.* New York: Simon & Schuster, 1975.

Gawain, Shakti. *Creative Visualization.* New York: Bantam Books, 1980.

LeShan, Lawrence. *How to Meditate.* New York: Bantam Books, 1984.

Peck, M. Scott. *The Road Less Traveled.* New York: Simon & Schuster, 1980.

Rogers, Ronald L., Chandler Scott McMillin, and Morris A. Hill. *The Twelve Steps Revisited.* New York: Bantam Books, 1990.

Satir, Virginia. *Self-Esteem: A Declaration.* Millbrae, CA: Celestial Arts, 1975.

Wallace, John. *Alcoholism: New Light on the Disease.* Newport, RI: Edgehill Publications, 1985.

Audiocassettes

Bloomfield, Harold, and Sirah Vettese. *Self-Hypnosis and Meditation* (read by the authors). New York: McGraw-Hill.

Dalke, Richard. *How to Use and Apply the Powers of Hypnotism, Tapes I, II, and III* (read by the author). Spokane, WA: Books in Motion.

Hazelden Audio Cassette Library Series. *Each Day a New Beginning: Audio Meditations for Women.* Minneapolis: Metacom, Inc.

Hazelden Subliminal Audio Library Series. *Self-Esteem*. Minneapolis: Metacom, Inc.

Hazelden Subliminal Audio Library Series. *Serenity*. Minneapolis: Metacom, Inc.

Jackson, T. H.. *How to Turn Off Stress*. New York: Simon & Schuster.

Mackoff, Barbara. *Leaving the Office Behind* (read by Donada Peters). Newport Beach, CA: Books on Tape.

Miller, Emmett E. *Letting Go of Stress*. New York: Simon & Schuster.

Subliminal Persuasion Series. *Self-Hypnosis*. New York: Warner Audio Publishing.

Videocassettes

Biofeedback: Waves of the Future. Dr. Barbara Brown. Garden Grove, CA: Trainex, 1975.

Biofeedback: Yoga of the West. Dr. Elmer Green. Cos Cob, CT: Hartley Film Foundation, 1975.

Lilias! Alive with Yoga. Lilias Folan. Cambridge, MA: Rudra Press, 1987.

Yoga Moves with Alan Finger. Alan Finger. Universal City, CA: MCA Home Video, 1983.

3. The Recovering Family

Books

Al-Anon Family Group Headquarters, Inc. Staff. *Al-Anon's Twelve Steps and Twelve Traditions*. New York: Al-Anon, 1986.

Beattie, Melody. *Co-Dependent No More: How to Stop Controlling Others and Start Caring for Yourself*. New York: Harper & Row/Hazelden, 1988.

Bepko, Claudia, and Jo Ann Krestan. *The Responsibility Trap*. New York: The Free Press, 1985.

Bradshaw, John. *Bradshaw On: The Family*. Deerfield Beach, FL: Health Communications, Inc., 1988.

Burgin, James E.. *Guide Book for the Family with Alcohol Problems*. Center City, MN: Hazelden, 1982.

Clarke, Jean Illsley, and Connie Dawson. *Growing Up Again: Parenting Ourselves, Parenting Our Children.* New York: Harper & Row/Hazelden, 1989.

Meryman, Richard. *Broken Promises, Mended Dreams.* New York: Berkley, 1986.

O'Gorman, Patricia, and Philip Oliver-Diaz. *Breaking the Cycle of Addiction.* Deerfield Beach, FL: Health Communications Inc., 1987.

Schlesinger, Stephen E., and Lawrence K. Horberg. *Taking Charge: How Families Can Climb Out of the Chaos of Addiction.* New York: Simon & Schuster, 1988.

Somers, Suzanne. *Keeping Secrets.* New York: Warner Books, 1988.

4. Improving Your Sex Life

Books

Drews, Toby R., and Lloyd Hildebrand. *Sex and the Sober Alcoholic.* Baltimore: Recover Communications, 1987.

O'Connor, Dagmar. *How to Put the Love Back into Making Love.* New York: Doubleday, 1988.

5. Finding a Job

Books

Bolles, Richard. *What Color Is Your Parachute?* Berkeley: Ten Speed Press, 1988.

Petras, Kathryn, and Ross Petras. *The Only Job Hunting Guide You'll Ever Need.* New York: Poseidon Press, 1989.

Videocassettes

The Winning Job Interview. John C. Crystal and Nella Barkley. Los Angeles: Star Video Productions, 1983.

6. Healthful Eating

Books

Brody, Jane. *Jane Brody's Good Food Book: Living the High Carbohydrate Way.* New York: Bantam Books, 1987.

Brody, Jane. *Jane Brody's Nutrition Book.* New York: Bantam Books, 1982.

Burros, Marian. *Keep It Simple: 30-Minute Meals from Scratch.* New York: William Morrow & Co., 1981.

Burros, Marian. *Twenty-Minute Menus.* New York: Simon & Schuster, 1989.

Carper, Jean. *Jean Carper's Total Nutrition Guide.* New York: Bantam Books, 1987.

Shulman, Martha Rose. *Fast Vegetarian Feasts.* New York: Doubleday, 1986.

Smith, Jeff. *The Frugal Gourmet.* New York: Ballantine Books, 1988.

Smith, Jeff. *The Frugal Gourmet Cooks American.* New York: William Morrow & Co., 1987.

7. Exercise

Books

Anderson, Bob. *Stretching.* Bolinas, CA: Shelter Publications, Inc., 1980.

Jonas, Steven, and Peter Radetsky. *PaceWalking: The Balanced Way to Aerobic Health.* New York: Crown Publishers, Inc., 1988.

LaLanne, Elaine, and Richard Benyo. *Fitness After 50.* Lexington, MA: The Stephen Greene Press, 1986.

McCullagh, James C.. *The Complete Bicycle Fitness Book.* New York: Warner Books, 1984.

Neiman, David C. *The Sports Medicine Fitness Course.* Menlo Park, CA: Bull Publishing Company, 1986.

Videocassettes

Gary Yanker's Walking Workouts. Universal City, CA: MCA Home Video, 1985.

Jane Fonda's Low Impact Aerobic Workout. Culver City, CA: Lorimar Home Video, 1986.

Jane Powell's Fight Back with Fitness. Culver City, CA: Lorimar Home Video, 1986. (For arthritis sufferers and others who need to start slowly)

Jazzercise. Judi Sheppard Missett. Universal City, CA: MCA Home Video, 1982. (Aerobic dance routines)

Richard Simmons & the Silver Foxes. Culver City, CA: Lorimar Home Video, 1986. (For age fifty plus)

Kathy Smith's Body Basic. Agoura Hills, CA: JCI Video, 1985. (Warm-up, toning, and light aerobics)

Start-Up with Jane Fonda. Culver City, CA: Lorimar Home Video, 1987. (For beginners)

Appendix B
Prescription and
Over-the-Counter
Medications to Avoid

1. Medications That Contain Alcohol

These are only a few of the most commonly used alcohol-containing medications. There are many similiar medications that also contain alcohol. Before buying any preparation, make sure it does not contain alcohol. For over-the-counter medications, read the label or ask your pharmacist; for prescription medications, check with your physician and double-check with your pharmacist.

Product	Alcohol Percentage
Actidil	4.0
Bayer Cough Syrup for Children	5.0
Benadryl Elixir	14.0
Benylin Cough Syrup	5.0
Bronkolixir	19.0
Cēpacol Mouthwash	14.0
Cheracol Plus	4.0
Cheracol D Cough Syrup	4.75
Chlor-Trimeton Syrup	7.0
Colace Syrup	1.0
Contac Nighttime Cold Medicine	25.0
Dimetane Decongestant Elixir	3.0
Dimetapp Elixir	2.5
Donnatal Elixir	23.0

Product	*Alcohol Percentage*
Feosol Elixir	5.0
Geritol Liquid	12.0
Listerine Antiseptic Mouthwash	26.9
Listermint with Fluoride	6.6
Novahistine Elixir	5.0
Novahistine DMX	10.0
Nyquil Cough Syrup	25.0
Robitussin Night Relief	25.0
Robitussin CF	4.5
Robitussin Syrup	3.5
Robitussin DM Syrup	1.4
Sudafed Cough Syrup	2.4
Tedral Elixir	15.0
Tylenol Adult Liquid Pain Reliever	7.0
Vicks' Formula 44 Cough Mixture	10.0

2. Over-the-Counter Medications That May Make You Feel Drowsy

Allerest:
- Allergy Tablets
- Headache Strength Tablets
- Sinus Pain Formula
- 12 Hour Caplets

Benadryl:
- Decongestant Tablets
- Elixir
- 25 Kapseals
- 25 Tablets
- Plus Tablets
- Spray

Benylin:
- Cough Syrup
- Decongestant

Bromfed Syrup
Cerose-DM
Cheracol Plus Head Cold/Cough Formula
Chexit Tablets

Children's CoTylenol:
- Chewable Cold Tablets
- Liquid Cold Formula

Chlor-Trimeton: Allergy Syrup
Decongestant Tablets
Long-Acting Repetabs Decongestant Tablets
Long-Acting Repetabs Tablets

Comtrex: Multi-Symptom Cold Reliever, Tablets, Caplets or Liquid
A/S Multi-Symptom Allergy/Sinus Formula, Tablets or Caplets

Contac: Capsules or Caplets
Severe Cold Formula Caplets

Coricidin: 'D' Decongestant Tablets
Demilets Tablets for Children
Maximum Strength Sinus Headache Caplets
Tablets

Demazin Nasal Decongestant/Antihistamine Repetabs Tablets or Syrup

Dimetane: Decongestant Caplets
Decongestant Elixir
Elixir
Extentabs
Tablets

Dimetapp: Elixir
Extentabs
Plus Caplets
Tablets

Dorcol Children's Liquid Cold Formula
Dristan Decongestant/Antihistamine
Drixoral Antihistamine/Nasal Decongestant Syrup

Fedahist: Decongestant Syrup
Tablets

4-Way: Cold Tablets
Fast Acting Nasal Spray, Regular or Mentholated

Midol: Maximum Strength Multi-Symptom Formula
Maximum Strength Premenstrual Syndrome Formula
Original Multi-Symptom Formula

Miles Nervine Nighttime Sleep-Aid
Novahistine Elixir
Nytol Tablets

PediaCare: Cold Formula Liquid
                    Cough-Cold Formula Liquid or Chewable Tablets

Presym PMS
Primatene Tablets, M Formula
Pyrroxate Capsules
Robitussin Night Relief

Ryna: Liquid
                    C Liquid

St. Joseph Nighttime Cold Medicine
Scot-Tussin Sugar-Free DM Cough and Cold Medicine
Sinarest Regular and Extra Strength Tablets

Sine-Off: Maximum Strength Allergy/Sinus Formula
                       Caplets
                    Sinus Medicine Tablets-Aspirin Formula

Singlet

Sinutab: Maximum Strength Tablets or Caplets
                    Tablets

Sleep-eze 3 Tablets
Sleepinal Nighttime Sleep Aid Capsules

Sominex: Liquid
                    Pain Relief Formula
                    Tablets

Sudafed: Plus Liquid
                    Plus Tablets

Teldrin Timed-Release Capsules

Triaminic: Allergy Tablets
                    Chewables
                    Cold Syrup
                    Cold Tablets
                    Triaminic–12 Tablets

Triaminicin Tablets

Triaminicol: Multi-Symptom Cold Syrup
                    Multi-Symptom Cold Tablets

Trind
Trind-DM
Tussagesic Tablets

Tylenol: Cold Medication Caplets or Tablets
                     Cold Medication Liquid

Unisom Dual Relief Nighttime Sleep Aid/Analgesic

Vicks: Children's Nyquil
                     Formula 44 Cough Mixture

3. Over-the-Counter Medications That May Make You Feel Jittery

A.R.M. Allergy Relief Medicine Caplets

Actifed: Capsules
                     12-Hour Capsules
                     Syrup
                     Tablets

Acutrim: Late Day Appetite Suppressant
                     16 Hour Appetite Suppressant
                     II Maximum Strength Appetite Suppressant

AllerAct Decongestant Tablets or Caplets

Allerest: Allergy Tablets
                     Headache Strength Tablets
                     No Drowsiness Tablets
                     Sinus Pain Formula
                     12 Hour Caplets

AsthmaHaler Mist Epinephrine Bitartrate Bronchodilator

Bayer: Children's Cold Tablets
                     Children's Cough Syrup

Benadryl: Decongestant Elixir
                     Decongestant Kapseals
                     Decongestant Tablets
                     Plus Tablets

Benylin Decongestant
Bromfed Syrup

Bronkaid: Tablets
Mist
Mist Suspension

Bronkolixir
Bronkotabs
Cerose-DM
Cheracol Plus Head Cold/Cough Formula
Chexit Tablets

Children's CoTylenol: Chewable Cold Tablets
Liquid Cold Formula

Comtrex: Multi-Symptom Cold Reliever Tablets, Caplets or
Liquid
A/S Multi-Symptom Allergy/Sinus Formula
Tablets or Caplets

Congespirin for Children: Aspirin Free Liquid Cold Medicine
Aspirin Free Chewable Cold Tablets

Congestac Caplets

Contac: Caplets or Capsules
Junior Children's Cold Medicine
Nighttime Cold Medicine
Severe Cold Formula Caplets

Coricidin: 'D' Decongestant Tablets
Demilets Tablets for Children
Maximum Strength Sinus Headache Caplets

Demazin Nasal Decongestant/Antihistamine Repetabs Tablets or
Syrup

Dexatrim: Capsules
Maximum Strength Caffeine-Free, Caplets or
Capsules
Maximum Strength Plus Vitamin C/Caffeine Free,
Caplets or Capsules
Maximum Strength Pre-Meal Caplets

Dimacol Caplets

Dimetane: Decongestant Caplets
Decongestant Elixir

Dimetapp: Elixir
Extentabs

| | Plus Caplets |
| | Tablets |

Dorcol: Children's Cough Syrup
             Children's Decongestant Liquid
             Children's Liquid Cold Formula

Dristan: Decongestant/Antihistamine
             Maximum Strength Decongestant/Analgesic
                 Coated Caplets
             Nasal Spray, Regular or Menthol

Excedrin Sinus Analgesic, Decongestant Tablets or Caplets

Fedahist: Decongestant Syrup
             Expectorant Pediatric Drops
             Expectorant Syrup
             Tablets

4-Way: Cold Tablets
             Fast Acting Nasal Spray, Regular or Mentholated

Mediquell Decongestant Formula

Naldecon: CX Adult Liquid
             DX Adult Liquid
             DX Children's Syrup
             Pediatric Drops
             EX Children's Syrup
             EX Pediatric Drops

Neo-Synephrine

Nostril Nasal Decongestant

Novahistine: DMX
             Elixir

Ocugestrin Solution
Ornex Caplets
Pazo Hemorrhoid Ointment and Suppositories

PediaCare: Cough-Cold Formula Liquid
             Cough-Cold Formula Chewable Tablets
             Infants' Oral Decongestant Drops

Prefrin Liquifilm

Primatene: Mist
                      Mist Suspension
                      M Formula Tablets
                      Regular Formula Tablets
                      P Formula Tablets

Pseudoephedrine HCL Tablets
Pyrroxate Capsules
Relief Eye Drops for Red Eyes

Robitussin: CF
                      Night Relief
                      PE

Ryna: Liquid
                      C Liquid
                      CX Liquid

St. Joseph: Cold Tablets for Children
                      Measured Dose Nasal Decongestant
                      Nighttime Cold Medicine

Sinarest: No Drowsiness Tablets
                      Regular or Extra Strength Tablets

Sine-Aid: Maximum Strength Sinus Headache Caplets
                      Sinus Headache Tablets

Sine-Off: Maximum Strength Allergy/Sinus Formula
                      Caplets
                      Maximum Strength No Drowsiness Formula
                      Caplets
                      Sinus Medicine Tablets–Aspirin Formula

Sinutab: Maximum Strength Caplets or Tablets
                      Maximum Strength Without Drowsiness
                      Tablets

Sucrets Cold Decongestant Formula

Sudafed: Adult Strength Tablets
                      Children's Liquid
                      Cough Syrup
                      Plus Liquid
                      Plus Tablets
                      Sinus Caplets or Tablets
                      12-Hour Capsules
                      Tablets

Triaminic: Allergy Tablets
                      Chewables
                      Cold Syrup
                      Cold Tablets
                      Expectorant
                      DM Cough Formula
                      12 Tablets

Triaminicin Tablets

Triaminicol: Multi-Symptom Cold Syrup
                      Multi-Symptom Cold Tablets

Trind
Trind-DM
Tussagesic Tablets

Tylenol: Cold Medication Tablets or Caplets
                      Cold Medication No Drowsiness Formula Caplets
                      Cold Medication Liquid
                      Maximum Strength Sinus Medication Tablets or
                        Caplets

Ursinus Inlay-Tabs

Vicks: Children's Nyquil
                      Daycare Daytime Cold Medicine Caplets
                      Daycare Multi-Symptom Colds Medicine Liquid
                      Formula 44D Decongestant Cough Mixture
                      Sinex Decongestant Nasal Spray
                      Sinex Decongestant Nasal Ultra Fine Mist
                      Vatronol Nose Drops

Appendix C
Sources of Help and Information

Alcoholics Anonymous maintains listings in local telephone directories. Calls are answered by an AA member who will give you information about meetings in the area and/or assist you in obtaining literature.

Alcoholics Anonymous World Services, Inc.
468 Park Avenue South
New York, NY 10016
(212) 686-1100
(Literature for recovering alcoholics)

Al-Anon Family Groups, Inc.
P.O. Box 862, Midtown Station
New York, NY 10018-0862
1-800-356-9996
(Information and literature about Al-Anon and Alateen)

American Association of Sex Educators, Counselors and Therapists
435 N. Michigan, Suite 1717
Chicago, IL 60611
(312) 644-0828
(Referrals to certified sex therapists)

American Society of Addiction Medicine
12 West 21st Street
New York, NY 10010
(212) 206-6770
(Referrals to physicians and psychiatrists with special knowledge of the needs of recovering people)

Cocaine Anonymous (CA)
6125 Washington Boulevard, Suite 202
Culver City, CA 90230
(213) 839-1141

Drugs Anonymous (DA)
P.O. Box 473
Ansonia Station
New York, NY 10023
(212) 874-0700

Employment Program for Recovered Alcoholics, Inc. (EPRA)
360 West 31st Street
New York, NY 10001
(212) 947-1471
(Information and assistance with employment opportunities, for New
York State residents only)

Families Anonymous
P.O. Box 528
Van Nuys, CA 91408
(818) 989-7841
(Nationwide referrals to self-help groups and meetings for families of
recovering people)

Hazelden Foundation
Box 176, Pleasant Valley Road
Center City, MN 55012-0176
1-800-328-9000 (continental US)
1-800-257-0070 (within Minnesota)
(612) 257-4010 (all other locations)
(Literature, tapes and educational materials for recovering people and
their families)

Incest Survivors Anonymous
P.O. Box 5613
Long Beach, CA 90805-0613
(213) 428-5599

Narcotics Anonymous (NA)
World Services Office
P.O. Box 9999
16155 Wyandotte Street
Van Nuys, CA 91409
(818) 780-3951

National Association on Sexual Addiction Problems, Inc.
22937 Arlington Avenue, Suite 201
Torrance, CA 90501
(213) 534-1792

National Council on Alcoholism
12 West 21st Street
New York, NY 10010
1-800-NCA-CALL
(Information on alcoholism and other drug addictions and referrals to services for recovering people through a nationwide network of local affiliates. To find the affiliate nearest you, call the 800 number listed above. Available services vary from affiliate to affiliate.)

Self-Help Clearing House
St. Clare's–Riverside Medical Center
Pocono Road
Denville, NJ 07834
(201) 625-7101
In New Jersey only: 1-800-367-6274
(Referrals to national headquarters of all self-help groups. Also publishes *The Self-Help Source Book*, a nationwide directory of self-help groups. In New Jersey, information on all self-help groups meeting in the state, as well as a statewide directory.)

Smokers Anonymous World Services
2118 Greenwich Street
San Francisco, CA 94123
(415) 922-8575

Survivors of Incest Anonymous
P.O. Box 21817
Baltimore, MD 21222
(301) 282-3400

Index

About the Authors

Anne Geller, M.D., was born in England and graduated from Oxford University with a Bachelor of Medicine degree. She trained in neurology and psychiatry at the New York University division of Bellevue Hospital. She did a postgraduate fellowship in psychopharmacology at Albert Einstein College of Medicine, and for several years did research on drugs and behavior for which she received a Research Center Development Award from the National Institutes of Health. In 1977 she reentered clinical medicine and joined the Smithers Center of St. Luke's Roosevelt Hospital in New York City, becoming its director in 1979.

Dr. Geller has published in basic research and more recently on clinical issues. She is a member of the board of directors of the American Medical Society of Addiction Medicine and is on the editorial board of the *Journal of Substance Abuse Treatment*. She has had a special interest in the area of impaired physicians.

M. J. Territo is an experienced free-lance writer who has collaborated on two previous nonfiction projects.